Romanesque Architecture

Hans Erich Kubach

Romanesque Architecture

faber and faber / **Electa**

Photographs: Bruno Balestrini
Drawings: Studio Lodolo-Süss
Layout: Arturo Anzani

Copyright © 1978 by
Electa S.p.A., Milan

Paperback edition first published
in Great Britain in 1988
by Faber and Faber Limited
3 Queen Square, London WC1N 3AU

This volume is the redesigned paperback
of the original Italian edition published in 1972
by Electa S.p.A., Milan,
and the English edition published in 1979
by Academy Editions, London

British Library Cataloguing in Publication Data

Kubach, Hans Erich
    Romanesque architecture.—(History of
    world architecture).
    1. Architecture, Romanesque—Europe
    I. Title   II. Series
    723'.4   NA390

    ISBN 0-571-15071-3

Printed in Italy

TABLE OF CONTENTS

INTRODUCTION

This book is the product of nearly fifty years of study, travel, and research in almost all the countries of Europe affected in any way by the Romanesque style. In many matters it expresses the not necessarily orthodox viewpoint of the author—a viewpoint that has no qualms about differing from several generally accepted scholarly notions and that is frankly skeptical about the possibility of making flat statements and neat distinctions when it comes to the complexities of Romanesque architecture.

Time, unfortunately, did not permit putting together a comprehensive handbook for scholars in this field. Nevertheless, if this English edition approaches that goal, it is thanks to the editorial assistance of the translator, Dr. Robert Erich Wolf, aided by Ronald Millen.

Hans Erich Kubach

Ten thousand or so Romanesque buildings have survived in Europe. Many hundreds of great cathedrals and monastic and collegiate churches are still standing, though often much altered in appearance. Traces and vestiges, old foundations brought to light by excavations, and early written accounts all tell us of as many more. With varying density, they may be found from halfway down the Iberian peninsula all the way to Ireland, Scotland, and halfway up Scandinavia; the eastern regions of Central Europe—the western Slavic lands, that is—have them too, from Poland through Bohemia and Moravia to Slovakia, as well as western Hungary and Slovenia; in the south they are found throughout the Italian peninsula and its islands. Their territory, in short, is that of the peoples who speak Germanic and Romance languages, plus that of the western Slavs and the descendants of certain other anthropological substrata—a territory that constituted nothing less than the domain of the Roman Church during the Middle Ages.

Historically, the Romanesque was the creation of very different lands and peoples: its nucleus was the Roman Empire in Italy and its extensions to the west, north, and northeast. If its hegemony in the western Mediterranean basin was reduced considerably by the Arab conquests after 711, this was compensated by the regions of northern and eastern Europe newly won over to Christianity.

To use modern geographical designations, the Romanesque style centered in France, the northern parts of Spain and Portugal, the western and southern parts of the German-speaking countries, the British Isles, Italy, and the lands between these—that is, those regions belonging to the ancient Roman Empire. To them we can add, in the north and the east, a belt of countries where the concentration of Romanesque monuments is less dense and where the style was, on the whole, less significant.

After the collapse of all existing social systems in consequence of the migration of the Germanic peoples toward the west and the south in the fourth and fifth centuries A.D., there arose throughout this territory a new political, social, and economic order whose conceptions of the world, of the life of the spirit, and of art were largely determined by the Christianity of the Early and High Middle Ages.

In our times, with the decline in culture and the progressive detachment from the tenets of Christian faith, the natural and secular familiarity with this art is likewise in decline. But the old world of Europe still differs from the other regions to which the white race has spread in that the basic urban nucleus of its towns and villages echoes a remote past that still is clearly apparent in their present form, and that its churches, both large and small, as well as other edifices have transmuted their original spiritual intensity into a form which links modern life with its ancient roots. Thus, the art of the Middle Ages, and architecture in particular, is not—or is not only—a cultural patrimony to be stored in a museum but rather a still active part of our life. The architecture of the Middle Ages is an exceptionally complex phenomenon. (In our present examination of it we shall reserve for a special chapter what little is known about the medieval city and castle and civil architecture as a whole.) As Greek architecture found its unique realization in the temple, so that of the Middle Ages found its own in the Christian church. It is precisely in the building of churches that the creative aims and abilities of the medieval period revealed themselves to the fullest and in purest form as the sum of all the intellectual, artistic, technical, and craftsmanly possibilities of the time.

Those ecclesiastical structures were not, however, created in a void. There is still much controversy over the part played in their conception by the prehistoric and primitive wooden architecture of the Germans and Slavs and by the primitive stone buildings of the Mediterranean region. Many significant features of Romanesque construction can be traced to earlier prototypes: the arch and the arcade (either open or blind) are familiar from ancient Roman architecture, as are the dome and barrel vaults as well as the more complicated cross-groined vaults in which the barrels intersect. Arches and barrel vaults can be traced back to Sassanid architecture, while arches and domes were often used in Byzantium, Armenia, and Asia Minor in the sixth century. The columns, made either from a single block of stone or from superimposed rounds, was widely diffused throughout Egypt, Crete, and Greece. With its lowest member (the socle) conceived as a so-called Attic base and its capital designed in the Ionic, Corinthian, or Composite order, it had existed in thousands of examples ever since the fourth century B.C. in Greece and had subsequently spread throughout the Roman Empire. Rows of columns supporting arches (or architraves) are found in the atria and basilicas of Early Christian times. Orders of columns superimposed over several stories are known as far back as the Hellenistic period, when they were used for rear stage walls, the exteriors of amphitheaters, and city gates.

Squared stone construction was already in use in the great edifices of Egypt's Old Kingdom, while brick construction was employed in the early cultures of the Near East as well as among the Romans. How all these forms and techniques came to be known to the medieval Occident is, however, impossible to ascertain, in either general or specific terms. Certainly a number of them were to be seen in all the provinces of the Roman Empire. One such form was the basilica, so long in favor for Christian churches. The organization of the basilica interior—atrium, transept, apse and tripartite choir, longitudinal galleries, and so on—was transmitted in this manner, as were the basic forms of central-plan construction, the Greek cross, the octagon with niches, the rotunda with ambulatory. Various other and more complex forms of the church with a centralized dome occurred in Asia Minor, Armenia, Byzantium (the so-called Justinian architectural system of Hagia Sophia in Constantinople), and Italy (San Lorenzo in Milan). The octagonal chapel of Sant'Aquilino alongside the latter church even displays the division of the wall into two shells by means of two superimposed ambulatories oriented both inward and outward, a pattern that was to become characteristic in certain regions during the eleventh and twelfth centuries. The original form of the twin-towered façade has been identified in Syria, as has the system of flying buttresses.

There is no reason to be astonished by the fact that the entire repertory of architectural forms and types accumulated in the countries of the Mediterranean from the third millennium B.C. onward should have been available to the Romanesque architects. What is, however, surprising is that such a limited selection was made from that available repertory.

On the whole, one can say that even the architecture of the Christian churches found in Egypt, Palestine, Syria, Asia Minor, Armenia, and Byzantium had little influence in the West, at least in the sense of direct imitations or further developments. Upon closer study, almost everything we know in Romanesque architecture proves to be a new creation which utilized and transformed whatever stimuli were received from elsewhere. The most significant exceptions are the column with base and capital and the colonnaded basilica. As long as scholarly interest was focused on these specific forms and this architectural plan (especially frequent in Italy), the impression was possible—even inevitable—that medieval architecture was a successor to Late Antique and Early Christian architecture, and often a poorly executed and even misunderstood imitation of it at that. However, since we have not only become acquainted with the entire wealth of medieval art but also learned to appreciate its uniqueness and special beauty, our judgment has been altered. Even when compared with the more or less contemporary parallel development of church architecture in, say, Armenia and Russia—notably in Kiev, Suzdal, and Novgorod—we find that there is often a disconcerting similarity but very rarely anything we can define as a truly tangible relationship.

Only in recent times have we become aware that there exist fundamental differences even where there is an apparently demonstrable dependence of the Romanesque style on its predecessors; one basilica is not necessarily the same as the other. The differences are likely to be obscured by erroneous interpretation of the facts: the Early Christian basilica should not be interpreted in the same terms as those applied to the romanesque churches of the eleventh and twelfth centuries. Unlike the latter, an edifice of the fourth, fifth, or sixth century is not a firmly assembled cubic box of space whose sides are made up of compact piers and walls. Rather, it is much more like an indeterminate intermediate space between two parallel walls which themselves rise almost incorporeally as if suspended above numerous slender columns, rendered unreal by glistening mosaics. The pavement of smooth, gleaming marble or figurative mosaics seems to glide underfoot. Above, an openwork construction of timber supports the sloping surfaces of the ceiling without really sealing off the space below. Therefore, although analogies exist between Early Christian and Romanesque basilicas—three naves separated by rows of supporting members, the central nave given greater importance and having its own windows, sometimes a semicircular apse with a half-dome to close off one end—it is not enough for us to insist

on them. The routes by which the multifarious forms and techniques could have reached the West were numerous. Despite the schism between the Byzantine and Roman Churches in 753, there continued to be links between Constantinople and Rome. And even after the Arab conquest of Spain in 711, pilgrims persisted in making their way by either land or sea to the holy places in Palestine. Commercial links are attested to not only by political history but also through the artistic evidence of imported textiles. Finally, when these connections were strengthened by the Crusades in the eleventh and twelfth centuries, many Europeans came to know firsthand not only the architecture of the Islamic East but also several ancient cultures, both pagan and Christian, which were older than their own. It says much for the incredible power of invention of the West that we almost never happen upon concrete and convincing ties with the East that are really more than a distant echo or a deliberate allusion: the central-plan church in the West is just such an allusion, based on the church in Jerusalem where Christ is said to be buried and on the Holy Sepulcher itself.

Viewed in modern terms, the link with Antique prototypes should have been especially close in those cases where the large buildings of ancient Roman cities were adapted to medieval functions. An instructive example is the early fourth-century Porta Nigra in Trier (today in southwestern Germany), which in Roman times was the northern gateway to the city and was transformed into a church in the eleventh and twelfth centuries. Here too there was multi-storied articulation by means of orders of columns and entablatures, galleries hollowed out of the thickness of the walls, and vaults. But the apse, added around 1150 as a presbytery, would seem to have been deliberately and conspicuously set off from the Roman gate: instead of horizontal stories, an emphatically vertical cohesion was achieved through the use of buttress piers; the various architectural components were no longer rounded off but angular. While a passageway was developed out of the so-called dwarf gallery that crowned the whole, it was so conceived that only the abstract analytical approach of architectural historians could have considered it a phenomenon parallel to the Roman roofed parapet walk. Thus, neither in appearance nor in construction is there any real connection between the Antique and medieval portions of the gate.

During the Middle Ages (and still today in some places), buildings from imperial times could be seen throughout the Holy Roman Empire. Their influence, however, as we have suggested, was relatively limited. Similarly, influences from another great cultural realm, Islam, made themselves felt only peripherally. Like the Christian church, though far more so, the significant functional part of the mosque is an interior space, yet that space is almost boundless, fluid, unmethodical; and, while there are certain grounds for comparison with the hall church, nevertheless all Western buildings are firmly circumscribed, with a clearer correspondence between exterior and interior, between the structure and the space it encloses. Islamic influence, in fact, was limited to a few isolated forms such as the pointed and horseshoe arches, the notched arch, and the ribbed star vault—though even these turn up only sporadically, mostly in border regions.

The art and architecture of the Middle Ages are unthinkable except within the total context of the medieval milieu, which was altogether distinct from that of antiquity. The medieval population itself was quite different, even if older strata lingered on to an extent that is difficult to define. There is much controversy over the role played by the new populations within whose area of settlement Romanesque art arose. Many scholars are convinced that they see Celtic or Germanic elements in Romanesque art; others passionately contest this claim, considering the transformation of ancient forms as merely a decline into the barbaric. What did the Celts, the Germans, the western Slavs contribute in their own right to the creation of this new culture? Romantic notions and nationalistic ambitions have led to much confusion in this regard, especially because certain modern nations have identified themselves with populations which, in prehistoric or even protohistoric times, had not as yet in any way come upon the social structure that permits us to speak of a "people" or a "nation." Today we need scarcely insist that the Celts and the French are not identical, nor Anglo-Saxons and English, Teutons and Germans, much less Longobards and Lombards. Granted this, we can reflect with considerable impartiality upon just what contribution the various peoples made to the development of medieval culture.

Protohistoric sculptures in stone and metal found in Gaul reveal forms blocked out in much the same way as those of the Romanesque of the eleventh and twelfth centuries. The Romanesque architecture of Normandy, and that of England after the Norman Conquest (1066), emphasized to an especially marked degree verticals articulated by round elements, a feature found otherwise only in the wooden stave churches which exist solely in the Scandinavian homeland of the Normans. And recently we have come to learn that early forms of the timber framework, the bay, and the hall plan—all of them associated with Romanesque church architecture—played a significant role in protohistoric secular buildings as well.

Organization of Bishoprics and Parishes

It was in the Carolingian period that the civil and administrative organization of the Church gradually took shape. The general diffusion of the diocese and of centers where bishops had their seats was approaching the system that was to prevail for so long during the Middle Ages. Some were relocated, others newly founded. Thus, the see of the bishopric of the Meuse Valley was displaced from Tongres to Maastricht and finally to Liège. In Italy and southern France many episcopal sees had been located in medium-sized, even small towns ever since Roman and Early Christian times, and had correspondingly small dioceses. On the other hand, in the regions that were not converted until the eighth and ninth centuries or later (in consequence of the missionary efforts of St. Boniface), the dioceses covered vast areas.

Often this was reflected in the greater dimensions of the cathedral churches, though more frequently the impressive size was the result of patronage by some great secular potentate.

The care of souls in the towns and countryside was assured through a dense network of parishes and affiliated churches. This likewise has its importance for the history of architecture, since wherever a parish is known to have existed once, there must also have been a church.

The connection between state and Church was close. Those who made financial contributions to the Church obtained various privileges. Thus, the German kings had a say in the selection of bishops, if not in their actual nomination—a situation which in the eleventh century led to open conflict over the right of investiture. Innumerable lords of small or large feudal territories exercised similar rights in the local abbeys and parishes. It is all too easy to conclude that such distribution of ecclesiastical authority and such legal interdependence must have determined certain important architectural variations, but this can seldom be demonstrated and has all too often led to erroneous conclusions.

Monastic Orders

The monastic system has its roots in the interpretation of Christian faith as promulgated in the theology of the sixth century, first and foremost in the East. Like theology itself, and like architecture, it too went through far-ranging transformations in the West, though we cannot consider those changes here except in terms of their consequences for our subject. For several centuries the Benedictine order led the field. Hundreds of abbeys and convents came into being all over Christian Europe, constituting nuclei of faith, Christian tradition, learning, and culture. Reforms were called for continually and carried through whenever and wherever laxity threatened to weaken the rigorous precepts of the monastic houses; those of the eleventh century which affected the Lotharingian monastery at Gorze and the Burgundian abbey at Cluny had especially notable consequences. The influence of such reforms on church architecture has been the object of much study and debate but seems often to have been unduly overrated, particularly in the case of those carried out in the Swabian abbey of Hirsau in the diocese of Speyer.

In the twelfth century the abbeys of Prémontré and Cîteaux became radial points for two new reformatory orders, the Premonstratensian and the Cistercian, which had immense success throughout the West and generated hundreds of other new monastic centers, thereby writing a fascinating chapter in the history of architecture. The thirteenth century was marked by the foundation of the Franciscan order, which was reflected in the rise of Gothic architecture—though some early Franciscan churches fit in perfectly with the local Late Romanesque style, as was the case with Sankt Marien zum Spiegel in Cologne (demolished) and the former abbey church at nearby Seligenthal on the Sieg River.

State and Nation

The medieval world knew nothing like the "national state" as we have conceived of it in the nineteenth and twentieth centuries. For us it is of such central concern that many historical studies confine themselves to the question of how the "national state" and "national consciousness" came into being.

Art historians were long dominated by the compulsion to consider the objects of their studies chiefly as manifestations of national superiority. This was not merely an invention of Fascism and Nazism; in France the phenomenon has been even stronger. The roots of the process leading to the formation of national entities go far back in time. In the centuries that concern us here, however, there was primarily a profusion of large and small territories on one side, and the Empire on the other. The Holy Roman Empire considered itself the successor to the Roman Empire and a governing power, but only occasionally was it able to assert this claim successfully, and even then never simultaneously throughout the territories of the Romanic, Germanic, and western Slavic peoples. It was not until almost the end of the Romanesque period that the largest of these feudal territories—the crown lands *(domaine royal)* of France, with Paris as its center, and the kingdom of England—rose to the importance of a monarchy. Hand in hand with the growing importance and territorial extension of these kingdoms went the disintegration and decline of the Holy Roman Empire of the Germans.

Viewed impartially, the history of art also shows analogies with this situation. The innumerable small territorial states may be compared to the multitude of art centers which likewise were often sharply demarcated from each other. Yet those centers were by no means geographically identical with the territories and, furthermore, display interrelationships on a higher level which have no parallel whatsoever with any ecclesiastical or civil entities to be found on the map.

The state was characterized by feudal obligations and chivalry, both of these being expressions of a rigid hierarchical order. This remained so throughout the Romanesque period, even if in certain regions—Lombardy and the Rhineland—the city began to acquire autonomous importance from the twelfth century onward. A dense network of fortified castles spread across the Continent, and in them the feudal nobility had their residence. There they administered their holdings and sat in judgment, afforded the population protection from enemy incursions, and controlled the routes of commerce. It was in the somber times of the late ninth and tenth centuries, when no one was safe from the raids of Normans or Hungarians, that the need for such organization had become obvious. Subsequently, feudal control was extended to the West's frontiers, to guard against the Islamic hordes and threats from the East, though often enough there were deadly feuds and wars within and between their own populations. Soon enough the expanding cities found that they too required fortifications.

The term "Pre-Romanesque" is of quite recent invention and is at best an expedient. Moreover, the concept itself is fluid and difficult to define. One can, of course, simply say that whatever is not yet, or not fully, Romanesque but that nevertheless points to it can be termed Pre-Romanesque. It is in this sense that K. J. Conant speaks of a Carolingian Romanesque; taken thus, the eighth, ninth, and tenth centuries can be grouped under that heading. For my part, I prefer to stress not so much the negative aspect—the "not-yet"—as the positive, the tendency that moves toward the Romanesque. Many aspects of Pre-Romanesque art in general and architecture in particular can if viewed within the broader context of a universal history of art be regarded as the ultimate manifestations of Late Antique art in the Mediterranean basin—an explanation which is valid as long as one keeps in mind the point to which the evolutionary process eventually evolved: the Romanesque itself.

Pre-Carolingian Period

Three main periods of the Pre-Romanesque can be distinguished. The first can be called Pre-Carolingian or Merovingian, if we accept the Frankish kingdom as its geographical center. We must keep in mind, nevertheless, that this period extended from the end of the barbarian invasions in the fifth century to the middle of the eighth century and, broadly speaking, coincided with the domination of the Longobards in Italy, the Visigoths in the Iberian Peninsula and what is now southern France, and the early years of Anglo-Saxon supremacy in the British Isles.

From this Pre-Carolingian period a few small stone churches survive in the Iberian part of the Visigothic dominions. To them can be added several churches in Ireland and England, though their dating is generally accepted only because no valid alternative has been proposed (it is difficult in any case to be sure that they belong to this time). Besides these, intensive excavations of medieval sites are bringing to light a steadily growing number of churches, for the most part single-naved and built in stone, as well as single- or triple-naved churches and dwellings in wood. Without exception, however, what survive are their foundations and not their walls, meaning that we can determine their ground plans but not their elevations. Not a single one survives sufficiently to be reconstructed except on paper.

Carolingian Period

The second Pre-Romanesque period is that of the Carolingians, who held power for almost two and a half centuries, from 750 to 987. These dates do not, however, apply to all of the vast empire ruled from 768 to 814 by Charlemagne himself—a territory which stretched from the Ebro to the Elbe, from the North Sea to Italy. After his empire was divided up in 843 and again in 871, a West Frankish kingdom was formed, ruled nominally by the Carolingian dynasty until 987, and an East Frankish kingdom, which died out in 911. The Carolingians were followed by the House of

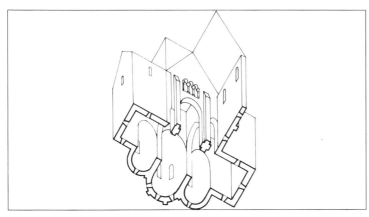

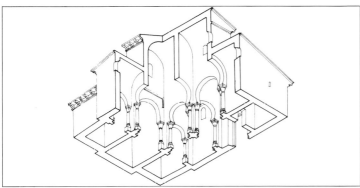

1. Meusnes, axonometric projection of the church (from Lesueur, 1969)

2. Lebeña, Santa María, axonometric projection (from Conant, 1959)

3. Cividale del Friuli, oratory of Santa Maria in Valle, drawing of the interior and plan (from Haupt, 1909)

Saxony—usually called the Ottonians—which ruled from 919 to 1024. Thus, it is on the basis of political history that French scholars tend to create a dividing line around the year 1000 and to date the onset of the Early Romanesque at the turn of the millennium, whereas the Germans see stronger links between the tenth and the eleventh centuries and have recently termed a large part of the latter century as "Ottonian" or, as in the case of H. Busch, "Pre-Romanesque."

This would restrict the concept of the Romanesque to the mature phase of the style. Personally, I should like to claim the entire Carolingian era as Pre-Romanesque, from the early Carolingians to the last rulers of the West Frankish kingdom, whose end would then coincide with the so-called Dark Ages in the middle of the tenth century. Thus, the Early Romanesque would begin in the late tenth century and comprise those works created when the Empire was dominated by the later Ottonians (up to 1024) and the first Salians (1024 to around 1060/80).

The Pre-Romanesque architecture of the Carolingian period is known to us through a few major works such as the Palatine Chapel in Aachen (Aix-la-Chapelle), the former abbey church at Corvey in Westphalia, and Santa Sofia at Benevento in Campania; through a few small but thoroughly harmonious edifices such as San Satiro in Milan, Germigny-des-Prés near Orléans, and the gatehouse of the Benedictine abbey at Lorsch in Hesse; through various groups of basilical buildings in Asturias, northern Italy, and the middle Rhineland; and finally through a profusion of buildings which are controversial either because we know only their ground plans (and that often far from any certainty)—as is the case with a considerable number of buildings whose foundations have been laid bare through excavations—or because we are dubious as to their dating, the true circumference of their original structures, and how they should be reconstructed, a situation especially frequent when it comes to Italian churches.

This state of affairs makes stylistic characterization extremely difficult. True, one can limit oneself to singling out what is clearly not yet Romanesque and at the same time no longer Late Antique. Or one can analyze one or another of the important churches mentioned above, or attempt to discover all the traits they have in common, and then—if one is bold indeed—try to set them against criteria drawn from painting and the applied arts. Attempts such as these have been made, and a few essential notions arrived at, though scarcely within a well-defined system of evaluation. Thus, for instance, the organization of the Pre-Romanesque interior tends to be multipartite and complex, and this accounts for the fascination of such buildings as the chapel at Aachen and the cathedral at Benevento. (There are certainly Romanesque buildings that outdo their Carolingian predecessors in the number of their spatial divisions, but at the same time they obviously strive to be clear and "readable.")

The predilection for complicated solutions is seen in the division and separation of space, particularly plain to read where projecting strips of wall

and deep-plunging arches cut off broad or high areas of the interior from each other, as in the clearly demarcated and segregated crossings found in many regions; the arches between different parts of Anglo-Saxon churches (nave and chancel, nave and transepts, nave and atrium), often no wider than doors—Saint Laurence's in Bradford-on-Avon in Wiltshire is a good example of this; and the openings in the walls between the central nave and the transept in San Julián de los Prados near Oviedo in Asturias, which were designed to be looked through but not traversed; to these can be added the large-scale division through a lattice of arches in the Palatine Chapel in Aachen. There is a notable frequency of narrow, shaftlike interiors in England and the Asturias region, and this is typical of the Aachen chapel as well.

Carolingian architecture is characteristically delicate, a quality still to be sensed, says O. Müller, even in the ruins at Steinbach in Hesse. The articulation of the wall surface is emphasized more than the compact mass of masonry. Though this was still often true in the eleventh century, walls of that period were no longer so conspicuously spun over with a net of fine details as they had been in the gatehouse at Lorsch. Vaults too show typical Pre-Romanesque features: when a barrel vault is intersected or traversed by another such vault, the result is often parabolic lunettes which delineate curved lines on the vault surfaces, thereby giving rise to a play of light and shadow. The ground plan and layout of the interior are extremely variable, quite unlike its Romanesque counterpart (a cross-groined vault between cross-arches over a square ground plan), in which everything is highly structured and the abstract form in large measure determines the external appearance.

Only a small number of Carolingian buildings are preserved well enough for us to reliably examine their structural variations. To go beyond this and to claim to be able to distinguish stages of development within Carolingian architecture is an interesting exercise at best, but one based far too heavily on subjective impressions. Moreover, one must always keep in mind the overwhelming disproportion between the few buildings that have come down to us by chance and the enormous number of those that once existed. A glance at A. Mann's map showing the "known" monasteries built in the Carolingian era would give a graphic demonstration of this.

Early Ottonian Period

The third phase of Pre-Romanesque architecture is represented by the early Ottonian period. These so-called Dark Ages, from which we know virtually no buildings whatsoever, extended from the late ninth century into the second half of the tenth. It was a time marked by Norman invasions in the North and West, the Arab domination of Spain (with sporadic incursions into southern Italy), and the onslaught of the Hungarians in southwestern Europe. Like the year 732 (when Charles Martel blocked the Saracens at Poitiers in their attempt to overrun Europe), the year 955 was another

turning point, marking the victory of Emperor Otto the Great over the Hungarians at the Battle of Lech. It was only then that a renewed consolidation of the Empire began, one which was to have clearly visible effects on art. The Ottonians were in power from 919 to 1024, but their first half-century of rule–up to around 960 or 970, when they governed the Eastern Empire–resembles the final Carolingian era in that it too belongs to the Dark Ages, a void as far as art history is concerned. Surviving buildings from the later ninth century and the first sixty years of the tenth century are extraordinarily rare. Almost the only exceptions are the small group of so-called Mozarabic churches (Chistian churches built under Arab domination) in northern and central Spain–at Berlanga, Mazote, Lebeña, Melque, Celanova, Peñalba, San Millán de la Cogolla–and at Lourosa in Portugal.

The State of Research: Excavations and Investigations

As with ancient architecture, yet far more than with succeeding medieval or late medieval art, the study of Pre-Romanesque architecture requires a critical analysis of the sources of our knowledge.

The primary fact to be remembered is that not one Carolingian or Ottonian building has come down to us unaltered. The number of surviving buildings which are essentially or even partially in their original state is small not only in comparison with the incalculable wealth of edifices of the twelfth century (to say nothing of the Gothic), but also in comparison with what once existed. Of this much we are sure. For more than a century scholars have striven, and with considerable success, to expand this knowledge. They have brought attention to more and more buildings of small or moderate dimensions, but also to others–large and of primary importance–which had been overshadowed or downright ignored. This holds true even for the eleventh century: Sainte-Gertrude in Nivelles, for example, along with an entire group of Early Romanesque churches in the Meuse Valley, has been given due attention only in the last few decades. Rediscovery has often been followed by restoration to the original state, as in fact happened at Nivelles. Nevertheless, by far the greatest increase in our knowledge is due to investigations into buildings that have survived only partially, are in ruin, or are extensively altered. Success in such cases demands exhaustive study and usually extremely laborious, time-consuming, and costly efforts. Even in studying an existing building, scaffolding may be required, which is generally available only if new construction or restoration work is going on at the same time and only if it is possible to work down to the original structure of the building. Excavations present the greatest problems. Very often, for external reasons and chiefly because of the expense involved, both types of investigation are forcibly limited in time or scope, so that the yield in new knowledge is all too fragmentary. But the investigative purpose itself has built-in limitations, since neither the utmost ingenuity nor the finest excavation techniques can succeed in bringing to light something that has disappeared forever. The deductions drawn from such material are often fallacious: the understandable inclination to come up with results—and wherever possible with respectable and conclusive ones—easily leads to hypotheses and immoderate claims. Hypotheses are indispensable in archaeological work, in which certainties are rare indeed, but the scholarly researcher must keep in mind that this is all they are. Reconstructions done on the drawing board have a way of getting into books and gaining general acceptance, after which they frequently prove hard to kill, despite becoming outdated. What is more, almost every excavation turns up little else than a ground plan—if we are lucky, a complete one, if we are luckier still, perhaps the remains of a portal, a pedestal, a plinth, or the base of a wall. But quite often there is simply nothing to go by in estimating the superstructures and their elevation. Conclusions drawn from typological resemblances between similar buildings are hypothetical at best. For this reason extreme caution should be exercised in any attempts at reconstruction and restoration. Thus, our presentation in these pages is based chiefly on buildings still standing, few as they may be. If we extend the scope further to include buildings whose foundations alone are known through excavations, or others of which only portions have been exposed by chipping away later rebuildings, then even more prudence is called for. Certainly we must take into consideration recent archaeological findings, but always with due critical objectivity.

However, from the standpoint of archaeological investigators, what is almost more important than the hypothetical and, as we have seen, limited possibility of reconstructing individual buildings is the glimpse their excavation may afford of the chronological sequence of constructions found in a particular area. A remarkable refinement in excavation techniques now permits us to read the strata chronologically. Today the first concern of excavators is no longer merely to lay bare the foundation walls; painstaking observation of the succession of strata from the lowest depths to the surface is now thought indispensable in order to introduce some degree of certainty into these usually very complicated findings. To grasp this stratigraphic approach one really needs to visit a digging site, but even then only the specialist can comprehend the entire process and, indeed, only one who explores every detail involved. The technique has in many cases revealed a clear succession from pagan Roman temples through churches of the Early and High Middle Ages to Gothic and even later constructions. Often there is a clearly readable sequence of increasingly larger and stronger foundations which can even be given relative dates. Absolute dating is often a special problem, which may be dealt with in a number of ways: through information transmitted by written sources; through the excavation of pottery and coins on the site; through vestiges of painting or sculpture that are turned up; or, finally, through comparison with related constructions.

In recent years there has been intense scholarly activity in the field of medieval archaeology. This does not mean, however, that none had preceded it: on the contrary, for a century now each decade has brought new stimulation, new investigations and excavations. But it was only the destruction done in World War II that opened up possibilities for architectural research to an extent previously undreamed of. The economic upswing that followed the war in many European countries provided the means for taking advantage of at least some of those possibilities. Stimulated by the work done in classical and provincial Roman archaeology and in prehistoric studies, researchers of early medieval architecture gained a new impetus. The long-standing and often deleterious barriers between the above-named disciplines and Christian archaeology and art history were by and large broken down. There were also incentives to a greater international exchange of methods and findings, with a general widening of intellectual horizons. We must remember that after World War I, Asturias and Catalonia, England, and even the Netherlands were still decidedly remote areas of study for German scholars, whereas Ottonian architecture within the imperial territories, for example, was by and large terra incognita for the French and Italians. In this light it is understandable how the opinion could arise that "national traits" in art already had their beginnings in very early times. The problems having to do with the nature and delimitation of what the French call *le premier art roman* and of Ottonian architecture are only now becoming clearly understood.

Equally meaningful, however, is the deepening and broadening of our objective knowledge. Admittedly, even the most thoroughgoing and successful excavations can never win back for us a long-vanished building. Nor can the interiors—with their original relationships in height, the doors and windows, the supporting members, the forms of the arches, the detailed organization—be imagined from ground plans alone. Some things can be arrived at by analogy, but even that is deceptive, since it presupposes an ideal excavation, one that turns up the entire ground plan, all the essential parts of the foundations, and that therefore permits the dating to be fixed with some degree of certainty: in short, the rare exception.

Be that as it may, and despite many reservations and doubts, we have been able to reclaim a large number of important churches, at least to the extent that we now know their chief features. The much built-over Carolingian cathedrals of Cologne, Hildesheim, Halberstadt, and Reims were once no more than vague shadows in our minds, or even entirely unknown, but today they have taken on precise forms. This is also true of the Carolingian abbey churches at Essen, Nivelles, Lorsch, Corvey, and Saint-Denis, as well as of the Ottonian cathedrals of Halberstadt, Minden, and Lausanne, and the abbey churches of Cluny (the building known as Cluny II), Vreden, and Oberkaufungen.

The excavations in Esslingen and at the Niedermünster in Regensburg revealed Carolingian and Ottonian edifices in regions which, like Swabia, had earlier been excluded from medieval archaeological research or had, like the Danube area, been explored with not very highly developed research methods. In Westphalia and Lower Saxony entirely unexpected

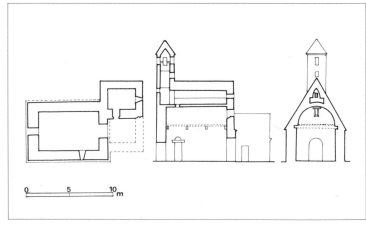

finds have come to light and in great numbers. The Dutch, Belgians, Swiss, and Austrians have opened up new realms, and not only with large churches—among which a few built in the wake of the Palatine Chapel at Aachen have aroused great interest—but also with a considerable number of smaller ones. As a result of all this, the question of the development of the various structural and formal types of Romanesque architecture had to be thrown open again. In many cases, however, even fundamental and crucial questions remain unanswered. The history of the building of the Carolingian cathedral in Cologne, whose excavation by O. Doppelfeld made a great sensation, is still a matter of discussion, and its architectural form throughout various periods has still not been fully explained. The dating—whether Carolingian or Ottonian—for the almost equally sensational excavation under the former Abdinghof monastery church in Paderborn carried out by B. Ortmann and H. Thümmler is still undecided. In addition, though various parts of the cathedral built under Otto the Great in Magdeburg are now known to us, precisely how they fit together is still much debated.

As one would expect, these recent findings have shed new light on older problems. The hypothetical reconstructions of the Upper Rhenish Ottonian cathedrals of Mainz, Worms, and Strasbourg, which had been accepted and published virtually without question in the manuals of art history, must all be thought through again, as must also those of the great Carolingian churches at Fulda and Sankt Gallen. Just how shaky even our apparently indisputable knowledge is was shown in an exemplary case, that of the ruins of the abbey church of Bad Hersfeld near Kassel in Hesse. D. Grossmann took a courageous step when he dared to claim that the present building, almost universally accepted as dating from the eleventh century, was in fact Carolingian. His grounds for this claim were decidedly convincing, and the scholarly discussion it provoked led to concrete action: new excavations carried out by Feldtkeller, Binding, and Von Winterfeld brought to light the foundation of a Carolingian church alongside the present church ruins.

Whole series of questions have come up in the last decades. The westwork and other related forms—such as the transverse west front and the three-towered west front, the exterior crypt, and the rotundaform choir—have been recognized as well-defined architectural types only in very recent years, with the result that our knowledge of early medieval architecture has gone through an extraordinary transformation.

In other respects too the numerous excavations have led to new points of view. While in many cases it was known that there had previously been one or more buildings on the same site—churches founded much earlier—this was thought of as a special field of study best left to specialists in church history. Now, however, for many important churches we have direct evidence of an unbroken sequence of buildings going back in some instances as far as Roman-Early Christian times. Thus, we can now see just how major cathedrals and great abbey churches grew out of very humble beginnings,

how a *cella memoriae* (a small votive chapel in a graveyard) could be repeatedly rebuilt in ever larger form, added to and expanded, to end up finally as a great Carolingian or Ottonian church. This first became clear in the Rhineland at Xanten and Bonn and then at Sankt Severin in Cologne, among others. The burial places of martyrs remain recognizable in many instances, and it is astounding how many of these earlier building strata have survived and can be identified despite all the rebuilding and changes. In other cases, the point of departure was a Roman temple, as in Elst in Holland, or a small single-naved Merovingian church, as in Nivelles in Belgium. Less frequent is the case in which a Roman-Early Christian church was already of considerable size and survived through numerous medieval alterations, as in Santo Stefano in Verona and San Simpliciano in Milan or, in France, at Saint-Pierre in Vienne on the Rhône. At Trier, T. Kempf not only proved that the legend of the founding of the cathedral by Empress Helena had historical grounds, but he also brought together and deepened most impressively the architectural research that had been going on there for all of a century. The hall-church character of the central-plan building erected in Trier under Constantine the Great (who had his residence there from 306 to 312) was preserved through all the centuries of the Middle Ages, whereas in Verona, Milan, and Vienne it is somewhat concealed by the medieval renovations. Thus, the much debated problem of the continuity between classical antiquity and the Middle Ages advanced to a new level.

Single-Naved Churches

It is really only in recent times that the aisleless church—a chancel linked to a single nave, a form often referred to by the convenient German term *Saalkirche*—has come to be appreciated as an independent architectural form. As a consequence of the extensive excavations carried out after World War II, the *cella* was found to be one of the basic forms of Early Christian churches, a discovery given further historical proof when, in a number of localities, the earliest places of Christian worship were found to have been small commemorative funeral chapels, *coemeteria*. Increasingly larger and more complex buildings were often developed out of these, and at times the later construction was simply built over the earlier. It is plain to see that many Pre-Romanesque and Romanesque churches are composed of just such cells in combination. It is extremely important to remember that such growth took place according to fixed rules: in fact, Romanesque architecture was based on the "addition" of spatial cells and cubes in rigorously symmetrical and lucid order, and never on the disorganized (or at least seemingly disorganized) conglomeration to be seen in ancient Near Eastern architecture or in the Cretan palace of the Minoan age.

The single-naved interior is found in chapels from the Pre-Romanesque and Romanesque eras in innumerable examples everywhere in Europe, often with an apse, a rectangular choir, or a tower added to it. Early constructions frequently differ from the full-blown Romanesque examples of the same type in one of two respects: the various components of the interior may not be decisively demarcated (they may, for example, all have the same width), or, on the contrary, they may be so separated as to communicate with each other only through narrow doorlike openings.

Several such buildings have survived either intact or partially, but we know many more of them through excavations carried out in many places since World War II which have disclosed entire strata of architectural monuments known previously only from early writings. Through them, whole regions that were once simply blank areas on the archaeological maps have turned out to contain churches dating from early times and have taken on for us a concrete identity. Thus, for instance, in the Lower Rhine and Meuse valleys we know an entire substratum of single-naved Pre-Romanesque and Early Romanesque church buildings existed, of which only a few still stand or are in such condition as to permit rebuilding from the vestiges of their walls. For these excavations we are indebted to W. Bader, G. Binding, H. Borger, L. Genicot, and J. Mertens, among others. The results in Westphalia have been scarcely less significant, thanks to the excavations and research of Claussen, Esterhües, H. Thümmler, and J.J. Winckelmann. Excavations in Swabia by G. Fehring and his assistants as well as by B. Cichy—with especially interesting results at the site of the early wooden church in Brenz—have exposed old strata; in Upper Bavaria, a few diggings, notably at Mühltal near Munich and in the Niedermünster (the old minster) in Regensburg, have yielded their first fruits.

We now know that quite early there were also single-naved churches of considerable size, and that they did not simply first appear in the churches built by the Italian mendicant orders in the thirteenth century. Examples can be cited from all previous periods: from Early Christian times we have such churches as San Simpliciano and San Nazaro in Milan and Santo Stefano in Verona, all three of which are still largely intact; from Merovingian times there is Saint-Pierre-aux-Nonnains in Metz, of which portions remain; from Carolingian times, the Niedermünster in Regensburg; and from Ottonian times, Sankt Pantaleon in Cologne, Sankt Patroklus in Soest, Meusnes in the Orléanais, and Saint-Généroux in the Poitou area. As for Romanesque aisleless churches of monumental dimensions, vast numbers are known, complete with barrel vaults, cupolas or cross vaults (above all in southwestern Europe), and with open trusswork roofs in Italy in particular.

Single-naved churches with annexes are also frequent. Among the examples cited above, several have symmetrical adjuncts to the east end. As a rule, however, such annexes are paired to give the effect of low crossarms and are treated as such, being marked on the exterior of the building by transverse saddle roofs and linked in the interior to the main area by arches. The result is a ground plan resembling a Latin cross, as in the first and second constructions of Sant'Abbondio in Como and the first two of Romainmôtier in Switzerland.

Annexes can also be joined up to churches in more casual ways. The earliest construction of the former collegiate church at Dietkirchen on the Lahn in Hesse seems to have had such adjuncts, which—because their floors were at various levels—had no relationship to each other in the interior of the church. In those aisleless churches that we know only in part on the basis of their excavated foundations, as in the case of Sankt German in Speyer, we simply cannot be certain that their basic plan was in fact symmetrical. From the Carolingian era we have examples in which a number of annexes were lined up in a row on a single side of the church, as in the former abbey church at Müstair in the Swiss canton of Graubünden. That such annexes could be lined up symmetrically along both sides is evident in a number of Anglo-Saxon churches, notably in Kent (the ruined monastery church at Reculver and the vestiges of Saint Pancras's in the abbey of Saint Augustine in Canterbury). Besides these, there are early aisleless churches with smaller and usually lower accessory structures on three or even all four sides, among them the Merovingian baptistery of Saint-Jean in Poitiers; a few Visigothic churches in Spain, such as San Pedro de la Nave at Zamora and Santa Cristina de Lena at Oviedo, the latter dating from around 800; and in Lombardy, Santa Maria foris Portam at Castelseprio (Varese). Also worthy of mention, finally, is the arrangement in which the aisleless main area is girdled on three or four sides by rows of accessory structures that when seen from the outside give the impression of lateral naves, though inside they are in fact linked only by doors.

A special form is the so-called tower-nave church consisting only of a chancel, nave, and tower, in which a square main room constitutes the ground floor of a tower, while the altar area gives the impression of being a lower-ceilinged annex. This is a reversal of the choir-tower church, in which the tower rises above the altar area—a type that became widespread in the Romanesque era but whose origins are not entirely certain. The tower-nave type was adopted chiefly in Mozarabic Spain and Anglo-Saxon England.

A further variant is the aisleless church with three contiguous apses attached to its east end. The best-preserved example of this is in Mistail in the Swiss canton of Graubünden: its juxtaposition of a tall hall with three slender apses is quite impressive. It belongs to a group of such churches in Graubünden—the former abbey church of Sankt Johann in Müstair, the Benedictine abbey church at Disentis—and in the adjoining areas, notably San Benedetto in Málles Venosta across the border in Italy. The type itself had forerunners in the Adriatic coastlands—at Cividale del Friuli, for example—where there was still contact with the eastern Mediterranean countries. Nor was it limited to the Central Alps, since it could also be found in the north, in the now-destroyed Sankt Clemens at Werden (North Rhineland) and at Oosterbeek in the Netherlands (of which only the foundations survive).

The aisleless church played a unique role in a few regions of special importance for the understanding of Pre-Romanesque architecture. Few

churches have survived in Spain from Visigothic times, before the Islamic conquest of 711. Those that have are small, for the most part without aisles, sometimes cruciform, their stones carefully hewn and fitted together. What is notable in them is the development of the crossing tower and, above all, the whole idea of the crossing (as will be seen below in our discussion of the disposition of the east end of the basilica). In none of them, however, was there anything like a self-contained, clearly demarcated, regular crossing with four equal arches on pilasters, the solution one would have thought most natural and inevitable. Furthermore, although the central area was emphasized by columns, they were disposed asymmetrically.

In Ireland the early churches are mostly single-naved, assembled from quarried stones but without mortar, with pointed barrel vaults held up on corbels and covered over directly by steep flagstone roofs. The longitudinal walls are often extended somewhat beyond the front walls to create an antenna-like projection. The entire conception is unique. Round yet very slender towers stand nearby, but they are entirely isolated from these single-celled churches. The chapel in Glendalough serves as a more or less typical example.

The situation is something else again in England. There, as in other lands of the Christian West, numerous large cathedrals and abbey churches were built during the time of the Anglo-Saxon kingdoms—from the fifth century until 1066, when the Norman invasion virtually put an end to the building fervor of this entire period. Not a single large edifice survives from this early time, because during the eleventh and twelfth centuries the new rulers of the country destroyed old buildings and constructed their own churches throughout the land; many of these were in turn covered over or replaced by new structures in the Gothic style. From the written sources and the few excavations undertaken thus far we have learned that the large Anglo-Saxon churches were by no means imitations of those on the Continent, but instead had characteristics all their own. Unfortunately, this can be demonstrated only in the churches of smaller monastic houses and in parish churches, though not many of these have even come down to us intact. However, English scholars have uncovered vestiges of more than four hundred ruined churches, enough to show that the artistic approach was highly individual and at the same time conservative: witness the tower at Monkwearmouth. This conservatism—a hallmark of other aspects of the English character as well—makes dating extremely difficult, with estimated dates for a particular church differing perhaps by centuries.

Almost all of these churches are surprisingly narrow and steep, with interiors like deep shafts, much like what we see at Escomb. Between the nave and altar area, and between the nave and crossarms as well, there are as a rule high, narrow arches that strike one more as doors separating the areas involved than as openings linking them. We are reminded of such Continental phenomena as the emphatically isolated crossing or the annexes of Carolingian aisleless churches.

The Westwork

The revelation of the westwork (the west section of the church, with its tower) as an architectural creation of the Carolingian era is due to a single scholar, Wilhelm Effmann, whose books on Werden, Centula, Corvey, and Hildesheim (in part published posthumously) stimulated research on these buildings from 1899 onward. Since then scholars have worked unflaggingly on this subject, and it can be said that today the westwork is judged one of the most significant phenomena of earlier architecture. This judgment remains despite the fact that few examples have adequately survived and despite the fact that we still do not understand with any certainty what its function actually was. As a constructional and architectural form, the westwork was something new and unique. No forerunners have been detected thus far, either in ancient Rome, Byzantium, or any other region. If today we comprehend the Carolingian era as a great creative period in art, it is due to some extent to our knowledge of the westwork. We now recognize the westwork to be neither a mere imitation of a misunderstood antiquity nor the first clumsy attempt of a half-savage people, but great art in its own right. Columns and vaults, basilicas and aisleless churches, and a good many other elements were adopted by Carolingian artists from the great reservoir of forms already at hand. But that the Carolingians did not alter them for the worse—transforming them instead into something relevant to their own culture and giving them another meaning—is something we have learned to appreciate much more since recognizing that these people were, in fact, capable of bringing into existence something new and entirely their own. Our enthusiasm may strike some readers as excessive, but is made necessary by the fact that by and large we are still under the influence of a point of view which, with complete disregard for history, takes the art of ancient Greece and Rome as absolute values, as norms. That Carolingian art signals instead a great renaissance is demonstrated today not only by its origins, but also because of its influence on the architecture of the succeeding period.

Architecturally, the westwork is a type of tower construction, and in medieval writings was in fact referred to as a *turris*. The tower, it so happens, is the form which medieval architecture often proved most impressive. It is found virtually wherever large-scale monumental architecture was built from Carolingian times onward: alone, in groups, isolated or—even more characteristically—incorporated into the structure of the church. Therefore, in these terms as well the westwork takes its place significantly at the very beginnings of medieval art.

The westwork of the former abbey church of Sankt Vitus at Corvey is the only one which can still convey an impression of the Carolingian form. The Benedictine abbey was founded in Carolingian times on the Weser River, namely at the eastern border of Westphalia, in what was at the time a newly conquered territory for the Frankish kingdom, not far from the Porta Westfalica (a pass between the high Westphalian hills where the river

flows down into the plain from the uplands). The church and the abbey we see there today are products of the Baroque era, but they cannot eradicate the majesty of the massive westwork, though even that is not unaltered. What we see today is a high façade wall with a narrow projecting structure in the center, flanked by two very tall towers between which stretches an arcaded bellhouse. As a whole, the effect is of a shallow transverse structure much like the transverse west fronts in Lower Saxony and Westphalia, which have been likened to a lock bolt (the German term is *Westriegel*). The arcaded story is a twelfth-century addition: before then, there had been a somewhat recessed square tower related to the lateral towers in such a way as to give them the full effect they do not attain today. The whole was a massive block on a square ground plan, shot through with a central tower and flanked by a tower at either corner. The result was a play of huge structural cubes instead of the present flat façade-like effect, something along the lines of Thümmler's reconstruction of the comparable westwork of the cathedral at Minden.

At Corvey, a tall atrium below the arcade projects from the main block. Behind it lies the vaulted ground floor often described as a crypt and, in fact, constructed like a Romanesque hall-crypt with nine cross-groined vaults on four columns along with lateral passages separated by pillared arcades. Unlike the more fully developed hall-crypts of the eleventh century, the interior has no cross-arches, and so there are no bays, the ceiling creating the effect of a single uniform vault funneling down to the columns. The capitals are the block-shaped Corinthian type. At one place a start was made at carving the feathery Corinthian foliage, and there are bead moldings that constitute further antiquicizing elements. Nevertheless, one has the impression that it is not by chance that finer decoration in the classical manner was omitted here. The boss or projecting capital seems, as a form, perfectly appropriate to the architecture, and in fact became the typical Pre-Romanesque and Romanesque form, the so-called Corinthian boss capital.

Behind the arcades of the transverse corridor lies the church which, though built in the seventeenth century, preserves the original elongated aisleless ground plan. When we ascend the vaulted winding staircases of the corner turrets, we are surprised to find a high, broad, and complex room, the so-called *Johanneschor*, the choir of St. John. After centuries during which it was known only in distorted form, it has been restored to its original appearance—at least to the extent permitted by the surviving parts. Only the columns of the upper arcades have been completed in modern form. The trabeated ceiling of the high square central area is problematical: did it lie immediately over the arcades (as it does today) and thereby close off the interior into a cube, or was it much higher, opening like a well into the central tower?

The impressive effect is due to the two stories of arcades that surround the central area. These open into what can be called side naves and galleries, which correspond on all four sides to the narthex and corridors of the ground

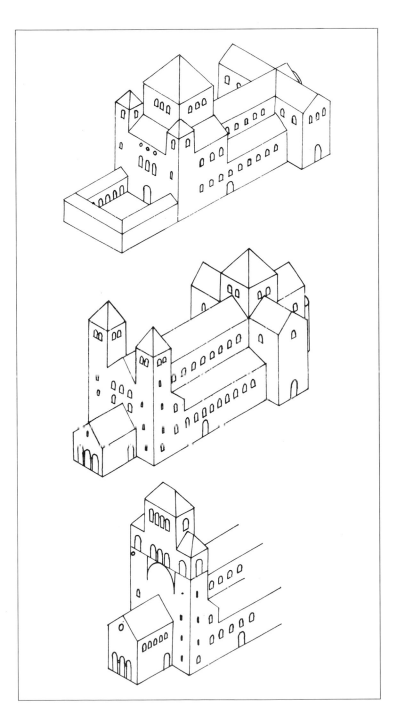

floor, though when taken point by point are conceived differently. Particularly prominent is the middle of the west gallery, which opens into a large arch not bisected by a central column. Since the westwork itself is deeper at this point (thanks to the tall projecting atrium), the interior too is deeper here. On the opposite side of the room, to the east, the chamber opened onto the nave of the church through a kind of lattice of arches, which here—unlike the system in the Palatine Chapel at Aachen, where columns were set into a round arch—consists of superimposed arcades.

The added emphasis given to the gallery on the west is the subject of a scholarly controversy revolving around the question of the significance and function of the westwork as a whole. Was it the seat of the emperor when, in the course of his travels, he visited this royal abbey? Should the entire structure be understood as a church reserved for the emperor? The latter hypothesis, accepted by many scholars, has no support from either written or archaeological findings, for which reason other experts view it with well-justified doubt and look instead to the rich and highly varied liturgy of the Early Middle Ages for an answer. We know that there were "families," or groups, of churches in immediate juxtaposition. From that standpoint the westwork would be a sort of auxiliary church directly adjoining the principal church and connected with it. As a matter of fact, in the further course of their development, westworks became ever more closely linked to the churches, though for a long time they continued to preserve a certain spatial autonomy. It is also perfectly possible to combine both scholarly explanations, since there was nothing to prevent the emperor and his entourage from making use of the westwork from time to time for their own purposes, even if its primary function was liturgical. Whatever the case, the westwork at Corvey was, and is, a multi-storied, many-chambered, more or less central plan edifice with a tower-like exterior.

A number of similar structures have been disclosed by excavations in recent years, all of them displaying the characteristic almost-square ground plan with foundation grid for the pillar arcades and the columns of the ground floor. Among them are the early cathedrals at Hildesheim, Halberstadt, and Reims, but it is only at Minden that portions of the original have survived in a later west front. From written sources and old views, as well as from the research of Durand and Effmann, we know that there was a westwork on the long-destroyed abbey church of Centula (now known as Saint-Riquier) in Picardy, making it the earliest of all those known. However, tradition is decidedly uncertain on this point, despite the fact that it rests on the interpretation of early texts and their comparison with certain seventeenth-century views that are said to go back to pre-Gothic drawings. Great care is therefore needed in evaluating all the evidence.

Basilical Churches

Although as a rule the westwork was completed on the east by a basilical nave, neither in Corvey nor elsewhere has such a nave survived from

11. *Corvey, former Benedictine abbey church, interior of the Johanneschor on upper story of the westwork, looking southwest*

12. *Corvey, former Benedictine abbey church, ground floor of the westwork*

Carolingian times. We are obliged therefore to examine other churches whose naves still exist. For the basilica—the three-aisled nave with its higher upper story pierced by windows for the central aisle—what we remarked earlier is even more true—namely, that the ground plan alone (that is, the excavated foundation) can lead to significant conclusions but cannot convey the artistic essence of an architecture that no longer exists, and that it usually tells us very little indeed about the height of the interior and its proportions, about the arcades and openings, and about the supporting elements.

Some basilicas of the Carolingian era are still standing in three regions of Europe: between the Rhine and Main valleys, in Asturias, and in northern Italy. We must exclude Roman churches from this brief survey, since there is much debate about precisely those forms of theirs which would be most revealing for our present inquiry—most notably the pier arches in Santa Prassede and the alternating supports in Santa Maria in Cosmedin. As for the churches in the three areas mentioned, they exhibit such characteristic differences that we find ourselves obliged to speak of regional traits as early as the ninth century. The most striking of these differences is that the Italian churches quite obviously carried forward the Early Christian tradition. San Salvatore in Brescia has the same sort of slender and narrowly separated columns and thin clerestory walls as the Late Antique basilicas. The apse connects directly with the middle nave, without a transept. There is neither tower nor westwork. Blind round arches frame the upper-story windows on the outside just as in the churches of Ravenna. Stucco ornaments decorate the undersides of the arches of the pier arcades, and especially the latter permit dating the building at shortly after 800, as proposed by Panazza and Peroni. Without those arcades, the date might seem all too dubious, as it is, in fact, when applied to almost all other North Italian basilicas commonly assigned to the ninth century, including San Vincenzo in Milan and San Vincenzo in Galliano near Cantù. In almost every case dating must be drawn from secondary evidence, because the stylistic traits continue to be ephemeral, even in later constructions.

All of the comparable basilicas in Asturias use pillars, not columns, as their supports. About six are fairly well preserved and are datable with certainty to the Carolingian era. The most important among them is San Julián de los Prados, known popularly as El Santullano, which King Ramiro built before the gates of his capital at Oviedo. The nave is short and broad (at the east end a transept cuts across it) and it is completed by three rectangular choirs of different widths. Here for the first time we can gauge the spatial effect of a full-fledged continuous transept, our only previous examples having come from excavated foundations or later additions. The juxtaposition of independent spatial areas is plain to see here; moreover, they are clearly cut off from each other by strongly projecting wall strips and separating arches, an impression in no way affected by the vistas seen through the small arches in the strips of wall. The plan of the interior is further complicated by upper-story rooms above the altar area and by

13. Oviedo, San Julián de los Prados,
exterior from the southwest

14. Monte Naranco, San Miguel de
Liño, reconstruction with interior
exposed (from Haupt, 1909)

narthexes at the west end and at the head of each crossarm, with the result that the exterior too looks like an accumulation of quite separate building components. There are vestiges of wall paintings containing illusionistic decorative architecture, rather like Hellenistic and Pompeian examples. It is thought that the original cathedral of Oviedo (replaced by a Gothic construction) must have been much like this.

The other churches are smaller and mostly narrow and tall, but each of them—and notably those in Tuñón, Gobiendes, Valdediós, and Priesca, as well as San Pedro de Nora in the city of Oviedo—repeats a few characteristics of San Julián de los Prados. Especially instructive is the church of San Miguel de Liño (also known as Lillo), adjacent to the great ninth-century royal palace on Monte Naranco near Oviedo. It survives only as a fragment, but in the original plan a number of steep bays, as in a basilica, alternated with transept-like structures in which, however, the pseudo-crossarms were isolated as shafts of space above the side aisles and were separated from the central nave by the latter's continuous dividing wall. There is also, above the west entrance, a very complicated tribune with highly detailed decoration. Together with the rich architectonic decoration, this treatment of separate areas as distinct shafts of space makes for a most impressive interior.

The third group of Carolingian basilicas includes the churches at Steinbach im Odenwald, Seligenstadt, and Höchst. That of Sankt Marcellinus und Sankt Petrus at Steinbach, in the region of Darmstadt, was founded and built by Einhard, the biographer of Charlemagne, as was also the church of the same name in Seligenstadt on the Main in the same region. The basilica at Steinbach is a ruin, but carefully looked after. Its pillars are constructed of Roman flat bricks. The central nave runs directly to the apse, and two lateral areas constitute low crossarms, though unfortunately the southern one is broken off and the northern one lengthened; the lateral naves and west end no longer exist. Nevertheless, all the conditions are present which would permit a reconstruction of the destroyed parts, thereby bringing back to life an important monument in the very heart of Carolingian territory. For anyone interested in the technical details of architecture, even the present ruined state of the basilica has a great deal to offer. Among other features, there is an underground galleried crypt that probably holds the graves of the founder and his wife.

Quite similar is the church at Seligenstadt, though there the transept is the same height as the central nave. A Late Romanesque choir and crossing tower, however, very much alter the original appearance. As for Sankt Justinus in Höchst, a suburb of Frankfurt-am-Main—in an almost unsightly architectural medley—there is still a Carolingian nave with powerful columns and handsome capitals as well as squat crossarms and a fully isolated crossing area. Its dating is much disputed.

Research and excavations have given us some idea of a considerable number of Carolingian churches, especially in Germany, and much the same

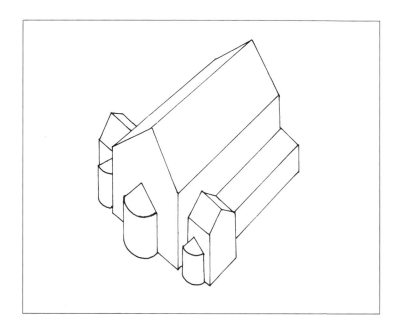

applies to these as to the ones discussed above. For decades now, several of them have been objects of particular study, revealing more and more new aspects of Carolingian architecture, especially the churches founded by the missionary St. Boniface in Fulda (the cathedral) and Bad Hersfeld. Of particular note in southwestern Germany is the former abbey church at Mittelzell on the island of Reichenau on Lake Constance; in Switzerland, the monastery at Sankt Gallen; in southeastern Germany, the church of Sankt Emmeram and the Niedermünster in Regensburg and the recently excavated colonnaded basilica at Solnhofen, of which considerable portions are still standing; and, in nearby Austria, the cathedral erected by Archbishop Virgil in Salzburg. The excavations of the early cathedral in Cologne have come up with increasingly diversified findings and are a clear demonstration of the difficulties encountered in diggings, even with all the technical advances of modern archaeology. According to the latest results, the original building was a very large basilica with piers as supports. The chief Carolingian monuments in northwestern Germany are the Abdinghof church at Paderborn and the convent church at Vreden, both in Westphalia, and the earliest cathedrals at Hildesheim and Halberstadt. In northern France we may cite the Carolingian original of the abbey church of Saint-Denis near Paris, as well as the no longer extant abbey church at Centula near Abbeville, these likewise highly problematical in many respects.

The surviving central nave with pier arcades at Brixworth (Northamptonshire) in England (which, like the basilica at Steinbach, is built of Roman bricks) shows that a fourth group—an Anglo-Saxon one—existed, though it eludes analysis only because so little of it has been preserved. This is true of other regions of Europe too, and therefore cautions us against broad generalizations. Nevertheless, it is striking that certain important characteristic traits were widespread except in Italy: these were the use of piers and pillars and a tendency toward a complex spatial system in the east end of churches. Along with these, certain key traits of the Romanesque basilica were laid down in advance, which means that in decisive ways that style did not grow out of the Early Christian colonnaded basilica but evolved independently with aims of its own. It is of interest in this regard to note that one of the surviving Visigothic churches in Spain, San Pedro de la Nave in the province of Zamora, likewise has piers in its nave. On the other hand, in San Miguel de Escalada the tendency of the colonnaded basilica to appear more plastic, even to soar, is further emphasized by the horseshoe-shaped arcades and the way they carry over into the open and airy transverse choir screen.

Organization of the East End

North of the Alps in particular, and in its more significant examples, the Carolingian basilica is as a rule cruciform, with the nave terminating at the east end in a transverse structure that is itself completed by an apse. There are a number of basic forms to this plan:

1. The main apse connects directly to the central nave, and the side naves are shorter than the central one. At the east end, to either side, there is an arch that is larger than the nave arches but that does not reach the height of the central nave. Each arch opens onto a lateral compartment that is usually square and likewise lower than the central nave but, at the same time, higher than the side naves. This is often marked by the fact that there are windows in the central nave clerestory as well, though usually smaller than those in the outer walls of the lateral naves. The adjoining compartments have apses of their own and can therefore be interpreted either as symmetrically disposed chapels, as accessory choirs, or as crossarms. The basilica at Steinbach is representative of this so-called cellular transept type. If the east end of the central aisle corresponding to such crossarms is separated off by a pier arch, as in the eleventh-century Belgian churches of Saint-Hadelin in Celles and Sainte-Gertrude in Nivelles, the result is a kind of crossing, though not as yet in the fully isolated form that would suggest a genuine transept. It is assumed that this type grew out of the basilica with pastophoria mostly confined to the eastern Mediterranean basin but present also in Ravenna. The interior effect is created through the many variations in height between the numerous distinct areas.

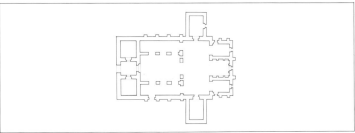

2. At the east end of a three-aisled nave there is a broad transept matching the central aisle in height and often also in length and breadth. Conceived by and large as an autonomous chamber, it is disposed unequivocally at a right angle to the main room. It is separated from the central aisle by a pier arch and terminates at the east in an apse or an altar area with various subdivisions. This type can be seen most effectively in, for example, the ruins of the eleventh-century Benedictine abbey church at Bad Hersfeld in Hesse and in the Carolingian church of San Julián de los Prados in Oviedo. Presumably, the plan derives from such large basilicas of the Constantine period as Old Saint Peter's and San Paolo fuori le Mura in Rome. Indeed, it is often argued that the expression *more romano* ("in the Roman manner") in early literary sources refers precisely to this plan, which in buildings such as the original Cologne Cathedral and the abbey church at Fulda is thought to represent a conscious and deliberate return to Roman prototypes. However, these German examples from Carolingian times are known only through portions of their ground plans, and so the interpretation must remain hypothetical. The type is designated as "continuous" or "attached" from the fact that the transept runs uninterruptedly through the nave or is firmly abutted against its end, forming either a Latin cross or a T. Characteristic of it is the marked isolation of its spatial components.

While the types with cellular or continuous transepts are typical of Pre-Romanesque architecture, they continue to be found well into the eleventh century and, sporadically, even later.

3. In a third type, the central nave and the transept are of equal height and width, and they intersect to create a square area, the crossing, which as a rule is surrounded by four arches of equal height. Differences in the

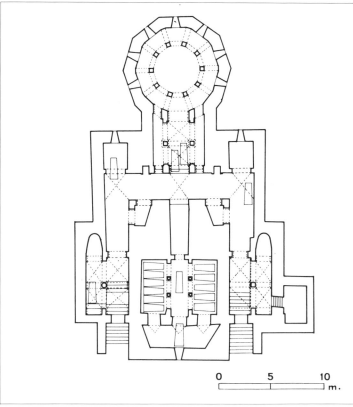

0   5   10
m.

form of these arches determine two sub-types. In one, the arches conspicuously separate the crossing area from the crossarms, central nave, and altar area inasmuch as they are quite a bit narrower or lower than the cross section of the interior. The piers that support them are extended to make strips of wall projecting into the crossing. This type of crossing is referred to as "tied off" *(abgeschnürte),* and good examples of it are the church of Sankt Georg at Oberzell on the island of Reichenau and Saint-Philibert-de-Grand-Lieu near Nantes in Brittany, both from the tenth century. In the other sub-type, the arches reach the full height of the interior, and their supporting piers project only slightly into the area (to judge by the naked eye alone, not more than the depth of their intrados). Here the arches do not tie off the contiguous areas but instead make them all seem like so many separate bays (to use a term appropriate only later in time). This "isolated" *(ausgeschiedene)* type of crossing appears in the clear, almost classical cruciform church plan. The culmination of a long development, it became the form for Early Romanesque architecture and the virtually mandatory form for the High Romanesque. Perfectly obvious, simple, and clear, this form was nevertheless not understood as such for long, even by specialized scholars. Today still it is debated whether the form was used only sporadically or was already being developed before the year 1000, perhaps as early as Carolingian times. There is no definite proof of the latter, and the arguments in its favor are in part pure hypotheses, based as they are on theoretical reconstructions such as that of the long-disappeared abbey of Centula. The fact is, we first find the "isolated" crossing with certainty at the start of the eleventh century, in Sankt Michael at Hildesheim, though from then on it was more and more frequent. Like many other forms of church architecture, this one too was not current everywhere in Europe but only in specific regions. Generally speaking, the transept and crossing were of lesser importance in southwestern Europe, where the aisleless and hall plans dominated. Even when there was a rectangular ground plan—often conditioned by the tower built over the crossing—the crossing seldom or never dominated the entire interior as it did in the basilical churches of northwestern Europe. Very often in southwestern Europe, and even in the twelfth century, it is "tied off" and set apart; south of the Alps, the crossing seldom was given the normative arrangement, and this is characteristic for almost all the regions of Italy. It is irrelevant to derive conclusions involving value judgments from this fact, but one must nonetheless recognize that the spatial problem of transept and crossing is by and large limited to northwestern and central Europe.

The Chancel

The crossing achieves its full effect as the center of a cruciform church plan only when it is joined on the east as well as on the west, north, and south by something larger than a simple apse. This explains why scholars are particularly interested in the development of the altar area. Here again, as

is so often the case, the broad lines of development are now clear, while the individual stages and their dating are still disputed. Actually, a number of characteristic forms existed simultaneously: the simple semicircular apse; the apse preceded by a short antechoir, which—when it is not flat-ceilinged but barrel vaulted—resembles more a deep arch than a distinct spatial compartment; the square or rectangular chancel with or without apse; and the tripartite choir (as in San Julián de los Prados).

Only a few of these formal dispositions have come down to us with full authenticity and in well-preserved Carolingian churches, and here again we often must rely on Carolingian ground plans that were later built over.

From Carolingian times onward, there were frequently two chancel areas, with apses and even transepts at the west as well as at the east end. Such double-choired churches were rare before that time, and are thought, quite rightly, to be the consequence of the adoption by a particular church of a second titular saint in whose honor, and for whose veneration, a second main altar was erected. With respect to the Early Christian basilica, this brings about a major alteration in the total plan: the main entrance is no longer in the middle axis of the building but displaced to one side. For this reason, it has been said that the Early Christian basilica is to be understood as a colonnaded passage from portal to altar, whereas in the early medieval church the central aisle invites the faithful to linger there or to walk about in the chapels and other areas around it. Though this is doubtless a somewhat exaggerated and subjective modern interpretation, it serves to cast light on a factual distinction that does indeed exist and is confirmed by the spatial organization of Carolingian churches, which in so many cases quite obviously point ahead to the Romanesque rather than merely looking back to Late Antique predecessors.

The Crypt

The main outline of the origin and development of the crypt can be easily understood, and, what is more, we have a good idea of what led to them. The point of departure was the persecution of Christians by the pagan state and priesthood, which ended by encouraging the veneration of the martyrs and early witnesses to the faith. As time went on, this veneration assumed precise forms. Quite early, churches were erected above the graves of martyrs or, vice versa, their bones were removed into churches. Often the relics were installed in the apse, in immediate proximity to the altar, while those of the most important martyrs or, later, of other saints or founders of the church were frequently put away in a walled and vaulted chamber called the *confessio*. Because the piety of the time demanded physical contact with the venerated burial place, whether direct or indirect or even purely visual, a partially or fully underground passage was constructed around the tomb or *confessio*. Often an opening (the *fenestrella*) permitted the tomb to be seen from the passage. The latter followed the inner or outer circumference of the apse, and where the altar area was rectangular rather

than semicircular, that form was respected. Niches were hollowed out of the walls to hold candles or devotional offerings, and stairs led down to the passage. The result was the so-called passage-crypt *(Gangkrypta)*, whose development began in Early Christian times and can be traced into the fourth century, though as a type it endured into Carolingian times, with well-preserved examples in the inner crypt of Sankt Salvator in Werden on the outskirts of Essen (North Rhineland); in the crypt of the titular saint in the former Benedictine abbey church of Sankt Emmeram in Regensburg (Bavaria); and in the former abbey church of Sankt Luzius in Chur in the canton of Graubünden (Switzerland).

Until that point, the crypt was not particularly interesting, being more a cellar-like passageway than a real room. For us its interest lies chiefly in the evidence it gives of early medieval faith. However, in the tenth century especially the chambers of the crypt were enlarged and connected to each other, with additional chambers linked to them. The altar area at the east took up more room, was divided up by columns or pillars supporting vaults, and not infrequently was even two-storied. Thus the external crypt (the French term is *crypte en hors d'oeuvre*) came into existence; often it was much like the later form of the interior crypt, the hall-crypt. Examples still in good state are found in the so-called Ludgeriden crypt of Sankt Salvator at Werden, in the church at Susteren in the Dutch Limburg, in Sankt Emmeram in Regensburg, and in Saint-Germain at Auxerre. This type of crypt, according to A. Verbeek, dates chiefly from the tenth and eleventh centuries, and recently Sanderson has connected it with the reform movement centering around the Lotharingian monastery of Gorze.

In other cases corridors or chambers lead off the rectangular passage-crypt at the east and the west to form another type called the gallery-crypt (like a mine, it has tunneled galleries going off in various directions). Carolingian specimens in fairly good condition are found at Steinbach, Echternach, and in the ruined abbey of Saint-Médard near Soissons. Where the barrel vaults of the corridors are of the same height and breadth, they create cross-groined vaults at the intersections, and these give us an excellent idea of the origin of this form of vault. However, if one corridor is lower or narrower than the other, its barrel vault cuts into the other one with roundish lunettes as in Sankt Willibrord at Echternach (Luxembourg), resulting in a play of curved lines that seems very characteristic of Pre-Romanesque architecture. This effect is carried further if there are niches that hollow out the walls, as in Saint-Médard. In the wavering light of candles or torches, such corridor systems seem virtually labyrinthine.

There is another significant variant: the ground traversed by these corridors may be so hollowed out that only narrow brickwork partitions remain between the tunneled galleries. If those partitioning walls are broken through for openings, the result is something very close to the fully conceived crypt. This is so in a number of well-known crypts from the tenth and early eleventh centuries, notably in the former Benedictine abbey

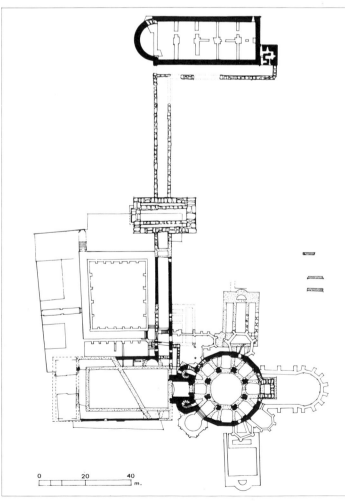

22. *Aachen, Palatine Chapel, axonometric projection with reconstruction of the west front (from Kubach, 1952)*

23. *Aachen, plan of the Palatine Chapel and the Imperial Palace (Aula Palatina) as reconstructed on the basis of excavations (from Kreusch, 1958)*

church at Muri in the canton of Aargau (Switzerland); in San Felice and the one time monastery of Santa Maria delle Cacce at Pavia; and in Sankt Dionys at Esslingen.

While in this type the impression still prevails of parallel and intersecting corridors, in the next stage it becomes clear that distinct spatial areas are separated by arcades, as seen in Sankt Wiperti in Quedlinburg and in Sankt Mang in Füssen, where one can already speak of hall-crypts. Much as in Romanesque hall churches in southern France, here too the separation of the aisles is marked by their barrel vaulting, though at eye level they are very much open to each other through the arcades.

This stage of crypt development goes on well into the eleventh century. Thus we still find barrel vaults with lunettes in the Early Romanesque east crypt of the Trier Cathedral and in the crypt of the Abdinghof church at Paderborn, both dating from the middle of the eleventh century and reconstructed in the present one. Short, thick, square pillars such as are found in crypts in Fosse (Belgium) and Susteren (Netherlands) are still reminiscent of the earlier corridor plan. Only at the next stage do we arrive at the authentic hall-crypt of the Early Romanesque; this will be discussed in the next chapter.

Early Central-Plan Buildings

With the central plan, as with the basilica, there were both strictly traditional buildings and others pointing toward the future. Characteristic of the former group are a number of baptisteries in northern Italy and southeastern France extending in unbroken continuity from the fourth or fifth centuries into the eleventh, though scholars may still vary in their dating of individual buildings by as much as hundreds of years. Most are vaulted, thus carrying on the tradition of the vault throughout the Dark Ages. The form most frequently adopted in the beginning was the octagon with niches, an eight-sided structure with cupola whose lower walls were enlarged into eight niches, all alike or else differing pair by pair. Often hollowed out of a solid wall, the niches were also frequently extended outward, being visible on the exterior of the building. Examples are found at Novara, Albenga, Biella, and Lomello in Italy and at Fréjus, Marseilles (Saint-Jean-Baptiste, known from excavation), Aix-en-Provence, and Mélas in France. Neither the oval decagon with niches used in Sankt Gereon in Cologne nor the centralized building over a square ground plan with vault and apses such as we find in San Lorenzo in Milan was taken up elsewhere during the Middle Ages.

The cruciform central-plan building with ambulatory—the Greek cross—can be traced back to Late Antique times. Santa Costanza and Santo Stefano Rotondo in Rome are the best-known representatives of this form, but there are others in Nocera Superiore (Salerno) and Perugia (Umbria). Characteristic of the post-Antique successors of that type seem above all to be the remarkably complex Santa Maria in Pertica in Pavia (though the building has been destroyed and its reconstruction is uncertain) or, far to the south,

Santa Sofia in Benevento, of which we shall have more to say below. Not until the eleventh and twelfth centuries did the clear basic form re-establish itself, as in the baptistery of San Tommaso near Almenno San Bartolomeo, in the province of Bergamo; that of San Pietro at Asti (Piedmont); and elsewhere.

The most famous representative of the basic central plan is the minster at Aachen, now the cathedral of that bishopric but erected around 800 as the chapel for the favorite palace of Charlemagne. It is the largest, most artistically significant, and best preserved construction of the Carolingian era to have come down to us. It is highly complex both from the standpoint of technique, as a freestone building, and from that of construction, as a quite complicated vaulted structure. In form it consists of a steep octagonal shaft of space that constitutes the core, and this is illuminated from above by eight round-arched windows set just under the level from which the cloister vault springs. The walls below have numerous conspicuous openings but are virtually flat, with scarcely anything in the way of projecting elements except for a strongly marked cornice separating the ground floor from the superstructure. All around the octagon, on two stories, there are round-headed arches—the lower ones quite squat, the upper ones tall and narrow. These give onto passages or galleries conceived in a quite different manner, having in common only the sixteen-sided outer wall. The linkage of an interior octagon and an exterior sixteen-sided polygon called for complicated solutions in the vaulting, whose immediate relationship is necessarily to the interior walls and vertical supports. On the lower level, between the sixteen-sided outer polygon and the eight-sided inner core, the spaces are vaulted by angled-off annular barrel vaults that, because of the lunettes on the eight main sides, come close to being cross vaults (though there are no cross-springers; many diagrammatic plans indicate them erroneously). Above, eight square bays with barrel vaults and eight triangular bays with vaulting cells fan out of radial pier arches. The barrel vaults lie very high and rise in height from outside in, which means too that the round arches of the upper gallery are necessarily stilted. Paired columns superimposed on two stories and separated by a kind of arched bridge constitute a sort of lattice or grille on both levels.

However, the whole is not a pure central-plan structure, as what we have said so far might suggest, for it is oriented on an east-west axis. At the west a porch rises in front of both floors of galleries and is flanked by large round turrets containing winding staircases. On the ground floor there is a kind of narthex with a portal, and above it lies a tribune. This was originally echoed on the east by a rectangular altar area that was replaced in the fourteenth century by a tall Gothic choir. Later, too, Gothic and Baroque chapels were added to the exterior of the building. Despite all this, the plan was axially determined in another respect: between the west towers on the exterior there was a tall troughlike recess, forming a kind of apse to the rectangular atrium, but only vestiges of this survive. On the north a long

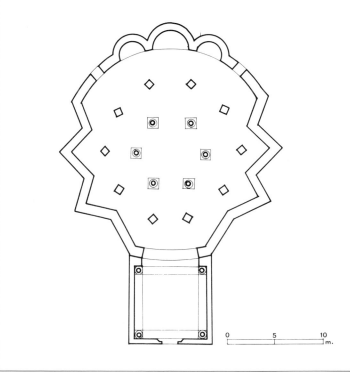

two-storied passageway connected the chapel with Charlemagne's residence, the Aula Palatina, but in its place now stands the Gothic town hall. In the lower ambulatory there were altars and shrines, and on the tribune across from the altar area was Charlemagne's throne, a simple construction of marble slabs, now largely composed of material from the tenth century. Only a few invaluable items from the original furnishings have survived, notably the simple bronze doors and the richly worked gratings around the galleries.

Scarcely another medieval building had so unmistakable and so easily discernible an effect upon subsequent developments as did the Palatine Chapel at Aachen. Central-plan churches were based on this prototype well into the eleventh century. Some of them were even so identified in contemporary sources, and while the actual formal evidence is admittedly vague in the case of the late tenth-century burial tower at Mettlach (Saarland), others were more closely dependent on it—for example, the former abbey church at Ottmarsheim in Alsace, which was dedicated in 1049; and the chapel at Nijmegen in eastern Holland, in which, however, the scheme was reduced to its essentials. Other such buildings in Belgium and the Netherlands—Saint-Jean in Liège, Sint Lambert in Muizen, Sint Pieter in Louvain, the chapel in Groningen—are known only through excavations or as foundations for Baroque remodelings. Not all of these are palace churches like that at Aachen, the one in Ottmarsheim belonging to a charitable institution for gentlewomen, and those in Mettlach and Louvain being cemetery churches (the latter, with its rotunda around the crown of the choir, belongs in fact to another group).

The central plan was used primarily for baptisteries, but also for chapels within palaces and citadels. By an exceptional stroke of good luck we possess three other palace chapels from Carolingian times that are also centrally planned, though otherwise very different indeed, none of them having upper stories. The most closely related is Santa Sofia in Benevento in southern Italy. A polygonal building with ambulatories, it was completed in 762 by the Longobard duke Arechis II, whose realm extended as far as Apulia. There the central hexagon is surrounded by a double ambulatory with columns and squared-off pillars. The outer wall has a star-shaped, many-angled form. Triangular vaults of varying sizes make up the stone ceiling in the interior. Thus everything is unlike the chapel at Aachen, and it is only in the extremely complicated interlocking of interior and exterior forms that their relationship can be recognized.

In Milan, an archiepiscopal chapel built around 875 and known as San Satiro—now incorporated into Bramante's basilica of Santa Maria presso San Satiro—follows an entirely different scheme. It is a square with four interpolated vertical supports and extended by four apses into a cross-form, the whole sheathed within a round wall whose exterior was devised by Bramante. If one grasps the basic relationships—and they only *seem* simple—and interprets them in the light of Chierici's research, one sees here as well a complicated interplay of forms consequent upon the differing

heights of the columns, of which four stand free in the center, surrounded by twelve others following the disposition of the walls.

Another building intended as residence or palace chapel is the well-known one at Germigny-des-Prés built by Bishop Theodulph of Orléans around 800. Again the plan is centralized, but the architectural type is different from those mentioned heretofore. Despite the fact that its ground plan is related to that of San Satiro in Milan, its interior organization is quite diverse. In Benevento and Milan the central lanterns we see today are of more recent origin and their initial design is not certain, but at Germigny-des-Prés there is a characteristic Carolingian square crossing tower. A square and a cruciform ground plan are combined as they are in Milan, but with piers rather than columns. In particular, the crossarms are very high here and separated by a trellis of arcades that recalls the chapel at Aachen, though there are no upper galleries. The building has been grossly over-restored, but still corresponds to the original in its principal features.

Here, then, we have the various forms the central-plan conception assumed in certain important works still surviving from the Carolingian era: the octagon with niches; the octagon with ambulatory; and the square with four vertical supports. Along with these, but surviving only in later constructions, are the simple cruciform round building, the Greek cross, and the quatrefoil. It can hardly be expected that all these designs were invented wholly without older models to go by. As the prototype for the palace chapel at Germigny-des-Prés, the Armenian cathedral of Bagaran has been proposed. While the origins of the design at Aachen are disputed, San Vitale (built in the Byzantine exarchate of Ravenna in the fifth century) has long been the most frequently proposed model, and this is still the most convincing explanation. Be that as it may, the Aachen chapel decisively transforms its model into a quite different conception: it has a steep, shaftlike interior instead of the almost rotund form of San Vitale; its octagonal walls are narrow and shallow instead of being gently hollowed out; and it has a clear axial orientation. Similar distinctions can be demonstrated in all its features and details.

Here, as in so many other instances, all talk of prototypes and influences clarifies only a restricted segment of the artistic creative process. For the most part, it gives no more than an indication in which something of the sort could have taken place, and by no means a concrete identification. Architecture cannot be fully grasped in one context alone, whether it be as art work or as technical achievement, as a representational object or according to its intended function, as a purely craftsmanly realization or as the product of economic and social conditions.

Carolingian Wall Articulation: the Gatehouse at Lorsch

Fortunately, we do possess a building whose exterior looks by and large much as it did in Carolingian times, when it was built: this is the gatehouse of the former Benedictine abbey at Lorsch, between Worms and Darmstadt.

Not much remains of the overall structure of this Carolingian imperial monastery and its church, though the excavations led by Behn have brought to light at least the main outlines of the church's plan: an elongated forecourt, a westwork, and an interior that is seemingly very simple or, at any rate, without transept. The general disposition is noteworthy, since it is axially oriented within the broad circle of surrounding walls. All that has endured relatively intact is the gatehouse, which stands free in the middle of what was once the forecourt of the church. This is a two-storied, houselike construction with a saddle roof and a small round staircase turret to either side beneath the open gable. The ground floor resembles a triumphal arch with three round arches opening onto the front and rear to create an open passage. However, unlike the Roman triumphal-arch gates, the passages are not vaulted, the space between the front and rear arcades being instead flat-ceilinged. Above it there is a similarly flat-ceilinged upper story whose interior has walls painted with architectonic pilaster motifs. The room itself was the chapel of Sankt Michael, a structure found at the west end of many churches in early medieval monasteries and whose function was to provide a post from which the Archangel could ward off the powers of evil. But what was the purpose of this entire building? Was it really a triumphal gate? Ginhart thinks the earliest church of Sankt Martin in Linz on the Danube in Austria must have been of the same type.

Not only the function but also the architectural form of the building at Lorsch is puzzling. It is obvious at a glance that Antique motifs are cited. The arcade is faced with half-columns having Composite capitals that support a cornice. On the upper story there are fluted pilasters over which rise triangular pediments instead of the usual blind arches. The entire building is overlaid with colored stone tiles in geometrical patterns that lend it an air of unreality. It is, in fact, ornamental rather than architectonically rigorous, and Frankl has described the building as having been conceived like a textile and not structurally. Similar or at least comparable conceptions are encountered often in the early period, and here already their fundamental traits were fixed.

Lorsch is a unique surviving example of the Carolingian style of articulating the exterior walls and is a work of great technical perfection, giving the impression that it was conceived aesthetically, with due concern for beauty. It shows how Antique and Roman three-dimensional articulation could be turned inside out to create a purely flat surface from which all structural import has been stripped away, resulting in something more like a woven textile pattern. Thus, elements were incorporated into architecture that can be compared with what is found in Carolingian miniature painting and the minor arts (for example, the reliquary Einhard had made for Sint Servatius in Maastricht).

Nonetheless, the articulation of the Lorsch gatehouse is carried through in a system scarcely to be found elsewhere. Most like it is the tower of the church at Earls Barton near Northampton in England—which, however,

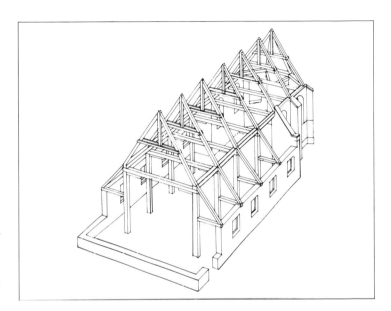

moves even farther away from the formulas of classical antiquity: there the pediments became zigzag lines; the pilasters, very slender stone strips; the columns, little balustrades with tiny barrel vaults. A similar though not quite so radical transformation appears in Saint-Laurent in Grenoble, with its new way of linking columns, architraves, and arches, and in the interior of the palace on Monte Naranco (Oviedo), which has pendant bands of decoration with ornamental disks. The plastic relationship between articulation and wall in all these cases does not as yet achieve the absolute abstraction so widespread in the Early Romanesque. Therefore, there is nothing amazing about the fact that fully developed round columns are incorporated into the articulation of the wall surface—as at Saint-Laurent in Grenoble and in the church in Jouarre (Seine-et-Marne)—or that buttresses articulate the exterior walls energetically at San Miguel de Liño on Monte Naranco and Santa Cristina de Lena, both in the province of Oviedo, as well as on the cupola drum of the minster at Aachen, while remaining isolated and unlinked by either arches or entablature.

Early Domestic and Military Architecture

In a survey of medieval architecture one does not usually find a summary of the findings concerning archaeological excavations of prehistoric and protohistoric buildings. Nevertheless, it is important to draw the reader's attention to these tentative beginnings. The stone architecture of the advanced cultures, as it appeared in all the provinces of the Roman Empire, is not all that was inherited from the past. Architectonic conceptions were already present in such elementary earthworks as the round citadel with wall, moat, and palisade. If a stone monument of some sort—a menhir, for example—was to be set up, considerable technical expertise was required to transport and raise its huge blocks into place. When such stones were combined into a kind of *allée* or avenue, this presumed not only the conceptions of "axis" and "orientation" but also a very decided will to think and to build in monumental terms. This was unequivocally true for the first time in the circular assemblages of huge stone blocks erected during the Bronze Age. With the vertical elements—the "pillars"—covered and linked to each other by horizontal stone beams, the result was a primeval architecture already foreshadowing the Greek peristyle temple. The best known and best preserved work of this sort is, of course, Stonehenge near Salisbury. Tombs covered by stone slabs—the so-called megalithic tombs of "princes"—also involve technical problems bordering on the domain of architecture. The spherical mounds of earth raised over them are not far from the idea of the Egyptian pyramids. If stone huts with conical dry-earth roofs—the *trulli* of Apulia and *nuraghi* of Sardinia—are late manifestations of an artistic approach from which such very early domed Mediterranean interiors as the so-called Treasury of Atreus in Mycenae likewise stemmed, then we may indeed speak of a far-reaching and ancient tradition of vaulting. In early historical times in the North, where wood was the basic material, there were not only primitive blockhouses or log cabins made out of entire tree trunks (such as are still lived in today in eastern Europe), but also buildings with timberwork framing, employing early forms of structural wall beams, vertical supports, and architraves and with their interiors divided into more than one aisle as well as what can be called bays. The analogy with medieval church design is obvious, but how much can really be deduced from this is a matter of argument. However, the Norwegian stave churches of the High Middle Ages utilizing pales or stakes, as at Borgund, are beyond doubt related to these early wooden structures, and to them is attributed the origin of the half-engaged supporting column, one of the most striking phenomena of the Early Romanesque (subdivision of the wall through vertical round elements is quite simply nonexistent in the stone architecture of antiquity). There do exist wooden churches of somewhat similar type, but built long afterward, at Honfleur in Normandy and Paaslo in Holland.

Our knowledge of Pre-Romanesque secular architecture is full of gaps. The protohistorical forms of the donjon or keep, the motte (the earthen conical mound of a castle), and the various forms of dwellings were carried over into Carolingian and Ottonian times. Along with these there were monasteries laid out in a manner we can ascertain from a few surviving Irish complexes, from excavations made at Fulda and Bad Hersfeld, and from an early drawing of the Sankt Gallen monastery (to which we shall have occasion to return later). We also have some acquaintance with the imperial palaces of Charlemagne and his successors.

The ground plan and model for the palace at Ingelheim, which one often finds reproduced, should be viewed with great skepticism. The palace at Aachen has been studied somewhat better: particularly striking there are the linkages and axial relationships. On the west in front of the surviving central-plan structure of the Palatine Chapel lay a two-storied porch. A long and likewise two-storied passageway, built partly of wood, linked this section with an aisleless building on the north, the Aula Palatina, of which considerable portions were incorporated into the Gothic town hall. In the cross-axis of the central-plan chapel there were auxiliary churches to the north and the south.

A royal hall survives in Asturias, in the celebrated royal palace on Monte Naranco near Oviedo, known from the thirteenth century on as Santa María de Naranco but now restored to its original designation. Both stories of the narrow longitudinal building are covered with barrel vaulting, have rich wall articulation and decoration both inside and out (using relief roundels as ornamental elements), and have buttresses and columns, transverse ribbing, open loggias, and double freestanding staircases. Thus, all in all, it is a building of rich conception and imagination. The secular constructions at Aachen and Lorsch lead us to suspect that there must have been others like them in the Carolingian realm, but even the Lorsch gatehouse must be thought of as belonging to a category somewhere between religious and civil architecture.

Chapter Two

EARLY ROMANESQUE ARCHITECTURE

There is a subtle transition between the Pre-Romanesque and the Early Romanesque, which were to set the stylistic bases for what we may call the "archaic" stage of Western art, extending from the late tenth century into the second half of the eleventh. The "Mature" or "High" Romanesque style developed between 1060 and 1080 and is characterized by such buildings as Speyer II and Cluny III. The transition to this latter phase is easily recognizable in the first Anglo-Norman edifices at St. Albans and Durham, as well as in the imposing new cathedral at Pisa and the hall churches with galleries in southwestern Europe, especially those in Conques, Toulouse, and Santiago de Compostela.

Pre-Romanesque art was diffused over an area more or less equivalent to that of the then civilized West, but without as yet really reflecting its inner regional differences. During the decades around the year 1000, however, certain centers or regions of decisive importance and influence on Romanesque art began to arise, to be followed by others in increasingly greater number. Chief among them were: Catalonia in the eastern Pyrenees and their northern and southern slopes; Lombardy, a name applied in these pages not only to the central part of the Po Valley but also to all of northern Italy because of what one finds in such churches as San Paragorio at Noli in Liguria and elsewhere; Burgundy in the river basin of the Saône; Normandy along the French coast of the English Channel; the lands around and between the lower courses of the Rhine and the Meuse; the Upper Rhine region between Basel and Mainz; and Lower Saxony between the Weser and the Elbe. Other regions, destined for greater importance, were still in their earliest stages of development. Without allowing ourselves to be influenced by their later achievements, we can scarcely dare distinguish in the eleventh century between Tuscany, Apulia, Provence, Westphalia, and Aquitaine.

Even more important than the regions as such are their supraregional interconnections and differences. In the eleventh century two focal centers developed, one in the eastern Pyrenees, the other in northwestern and west-central Europe. Thus, the Loire came to demarcate the boundary between a region comprising northern Spain and southern France and another region made up of northern France and western Germany—a separation that was to become even more decisive from the twelfth century on. Similarly, we can already discern links between southern Germany and northern Italy in certain significant aspects. If we follow only the dictates of art and override or ignore present national boundaries, Italy likewise proves to be not a firm unity but a loose conglomerate of individual regions. These are phenomena that prevailed to the very end of the Romanesque era and, in part, during the Gothic period and even beyond.

In the decades around 1000 the German Saxon kings—designated Ottonians, after Emperor Otto the Great—consolidated their dominion over the Empire and confirmed their authority by refurbishing everything to do with the dignity of the Roman emperor. Under their jurisdiction, the Church became an official organ of the state, to which it was almost indissolubly bound, and the bishops were made dukes. Consequently, the glory of imperial power was given concrete form in the visual arts, above all in the building and furnishing of churches.

Ottonian and Early Romanesque Art

The Ottonians ruled in their German lands from 919 to 1024. This is a fundamental datum for our study, since in recent decades the notion of "Ottonian art" has become greatly, indeed inadmissibly, extended. As regards architecture, the entire first half of the century of Ottonian rule is a virtual void, the Dark Ages that began with the Norman invasions around 880 and did not end until well into the second half of the tenth century with the last of the Hungarian invasions and, specifically, with the Battle of Lech in 955.

It is only in the later tenth century that we begin to find isolated but very important buildings: in Lower Saxony, at Gernrode and Quedlinburg; on the Upper Rhine, at Oberzell on the island of Reichenau; in Normandy, at Saint-Pierre in Jumièges; in Aquitaine, at Saint-Généroux; along the lower reaches of the Rhône, at, Saint-Pierre in Vienne; in the Pyrenees, at San Miguel de Cuxá; in Lombardy, at Galliano. In all of these, what still basically dominates is clearly Pre-Romanesque, and in none of them do we have any difficulty in singling out the elements that can be defined as Ottonian. The style persisted far into the eleventh century, and it is especially evident where, as in the minster in Essen or the convent church at Ottmarsheim, the tradition of the Palatine Chapel at Aachen is still plain to see.

What the German scholar H. Jantzen designates as Ottonian is chiefly a product of the years after 1024 and even (in part) from the middle of the eleventh century or thereafter. This art—until now better if less impressively termed Early Romanesque—presents certain problems as soon as we call it Ottonian. Judged in terms of their own characteristics, certain important works—the Benedictine church at Limburg on the Haardt, the early cathedral at Speyer—simply do not fit into that style. Furthermore, the years around 1024 do not mark any stylistic change; the creative highpoint was, in fact, later, during the time of the Salians—at least as far as the surviving works are concerned. Finally, too, all the monuments throughout northern France constitute an inherent part of the art of the German Empire, sharing with it the standard form of the flat-roofed basilica with towers, a form wholly unlike the hall plan favored in the South and one that early on was characterized by a tendency toward vaulting. Here too, then, the designation Ottonian is difficult to justify.

Nonetheless, the notion of an "Ottonian" art is more colorful than the vague term "Early Romanesque," and for that reason the designation has been adopted by many more recent scholars, even outside of Germany. For out part, we feel it should be ruled out since it carries with it all too many contradictions. In recent years even the term Early Romanesque has been

dropped altogether. Consequently, and with somewhat more logic, this means that eleventh-century buildings would have to be considered Pre-Romanesque.

Early Romanesque architecture takes its place between the Pre-Romanesque and the High Romanesque periods not only on factual grounds—that is, its historically chronological position—but even more for reasons of style. Many of its creations, whether actual buildings or architectural types and forms, quite plainly go back to Pre-Romanesque phenomena, whereas the transformations it underwent had great influence and in turn set forth the basic principles for the architecture of the twelfth century.

The Early Romanesque forms for the west end of the church—the reduced westwork, the triple-towered west front, the twin-towered façade, the transverse west front—were already all present in their essentials in such Carolingian solutions as the fully developed westwork and west front of the minster at Aachen. They can be thought of as originating through simplification, clarification, or differentiation of specific structural elements, though any decision as to whether in fact they did so arise is bound to be more or less subjective. Although the flat-ceilinged basilica goes back to the Early Christian form in the Mediterranean area, as early as Carolingian and even pre-Carolingian times there were modifications especially evident as far as the vertical supports were concerned: columns were superseded by piers or pillars. Whether examples existed before the tenth century of a system of regularly alternating supports—strong and weak, piers and columns—is another question that is still open, and this is true too of the longitudinal gallery and (although the question has not been much discussed) the wall articulation: vertical through the use of responds (engaged piers), horizontal through the use of blind arcades. An impressive number of such Early Romanesque basilicas have survived, but many aspects of their architecture have been insufficiently studied, especially the ceilings. Italy was partial to open timberwork, as, presumably, was Normandy also. In other regions we lack factual information as to whether beams or flat board ceilings closed off the interior into a solid box of space or whether a vestige of the Pre-Romanesque plastic conception lived on in the guise of open raftered ceilings.

As for the cruciform basilica, in Carolingian times there are three, possibly four, types of transept design, and these are determined by the character of the crossing. They persist throughout the eleventh century, while the emphasis shifts more and more clearly to the fully isolated crossing and the uniform square crossarms. The clarification of the form resulting from this has its effect on the crossing tower, especially on its position and arrangement, as well as on the conception of the altar area. When and where the apse became dissociated from the transept to become an oblong and then square chamber of independent stature, and when and where the tripartite choir, the choir with staggered apses, and the choir with ambulatory were developed into richer and more extensive forms—these are all questions that have been troubling architectural historians for a century now, and all the answers have been at best provisional. Be that as it may, all these phenomena belong incontrovertibly to the Early Romanesque—as does the hall-crypt, the finest examples of which date from the eleventh century.

Another problem involves the transformation of shimmering, sparkling, weightless screens of masonry into compact walls of solid substance that utilize apertures of various sorts precisely with the aim of elucidating their own mass by means of such articulations and subdivisions. This process was quite obviously going on in the eleventh century and was in fact in its decisive phase; it was over by the twelfth. When, however, did it begin? This question surrounds one of the most fascinating developments in Romanesque architecture: the solid walls begin to break down into surface strata, the space they enclose begins to burrow into them by means of niches, wall and space interpenetrate in arcaded galleries. Thus, no sooner did the wall arrive at a real consistency than it once again began to dissolve, or in some instances was broken down into a skeleton-like arrangement of piers and solid walls (Speyer Cathedral) or of piers (Saint-Etienne in Caen). Researchers have done their utmost to trace almost all of these phenomena further back, but they have succeeded in only a few cases. On the whole, however, we do get the impression that many strands in the developmental process go back in fact to Pre-Romanesque times.

While those processes were evolving principally in west-central and north-western Europe, in the southwest (Spain plus France up to the Loire) an entirely different but equally revolutionary development was in motion: the complete vaulting of the single- or triple-naved church interior was realized at a single stroke, something known on a large scale only in central-plan buildings and seldom in small basilicas (though it may be found in San Salvador de Valdediós). From the late tenth century on, longitudinal and transverse barrel vaults were erected, and in most cases this meant that the high, gradated, and well-lit interior of the basilica form was replaced by the much lower and usually dark interior of the hall form. The centers that adopted this new approach were at first Catalonia and Burgundy, but soon the entire southern part of present-day France as far north as the Loire was won over to the form. In the rest of northern Spain and in northern and central Italy, similar forms arose and continued to be in use well into the twelfth and thirteenth centuries.

The new style had little if anything to do with the various forms hitherto discussed. Monumental westworks were rare, and even in larger churches the transept was not considered an integral component of the structure as in northern basilicas; therefore, the problems of conception and design of the crossing itself were of much less importance, though there was the same sort of orderly organization, or at least a square form demarcated by four similar arches. The three naves covered by a single shallowly sloping saddle roof were only slightly surpassed in height by a crossing cupola (usually octagonal).

Towers, singly or paired, were duly imposing, though as yet they scarcely made contrasting groups as in the North. Wall decoration was confined to neutral framing of flat surfaces through the molding and arch friezes characteristic of Romanesque architecture all over Europe. The accentuated mass of the walls, the conception of interior areas (singly or in combination) as closed cubes, and the firm cohesiveness of the interior design—all these were at least as evident as in the North, but as yet with scarcely any indication of the eventual dissolution of the wall surface. This explains why the architecture of southwestern Europe strikes one as more "original" than that of the North, and this may also be why, when audiences first became aware of its artistic identity and qualities, it had such a sensational impact.

The Italian peninsula was decidedly conservative and took part in the above-mentioned innovations only occasionally and with hesitation. Scholars such as P. Frankl who are entirely persuaded by the idea of the dynamic development of the North tend necessarily to minimize the importance of Italy within the overall Romanesque picture, a position which at times has been carried to exaggerated lengths in an effort to counter the disproportionate overvaluation given to the South in the earlier literature. Nonetheless, even if this approach is adopted, there is no denying the high artistic gifts of the Italians.

If we examine without bias the churches built throughout Europe between 960 and 1060, we find extraordinarily sharp distinctions. In the main, they can be separated into regional groupings, with wooden-ceilinged basilicas on the one hand and barrel-vaulted halls on the other. One wonders if this distinction is not far more decisive than the changes that occur in time and by which we define the history of "style." But even the study of stylistic evolution furnishes us with important clarifications, focusing on common principles and comparable transformations in the composition of interiors, and in the articulation and conception of walls.

Early Romanesque West Fronts and Towers
The westwork is one of the architectural conceptions through which we can grasp the development of Carolingian ideas into Romanesque forms—clearly and directly in the tenth and eleventh centuries, somewhat less so in the twelfth and thirteenth centuries. The most fully developed prototype, as we have seen, was that in Corvey. The ground plans of the foundations excavated at Halberstadt, Hildesheim, and Reims are by and large so similar to it that we can justifiably reconstruct them according to that model. In the tenth century the series of westworks continued with the cathedral of Minden and with the first stage of Sankt Pantaleon in Cologne. However, three surviving Early Romanesque buildings show a significant modification: the lower story with the so-called westwork-crypt is omitted. This is the case at Sankt Peter in Werden (the westwork of Sankt Salvator; it was separately dedicated and given a name of its own), at Sankt Pantaleon II

36. Jumièges, ruins of the abbey
church of Notre-Dame, the west front
from the west

37. Reichenau-Mittelzell, minster of
Sankt Maria und Sankt Markus, the
west front from the southwest

36. Jumièges, ruins of the abbey
church of Notre-Dame, the west front
from the west

37. Reichenau-Mittelzell, minster of
Sankt Maria und Sankt Markus, the
west front from the southwest

in Cologne (the building that is still standing), and the former abbey church of Münstereifel in the Cologne area. While the Werden westwork, dedicated in 943, still had a complicated system of pier arches and barrel vaults in the side rooms and galleries, Sankt Pantaleon was refined to a virtually classical beauty and maturity (an impression certainly aided by the fact that the west crossarm, shortened in the nineteenth century, has been reconstructed), qualities in which it was followed by the former abbey church of Sankt Chrysanthus and Daria in Münstereifel. The large dressed-stone arcades of the interior and the articulation of the outside wall with moldings and friezes around the round arches show that, in these respects also, Sankt Pantaleon represented a significant phase in the development of Romanesque art. Unfortunately, in all three buildings, as in the crossing towers of Sankt Michael at Hildesheim, it is not known if the room formed by the central portion of the westwork was divided into stories or was simply a steep light shaft attaining the full height of the tower building.

Conceptions resembling the westwork are found in other important buildings of the eleventh century, though at first glance they would seem to be quite differently laid out. Of the west front of the first cathedral at Speyer (the scholarly designation is Speyer I), dating from around 1050, the porch on the ground floor still exists but in altered form, as does the high middle room upstairs flanked by multistoried side rooms. On the exterior, all of this is encompassed within a powerful block lying athwart the main body of the church. We do not know if it was originally crowned with three towers as it has been since around 1100; though they are set back from the front, they nevertheless are clearly suggestive of a fully developed westwork. At Saint-Philibert in Tournus, the two-storied narthex from around the year 1000 gives the impression, from outside, of being a twin-towered façade, though not yet in definitive form. Inside, a barrel-vaulted basilical upper church is superimposed upon a hall-like vaulted lower church, again calling to mind the westwork. Even the west front of the abbey church of Notre-Dame at Jumièges, dating from around 1070, which can be claimed as an early twin-towered façade, has a projecting structure in the middle and an interior disposition that are still very suggestive of the westwork. Here it is apparent that the twin-towered façade likewise has its roots in the earlier structure.

As we have seen, the Romanesque type of west front can be derived, in theory at least, from Pre-Romanesque types. Thus, already in the Carolingian Palatine Chapel at Aachen we find a tower-like square structure, in the same axis as the central pile, linked to two symmetrical round staircase turrets. If all three structures were fully developed towers—which at Aachen is debatable—there would already have been a definitive three-towered west front, a form which appeared impressively in Maastricht around 1000, slightly later at the cathedral in Paderborn, and for the next two hundred years was used in countless instances in the territory between the Schelde and the Elbe rivers. Even something as simple as the three-towered front, however, proves extremely variable in the relations between ground plan, dimensions, height, articulation, and the distance from each other of its three components.

The twin-towered west front is known with certainty only from the late eleventh century and appears with overpowering grandeur and clarity in the abbey church of Saint-Etienne at Caen, though—despite the fact that it dates from the last third of the eleventh century—its rigorous form stamps it as still essentially Early Romanesque. It may be that even the twin-towered façade was a Carolingian invention. There are many examples from the twelfth century, and the High Gothic cathedrals of northern France made the form virtually the standard by which all others are to be judged—whence its widely diffused overvaluation. The effort to detect, at any price, the earliest possible origin and the widest possible dissemination of the form has led researchers astray. We shall never know with certainty if the ruined church at Limburg on the Haardt and the Strasbourg minster had Early Romanesque twin-towered façades, and there has been much debate as to whether what was involved was a transverse front with central tower or a genuine twin-towered façade. However, what is clear is that transverse west fronts of various forms and arrangements played an extremely important role. We know that the Early Romanesque cathedral at Speyer had a blocklike west front resembling a transept (no longer in existence) that, around 1100, was given three towers. The collegiate church at Bad Wimpfen (North Württemberg), from around 1000, has a west front that is by no means large but is highly impressive with its massive block form, large central recess, and two octagonal towers. The cathedral at Trier has by all odds the loftiest, noblest, and largest Early Romanesque west front of this sort, elaborately decorated with a west apse, four towers, recessed portals, and galleries; it dates from around 1050.

The multi-towered building unquestionably ranks among the highest achievements of medieval architecture. Six towers, three on the east and three on the west, make Sankt Michael at Hildesheim the earliest surviving example of this form. Notre-Dame at Jumièges, with its crossing tower to the east and its two towers to the west, gives an impression of contrast despite the symmetrical grouping. Innumerable churches are presumed to have had three or more towers built in the Early Romanesque period, but proof is lacking for most of them—even for the cathedral of Speyer—and their towers were either added or rebuilt at a later time.

Even the simplest form, the single tower at the west or east, is not without its eccentricities. In the period that concerns us here, it took the form of an independent structure isolated from the church, as was often the case with the Italian campanile, while north of the Alps—in France, Germany, and elsewhere—it was as a rule situated in the axis of the central nave, either preceding it, as a west tower, or at the east, crowning the altar area to create a so-called choir-tower. Here again the genesis is controversial, and the documented examples date only from the Early Romanesque.

40. Pomposa, Benedictine abbey
church of Santa Maria, the bell tower
and church

41. Pomposa, Benedictine abbey
church of Santa Maria, interior
looking west

As a rule, the tower is usually a solid cube (though there are oblong, round, hexagonal, and octagonal examples). In the early period it is often a single unarticulated block of masonry, relieved only by its apertures. As early as the eleventh century it begins more and more to be multi-storied, prismatic, or drum-shaped, with surfaces articulated by moldings and arch friezes or blind arcades and with increasingly numerous and large openings. Only seldom, however, does a Romanesque tower depart from a closed contour. Most are bell towers, especially if they are the only one on a church, and many are provided with stone stairs leading to the upper stories and roof. Others surmount the altar area (and are therefore known as choir-towers) or other portions of the interior, and their upper stories may contain the west tribune or a tower chapel. Even defensive military functions are not alien to church towers: they have always been utilized as watch-towers and, in many cases known from specific evidence, for the city fire wardens. Yet a good many are to be understood as far surpassing these utilitarian functions, as landmarks or monuments calling to the eye and mind the presence of the church in city or countryside, and some must have been added for purely aesthetic reasons, particularly where there are a number of towers.

A tower over the center of the church or over the crossing of nave and transept makes a particularly strong bid for monumentality. At Sankt Michael in Hildesheim, two crossing towers, one east and one west, achieved a kind of climax never matched elsewhere. If such a crossing tower opens like a shaft into the interior below, the effect on the interior is architectonically most impressive. Unfortunately, as concerns a number of important towers—among them those of Sankt Michael and of Speyer I—we simply do not know if they were opened or sealed off.

The history of tower construction in all these aspects remains to be written. Many phenomena are not yet sufficiently understood even by specialists in the field. Thus, for example, Italy and southern France are known to have been backward in the construction of towers—but where was there a more grandiose isolated tower than at the abbey of Pomposa? And there are considerably more twin-tower groups in this region than is commonly thought—one can cite the cathedrals at Ivrea and Aosta as well as San Miguel de Cuxá.

Essentially, however, towered west fronts and tower groups are a feature of the landscape north of the Alps, and they are one of the most magnificent manifestations of Early Romanesque architecture. Italy adopted such schemes much more rarely, and in this too we can observe how much later developments owed to Early Romanesque origins. The simple basilical façade aligned with the cross section of the nave remained characteristic of Italy. Two towers flanking the apse are to be most expected in this region, as in the previously mentioned cathedrals at Ivrea and Aosta and, from a later time, Sant'Abbondio in Como. Where large monumental towers were built, they were by preference isolated and set alongside the church. That

42. Château-Landon, abbey church of
Saint-Séverin, interior, wall of the
central nave (from Enlart, 1902)
43. Surbourg, former priory church,
interior looking east

at Pomposa is certainly the finest instance from the Early Romanesque, succeeded in the High Romanesque by the campaniles in Venice, Modena, and Pisa.

The Wooden-Ceilinged Basilica

In large stretches of Europe, from the southern tip of Italy to the North Sea and the Baltic, from the Loire to the Elbe, the dominant form was the basilica. Wherever that form appeared in Carolingian times, it underwent profound transformations—except in Italy. Piers very often took the place of columns and thereby decisively altered the entire character of the building. Vertical slabs of wall pierced by arcades and windows closed in the boxlike interiors—witness Sankt Leodegar in Schönenwerd or the abbey church in Château-Landon—instead of seeming to soar above long rows of columns like the insubstantial walls of the Early Christian basilica. If this insistence on a fundamental difference seems exaggerated, objections are overruled by the fact that the succeeding period carried further the same tendency with perfect unambiguousness. Not even the Italian centers escaped this process, even if important buildings still often reverted to the antiquated type of colonnaded basilica as in San Piero a Grado near Pisa, the cathedral of Torcello, and the abbey of Pomposa.

A number of decisive transformations took place in the eleventh century in buildings widely separated from each other geographically. The sequence of square piers is interrupted in the middle by a cruciform one at Sainte-Gertrude in Nivelles in Belgian Brabant, and the succession of columns is broken by a pier in the cathedral at Gerace in Calabria. Not only does the pier in the middle break the series of supports into two equal halves, but it also bisects the entire area of the central nave. One is no longer conscious of a long row of arcades but only of groups of supporting members seen together. This is decisive precisely in elongated buildings with eight or more arcades. The more prominent middle support acts furthermore in such a way as to draw the two arcades and the two central nave walls into relationship, thereby making one view the front end of the interior as an area in itself, a clearly demarcated boxlike room closed on all four sides and corresponding to the architectonic cube of the exterior.

At Sainte-Gertrude in Nivelles the middle pillar is cross-shaped: four rectangular projections around a square core make the pillar particularly substantial and solid. The projecting engaged shaft facing the nave breaks through the impost stone to climb high up the wall. Consequently, the central nave appears to be composed of two spatial cubes (though these are not yet the "upright" spatial bays of the High Romanesque). If both pillars are linked by a pier arch, the impression becomes even stronger, as indeed it is today at Sainte-Gertrude, where such an arch was added in modern times though it is absolutely certain that nothing like it existed previously. By arbitrarily adding this arch, the architect who conducted the restoration, S. Brigode, strengthened our argument by exemplifying it in actual fact.

Obviously, however, in the eleventh century the builders had not yet learned the full consequences of their actions.

In another innovation, the row of supports is infused with rhythm by alternating piers or pillars with columns. The simple type with a regular 1:1 alternation is found especially in the Lower Rhine and Meuse valleys, with well-known examples in Susteren (Dutch Limburg), at Sankt Luzius in Werden near Essen, and in Sankt Willibrord in Echternach (Luxembourg), but also along the Upper Rhine—in the former abbey church in Surbourg in Lower Alsace—and in Lower Saxony in the abbey church at Drübeck. In this type, the wall of the central nave becomes additionally consolidated and stabilized. However, there also exists another system, a 1:2 succession with units of pillar-column-column, whose most famous and earliest documented example is Sankt Michael in Hildesheim, of around 1000. In this form, which became a virtual hallmark of the Lower Saxon Romanesque, it is easy to overlook the linkage of the two rows of pillars with each other until one realizes that the pillars rise at the corners of ground-plan squares, a most effective solution.

The oldest church still standing in Paris, Saint-Germain-des-Prés, has a projecting engaged shaft running up the upper wall not merely once in the middle, as in Sainte-Gertrude at Nivelles, but a full four times, that is, with each recurrence of a pillar. Thus, the central nave wall becomes sliced into vertical compartments, and here we are already very close to the mature form of a succession of bays, though there are no pier arches yet.

In yet another variant—besides alternating supports, articulated pillars, and shafts rising the height of the wall—there are transverse pier arches, as in Santa Maria Maggiore at Lomello near Pavia in Lombardy, where the longitudinal walls are already mutually supported and the bays already well demarcated. True enough, the whole remains fairly light and delicately articulated, and the exceptionally oblique angles create a certain impression of instability. Nevertheless, the combination is decisive. Comparable with this is the ruined abbey church of Notre-Dame at Jumièges in Normandy. There the pier arches are not reinforced, and the entire building is a ruin, but it gives the impression of remarkable strength and solidity. Its lordly steep height reminds us that its builders were the conquerors of England. And in the former abbey church of Saint-Philibert in Tournus powerfully high and strong round brickwork pillars strike the keynote. From the top of each pillar there rises a small half-column engaged in the wall. Today they support pier arches, but those as well as the transverse barrel arches are later additions, there being originally a wooden ceiling or open timberwork. The half-columns rise to the crown of the wall and have a function much like that of the respond.

Along with the alternation of supports and the various ways of dividing up the central nave must be included the further development of the pillar itself as a three-dimensional structure. Pillars may have projecting engaged shafts not only on the side facing the nave, where the shafts extend above

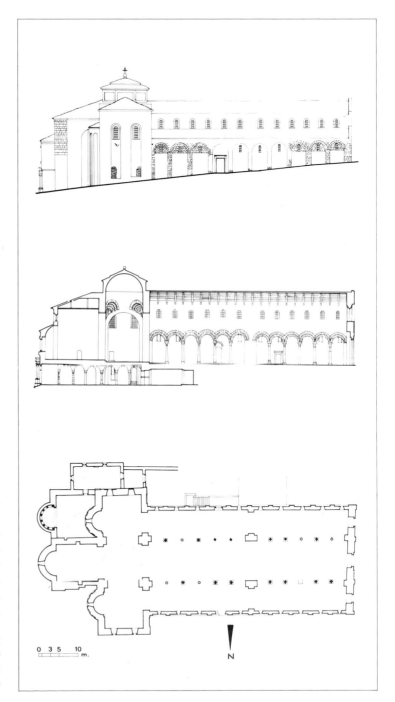

the impost, and not only on the side facing the lateral nave, where they generally have to do with vaulting and transverse arches, but also on the other two sides—that is, those supporting longitudinal rather than transverse arches. When the pier thus becomes compound, with rectangular or half-round shafts engaged in it on all sides, it assumes a fully developed configuration as a massive element in itself, as in the early example of the former abbey at Bernay (Eure). When these lateral shafts are present, it is virtually inevitable that they should carry over to the underside—the intrados or soffit—of longitudinal arches and take on a more corporeal, three-dimensional, contoured form. But who can say if this process initiated in the pier or in the arch? In design and cross section, such compound piers may go so far as to be bundles of shafts or even more complicated forms, something fairly frequent in crypts but rare in naves, though witness Saint-Remi in Reims.

As we see, there can be a great many variations in a simple basilica-form interior that, to a greater or lesser degree, originate in the supports. Others may be conditioned, directly or indirectly, by the general spatial plan of the interior, and there are still others having to do with the relationship between the central nave wall and the interior as a whole.

Basilicas with Galleries
Many medieval churches have chambers or passageways on an upper story that open onto the main room. These galleries, tribunes, triforia, or lofts may be located in the west front and west tower, in the crossarms, all around the circumference in central-plan buildings, at the west over a porch or similar element giving onto the central nave, longitudinally over the side naves, or even on occasion as part of an elaborately organized chancel. They are frequent also in the chapels of citadels and palaces and similar edifices. It is difficult to believe that they had no practical purpose, but in many cases we have no factual evidence as to whether and how they were put to use. Tribunes at the west end were evidently often intended for eminent individuals and their escorts or for nuns and canonesses. As a rule, tribunes are reached by steps cut into the wall or by circular staircases, and the more elaborate these are, the more one can presume they were in frequent use, as in the Late Romanesque gallery churches of the Lower Rhine region.

It has often been debated whether the gallery as a form is to some extent interchangeable between one type of church building and another—can the galleried basilica, for instance, be explained simply as having adopted the gallery from centrally planned churches?—or whether in medieval thinking architectural types were so firmly fixed that a central-plan church with circular galleries would be thought of as something very different from a basilica with longitudinal galleries, and that therefore an offshoot must be sought farther afield, not in the simple carry-over of a form but in historical and geographical factors. If the latter is true, then some sort of connection must be established between, say, Salonica or Rome of the Constantine

period and the Early Romanesque churches in Gernrode and Reims. I would not dare attempt to prove such a point but nevertheless seize this occasion to insist that there are great gaps in our knowledge of early architecture. How can one even propose to settle such questions knowing that, out of hundreds of early churches, at most one is known to us? Who can claim in all seriousness that the gallery basilica was not known to Carolingian architecture? Look at the map of monastic foundations of the Pre-Carolingian and Carolingian periods drawn by A. Mann and compare it with the buildings we know with any surety: the proportion is about eight hundred to ten. Anyone who claims that of the ten basilicas we know none have galleries and therefore the other seven hundred and ninety had none, must not expect to be taken seriously.

What we do know for certain, however, is that in the eleventh and twelfth centuries there were a great number of galleried churches of which the overwhelming majority fall into regional groupings; beyond this, they can most conveniently be divided into those with wooden ceilings and those with vaulted central naves.

Early Romanesque gallery basilicas are known in three regions: Lower Saxony, Champagne, Normandy. The earliest well-preserved example from each is, respectively, the abbey church in Gernrode at the foot of the Harz Mountains in East Germany, Saint-Remi in Reims, and Notre-Dame in Jumièges. The church at Gernrode, consecrated in 963, is especially striking because of the complicated rhythm of the arcades, which is not the same in the side aisles as in the gallery zone. The central nave wall is extensively opened up and almost playfully animated, whereas its topmost stretch is flat, with only a few small windows. Similar examples are the Heiligkreuzkirche at Hildesheim and Sankt Marien at Münzenberg on the outskirts of Quedlinburg.

Saint-Remi in Reims was begun in 1005 and consecrated in 1049 (the churches at Montier-en-Der and Vignory are not unrelated to it). Its plan is quite individual, and in its gigantic elongated central nave there is an uncompromising axial division: above each of its arches is a double opening of the gallery. Worthy of note too is the rich fashioning of the piers in the side nave, though the vaults and their responds must be excluded since they are Early Gothic additions. On the upper story, as can still be seen from outside, there were two rows of semicircular and round windows, one above the other. This produced a quadruple sequence of openings. Saint-Remi, like the church at Gernrode, gives an overwhelming sense of spaciousness.

The nave of Notre-Dame in Jumièges, on the other hand, is exceptionally steep and narrow. Here too tripartite gallery arches are directly above the semicircular pier arches, each time forming a powerful pairing that is further emphasized by the pronounced alternation of pier and column and by the round shafts projecting from the piers and rising straight up the nave wall. The church is in ruins, and the upper delimitation of this vertical articulation has been destroyed. It has long been debated whether the shafts ran up to the crown of the wall without supporting anything, or if they ended below the windows on the upper story and supported transverse arches spanning the central nave. The question cannot be decided with certainty. French and German scholars alike (notably E. Gall and R. Liess) hold different opinions. In one case, greater prominence would be assumed by the vertically articulated and braced wall, in the other by the emphatic division of the interior into bays. The question is important, as much because of the supra-regional distribution of the type—witness Santa Maria Maggiore in Lomello and Modena Cathedral—as of the central nave vaulting introduced a few decades later.

Among earlier gallery churches can be mentioned the cathedral of Coutances in Normandy, dating from the second half of the eleventh century, Saint-Etienne in Caen, and Saint-Vigor in Cérisy-la-Forêt; in southern England, the cathedral of St. Albans; in the Schelde Valley in Belgium, Saint-Vincent in Soignies, though the latter represents a variant.

If we compare these churches, we see how false it is to associate the presence of galleries with a steep interior, and the reason is easy to appreciate: the walls of the middle nave, whether high or low, can be set as close or as far apart as the roof-tree or other type of roof construction permits. Therefore the question of whether an interior is narrow and high or broad and squat has nothing to do with the galleries. As experience has shown, the blank walls between the nave arcades and upper-story windows can also be high or low, like the side naves and the nave arcades themselves. Not the gallery as such, but the disposition of the ceiling and roof over the side naves or galleries, and the height of these naves and galleries, influence the absolute height of the interior. The spatial proportions in the middle nave are exclusively the product of its height and scale. As this demonstrates, the gallery creates an effect not only as a space that has been opened up but, even oftener, as a row of subdivided apertures. For the principal effect of a church interior, what is frequently more important than the spatial relationship between central nave and gallery is the manner in which the elevation of the central nave wall was conceived. If one looks at the hall churches of southwestern Europe, it becomes clear that the decisive elements there are the towering basilical walls through which light streams down and, along with this, the contrast between the side naves lying in shadow, the high smooth walls, and the clerestory windows or other apertures arranged in ascending tiers on the walls. This distinction is not something merely read into these edifices as a consequence of subtle scholarly and aesthetic investigation, but was the direct intention of medieval builders. This is proven by two important phenomena: the first of these is the so-called false gallery that lacks a floor, so that, to all intents and purposes, the nave arcade is split into two tiers of apertures, which is the case at Vignory and in the Early Gothic examples of the collegiate church at Eu and Rouen Cathedral. The second proof is the blind triforium that articulates the wall between the nave arcade and the row of windows above, of which we shall have further occasion to speak. A rare secondary form of the gallery church is the triple-naved gallery type completely lacking in a clerestory, as in Santo Stefano and San Lorenzo in Verona.

Wall Articulation in the Central Nave

Medieval architecture achieves its effect not only through the succession of spatial units but, to a greater extent, through the conception of the walls as such. In this their sheer size plays an essential role. Among the largest walls that exist are those of the central nave of basilicas, along with a few façades. For that reason it is important that they be not merely impressive in themselves, but also to the highest degree related spatially to the interior as a whole. The central nave wall does not exist in isolation and is not viewed frontally—cannot be, in fact, or at least only in sections. There are always two parallel walls involved, which together shut in the interior at either side and so can be seen (and photographed) only in diminishing perspective or in isolated sections. As always with architecture, one must know how to see but also how to imagine what cannot be seen at a particular point. It is of decisive importance precisely here that impression and conception be brought into proper balance, something not all scholars have done.

In the hall church, unlike the basilica church, there is no central nave wall but rather a succession of arcades. The wall above the arcades is peculiar to the basilica and subject to specific conditions. Below, it opens into the side aisles just as in the hall church. Above those openings the wall must be high enough to connect with the highest point of the single-sloped (lean-to) roof always used for Romanesque side naves. Not until the Gothic period were side naves sometimes covered by a double-sloped saddle roof either longitudinally (which introduced complicated problems in water run-off, which the Romanesque did not understand) or transversely, which meant that the cube and contour line were broken—something that before Gothic times occurred only once, in the Late Romanesque former Cistercian church at Bronnbach in North Baden.

Inside the church, the lean-to roof is supported along the wall by a horizontal fascia, which—being usually a few yards high—forms a considerable part of the elevation of the central-nave wall. It can be omitted only when the side nave is covered by open timberwork rather than a flat ceiling and when the outer wall is lower than the nave arcade. This is found in Italy, with its predilection for a less weighty architecture, but is unacceptable to architects in the North.

Only above this middle zone are there window openings; lined up across the upper level, they create another story. Thus, exceptions aside, the central-nave wall in the basilica is three-storied: arcades, middle zone, window level (clerestory), a subdivision open to all sorts of variations as far as the height of the separate zones is concerned.

Because structural necessities made this division unavoidable in the basilical central-nave wall, an obvious consequence obtained in a number of buildings: the middle zone was made clearly readable as a separate story, articulated with blind arches or niches and, furthermore, delimited by lower and upper cornices. The articulation employed in it is called a triforium—a term which has been appropriated for Gothic architecture, though it is not linguistically justified. In Romanesque architecture it can perfectly legitimately be applied even where there is no passageway but only blind articulation. A misunderstanding can occur, however, if paired openings, so-called twin apertures, are described as biforia.

Instead of blind arches or niches, there may be rows of openings between the central nave and the roof area of the lateral naves. Due to their affinity with the arches of longitudinal galleries, these openings are termed false galleries. Structurally, however, they are more like triforia than galleries since, to all intents and purposes, space as such is less important in them than the function of articulation. Furthermore, this linkage of the roof area with the church interior has disadvantages—drafts of air, cold—that have often led to walling up the openings. The openings in the false gallery are frequently closer to the triforium in form when they are lined up in a series and fill the wall of the bay from one respond to another. If they are isolated and conceived as double or triple arches, the relationship with the true gallery is greater.

In any event, as far as form is concerned, there are so many transitional stages between what we call triforium and what we call false gallery that even specialized research often yields vagueness and confusion.

When these structural preconditions of the triforium are clearly understood, it becomes evident that it can also be incorporated into a two-storied elevation of the side naves, that is, together with longitudinal galleries. The result is the four-storied elevation of the central nave wall, which became important in the twelfth century. On the other hand, a combination of "true" gallery as a second story with "false" gallery as a third story is rare, though there are exceptions in the original Notre-Dame in Paris, in Chars (Normandy), and in Saint-Germer-de-Fly (Ile-de-France). It is worth noting that triforia seldom appear on the continuous walls of flat-ceilinged basilicas; the exceptions, other than at Bernay (Normandy), are mostly from the twelfth century, among them Tournai Cathedral (Belgium) and churches at Maule (Ile-de-France) and Lillers (Artois).

As a rule, articulation into overlying stories—arcade, gallery and/or triforium, clerestory—was adapted only where there was also articulation into bays by means of wall-high engaged shafts, high blind arcades, or central-nave vaulting. Geographically, the Romanesque triforium is clearly restricted to a few regions, essentially the Lower Rhine, Burgundy, and Normandy, where it appeared first and became most widespread, joined in the mid-twelfth century by the region famous as the birthplace of the Gothic, the Ile-de-France and Champagne. Where the hall church was the fundamental form, there was no central nave wall and hence no place for the triforium. Though the basilical form was almost the rule there, Italy

remained by and large indifferent to the triforium, averse as it was to anything that would emphasize the structure. However, north of the Alps also there were broad regions—the Upper Rhine and everything east of it—that continued to ignore such articulation. Was this by pure chance or the expression of a historical situation? I believe the latter and, in accord with the Swedish scholar J. Roosval, have on occasion described the territory that did not accept the triforium as the "European heartland." No doubt southwestern Europe (Spain and France south of the Loire) and Italy are no less "European," no less "Occidental," and yet one must concede that there is some special quality to the land between the Loire and the Rhine: the nucleus and point of departure for the Carolingian Empire at the start of Western history, it also became the cradle of the Gothic and the realm throughout which High Gothic cathedral architecture and sculpture was most diffused.

Thus, the indispensable precondition of the triforium is the multi-naved and multi-storied basilical interior to whose walls it lends a heightened formal weight and a more emphatically subdivided elevation. Only a few groups of buildings, concentrated in certain regions, give intensified value to their interior walls by means of the triforium. Nevertheless, they also introduce still other types of wall articulation in the nave and extend the division into the various stories to other portions of the interior.

There are Early Romanesque triforia in Normandy, the Lower Rhine, and the Meuse region. The wood-ceilinged nave of the eleventh-century Benedictine abbey church at Bernay (Eure) is still without the responds (columns or shafts half-engaged in the major supports) that around the middle of the eleventh century became a hallmark of Norman architecture. Rhythmically grouped blind arches articulate the central nave wall between the arcades and the clerestory without, however, really dividing it horizontally into anything one could call a story. The blind arches merely swim, so to speak, across the flat surfaces. This is clearly an early form, echoing the Ottonian. In Normandy—in the Benedictine abbey church in Lessay, in Saint-Georges at Saint-Martin-de-Boscherville, and in the nave of the Sainte-Trinité at Caen—quite the opposite is the case: the blind arches are tightly framed above and below by cornices, and they articulate the wall of the bay between two engaged columns, grouping the arch and the window zone in regulation manner. Here the triforium reached its mature form, and we are already on the verge of the High Romanesque.

At Sankt Luzius in Werden, dating from around 1060, the elevation of the tripartite choir is much like that of a basilica nave: two pier arches, above them three shallow troughlike niches, at the top again two openings, those of the windows framed, so to speak, by pilasters. Clearly, something equivalent to a bay has been made to stand alone here between the chancel arch and the apse, with a perfectly obvious three-storied articulation typical of a basilical nave wall. Much the same thing is found in the rather similar church in Susteren.

49. *Werden, Sankt Luzius, longitudinal section (from Zimmermann, 1959)*

50. *Zyfflich, Sankt Martin, reconstruction of the original Benedictine abbey church, axonometric projection, plan (from Schaefer, 1963)*

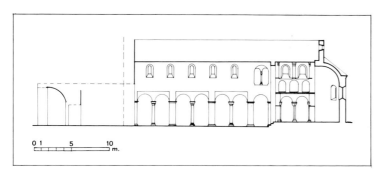

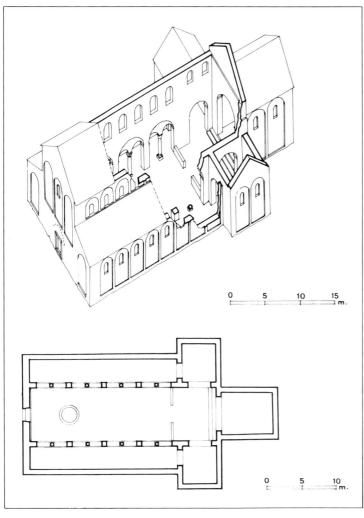

These examples from Bernay, Caen, Werden, and Susteren all show clearly how the triforium resulted from the effort to minimize the abrupt contrast between the smooth flat surfaces of the wall and the openings of the arches by means of a thoroughgoing and homogeneous articulation. This was done with very different means and in very different ways in the two regions, and there is no reason to suppose any contact between Normandy and the Rhine and Meuse basins.

The Forms of Transept and Crossing in the Flat-Ceilinged Basilica

These forms were established in Pre-Romanesque times, and we have already outlined their characteristics, so that a short summary suffices here. The cellular transept with low arms was favored particularly in the Lower Rhine and Meuse valleys. Even such a large edifice as the collegiate church at Nivelles clings to this form. Along with its two-choir plan, there are transepts at both east and west. Both are lower than the central nave, but whereas the arms of the west transept are short and narrow, those of the east are longer and broader—something very characteristic of this type, which is attuned to fine gradations and differentiations. Further examples are found in the Meuse Valley at Celles and Hastière; in the Rhineland at Zyfflich, where the crossarms were destroyed long ago; and in Luxembourg at Echternach, though there the transept may be of earlier origin. The plan is not unknown on the Upper Rhine, at Eschau near Strasbourg for example, but is rarer.

In Italy there are plans that appear very closely related to those of the Lower Rhine, though this fact passed unobserved for long. On the exterior, the transept of the cathedral of Acqui is well preserved, and Santa Maria Maggiore at Lomello shows the characteristic gradation in the interior as well. But even in the south there are similar plans, and the cathedral of Gerace in Calabria has quite rightly been compared with Nivelles.

The continuous and markedly projecting transept is represented in its most monumental form by the former abbey church at Bad Hersfeld (Hesse), of around 1040. The effect of this famed ruin depends principally on its huge transept and the two great arches that divide it from the (now destroyed) nave and elongated choir. The same disposition can be observed on the exterior of the cathedral of Würzburg, though the interior was remodeled in Baroque style. The continuous transept can be found also at the west end of churches with double choirs. A well-preserved example is that of Sankt Emmeram in Regensburg, and in Sankt Aposteln in Cologne one can still grasp the original Early Romanesque plan despite the Late Romanesque rebuilding with vaults. Other cases—such as the cathedrals at Strasbourg and Bamberg—are questionable. A very impressive example can be found in southern Italy also, in the cathedral of Salerno. There the transept does not project so much, but it is broader and forms a grandiose boxlike chamber to which three high apses are directly attached. This is

51. Acqui, Cathedral of L'Assunta,
exterior of the apses
52. Bad Hersfeld, ruins of the
Benedictine abbey church, interior, the
transept and choir looking northeast

presumed to be the source of inspiration for the churches in Apulia.

The square crossing that is of the same height as the central nave, crossarms, and altar area but that is separated from them by corner arches is likewise found in characteristic examples, a few of which are on the border between Pre-Romanesque and Early Romanesque art—for instance, Saint-Philibert-de-Grand-Lieu in Brittany or Sankt Georg in Oberzell on the island of Reichenau. To these can be added a few Mozarabic churches of the tenth century mentioned in the preceding chapter. In the church at Susteren it is difficult to say if the crossing should be described as "segregated" or as "isolated," which shows that the transition from one to the other form is fluid. Where it appears unequivocal, it is obvious that the "segregated" solution is retrograde, looking backward to Carolingian architecture, while the "separated" form is just as obviously progressive.

If the crossing is short and fairly narrow but well defined by projecting elements (though not by strips of wall impinging on the space) and demarcated by four arches of similar dimensions, we sense it to be a central bay of the interior conferring order and proportion on the entire edifice. Sankt Michael in Hildesheim and the former abbey church at Limburg on the Haardt have always been taken as early classical examples of this. In the High Romanesque phase, this "isolated" crossing becomes the norm. It appears in Sankt Marien im Kapitol in Cologne around the middle of the eleventh century, but in the cathedral at Speyer, begun around 1030, we can see how this plan still had difficulty in being established and how it had to compete with other conceptions.

Extraordinary pains have been taken by researchers to clarify the history of the rise of the so-called isolated crossing and the time of its appearance— one need only mention Boeckelmann's writings in connection with his investigations of the ruins of Sankt Peter und Paul at Neustadt on the Main—but much has remained hypothetical. This problem scarcely arises in Early Romanesque architecture in southern Germany, and this is also decidedly true of Italy, where ground plans without transept are in the majority, even in such large churches of the eleventh and twelfth centuries as San Piero a Grado near Pisa, and those at Torcello and Pomposa. In the early barrel-vaulted halls of the Pyrenees region it is natural that the transept and crossing should be of far less note in the overall conception. There, in the eleventh and even in the twelfth century, the transept seems to have retained its low form and the crossing often appears to be sunken in, as it were, rather than given prominence in relation to the nave, even when it is crowned by a cupola or an octagonal cloister vault. Seemingly, however, scholars have not yet dealt with these matters.

Closely connected with the problem of the isolated crossing is that of the crossing tower. It is easy to understand that none of the other plans even permits a crossing tower, let alone calls for one. At the most it can be combined with a segregated crossing—as in Saint-Martin in Angers and Sankt Georg in Oberzell. The crossing with a true and proper tower opening

53. Hildesheim, Sankt Michael, interior looking east

54. Utrecht, Sint Pieter, axonometric projection reconstructing the original state (from Ter Kuile, 1959, drawn by Van den Voet)

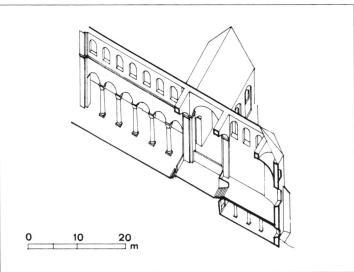

as a light shaft into the church interior was a remarkable idea to have arrived at, and must have been envisaged purely for its monumental effect and exclusive of any practical purpose, since bells cannot be installed in a crossing tower because of the practical obstacles to tolling and to maintenance.

Early Armenian churches had already established a prototype for the crossing tower in smaller central-plan buildings, which chiefly took the form of the Greek cross or the related form of a square with four supports. The Carolingian Palatine Chapel at Germigny-des-Prés has a square tower, the Early Romanesque Heiligkreuz chapel in Trier has an octagonal one, and more examples could be mentioned.

The decisive step was taken when the tower was raised over the high crossing of a cruciform basilica and devised not as a wooden rooftower or ridge turret but as a genuine piece of stone architecture. We simply do not know if that occurred anywhere before the eleventh century. Again we must look to Hildesheim, Limburg on the Haardt, and Speyer for our examples. However, it is not known if the square tower in Sankt Michael at Hildesheim was open below, if the octagonal tower (since destroyed) in Limburg really belonged to the Early Romanesque building, and if the crossing tower in Speyer Cathedral was actually executed (the present octagonal tower was erected only around 1100). It is alone with Notre-Dame in Jumièges that we find a high square crossing tower which, as far as can be judged, was open below, as evidenced by the absence of beam holes in the ruins. Many important churches in the South lacked both transept and crossing tower. It should be noted here that the round towers of the no longer existing Carolingian abbey church of Centula (the town today is known as Saint-Riquier) must have been built of wood.

The Enlargement of the Altar Area

Among the greatest "inventions" of Romanesque architecture were the new arrangements of the east end of the church, specifically the so-called staggered choir, the choir ambulatory, and the towers over the corners or flanks of the choir. In part they undoubtedly have earlier roots, like so many innovations, but they are all first found in concrete form in the Early Romanesque. In association with the transept and crossing tower, especially when there is a choir ambulatory, they result in new and remarkably differentiated forms in the interior and highly diverse structures on the exterior.

In treating the choir interior, abstract thinking based exclusively on studies of the ground plan led earlier and even more recent art historians to disastrous conclusions, aggravated often enough by a lack of perception or a deficient grasp of the liturgical functions for which that part of the church was designed.

What today we call the choir was, in the Early and High Middle Ages, simply a place with the altar (sanctuary, presbytery). The high altar stood in the apse or immediately in front of it. Separate from it was the place where

55. *Quedlinburg, Sankt Wiperti, interior of the crypt looking east, perspective drawing, detail (from Ostendorf, 1922)*

56. *Füssen, Sankt Mang, perspective drawing of the central part of the crypt (from Lang, 1932)*

57. *Saintes, Saint-Eutrope, crypt*

the chapter of the cathedral or collegiate church or—in the case of an abbey—where the *patres* had their seats. Their choir stalls were to the west of the altar area, in cruciform-plan churches usually in the crossing itself (though it should be noted that "crossing" is a modern art historical term for what, in the High Middle Ages, was called the *chorus* since it was there that the choral prayers were intoned). In special cases, above all when there was no transept and therefore no crossing, the choir stalls were placed in a "long choir," and this was so among the Benedictines as well as among the followers of the early monastic reforms (those of Cluny and Hirsau), the later reform orders (Cistercian, Premonstratensian), and such others as the Augustinians.

Three-Naved Choir Plans

The altar area was generally no more than an apse in Early Christian times but was soon expanded by the addition of an oblong or square area usually called by art historians an "ante-choir" or "choir-square," terms that are erroneous in a strict sense but so much in use that it would be difficult to eliminate them now (moreover, there are often other places for altars in secondary apses or chapels in the crossarms). Another line of development may stem from the pastophoria: in the Early Christian basilica, chiefly in the eastern Mediterranean but also in Ravenna, they flanked the main apse as separate chambers (designated *prothesis* and *diakonikon*).

Frequently, such apses or chapels were built in the middle of the east wall of the crossarm, though often they were also shifted to the side to allow room for the mouth of the stairs to the crypt, as in Limburg on the Haardt, or for the corner towers, as in Speyer. However, they could also be relegated to the choir itself, to which, if lengthened, they gave a three-naved ground plan. True, this is a three-naved chamber only if—and this is relatively rare—the separating walls are pierced by arches, in which case they are usually called collateral choirs, though in practice they are really only accessory chapels.

Cluny II is a well-known example, yet its influence has been exaggerated. A Lower Rhenish group is characterized by the fact that the three-naved arrangement affects the crypt likewise and involves a gradation in height. Thus, there are four distinct levels: crypt, lower collateral choirs, main choir, upper collateral choirs. The best preserved example of this is Sankt Georg in Cologne, and it appears in simpler form in Susteren and in Sankt Luzius in Werden.

The Staggered Choir

By displacing the apse or chapels to the middle, room is left on the east wall of the transept for additional apses or chapels. In larger churches two or three such altar places can be accommodated easily in each crossarm. Thus, there can be three, five, even seven altars with their relative surrounding areas, and a good example of such a threefold resolution with seven

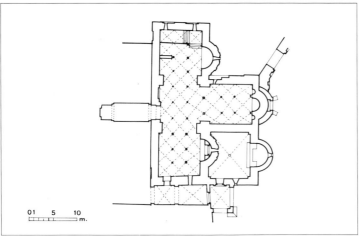

01 5 10
m.

chambers is Saint-Sever-sur-l'Adour. Such chambers along the east wall of the transept can be all the same size and disposed in a row, as was the Cistercian practice, or else staggered to the middle, as is the case in many Benedictine abbeys, which justifies the French use of the term *choeur bénédictin.*

We see from this schematic survey that the possibilities suggest themselves virtually automatically. A posteriori conclusions based on monastic, artistic, or other relationships would therefore appear scarcely called for, and this has proven true in practice: before Lanfry's excavation brought to light choirs with ambulatories at Jumièges and Rouen, it had seemed that the tripartite choir was the only type built in Normandy, for which reason many researchers concluded that there must have been very close relationships with Burgundy, and with Cluny in particular. Thus, earlier scholars tended to link the tripartite choirs in the Lower Rhine and Meuse regions—Sankt Georg in Cologne, Deventer, Utrecht, and others—with Cluny II, often drawing far-ranging conclusions from that deduction, until more recent writers, most notably A. Verbeek, pointed out that these structures were two-storied "collateral choirs" and therefore had decidedly different floor levels, which means that it is in their ground plans that these churches are similar to Cluny II and not in their elevations and spatial dispositions. Thus, they constitute a group in themselves. Elsewhere in the Lower Rhine and Meuse regions, for example in Sankt Luzius in Werden and the church in Susteren, the choir wall is typically basilical, and its three stories composed of arcades, niches, and windows, respectively. In the Romanesque all these possibilities were employed at will, as we see in the abbey church at Brauweiler in the North Rhineland, in Piacenza Cathedral (Emilia), and elsewhere.

The Choir Ambulatory

An ambulatory is created by extending the side aisle around the apse. This was the simple result of a long and varied development. One of the roots in certainly the Pre-Romanesque ring-crypt (discussed elsewhere), probably along with the ambulatory found in a few early hall-crypts from around 1000 (for example, those in the cathedral of Ivrea, Santo Stefano in Verona, and Sankt Michael in Hildesheim). Remarkably enough, all three of these are two-storied. The upper story, however, is neither a regulation prolongation of the side nave nor a tribune, nor does it open onto the apse by means of arcades as in genuine choir ambulatories. The latter are found principally throughout present-day France, in both the north and the south, which is why scholars have confined themselves by and large to French churches in exploring the origin and development of the choir ambulatory. To arrive at definitive conclusions one has to rule out such uncertain cases as the cathedral of Clermont-Ferrand. On the other hand, the excavated ambulatory of Saint-Martin in Tours, from around 1000, has for long been our earliest traceable example and is considered one of the most important points of departure. Already present in it are the semicircular chapels that are vital parts of the fully developed choir ambulatory (though they may be replaced by or alternate with rectangular ones, as in Auvergne).

The Romanesque choir ambulatory in a plan like that of Saint-Aignan is one of the handsomest achievements of Romanesque architecture. Viewed from the outside, the staggered sequence of absidioles around the ambulatory rising to the dominant projecting apse, itself often surmounted by a crossing tower, creates an unforgettable image—one need only think of Saint-Savin-sur-Gartempe, Saint-Philibert in Tournus, and Notre-Dame du Port in Clermont-Ferrand among many others. In the interior, to look through the arcades opened in the apse wall and see yet another space beyond it—the ambulatory—and to follow the changing perspective as one walks around that corridor, is itself an architectural experience of a special quality. It is difficult to imagine that this was not an important factor for the builders themselves. But just as certainly there were also functional considerations involved. From that standpoint, the choir ambulatory is presumably nothing else than a passageway leading to the altars in the chapels. We have already seen, in discussing the west end of the church and the crypt, that an increase in the number of altars and altar areas, and their incorporation into the ground plan and general architecture, was often a significant spur for the builders. In that sense it is natural that something like the domed single-naved churches of the Aquitaine region should as a rule also have single-naved choirs in which the absidioles open directly into the main room.

Unlike the great number of choir ambulatories built throughout France from the eleventh century on, only a few may be cited in Italy and Germany: in the cathedrals of Aversa near Naples and Acerenza near Potenza in Basilicata, the Chiesa Nuova of the abbey at Venosa (never completed), likewise in Basilicata; Sant'Antimo in Tuscany; Sankt Godehard and Sankt Michael in Hildesheim; Sankt Marien im Kapitol in Cologne; and the former abbey churches at Brauweiler in the North Rhineland and Stavelot in the Belgian Ardennes. In these latter there is obviously a connection with triple-aisled transepts such as one also finds in galleried hall churches in southwestern Europe. The Cologne church represents a high point of the form, since there each crossarm also terminates in an apse, making a total of three apses each with an ambulatory.

The Romanesque choir with ambulatory may take the form of either basilica or hall. Thus, Notre-Dame-la-Grande in Poitiers has a hall-type choir and ambulatory, but very often the choir in hall churches in southwestern Europe is basilical and decisively marked off from the nave. If a basilical choir with ambulatory connects up with a single-naved domed church, as in the abbey church at Fontevrault in Anjou, it is doubtless to be explained by a change in plan during the course of building, though such juxtapositions of dissimilar spatial designs within a single building can be due too to the

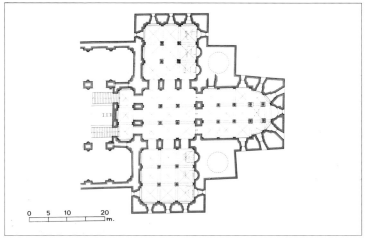

0 5 10   20
              m.

62. Sant Pere de Roda, ruins of the
Benedictine abbey church, interior
looking west

builders' intention to raze an older portion of the edifice and replace it by something more akin to the new parts.

The Norman Romanesque was familiar with the choir ambulatory, as recent investigations in Jumièges and Rouen have demonstrated, and from France it was transplanted to many great cathedrals in England. The Early Gothic of the French crown lands took up the ambulatory and, in logical fashion, extended the nave and transept galleries around it, as in the cathedrals of Paris, Mantes, Laon, Noyon, Soissons, Reims (Saint-Remi), and elsewhere—creations which, appearing on the threshold of the High Gothic, belong among the most splendid achievements of medieval architecture. Though these remarks bring us far along in time, we must remember that the premises on which future developments are based are essential elements in our total picture of Early Romanesque art.

After what we observed about Early Romanesque churches in Italy, it comes as no surprise to learn that we seldom find altar areas there in their more elaborate forms, a trait so characteristic of the regions north of the Alps. Italy was consistent in clinging to the simple apse directly juxtaposed to the naves or even to the central nave alone. The rule was one or three apses preceded by, at most, a short barrel-vaulted bay, as at San Pietro in Agliate near Milan. In Salerno Cathedral, and later in the Apulian churches, these apses are even linked with the continuous transept.

The Hall-Crypt

The Romanesque hall-crypt, as found in hundreds of examples throughout Europe, had already achieved its fully developed form by the start of the eleventh century, a form that was to continue with only minor modifications into the twelfth and thirteenth centuries. The Early Romanesque ideal plan is the multi-naved hall interior covered at the same height with cross-groined vaulting. Cross-arches and longitudinal arcades of similar form and breadth define square bays. The point of intersection of the vaulting groins unobtrusively signals the middle of each bay. The arches have as a rule just enough physical body so that they do not decompose the hall interior into separate segments but at the same time clearly reveal the arrangement in bays.

Thus, hall-crypts are distinguished from the hall churches of southwestern Europe by their "purer" expression of the hall form, since spatially the naves are as intensively linked to each other as are the bays. The reason is easy to comprehend: the crypts are generally lower stories beneath the main church whose floor they support, and this means that differences in height (such as occur when there are barrel vaults of differing breadths) are simply not possible here.

As with the so-called isolated crossing, the earliest genuine existence of the hall-crypt has been a matter of much discussion, among German scholars in particular. The proponents of an earlier Pre-Romanesque origin would seem to be in retreat now, because the fully developed form described above cannot be traced back before 1000 with any certainty. Nevertheless, Italian scholars apparently still hold that crypts of this sort were built in Carolingian and even Pre-Carolingian times, citing such examples as San Giovanni in Conca in Milan, Sant'Eusebio in Pavia, and Sant'Antimo. One can only think that Italian crypts must mostly have re-utilized older columns, and that therefore the usually reliable means of dating furnished by the capitals cannot apply there. It is clear that with methodical and irreproachable procedures one can arrive at the date of the earliest form of a work of architecture and thus be able to detect later accretions.

The most important predecessor of the authentic hall-crypt, which as a rule lies half-buried beneath the altar area, would seem to be the so-called westwork crypt of Carolingian times. Even down to the cross-arches, all basic traits are already defined in it, except that these chambers are at ground level and are in fact atria or corridors preceding the main edifice. Likewise, the two-storied exterior crypts mentioned earlier may have made a contribution to the development of the authentic hall-crypt.

As one might expect, the dimensions and plan of the crypt are dependent on the church of which it is a part. Occasionally, one has the impression that the location of the stairs in the church and the gradations in floor level were more important than the interior of the crypt itself. It is significant enough that we know little of the purpose and use of the crypt in its fully developed form. Thus, it is precisely the large hall-crypts that often do not contain, as justification for their existence and their plan, the tomb of a martyr or a sainted founder. Every crypt has one or more altars, and so services must have been held in them. As with the choir ambulatory, crypts may have taken their form and been enlarged as a consequence of the need for additional secondary altars. As for the location of the crypt within the church building, it is much more varied than one might at first suppose. A crypt of three bays by three bays beneath a square choir is the simplest case, and can be exemplified by the church at Limburg on the Haardt. The introduction of an apse, as in Maria Laach, or of an elongated oblong choir, as at Nivelles and Bad Hersfeld, brings about an increase in the number of bays. Crypts of this sort are usually reached by winding stairs from the transept, and another flight leads from the crossing to the altar area.

A further extension of the crypt occurs almost through necessity when the choir is tripartite as in Sankt Georg in Cologne. To underpin the walls or arcades of the upper church, similar walls or pier arcades are needed in the crypt, and this holds true also for choirs with ambulatories such as are found already in the tenth century at Sankt Wiperti in Quedlimburg, the cathedral of Ivrea, and Santo Stefano in Verona, or in the early eleventh century at Sankt Michael in Hildesheim, the cathedral of Auxerre, and Saint-Eutrope in Saintes. Besides these crypts with regulation ambulatories, sometimes even in the guise of a separate chamber as in Ivrea there are special cases (for example, Sankt Marien im Kapitol in Cologne) in which the area beneath the ambulatory has been broken up into separate chapels.

The crypt is often moved forward into the area beneath the crossing (or the easternmost bay of the central nave) as in Augsburg Cathedral (the west transept), the Neumünster in Würzburg, and, later, the abbey church at Jerichow. The crossing-crypt is then often opened onto the crossarms through pier arcades, affording "interesting" vistas that are essentially non-Romanesque. It almost seems, in these cases, as if the decisive factor in extending the crypt was more the creation of an elevated choir in the church proper than the enlargement of the crypt itself. There are, in fact, churches in which such a "stage," the depth of a single bay, projects into the altar area from the external crypt, as in two Belgian examples, the collegiate church at Fosse and Saint-Barthélemy in Liège (in neither is the elevated part of the crypt preserved), or from the crossing-crypt into the central nave as in Speyer I (likewise not preserved).

In all cases, the crypt thereby acquires a closer spatial link with the upper church, though mostly this occurs where the crypt occupies the entire

transept area. Early examples of this are found in the initial state of Speyer Cathedral, the part done during the second phase of building, around 1030-35; at Acqui Cathedral in Piedmont, dating from before 1067; in the abbey church of San Salvatore on Monte Amiata in Tuscany, dedicated in 1036; and in the cathedrals of Otranto in Apulia and Gerace in Calabria, the latter from the eleventh century. In the later eleventh century and in the twelfth, the fully extended elevated choir became virtually the rule in large churches in Italy, as one sees in Modena Cathedral, San Marco in Venice, San Zeno in Verona, and Bari Cathedral and its successors. If there is no transept, the east bay of the three-aisled nave is filled with the elevated crypt, resulting in something that at least resembles a real transept. Usually the transept crypt opens onto the middle nave, as was also the case in the second plan of Speyer.

Since we have mentioned the relationship between this Italian plan and Speyer, we must also stress their differences. In fact, the most distinctive of all the differences in their architectonic character resides precisely in the fact that, south of the Alps, Antique or Pre-Romanesque remains were frequently re-utilized in crypts as supporting elements, with bases, shafts, and capitals, either intact or, just as often, as separate components. Suitable shafts of uniform size were not always easy to come by, and so in order to adjust the height the base or even the capital was discarded and replaced by a simple stone slab. Columns of entirely different origins, materials, and strengths were utilized together, often with some semblance of rhythmic arrangement but just as often combined randomly. If the piers of the upper church required some supporting substructure, it was built in the crypt with no attempt to harmonize with the architecture there, as can be seen in Santa Maria in Siponto, the cathedrals in Otranto and Acqui, and San Miniato in Florence.

The result, obviously, was an architectural conception that did not stand on ceremony, that took pleasure in the diversity of materials and shapes of the vestiges it utilized, and that preferred a fleeting play of forms to a rigorously fixed system. Precisely this approach—and it is found also in many other places—would seem to be a common characteristic of the architecture of many regions south of the Alps and to be perfectly in accord with a more easygoing or more human conception, one with greater resistance to rigorous or even rationalistic systems. If it is not too much of a generalization, we can say that this goes along with many traits of the national character that are expressed not only in the arts and literature but also in everyday living.

The crypt in Speyer is something quite different. Instead of a many-columned fluid space seeming almost undefined, something in the manner of a Moslem mosque, here we have a severely ordered and clearly delimited interior. Powerful pier-arches separate the crossing from the crossarms, the east arm, and the antechamber to the west. The basic overall design of the huge interior can be read as composed of ground-plan squares each

65. Caen, Saint-Etienne ("Abbaye aux Hommes"), axonometric projection reconstructing the original state (from Gall, 1925)

66. Speyer, cathedral, reconstruction of the central nave of Speyer I looking east, drawing (from Kubach and Haas, 1972)

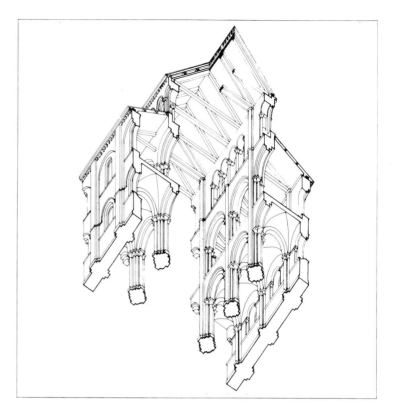

consisting of three by three bays, to which were added an apse and an antechamber. The mighty columns are put together out of superimposed stone drums, and powerful bases and cuboid capitals of consistently unified form give the construction its uncompromisingly solid and severe appearance. The outer walls are articulated to correspond with the pier-arcades, and make the spatial limits appear unobtrusive by means of a double tier of projections, specifically blind arches and half-columns.

Again different are the crypts of the cathedral of Auxerre on the eastern border of Burgundy and of Saint-Eutrope in Saintes in the heart of Aquitaine. In contrast to both the abstract language of the crypt of Speyer Cathedral and the animated interplay of that in Acqui, here the chief concerns are precise articulation and functional rightness: pier-arcades at Auxerre separate the three-naved main room of the crypt from the ambulatory in the same way as, in the Speyer crypt, they mark off the crossarms from the crossing. However, the piers are not powerful square blocks with projecting shafts but instead are entirely made up of round elements whose profile continues into the bulging longitudinal and cross-arches, stressing the connection of wall, supports, and ceiling.

Because our only sources are the few monuments that have survived, we cannot say where the crypt was first extended to fill the space under the choir and ambulatory or under the transept; but while the results were the same, the architectonic treatment is so diverse that the examples at Acqui, Speyer, and Saintes must be understood as expressions of starkly different types of temperament.

Comparison of Early Romanesque crypts in Piedmont, Burgundy, Aquitaine, and the Upper Rhine has yielded still more information about the stylistic elements of crypt architecture, notably that the surrounding walls and the forms of support can play an important part. The region in which a great many Early Romanesque crypts have survived, the Lower Rhine and Meuse valleys, can make this clear. Round and octagonal columns and square piers, piers with columns, pillars with half-columns projecting, bundle piers—they all exist alongside each other, and there are even numerous vertically or spirally fluted columns.

Vaulting, Articulation, and Specific Forms
The unified stylistic character of Early Romanesque architecture, especially in the Romanic regions, was very much the consequence of the gradual disintegration of Antique forms. Earlier generations, still under the influence of the notion that "classicism" was the norm in "classical" antiquity, judged this to represent a throwback to barbarity, to primitive times, and this notion is still present in the study, *Frühzeit des Mittelalters*, published by J. Hubert, J. Porcher, and W. F. Volbach as recently as 1968. Cultural-morphological study has taught us to stress things quite differently, and we are now able to see how it was precisely the Antique inheritance, with the immeasurable power of its tradition, that acted as an obstacle to

the discovery of a new and independent language of forms.

True enough, the canon of classical proportions as applied to the column remained somehow in force at one place or another during the Middle Ages, but when the capital no longer conformed to the classical orders, something essential disappeared, even though abstract formulations did arise to replace them, namely the cuboid capital (also called cushion or block), the pipe-bowl, the goblet, and later, the trapezoid forms. Even with the Romanesque Corinthian capital, the organic life of the form, the exuberance of the leaves, the feathering of the volutes were replaced by the solid volume of a geometric form. As for the column, although it never became entirely obsolete as a support, its significance was profoundly modified when it was placed on a par with the pillar in the system in which they alternate. An even more decisive blow to the autonomy of the column occurred when it became demoted to an accessory feature, to a half-column engaged in a wall or pier and robbed of its capital and base. How far that process went in the eleventh century is attested by the controversy among scholars concerning the genesis of the Norman architectural feature known as a respond: was it an engaged half-column very much lengthened, or a wooden prop translated into stone? Although this question can never be decided with full objectivity, one thing remains clear: in the Norman church of the eleventh century we have something very different indeed from Sant Pere de Roda in the Spanish province of Gerona, where only a few decades earlier columns (as we understand them from Hellenistic and Roman architecture) were placed entire and intact and completely free on all sides directly in front of piers and walls. Undoubtedly, they had already undergone a certain revaluation there, but the fact remains that they were still used. Around 1100 there was to be a new appreciation of the column, as we see in the interior of the transept apses in Speyer Cathedral.

Like the column, the pilaster too declined in importance. Not that it disappeared completely, but it no longer played the role it had in the Palatine Chapel at Aachen or the Lorsch gatehouse, though it still figured in the Essen minster or the Heiligkreuz chapel in Trier.

In seems characteristic that the leading elements became, instead, the abstract vertical wall band, the simple pilaster-strip, and the frieze of blind arches. Instead of an armature of pilasters and beams projecting well out from the wall, there was a thoroughly flat surface framed with forms about which it is difficult to say if they are laid over the wall or, conversely, sunk into it as blind elements. Shallow blind semicircular arches in simple rows characteristically tally with the fact that, as a rule, there were as yet neither plinths nor cornices on the exteriors of buildings. The slabs of wall rise directly from the ground like abstract forms, and the roofing is simply laid over them with a considerable overhang but no cornice. In the same way, the Early Romanesque pier often has no base or at the most a hewn stone step at its foot and a flat impost slab at the start of the arch, both of them frequently without even a molding and projecting only into the embrasure,

so that otherwise they are totally identified with the wall surface.

In general, the base of the column clung to the fundamental ancient Attic form. Nevertheless, it too went through a characteristic transformation in which its torus and scotia, its convex and concave moldings, became shallower and higher and the whole base much less undercut. More significant is the metamorphosis of the capital: along with the Antique types frequent in Italy either as actual vestiges or as imitations of the ancient forms, there were also, particularly north of the Alps, decided innovations in the shape of cube (or cushion), pipe-bowl, trapezoid, and goblet capitals. Even the names tell us that these are rigorously three-dimensional geometric shapes whose uncompromising abstractness constitutes the extreme opposite of the organically burgeoning Corinthian capital.

The wall, understood as mass and not as a surface plane without body, was an essential achievement of the Early Romanesque, though not arrived at everywhere with the same logical consistency. Out of this mass developed, in principle, its articulation, either through the stripping away of layers—fields defined by pilaster-strips and arch friezes—or by bringing forward elements—projecting shafts and blind arches—that likewise create the effect of differentiated strata. From that standpoint, an armature of forms standing free in front of the wall—columns with entablature or arches—strike one as remnants of the Pre-Romanesque style. This is felt quite clearly in Sant Pere de Roda, where one is reminded of Hellenistic or other Late Antique architecture.

The process by which new and more independent articulating forms came into being (or, at any rate, forms more appropriate to Early Romanesque architecture) is one of the most interesting in the history of medieval art. Of similar interest is the niche, which hollows out the mass of wall more deeply than does the blind recess. It is found in Catalonia, in the Lower Rhine and Meuse valleys, and quite isolatedly in Speyer and such Early Romanesque buildings in Regensburg as Sankt Stefan. When used as a wreath of rectangular niches above the apses it constitutes a predecessor of the dwarf gallery, especially in Lombardy and the Alpine districts.

Another fascinating chapter in the history of architecture is the story of the double-shell wall, which is bound up with the names of Ernst Gall, Jean Bony, Paul Rolland, and Pierre Héliot. In essence, the wall is no longer a compact mass between two parallel surfaces but is split into two with a cavity between the vertical strata. On one side there remains a thinner wall defining the interior area and containing the necessary openings for windows. On the other, in place of the wall, there is a hollow space that can usually be walked through—whence Rolland's term le mur évidé, the hollowed-out or cut-away wall. The arcade can open indoors or outdoors. In medieval architecture the double-shell wall was always associated with an articulation into stories. As a rule, it is the height of a single story, but it may also comprise several superimposed stories as well as change its orientation to the interior or exterior. Often the strength of the wall is reinforced through deep blind openings, which in the upper story would seem to aim at carrying the stratification to the upper wall. In any case, a relatively thick wall is the prerequisite for this, for which reason Bony speaks of le mur épais, though that is a misconception because, as a result of the strenuous opening up and hollowing out, the wall can no longer effectively be thick.

This double wall has been used on occasion for almost every part of a building, but not all regions were familiar with it. As so often occurs in the history of art, there is dispute over where the various forms appeared first, if they had to be invented anew each time, and whether and to what extent there was mutual influence between regions. Here again we must remember that countless buildings have been lost, and precisely from the earliest period. It is almost certain that they would have provided the key for the solution of many enigmas. For this reason, any attempt to trace the question all the way back to bedrock, so to speak, is at best work for idle hands.

For this new structural approach too there were prototypes in Late Antiquity, and the octagonal chapel of Sant'Aquilino adjoining San Lorenzo in Milan is by all odds the best preserved and best known of them. A barrel-vaulted inner passageway runs between the walls in front of the upper windows. An external passageway runs around the base of the cupola with depressed round arches (transverse barrel vaults) on slender columns. Here the system of the Romanesque passageway is to a great extent anticipated and must have provided a prototype for at least the Lombard galleries of the twelfth century.

So far no intermediate link has been found between the fifth-century Sant'Aquilino and Early Romanesque examples in the eleventh century when passageways in the walls (actual or in embryo form) began to appear in various parts of Europe. The most important are within the sphere of Norman, Lower Rhenish, and Mosan art, notably on the west front of the cathedral of Trier, that of the minster at Essen, and in the transept of the abbey churches of Bernay and Jumièges. All of them obviously came into being because of the need to provide passageways linking various parts and staircases in the interior. What matters, however, is that these connecting galleries assumed the architectonic form of open arcades, made up additional stories, and articulated the walls. Already with these beginnings the orientation is interchangeable: according to their position and purpose, the arcades can open either to the outside or the inside. The west front of Trier Cathedral carried these new possibilities to their highest point artistically, but it remained an isolated case that found its successors only about a hundred years later, in the Late Romanesque dwarf galleries outdoors and the galleries indoors.

In Normandy, the decisive step came when the passageway was extended from the transept to encroach on the central nave. This is found at its earliest in Saint-Etienne in Caen, dating from after 1057, though it is possible, according to Liess, that the Early Romanesque cathedrals at Bayeux and

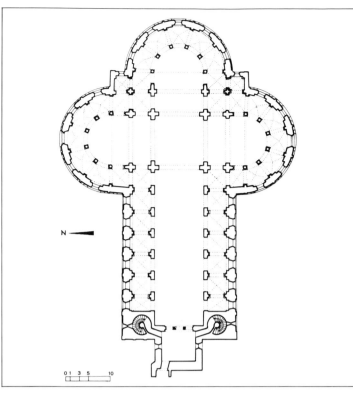

Coutances may have preceded it. From 1060 on, the indoor passageway in front of the clerestory windows became a characteristic of Norman and then Anglo-Norman architecture.

In terms of historical development, this passageway marked an important advance. The central nave wall had already been opened up by gallery arcades and articulated horizontally by blind triforia and vertically by tall shafts; now the clerestory level too came to be split into strata. In Trier Cathedral, the façade wall likewise was stratified in just this manner, preparing the way for the dwarf gallery typical of the Lower Rhineland. It was, however, on quite different bases that that type of gallery originated around 1080 in the Upper Rhineland, at Speyer, and then again, somewhat later, when a North Italian type appeared in Lombardy, though Pisan models must have preceded it.

The Problems of Vaulting

In large parts of Europe, from Carolingian times to late in the eleventh century or even the twelfth, architecture had to make do with a combination of stone and wood construction. Ceilings and the timberwork of the roof had to be laid over stone walls and wooden supports. To build the interior, including the ceiling, entirely in stone depended on mastery of vaulting, and this—not everywhere, but certainly in the West—meant the retrieval of a technique once known and now unlearned. Contributing to its recovery must have been not only the inner logic of working in stone, but also the stylistic desire to create imposing and solidly secure buildings as well as to satisfy practical necessities, chief of which in those times was protection against the everpresent threat of fire. Militating against such an innovation must have been the tradition-bound ways of working but also, no doubt, the aesthetic pleasure afforded by a flat-roofed, rigorously cuboid interior.

Lack of technical knowledge was only a minor hindrance, because in fact excellent vaultings were known from all centuries. The central-plan Palatine Chapel in Aachen combined level and stilted barrel vaults, cross-groined vaults, and triangularly segmented and octagonal cloister vaults with such assurance that they have never endured any appreciable damage in all these centuries. The Carolingian westworks have cross-groined vaults over their ground-floor chambers. Crypts are often covered with complicatedly cut barrel vaulting, though admittedly always of modest breadth. In the eleventh century, lateral naves were covered with cross vaults over rectangular bays twenty-six feet or so in width, and without difficulty, as in Speyer Cathedral. As early as the tenth century, southwestern Europe had developed for its hall churches the system in which barrel vaults, laid side by side, buttress each other reciprocally. Proceeding from this, here and there the step was taken to cover a basilical (or semi-basilical) central nave with barrel vaulting—in Cardona, Payerne, and Tournus, for instance. However, vaulting of the basilical central nave in large dimensions was a task effected only during the High Romanesque.

V. Jumièges, ruins of the abbey church
of Notre-Dame

72. Nivelles, Sainte-Gertrude, view
from the southeast
73. Essen, minster, interior of the
west choir

REGIONAL DIFFERENCES

Normandy

The region along the French side of the English Channel has a distinctive
history of its own. It was among the last to enter into architectural history
in Europe. In 911, the French king of the Carolingian house invested the
Norman duke Rollo with these lands as his fief, thereby inducing this
Germanic people to settle down finally in one place. Until then, they had
exploited the weakness of the late Carolingian rulers. In their swift ships,
these Normans—also known as Danes or Vikings—had sailed along the
coasts and up the rivers, putting towns and abbeys to the torch, spreading
fear and insecurity everywhere. This devastation now came to an end, but
a century had to pass before the Norman lords erected buildings of which
we have some remains. While there are interesting early accounts, nothing
survives from the tenth century except the vestiges of the small church of
Saint-Pierre in Jumièges. Thus, here as elsewhere, the first efforts at
architecture remain an enigma. Even the few buildings that can be dated
to the early eleventh century have come down to us in fragments only,
specifically parts of the Gothic cathedrals of Bayeux, Coutances, and Rouen,
and the abbey church at Bernay. Apparently, certain dominant motifs of later
Norman architecture were already launched in these buildings: the
twin-towered façade and nave gallery in Bayeux and Coutances, the tripartite
choir, blind triforium, and wall passageway in Bernay, the hall-crypt and
choir ambulatory in Rouen.

The earliest building that is firmly dated and that, though in ruins, retains
at least its most important parts is near Rouen: the abbey church of
Notre-Dame in Jumièges. Except for the crypt, it reveals all the architectural
components mentioned so far. Here, for the first time, they appear with full
effect: the central nave is a steep area between high walls, and arcades and
gallery openings are grouped in pairs by means of round engaged shafts
running up the walls. These latter are known as responds, engaged columns,
or auxiliaries, and later—in vaulted buildings—would serve to bear the
groins. Here they end at the crown of the wall, below the open timberwork
ceiling we must presume existed. These shafts have various functions. In
the first place, they reinforce the rhythm of the alternating supports—piers
and columns—by emphasizing the vertical axis of the pier to the full height
of the wall. They articulate the wall into vertical fields, and since the eye
inevitably perceives and understands the shafts to the right and left of each
column as a pair, they serve also to define the bays. (This function is
something that can be denied only if one comprehends architecture in a
purely "impressionistic" manner and rules out the rationality without which
it simply cannot exist). From the standpoint of construction, these engaged
columns constitute a point-for-point reinforcement of the cross section of
the wall. And since the lateral naves and galleries are vaulted, this is certainly
no small gain. What the arrangement into bays is to the aesthetic aspect of

74. *Hildesheim, Sankt Michael, interior, view into the south crossarm of the east transept*

75. *Gernrode, abbey church, interior looking toward the east choir*

76. *Hildesheim, Sankt Michael, reconstruction of the original exterior as viewed from the southeast (from Beseler and Roggenkamp, 1954)*

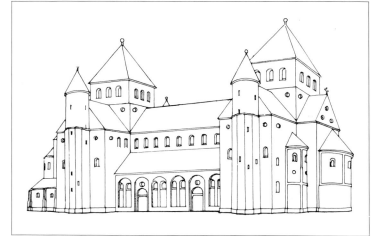

the building, this method of bracing is to its constructional aspect. Many researchers assume that the shafts did not originally reach the crown of the wall but instead supported the pier-arches. Unfortunately, this is no longer verifiable since the original shafts were replaced by thinner ones in the late seventeenth century. However, if that were so, then we would understand much better just how the systems of bays in the interior and the buttressing on the exterior developed.

The west front has two square towers topped by octagons. At the lower level, they embrace a somewhat projecting vaulted porch and gallery, and the reminiscence of the westwork seems still as vital here as in the west front of Saint-Philibert in Tournus (Burgundy). Not much later, in Saint-Etienne in Caen, what we may call the "pure" form of the twin-towered façade was realized by means of a grandiose abstraction of the cubes of wall and with a full equilibrium between the ideas of transept and twin-towers.

At Caen, in the two large abbey churches of Saint-Etienne (the "Abbaye aux Hommes") and Sainte-Trinité (the "Abbaye aux Dames"), founded in 1062 by Duke William the Conqueror and Duchess Matilda as expiation for their technically incestuous marriage, we find virtually all the characteristics of Norman architecture in synthesis, due to some extent to the fact that construction went on into the twelfth century. Both churches have been altered through rebuilding and vaulting. The original aspect with open timberwork ceiling can be reconstructed, though perhaps not with ultimate certainty. Saint-Etienne, like the cathedrals at Coutances and Bayeux preceding it, has a galleried interior with two tiers of large round-arched arcades without internal subdivisions. The piers and arches are plastically enriched by round engaged columns and shafts, the latter here too continuing upward through all the stories. The wall of the topmost story is opened up into a thin outside wall with windows, an arcade of columns

77. Drübeck, abbey church,
perspective drawing reconstructing the
original interior (from Feldtkeller,
1950)
78. Bad Gandersheim, minster, west
front

toward the inside, and passageway between them. The typically Norman passageway or gallery, known definitely before this date only in the transepts at Bernay and Jumièges, is incorporated here in the nave as well. Galleries fill the outer bays of the crossarms, so nave and transept are unified in very effective fashion, and blind arches on the ground floor of the crossarms continue the arcades of the nave. Thus, after the middle of the eleventh century, an important step was taken toward the unification of the entire church interior, just as in the great galleried halls of the South, where the same end is attained with three-naved transepts. This can be understood as one of the great advances leading to the Gothic cathedral, or at least helping to prepare the way. The auxiliary engaged shafts and the overall articulation and organization of the central nave wall by triforium, gallery, and ambulatory at the window level constitute a second element pointing in that direction, and the ribbed ceiling is a third.

The French Crown Lands

The lands between Burgundy and Normandy—Champagne, Ile-de-France, and Picardy—are designated as the French crown lands, the royal domain. They embrace innumerable territories and small holdings, but in terms of art this region is more of a unity with local shadings than a multiplicity of independent but related territories. As a whole, it belongs without question to the area of diffusion of the Early Romanesque flat-ceilinged basilica, an area stretching from the Loire to the Elbe and exhibiting an overriding unity. In the past, German and French art were interpreted as expressions of quite opposite national tendencies, and so it was easy to overlook the unity of this area. Earlier French scholars, however, did sense rightly that the Rhineland, and especially the area of Cologne, the Lower Rhine, and the Meuse, had a close inner connection with northern and northwestern France that, in architecture, is most apparent in the emphasis on articulation of the wall surface. On the other hand, they often minimized the fundamental distinction between the lands north of the Loire and those to the south, where the vaulted aisleless or hall church predominated.

In the French crown lands, small flat-ceilinged basilicas were densely diffused throughout the eleventh and twelfth centuries. Among larger Early Romanesque constructions, the outstanding ones were at Montier-en-Der (the nave) and Vignory in Champagne (both of these with galleries); Saint-Germain des Prés in Paris; and the old cathedral (the "Basse Oeuvre") in Beauvais. The largest surviving onetime flat-ceilinged basilica is Saint-Remi in Reims, a galleried building of immense significance that gives us an idea of what the predecessors of the High Gothic cathedrals were like, though we should think of it without its Gothic vaults and shafts. Besides these, we know the earlier cathedrals at Chartres and Orléans in ground plan at least. Just as in the Rhineland, occasional buildings continued to cling to this tradition during the twelfth century—for example, the collegiate church at Lillers in Artois. In the east, there were churches of this sort as

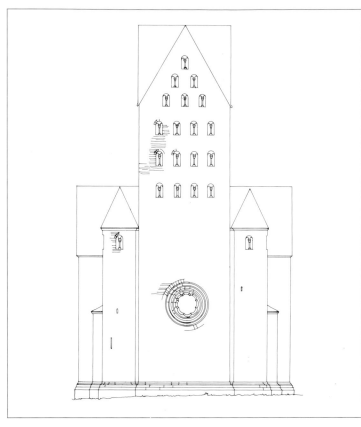

79. Paderborn, cathedral,
reconstruction of the original elevation
of the west front (from Ostendorf,
1922)
80. Paderborn, chapel of Sankt
Bartholomäus, interior

far as the border zone of Burgundy—at Bourbon-Lancy and Perrecy-les-Forges—and in the south as far as the Loire, notably at Lavardin.

The Upper Rhine

The developments in the decades around the year 1000 are very clear to grasp in the Upper Rhineland, or at any rate better than elsewhere, as has become evident in recent years. In Alsace, it is true that besides the east part of the crypt in Strasbourg Cathedral we have only minor and scattered vestiges that R. Will has collated in instructive fashion. But Sankt Georg at Oberzell on the island of Reichenau and Sankt Cyriakus in Sulzburg near Freiburg-im-Breisgau convey, like few other buildings from around the turn of the millennium, an impression of what we might call the "looser" system of the so-called Ottonian basilica, in much the same way as the crypts at Sankt Gallen, Oberzell, Constance, Strasbourg, and Salzburg show the hall form in the state before its Early Romanesque consolidation: the columns are still without cuboid capitals, the vaults are still without cross-arches and are simply interpenetrating, intersecting barrel vaults. The only way to explain the central-plan church in Ottmarsheim is as a holdover from a still very effective Carolingian tradition, in the wake of the Aachen minster. The slender pilaster-strips of the apse articulation in the church at Eschau near Strasbourg belong to the same tendency, as does also its pillared basilica interior, whose character is determined by its low crossarms.

The cathedral at Speyer is the largest Romanesque church in Europe, in length and height not far behind the greatest of the Gothic cathedrals. Surpassed by the third construction at Cluny in total length, its interior nevertheless doubtless was superior in the breadth of its vaulting and in its powerful spatial impression. Its grandeur is owing to the fact that the Salic dynasty had chosen as its seat the territory of the small diocese of Speyer; when the Salic Conrad II became king in 1024, he immediately began to build the cathedral as an imperial foundation. His two successors, Henry III and Henry IV, who are numbered among the outstanding ruling figures of the Middle Ages, enlarged and completed the edifice. It was only under them that it took on the form of an elongated structure stretched out between two groups of towers, and it was not until the last stages of building, around 1100, that it was completely vaulted over.

Conrad's cathedral was planned to be much smaller at the outset. We now know its development through a number of building phases and thus can observe how Pre-Romanesque and Early Romanesque conceptions came to be linked there. Still rooted in the past are the trapezoid ground plan of the altar area, the broad side naves, the contrast between entirely smooth outside walls and markedly articulated inside walls. Pointing toward the future are the huge hall-crypt that in the fourth decade of the eleventh century was extended under the entire transept, the fully isolated crossing (with open tower), and the increasing relief of the interior walls. The development of the Early Romanesque can likewise be followed here step by step: how the hall-crypt encroached from the altar area into that of the transept; how it came to mark off the square crossing by means of powerful pier arcades; how only during the actual building was it decided to raise a tower above the crossing; how the articulation of the inner walls in the east arm of the crypt began with half-columns, while those under the transept became double-layered through blind arches; how, in the lateral naves, blind arches combine into a blind arcade that symmetrically echoes the pier arcades of the central nave, finally achieving in the almost hundred-foot-high central nave a truly impressive height and colossal magnitude. Here, around 1040, a high point was reached in the centuries-long process of transformation of the Early Christian basilica into the Early Romanesque one.

In the considerable diversity of its spatial plan, the west front was still reminiscent of the Carolingian westworks. Externally, it was originally a single transept-like block over a hundred feet high and of comparable breadth, closing off the main street of the city leading to it like the curtain wall of a citadel. When the cathedral was set on fire by the army of Louis XIV, this great and awesome structure was lost. A new west front was built in 1772-78, but the nineteenth century, intolerant of what was judged its fortress-like massiveness, replaced it with a Neo-Romanesque academic and eclectic creation designed by Heinrich Hübsch in 1854.

The Early Romanesque on the Upper Rhine came to a climax with the cathedral of Speyer. Earlier and contemporary with it were the cathedrals of Mainz, Worms, Strasbourg, and Basel. Not much of the early form of those churches has survived except for important parts of Mainz Cathedral, where the monumental three-towered transept at the east links portions from around 1000 to others dating from the end of the eleventh century. Scholars have expended much effort on the study of the earlier form of this cathedral, but their reconstructions in drawing must be viewed with due skepticism. We get a fuller impression of the buildings of the time from monastic churches such as the ruins of the abbey church at Limburg on the Haardt (1025-43) and the priory church at Surbourg in Lower Alsace, built after the middle of the eleventh century, whereas the three churches on the island of Reichenau on Lake Constance are much harder to understand because of their more complicated building history.

The Lower Rhine and Meuse Valleys

If, in Early Romanesque architecture, we can distinguish a conservative orientation looking back to the Carolingians from a progressive one aiming at the logical development of the isolated crossing (Hildesheim) or of wall articulation and formation of bays (Normandy, the Upper Rhine), then the region under discussion here certainly belongs to the former. Scarcely anywhere else was there such a sharply differentiated gradation of interior spaces and constructional cubes as is found in Sainte-Gertrude in Nivelles and the other churches with low crossarms. Here too the complicated centralized plan of the minster at Aachen had its strongest influence (as

already noted above) with reference to both the general plan of the interior and the combination of gallery arches into a kind of grille, as in the minster at Essen or Sankt Marien im Kapitol in Cologne.

Along with Sainte-Gertrude in Nivelles (to which we shall have occasion to refer as the antipode of Sankt Michael in Hildesheim), there are smaller pier-basilicas of a similar sort, the best preserved of which are in Belgium: Saint-Hadelin in Celles, followed by the former abbey church of Hastière on the Meuse. There is an entire group of such smaller churches scattered between Brussels and Liège. Sankt Aposteln in Cologne, despite its Late Romanesque rebuilding, still shows clearly the loose and transparent structure of the Early Romanesque pier-basilica—which here, however (exceptionally), has a continuous transept at the west.

A second group of flat-ceilinged basilicas has columns with cuboid cushion capitals. Sint Pieter in Utrecht gives a good idea of this: the nave, taken in itself, would seem to be quite like what one finds in Upper Rhenish churches of the same sort, but the tripartite choir with crypt and two-storied secondary choirs belong unquestionably to another group represented by churches such as Sankt Severin in Cologne, Sint Lebuinus in Deventer, and Sankt Martin in Emmerich, to which can be added Sankt Georg in Cologne, with its elegant, presumably Roman, columns in the nave. We know that there were other naves with columns—in the now destroyed abbey church at Sint Truiden in Belgium for one—for which the shafts were brought from a great distance, first down the Rhine and then overland.

A third type, using alternating supports, shows most clearly the homogeneity and indissoluble linkage of a region that today belongs to four different countries. Representative examples are found, in the northern Rhineland and Westphalia, in Sankt Luzius in Werden, which has been well restored, and Sankt Martin in Zyfflich, which has been almost entirely altered; in the Netherlands, in the church at Susteren; in Belgium, at Saint-Ursmer in Lobbes (though there the intermediate columns were carved out around 1870); in Luxembourg, at Sankt Willibrord in Echternach. In all these churches, and in others besides, columns and pillars alternate in a simple sequence. Each pair of arches is embraced by a third stretching from pier to pier as a blind arch or, in Sankt Luzius, a blind rectangular field. Viewed as an isolated form, this is the twin-arch we know from innumerable nave galleries and from even more numerous bell towers and many other parts of the Romanesque church. Utilized for longitudinal pier-arches, it both separates and links the naves, thereby acquiring greater dimensions and increased importance. It is found occasionally elsewhere, in Lower Saxony and the Upper Rhine in particular.

Here, as in other regions, particular types have been developed, but for the larger and multipartite churches one can scarcely designate any fixed type of overall plan. In any given situation, there is a combination of structures in which especially the west end, nave, transept, choir area, and crypt may tend to different types. Nor is there often any firm linkage between parts, but rather the free variations that make the study of this architecture so fascinating.

In the Lower Rhine and Meuse area there are interesting examples of the three-towered westwork, and likewise of the hall-crypt, but two outstanding instances deserve fuller mention: the cathedral of Trier and Sankt Marien im Kapitol in Cologne.

Trier Cathedral is a unique case. Its original nucleus is a Late Roman hall over a square ground plan. Tall supporting members—first columns and then cruciform piers—supported large semicircular arches over which lay wooden ceilings or open timberwork. Huge walls, piers, and arches were of far greater interest to Early Romanesque architects than were the Late Antique naves with their columns added to the west. In a series of intermediate stages, these disappeared completely and have become known only in recent decades through the excavations of T. Kempf. The process seems symptomatic: the huge hall with its arches was extended to the west in the first half of the eleventh century by repeating the same interval between the alternating supports, which produced a rhythm of arches and bays in the form of A-B-A-B-A. Over the narrower bays of the lateral naves there were galleries (false perhaps), and the ceilings were graduated instead of being all at the same height. Not everything is known with certainty about Trier Cathedral, since it was vaulted in Late Romanesque times and its interior subsequently modified in the Baroque style. The basic elements are still clear, however.

The west front was conceived by the same unique fusion of Roman and Early Romanesque architecture. The large rectangle of the hall-like west wall is flanked by two round stair-turrets and broken through in the center by a large apse. The westernmost bays of the side naves are surmounted by large tall rectangular towers, with the stair-turrets emerging from them diagonally at their respective outer corners. There is surface decoration with pilasters, pilaster-strips, blind arches, and arch friezes. Between the stair-turrets and the apse, the real wall of the façade is concealed behind a blind architecture of large semicircular arches over the portals and arched galleries above them; together with the stair-turrets, the inner tribunes, and yet another gallery over the apse, these create a whole system of linkages.

Although this west front obviously grew out of a number of conjoined elements, its linkages likewise are true to type. While the west front at Limburg is very different, replacing the apse with a central porch, the relationship between the large towers and the stair-turrets must have been comparable. The east choir of Mainz Cathedral links its transept with an apse and flanking stair-turrets built at different times during the eleventh and twelfth centuries. Maria Laach and Sainte-Gertrude in Nivelles exhibit Late Romanesque transformations of this pattern.

Sankt Marien im Kapitol in Cologne, originally a convent church for noblewomen, was founded in Merovingian times but owes its fame to the rebuilding carried out in the eleventh century. With its narrow arcades and

84. *Sant Llorenç del Munt des Vallés, Benedictine abbey church, axonometric projection reconstructing the original state (from Puig i Cadafalch, 1909)*

85. *Sant Pere de Roda, Benedictine abbey church (ruin), axonometric projection reconstructing the original state (from Conant, 1959)*

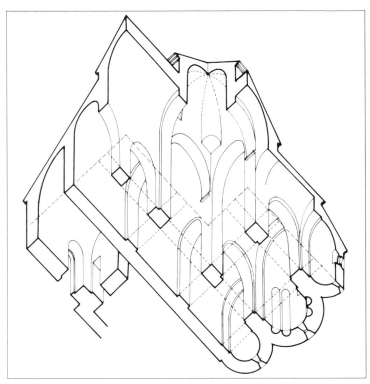

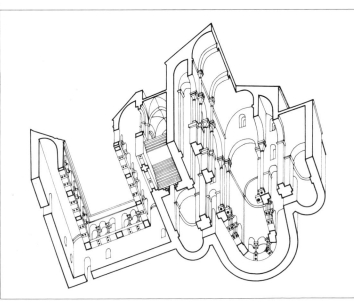

longitudinally oblong piers stretching out like walls, the nave offers a variant on the pier-basilica that strikes one as astonishingly harsh and austere for the Cologne region. The side naves, with their cross-groined vaults and marked wall projections, and the hall-crypt at the east recall Speyer I, but the latter's central nave and east end have nothing in common with Sankt Marien, whose east end is justly famous. It is a cloverleaf structure with three apses at right angles to each other, two of which make up a transept, and the third the choir. From the central nave, arcades supported on columns open onto side naves that run around the entire church to make kind of continuous vaulted ambulatory. Half-domes over the apses, barrel vaults over the intermediate bays, and a crossing tower that formerly was probably open make up an elaborate but rigorously graduated design.

Hugo Rahtgens, the author of a monograph on Sankt Marien, was able to gather a rich lode of prototypes and parallels for the building but not to explain its uniqueness as a creation. Nor, even less, was it explained by the suggestion of W. Effmann and A. Fuchs that the original crypt stairs would have called for an unconventional solution. Be that as it may, it should be kept in mind that, beginning with the middle of the eleventh century, three-aisled transepts were very much a part of the vocabulary of churches of the highest rank—the cathedral at Pisa, Saint-Sernin in Toulouse, Santiago de Compostela, the English cathedrals. But one need not look so far afield from the Lower Rhine and Meuse region for connections: the church of the former Benedictine abbey of Stavelot in Belgium preceded it with a choir ambulatory and three-aisled transept, while the church at Brauweiler near Cologne followed with both of these features.

Nivelles and Hildesheim

The convent church of Sainte-Gertrude in Nivelles (Belgian Brabant) and the Benedictine abbey church of Sankt Michael in Hildesheim (Lower Saxony), both of them well restored after the severe damage sustained in World War II, invite comparison, and A. Mottart has done so point by point. Sainte-Gertrude dates back further, all the way to Merovingian times, whereas Sankt Michael was initiated by Bishop Bernward (933-1022). Nevertheless, the Early Romanesque portions of both churches date from almost exactly the same time and—as flat-ceilinged basilicas with a choir and transept at either end and with crypt and towers—both aim at monumentality. Within that basic framework, their plan is so different from any other as to appear unique, typical above all for the broad gamut of possibilities in the early eleventh century but also in terms of regional differences.

Quite rightly, the abstract clarity of the Hildesheim church is admired as one of its basic traits. The central nave is hemmed in at either end by an isolated crossing, each giving onto equally high and square crossarms. The east and west ends are terminated by high though not square choirs with apses, and these serve to clarify the function and design of the intersection of the longitudinal and transverse components. In the nave,

86. Saint-Martin-du-Canigou, Benedictine abbey church (remains), axonometric projection reconstructing the original state (from Puig i Cadafalch, 1909)

87. Sant Père de Cassérres, monastery church, plan and transverse section (from Puig i Cadafalch, 1909)

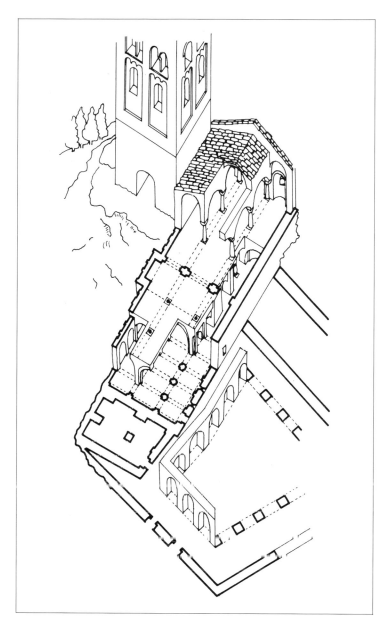

piers are interposed in a row of columns in such a way that, three times in all, there are two columns between each pair of piers, making a rhythmic meter of A-B-B-A. But one can—and must—also see that the piers give rhythmic accent and a firm regular measure to the whole interior, and the way in which this comes about can be read from the ground plan, where it is clear that the piers stand at the corners of the basic squares of which the plan is composed. Seen from outside, square towers over both crossings emphasize the equilibrium of the structure as a whole. At the head of each arm of each transept a stair-turret helps to confirm that impression.

At Nivelles, everything is different as far as details are concerned. The transepts are of different widths, heights, and lengths. Most important, their arms are lower than the central nave, and this is something made evident by the arches. The west transept was linked to the towered west front, which was carried over in the early rebuilding from the previous church but was eventually replaced by a gigantic Late Romanesque construction. At the east end there is an elongated rectangular choir over the crypt. The nave has slender round arches—there are eight as against Hildesheim's nine—set on piers whose succession is interrupted by a single cruciform pier in the center. On the side facing the central nave, the projecting shaft of that pier is carried halfway up the wall. When the church was restored in recent times, the shaft was utilized to support a transverse arch that surely never existed there before, though it cannot be proved that it was never intended for some stage or other of the building.

In Sankt Michael, what we may call the beauty of the spatial effect is in large part a product of the abstract clarity of the original plan. At Nivelles, on the other hand, it is much more the play of the sharply differentiated spatial cubes that creates so fascinating an effect. Interpreting the two churches in terms of opposites as we do, we must also add that there are other traits that likewise oppose each other. At Hildesheim, there are complications due to a number of factors: there are differences in the floor level because the west choir is elevated above the crypt; the ambulatory around the crypt led from the west entrance to the west transept and had an upper story; on the end walls of all four crossarms there are three stories of arcades; the lateral naves are broad, not as yet respecting the Romanesque norm of being half the width of the central nave; and so on. Certain factors remain unknown, such as whether the crossing towers were open to the interior. At Nivelles, the outstanding factor is that the pier-arcade is of great austerity and strength. Slender as are its supports, the crypt there—because of its square bays demarcated by cross-arches—has a more rigorous form than at Hildesheim, where transverse arches were not yet used.

Lower Saxony, Westphalia, and the East

Lower Saxony, the eastern part of Saxony between the Weser and the Elbe rivers, was one of the important centers of Early Romanesque art. Its outstanding monument is Sankt Michael at Hildesheim, which we have just

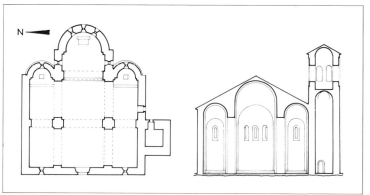

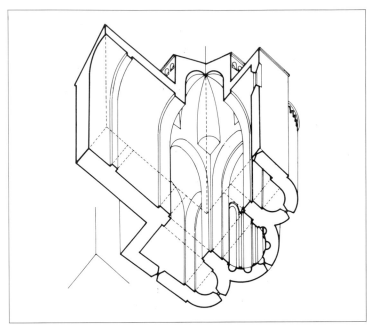

88. Sant Jaume de Frontanyá, axonometric projection (from Puig i Cadafalch, 1909)
89. Sant Jaume de Frontanyá, interior looking east

discussed. Built around 1000, its forward-looking stylistic elements are plain to see. In contrast to it, the galleried abbey church at Gernrode in the Lower Harz (East Germany), founded in 963, is more strongly linked with Pre-Romanesque art, as we have already seen.

An entire galaxy of flat-ceilinged basilicas has survived in this region along with these two, either with the same sort of simple alternation of supports found in Gernrode—for example, at Drübeck and Ilsenburg—or with the double alternation seen in the minster at Bad Gandersheim near Braunschweig and in the Benedictine abbey church at Gröningen near Magdeburg. Along with these, but rarer, are pier-basilicas such as the former Benedictine convent church at Kemnade near Hildesheim. As for the great cathedrals—Magdeburg, Hildesheim, Merseburg, Bremen—their Early Romanesque structures have either disappeared or survive only as modest vestiges.

Westphalia, the western part of Saxony, offers no such well-defined picture in its surviving Early Romanesque churches. Among these, the most important are three churches in Paderborn: the pier-basilica of the Abdinghof church, the three-towered westwork of the cathedral, and the entirely unique chapel of Sankt Bartholomäus, a small hall church (1017) with pendant cupolas on columns. Although it was vaulted over and rebuilt in the twelfth century, the original single-naved cruciform plan of Sankt Patroklus in Soest can still be made out. It is only somewhat tentatively that one can decipher the characteristics of Westphalian architecture in these buildings.

As for the former territory of the Polish Empire, recent Polish research has established the presence of Early Romanesque buildings from Ottonian times in so-called Great Poland around Gniezno and Poznań, that is, in the Warta River basin, and in Little Poland around Cracow. Little, however, has survived, and for the most part we know only ground plans and even these in fragmentary or hypothetical form. The first cathedral in Cracow, Swaty Gereon on the Wawel, has a long west transept recalling that of Sankt Michael in Hildesheim, because in both columns partition off the end of the crossarms (they doubtless also supported tribunes) and stair-turrets are centered at the end of each crossarm.

The Regions of Italy

The overall picture of Early Romanesque architecture in Italy was not sketched out satisfactorily before the article published by Thümmler in 1939. Since then, research has gone on without interruption, though the basic traits remain those he indicated. Now, as earlier, one thinks first of the great colonnaded basilicas at Pomposa, Torcello, Aquileia, San Piero a Grado near Pisa, and Otranto, most of them without transept and westwork and thereby carrying the Early Christian tradition into the tenth, eleventh, and even twelfth centuries. Not that there are entirely lacking the elements that brought about such an immense change in eleventh-century architecture

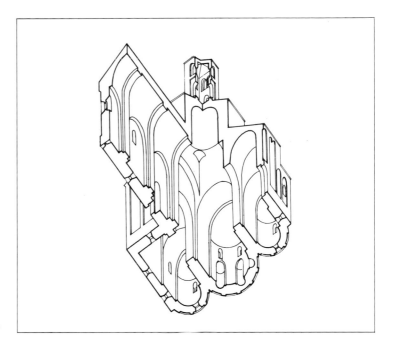

90. *Sant Ponç de Corbera de Llobregat, axonometric projection (from Puig i Cadafalch, 1909)*
91. *Sant Ponç de Corbera de Llobregat, interior looking east*

north of the Alps: San Pietro in Acqui (Piedmont) is a basilica with sturdy piers; there are alternating supports and a pier-arch system in Santa Maria Maggiore at Lomello in Lombardy, in the recently reconstructed San Piero Scheraggio, and San Miniato in Florence (Tuscany), and transverse arches also in the side naves of the cathedral of Gerace in Calabria; the church at Lomello and the cathedrals of Acqui, Gerace, and Aquileia (Friuli) all have low crossarms of the sort familiar in the Lower Rhine and Meuse valleys, and there are continuous transepts in the large single-naved churches at Farneta and San Salvatore on Monte Amiata (both in Tuscany) as well as in the late eleventh-century cathedral in Salerno far to the south; San Salvatore is especially noteworthy for having two west towers. The rows of niches in Sant'Ambrogio in Milan, in the abbey church at Nonantola (Emilia), and elsewhere were the first steps in the development of passageways. The large transept crypts in the cathedral at Acqui, in San Salvatore, and in Gerace began a series that continued into the twelfth century, and we have already pointed out their particularities, chiefly in contrast to Speyer.

It tell us a good deal about the state of scholarly research that for many years all these elements, while not overlooked, were nevertheless not assimilated and coordinated. Not until the intensive study of Romanesque architecture in the North, and its comparison with buildings in Italy, were scholars' eyes opened to the fact that these forms are not to be interpreted as bastardizations of a classical norm but as symptoms of a change in style that admittedly can be grasped much more unequivocally in the North.

Christian Spain

In Catalonia, between the Pyrenees and the Ebro, an extraordinary number of churches were built during the tenth and eleventh centuries in a rush of enthusiasm that also affected the closely related territory of Roussillon on the northern side of the mountains, in France. Because these areas subsequently lost a large part of their political importance, little in them has changed and their early buildings survive as relics of the past. Thus, there are still a great many Pre-Romanesque and Early Romanesque churches that not only warrant study in themselves but also help to compensate for the great losses of early buildings in most other regions. What is more, they continue to impress us through their rustic simplicity and grandiose natural settings, still often unspoiled.

There is scarcely any connection between the architecture of Asturias, which strikes one as the product of a refined court culture of the Carolingian era, and the rustic Early Romanesque of Catalonia. Between them is the so-called Mozarabic art that flowered in the tenth century in the border areas between Islamic and Christian regions among the local populations whom the Arabs permitted not only to continue as Christians but even to build new churches. Here there are remarkable parallels with Anglo-Saxon and Ottonian buildings.

Until the middle of the eleventh century, the Romanesque style affected Spain only in the higher reaches of the Pyrenees and in the eastern part of the territory immediately to the south, that is, in Catalonia. It was only around then that the Reconquista, the winning back of the peninsula in the name of Christianity, took on serious proportions. In 1036 a first slice of territory was reconquered, up to the Ebro and Duero rivers, and this meant that the cities of Barcelona, Jaca, and León in the north, and Ávila, Segovia, and Ciudad Rodrigo in Castile became Christian again. However, the effect of this was felt fully only in the High Romanesque architecture that began at the end of the eleventh century.

Catalonia and Early Romanesque Art

In art history too, the unity of Europe takes shape only slowly. National and linguistic borders divide what belongs together: we continue to feel things to be separate that we know perfectly well are closely linked to each other. That is why the art of the Catalans who live to either side of the eastern stretches of the Pyrenees (like that of the Basques in the western stretches) was for long classed as no more than the primitive folk art of remote provinces of France and Spain. In reality, the Pre-Romanesque and Romanesque art of the region between Perpignan and Barcelona provides the key to the understanding of art history in large parts of the West from the tenth to the twelfth centuries. It was a Catalan architect, Puig i Cadafalch, who acquainted us with this architecture in the numerous books and articles he published from 1906 on, and who was the first to give it its rightful place in the general history of art in Europe. Even more remarkable, it was not the total organization of the churches (their spatial and ground plans) that he focused on chiefly, but rather on certain motifs of the wall articulation, specifically pilaster-strips and friezes of blind arcades. The maps he made to show the diffusion of these architectural forms and their various combinations are highly informative yet vastly overrated. Obviously, he simply did not see that, in Catalonian architecture of the tenth and eleventh centuries, we have the earliest evidence of a spatial form of fundamental and wide-ranging importance for the history of all European architecture: the hall church.

An immense distortion has become customary in current art historical conceptions: the Early Christian basilica is taken to be the one and only point of departure, which—through transformations and additions—finally culminated in the diversity of forms definable as Romanesque. Meanwhile, the fact is often scarcely noticed that a radically different and in many respects diametrically opposed basic design—the hall form—had been present almost from the beginning. The only thing these two basic forms of the Western church have in common is the use of three naves separated, obviously, by arcades. Everything else is different.

From the outside, most Early Romanesque hall churches appear remarkably squat and unaccented: the four walls are topped by a large saddle roof; the two small end walls are quite simple under large triangular gables; at the east end there are three apses; finally, semicircular-arched windows and a portal—nothing more. Inside, there are two parallel arcades on sturdy supports, above them three parallel longitudinal barrel vaults. No upper story adds a special accent to the central nave, no light falls into it from high above; instead it seeps in through the outside walls, filtered and washed out to a uniformly modest intensity as it passes through the side naves. The windows lie below the impost line of the vault, so that the vault itself is dark, often more a zone of shadow than anything recognizable as a ceiling. The stone barrel vaults lie like a heavy lid over the walls and arcades. The naves all appear to be the same height, even when the central one is broader so that the round arches of its barrels become, necessarily, somewhat larger and higher than in the side naves. The small windows in the apses at the east end admit a bright light only in the morning, while in late afternoon and evening the sun's rays penetrate from the west, parallel to the walls, arcades, and barrel vaults. In the side-lighting that results, one does not notice the originally raw rubble walls that must be thought of as at least roughly plastered over, even if today's restorers are partial to a coarse stone effect.

This is by and large what we still find in many Early Romanesque churches in Catalonia. Santa María in La Tossa de Montbui in the province of Barcelona is certainly one of the earliest and best preserved among them. Set in the majestic barrenness of the steep mountainous landscape of the Pyrenees, its gloomy interior—entirely of stone—has a feeling of mystery about it. The church, inside and out, has an atmosphere uniquely its own, redolent of the magic of its ancient origins. How did it assume this form? Is it a reduction of a basilica? The latter is difficult to accept. With such "original" architecture, should one not rather think back to the very basis of stone construction. Walls were composed of hewn stone, and there were stone pillars and arches. Stone barrel vaults were raised over a continuous line of walls. Buttresses were not needed, since the three barrel vaults buttressed each other mutually, and the rest of the thrust was borne by the powerful walls. The church had to be large enough to accommodate a monastic or parish congregation, and if more space was required than could be covered by a single vault, three were built and held up by rows of supports and arches. The space above the barrel vaults was filled by brickwork or even by rubble or dirt, and the stone slabs of a single shallowly sloping saddle roof were laid over this directly, thereby producing a very secure construction entirely impervious to damage by fire since it required no timberwork roofing. Compared with the elaborately articulated constructions in the North, this may seem primitive, but it is also closer to its spiritual origins and it is precisely this that makes a powerful impression in churches such as Sant Llorenç del Munt des Vallés and Sant Pere de Cassérres.

Is more needed to explain such buildings? Naturally, they presuppose the ability to erect walls and vaults. Vaulting was already a matter of necessity

VII. Trier, cathedral, exterior

VIII. Speyer, cathedral, interior

at that time, partly because of lack of wood, partly because it was the tradition in the lands bordering on the Mediterranean. Through centuries and millennia vaulting had survived as a sort of elementary technique, something virtually part of folk knowledge. This explains such vaulted stone houses as the *trulli* in Apulia, the *nuraghi* in Sardinia, and similar constructions elsewhere; these are not without connection to the earliest vaulted structures known. Are not the stone tombs, dolmens, and monuments of megalithic culture a parallel to this? Certainly the missing link in this evolution is not something easily found. For many, such notions are purely romantic, but without hypotheses one cannot write history, and we are indebted to H. Glück for expounding these connections.

The barrel-vaulted hall church in Catalonia went through many transformations in the late tenth and in the eleventh century. As in other regions in the Early Romanesque period, projecting engaged shafts were added to the piers, which thereby took on a more elaborate plastic form. Along with these, however, square or round pillars or even columns continued to be used very often. An interesting special case is found in Sant Pere de Roda, where two tiers of columns were placed against the walls and piers to create a kind of articulated scaffolding that almost recalls Hellenistic architecture (we ought to remember that Catalonia too was a Roman province). The vault is divided by cross arches that in turn demarcate bays.

Along with the hall church, the barrel-vaulted church with a single nave is also a widely diffused form, of which many examples from the late eleventh and twelfth centuries can be found in the southern half of France and the northern half of the Iberian peninsula.

The hall church is insufficiently appreciated in non German research, and in fact many languages do not even have a special term for what is so aptly evoked by the German word *Hallenkirche.* Its essential features are already present in the Carolingian westwork, where there is a crypt-like chamber (at ground level, however) with more than one nave and with vaults over supports of equal height. The full-fledged Romanesque hall-crypt appeared all over Europe from the end of the tenth and the beginning of the eleventh centuries, and is known in countless examples. The largest are not restricted to the space under the choir but extend beneath the crossing or the transept and in exceptional cases, as in the cathedral at Trani, across the entire nave. As a porch in the westwork or as a lower church (crypt), the hall form is limited by the fact that the church interior lying over it must of course have a level floor, though it may be raised. This means that the hall can become a spatial form in its own right only where it constitutes an independent interior, most especially the main chamber of a church. As we have seen, this occurred first in Catalonia in the decades around the year 1000. This is undoubtedly the origin of the innumerable hall churches built throughout southern France and, subsequently, in northern Spain as well as in scattered locales throughout Italy during the eleventh and twelfth centuries. In the lands between the Loire and the Duero, the hall church, together with the

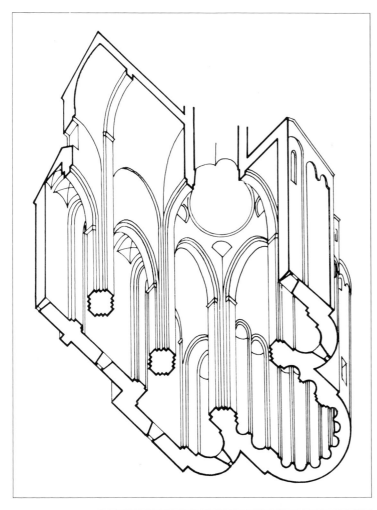

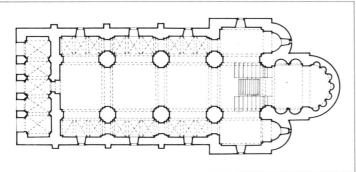

single-naved church covered by barrel vaults and cupolas, was the dominant form of Romanesque architecture, while the basilica form declined to no more than an occasional secondary phenomenon and seldom appeared in truly pure form. This is all the more remarkable in that the basilica is generally taken to be the one and only basic design for churches in the West in medieval times. To grasp the real situation, one must stop relying on the ground plans drawn by scholars and instead think of the interior as a three-dimensional reality. For this, besides actual study of the original building, one can use photographs, isometric diagrams, and cross sections.

Early Romanesque barrel-vaulted aisleless churches are especially numerous in Catalonia, often with a cruciform plan, meaning that at the east end, chapels open to either side in front of the apse and are usually covered by barrel vaults at right angles to the main vaults; this makes them look like transepts, as in Sant Jaume de Frontanyá and Sant Ponç de Corbera de Llobregat. Often these crossarms broaden to become two-aisled chambers resembling hall-form interiors, in which case the aisleless longitudinal nave may end up as no more than a short appendage to the west of this main chamber, as at Santa Cecilia in Montserrat. Thus, one finds oneself hesitating between describing this plan as a short hall church with elongated central nave or as a barrel-vaulted aisleless interior with an extended eastern part that, in turn, can be defined as either a hall-choir or a hall-transept. Above the crossing, if that is what one can call it, the interior frequently expands in the upper zone into an octagonal cupola on squinches, which looks like a low crossing tower when viewed from outside. But this pseudo-tower admits little light to the interior and should not be thought of as being like the huge light shafts that constitute crossing towers in the North, as at Jumièges, Caen, Hildesheim, or Speyer. Therefore, even this type of Catalan church, for all its more elaborate division of space, is still as dark and enclosed as a stone cave and quite unlike the high and much better illuminated basilicas of the North.

The barrel-vaulted aisleless church may also be combined with the clover-leaf plan familiar in flat-ceilinged aisleless churches south and north of the Alps. Granted that the Early Romanesque barrel-vaulted hall church is cavernous, but it is not unorganized. Round-arched arcades and round-arched barrel vaults convert the interior into the rigorous form we know to be a rule of Romanesque architecture. The central nave is usually broader than the lateral naves, and often it is also higher, even twice as high as in the upper church of Saint-Martin-du-Canigou. The interior then becomes graduated without, however, losing its hall-church character, because despite the fact that the walls rise steeply to either side of the central nave, they have no windows. Here too the three barrel vaults of the naves are covered over by a plain saddle roof.

Admittedly, not even this is a hard and fast rule. A central nave may occasionally rise higher than the roof and incorporate a few windows. The most important example of this sort is San Vicente in the castle at Cardona,

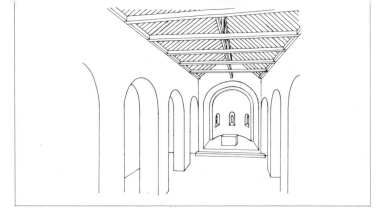

which—according to the usual classification—would be identified as a barrel-vaulted basilica. Indeed, it does look as if the basilica form was not simply used here as an existing type but as if it were a special form of the hall type in which the central nave happened to be elevated—an impression furthered by the fact that often in these churches there are windows on one side only (the south). Thus, it is as if the builders had found the gloom of the central nave excessive in larger churches and had taken steps to remedy it by a simple expedient without, however, following through logically and opening windows symmetrically in both walls of the upper story. Such exceptional plans are found even more often in the High and Late Romanesque period in the South, notably in Saint-Trophime at Arles, in the cathedral at Seo de Urgel, and in a few Cistercian churches.

Common to all Early Romanesque churches, whether they have plain or graduated halls, basilica-like plans, or aisleless chambers, is the barrel-vaulted ceiling. As an unarticulated half-cylinder, it has the simplest stereometric form and gives the effect of a kind of lid, so much so that if we envisage it in rough stone it calls to mind the monolithic lids over prehistoric tombs. Usually, however, it is articulated by means of cross-arches, which continue down to the floor in the form of rectangular shafts and which articulate the walls and piers also. The round-arched arcades, often without impost, can give the effect of something cut out of the walls themselves. Even when the piers have projecting engaged shafts and so become cross-shaped, they have little structural autonomy at first. They still continue to resemble walls even when, together with the shaft, they become a two-level relief. The phenomenon of the longitudinally elongated pier, and even the pier without impost stone, is also familiar in Early Romanesque examples in the North. As in southern Europe, the pier coheres with and is incorporated into the wall, though an element of future autonomy is latent in the crosslike shape of the pier. In any event, the projecting shafts and the cross-arches divide the interior into bays, even if the relationship between the space of the nave and that of the bay—between the whole and the part—remains indeterminate, just as one also finds oneself hesitating at times to know if the pier was intended as an autonomous supporting structure or if it simply represents what was left of the wall after the arcades were, so to speak, cut out. If we restrict ourselves to an abstract stylistic comparison, it is precisely this ambivalence that must be considered the decisive parallel between the North and the South, however much the architecture would appear to differ otherwise.

Of the numerous smaller Early Romanesque buildings in Catalonia, three large constructions stand out. The church of San Vicente, mentioned above, was built between 1029 and 1040 and is in good condition. It is distinguished from the throng of other churches by its crypt, a crown of niches in the apse, and cross-groined vaulting in the side naves and crypt. Despite the unfortunate restoration done in the late nineteenth century, the monastery church of Santa María at Ripoll is still very impressive, especially

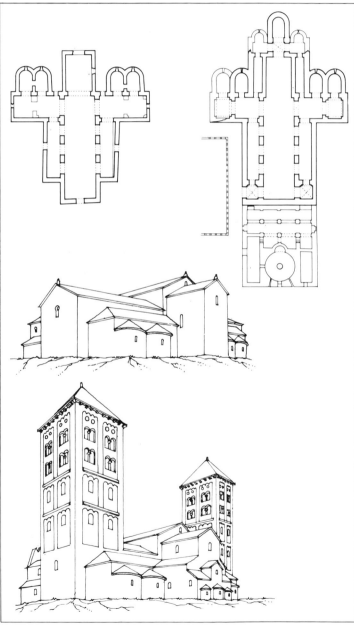

99. *La Tossa de Montbui, Santa María, the east end*

100. *La Tossa de Montbui, Santa María, interior looking east*

in its exterior aspect (it has a markedly projecting transept from which seven apses emerge). The interior was treated much more cavalierly by restorers, and the shallow barrel vault over the central nave is poorly documented and unconvincing, though the five-aisled nave is certainly authentic. The alternation of rectangular piers with columns is unique. The third of the large churches, the abbey church of San Miguel de Cuxá in French Roussillon on the northern slopes of the Pyrenees, is the product of the alteration and enlargement of an earlier church, completed in 974, and was finished in its new form in 1040. The axial disposition of quite different portions of the building is remarkable here and is comparable with the minster at Essen dating from the same time. At the west there is a round chamber with barrel vaulting springing from a column in the center, and this lightless room is referred to as the manger-crypt, the *iglesia de pesebre*. Barrel-vaulted lateral passageways lead to a kind of west crypt consisting of two north-south oriented chambers with barrel vaults on piers. This lies between the central-plan structure and the nave, below the atrium. Upstairs this plan was repeated, with a central plan structure and atrium, though this survives only in fragments. To the east there is a three-aisled nave that today has the form of a pillar-basilica. The original disposition is not entirely certain. The choir and secondary choirs connect with the transept and are surrounded by a U-shaped exterior crypt. Inside, the diversely grouped and graduated chambers are linked by horseshoe arches. In appearance as in fact, these relate the church to the Mozarabic style. On the outside, there is a highly impressive group of structures framed by two powerful towers over the ends of the crossarms. If this plan is kept in mind when viewing this partly ruined complex, it is evident why it was one of the most significant constructions of the Ottonian period. Parts of the cloisters, a later addition, were sold to the Metropolitan Museum of Art in New York, where, together with portions of other ruined churches, they now make up the medieval branch of the museum, known as The Cloisters.

Burgundy

The early buildings of southern Burgundy must be seen in connection with those of Catalonia to be understood properly. Between the upper course of the Loire and the Alps, the Rhône Valley provides a strong link between the Mediterranean region of Provence and the Jura Mountains, Lorraine, and, indirectly, the Rhineland. In Early Romanesque churches in Burgundy we find stone vaulting, barrel vaulting, and frequent use of the hall form. Examples of this can be seen at Farges in Burgundy and Saint-Hymetière in the Juras. There are also hall churches with elevated barrel-vaulted central naves, at Chapaize for instance, and barrel-vaulted basilicas, as at Uchizy.

If this is clearly understood, the most famous surviving Early Romanesque building in Burgundy—Saint-Philibert in Tournus on the Saône River—no longer seems an isolated phenomenon but rather the crowning point and synthesis of this entire phase of architecture. Its powerful west

front was built in the decades around 1000. From the outside, it is a massive block of masonry relieved by flat pilaster-strips and round-arch friezes, and with a tower over each of the western corners. Inside, the low ground story is a vaulted hall with round pillars and cross-groined vaulting in the central nave, and transverse barrel vaulting in the side naves. Thus, the vaulting system is different from that found in Carolingian westworks, though we are nonetheless reminded of the westwork crypt. The upper story is a church in itself, a basilica with longitudinal barrel vaulting in the high central nave and quarter-circle barrels in the side naves. This too is quite different from the flat-ceilinged upper story in the German westworks with their surrounding galleries. However, we must remember that even Sankt

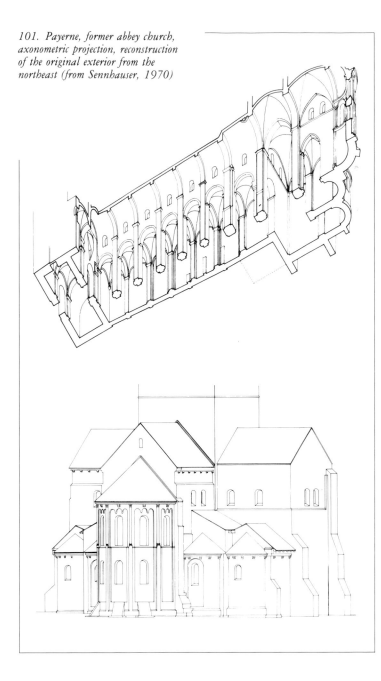

to a greater height and a hall-like form. However, there are windows in the low clerestory that illuminate the interior brightly. Above the round pillars rise smaller ones, but these are so engaged in the wall that no more than a quarter of their volume emerges. Originally, they rose to the crown of the wall, over which lay a wooden ceiling that was either of open timberwork or entirely flat. Later, though still in the eleventh century, they were shortened and utilized to support transverse arches across the nave; in turn, these support transverse barrel vaults that carry the eye upward. This creates a fantastic effect, something like the later cupola-vaulted hall of Saint-Hilaire in Poitiers or the church of Saint-Ours in Loches with its steep conical vaults. Aesthetically, the solution here is decidedly daring—doubtless a factor in its fame. However, it had no followers though, from the standpoint of technical construction, it is quite like the globe of Columbus: the barrel vaults buttress each other mutually so that the problem of statics is simply eliminated. Only a single (and smaller) building, at Mont-Saint-Vincent not far from Cluny, adopted the idea.

The eastern portions of Saint-Philibert, the transept, the choir with ambulatory and chapels, and the crypt were all built in the twelfth century. It is worth noting that they do not reach the height of the nave and that, indoors, even the open crossing tower gives the impression of being squat and concave, something it has in common with many crossing towers in southwestern Europe. In this, as in the preference for barrel vaulting, there is tangible evidence of links with the South, whereas the westwork-like front and the strong emphasis of the basilical interior demonstrate the connection with northwestern Europe. On the whole, then, there is already proof here of the intermediate position of Burgundy between North and South.

Among Burgundian barrel-vaulted basilicas of the eleventh century, the former abbey church in Payerne in western Switzerland is the most important. Like other buildings of this type, it shows a certain indecision in the way the upper-story windows cut into the barrel vault and thereby assume parabolic arch forms. This undoubtedly is to be interpreted, within the context of Ottonian art, as a holdover from Pre-Romanesque conceptions. Related to this was the third construction at Romainmôtier, likewise in western Switzerland, which constitutes the main core of the church as it stands today.

The approach used in these churches may provide some clue as to the nature of the second construction at Cluny. The research and excavations of the American scholar K. J. Conant—unfortunately still not well enough known—have confirmed the existence of a tripartite choir plan, but with regard to the form taken by the interior of the nave, they have scarcely advanced matters beyond the point where we can now propose a hypothetical reconstruction of the destroyed Cluny II on the basis of known portions of the ground plan interpreted by analogy with surviving churches. Conant's visualization may well reflect what the church really looked like, but there is no use denying that it could also have been entirely different.

Pantaleon in Cologne and other Ottonian westworks display decisive modifications in the architectural organism. At Tournus, what is outstanding is the rich invention displayed in the combination of such different forms of vaulting. The predominance of the barrel vault points to the connection between the Saône Valley, the lower Rhône, and the Pyrenees where, during this same period, the barrel-vaulted hall church predominated and barrel-vaulted basilicas were also found.

The nave of Saint-Philibert produces an astonishing impression—even in a period such as the Romanesque, so rich in impressive monuments. Powerful round pillars composed of small stone bricks drive the side naves

The term "High Romanesque" (roughly designating the period from 1070 to 1150) is, like "Early Romanesque" and "Late Romanesque," a concept of some use in bringing order to the mass of material to be dealt with. All three are, however, arbitrary terms that should never have been given as much importance as they have; they are useful only in that they help in making distinctions between one phase and another.

In 1061 the Early Romanesque wooden-ceilinged cathedral known as "Speyer I" was consecrated. Twenty years later rebuilding began—giving rise to "Speyer II"—and led promptly to the covering of the upper reaches with cross-groined vaulting. This signified a veritable revolution in the basilica plan. The central nave and transept were sealed off above, and at greater height than was possible before, by a concave stone vault. Instead of an abstract cube closed off by a level ceiling, a round-arched vault now delimited the interior. The side walls were linked to the central nave by a ceiling of the same solid, weighty material. The round arches achieved to some extent a true feeling of the third dimension. What is more, the vertical "spatial cells," the bays, became as dominant in the central nave as they had been previously only in the crypt and the side naves, thereby exemplifying clearly and tangibly the Romanesque principle of "addition": the bays were no longer sliced one by one out of the total interior space by the transverse arches—which meant that, as Frankl has pointed out, a vestige of spatial division still made itself felt—but for the first time themselves composed the total interior as a succession of distinct entities.

This was something anticipated in the crypt and the side naves, while the so-called wall bay was prefigured in Speyer I. In Speyer II, the articulation of the apse was connected with the relief elements of the central nave wall of the earlier construction, carrying over the colossal order of shaft and blind arches from the straight to the curved wall, outdoors as well as indoors.

With this, a further decisive step was taken: the transformation of the wall itself. Pre-Romanesque architecture had already established the bases for treating the wall as something more than a flat screen closing off an interior, as a surface more than a solid substance. Early Romanesque architecture had gone beyond this and conceived the wall as a three-dimensional "pane" with, already, occasional elements in relief. The mature phase of the Romanesque then proceeded to treat the wall as a plastic, sculptural mass to be shaped and modeled both inside and out. As a third step in the process, the space enclosed by the walls no longer merely penetrated the wall from the outside in, in layers, but was itself hollowed out of the inner core of the wall. With this, the technical structure of the Romanesque wall is visually exposed to some degree, since whether the wall is made of rubble, bricks, or large or small hewn stones, it always has an inner and an outer shell, painstakingly built up and consolidated, with the core between them filled with rubble and masonry debris. Where here and there the core is omitted, there are voids within the block of wall that, as

one would expect, are given specific forms. In Speyer II, they take the form of chapels with two bays and two minor apses that open on the church interior through twin arches on central columns. Or they may slit open the wall along its entire length to make arched galleries below the crown of the wall, the so-called dwarf galleries opening on the exterior. These likewise, as we have seen, were occasionally anticipated in the Early Romanesque, notably in the westwork of Trier Cathedral and the transepts at Bernay and Jumièges. With the passageway in front of the clerestory windows at Saint-Etienne in Caen, built in the 1060s, this cleave of the wall was introduced into the architectural system of the entire central nave. Then, however, around 1080/90, in the altar area and subsequently in the transept of Speyer II, a temporary halt was called to the process: this hollowing out of the wall was coupled with the vaulting of the high nave and utilized simultaneously for both the interior and the exterior of the church.

There was one more stage, however. In Speyer I the relief articulation of the central-nave wall had been carried through along with what can be called a kind of skeletal construction technique, meaning that even before 1050 piers and walls with rubblework filler had taken the place of the Early Romanesque solid-screen wall. Something similar had been done already in the galleried church at Jumièges, and it was quite tangibly realized at Saint-Etienne in the large gallery arches, which reduce the wall to a succession of piers. Piers instead of walls thereupon became the basis also for the transept at Speyer, where massive corner and central piers project both inside and out. If the many large windows in the transept are conceived as arched gates, it is reasonable to read them not as windows opened up in a continuous wall (like the Norman Romanesque windows with inclined sills) but as arches linking the enormous pilasters between them and at the corners.

This indicates how far back the bases of the High Romanesque extend, and also that was only after 1060/80 that the preconditions for a new conception all finally came together. If we demonstrate this innovation in a single truly outstanding example, it is because it was not the rule but the exception at the time, something really achieved only in Speyer II and in the Norman examples.

Turning to a quite different case, in Paray-le-Monial and the related Burgundian churches the entire central-nave wall is covered with a uniform network of articulation, distributed horizontally in bays and vertically in three stories. The outer wall of the apse of Sainte-Trinité in Caen is likewise articulated in narrow vertical sections corresponding to the bays inside and divided into four stories. Thus, possibilities were mastered around 1100 that were to remain essentially valid for the Late Romanesque also, as can be seen in the central-nave walls of the cathedral at Le Mans and the abbey church at Brauweiler of around 1150 or in apses along the Lower Rhine as late as 1250.

We see, therefore, that there were continuous lines of development in

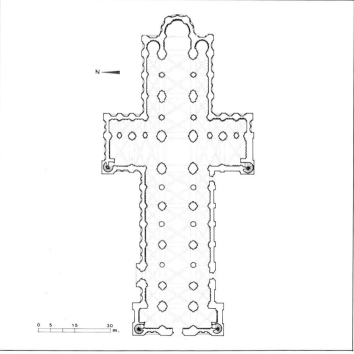

Romanesque architecture from the first to the second and then to the third stage. If judged by the actual date of their creation, many phenomena would belong to another stylistic stage than that in which, according to an ideal chronological scheme, they should have their place. Nonetheless, if only in the interest of clarity, the more or less abstract scheme should be retained as an aid in orientation.

As indicated, Speyer and a few vaulted Norman and Burgundian churches are really exceptions, the superlative examples of an aristocratic architecture. Wherever the basilical form prevailed, the overwhelming majority of new churches, even very large ones, continued in the late eleventh century and well along into the twelfth to be faithful to the wooden ceiling and, along with it, to the boxlike plan for the central nave. As was already the case in many Early Romanesque buildings, the crypt, the side naves, and the ground floor of the westwork—possibly too the altar area and often the crossing—were vaulted, these being the portions of the building that either had smaller spaces to span and narrower intervals between their supports or else had some particularly important ecclesiastical function. Buildings of this sort appeared throughout the regions favoring the basilica form, from Scandinavia and England through northern and central Europe and across the Alps into all the various provinces of Italy, to which can be added those parts of east-central Europe where building in the basilica forms was practiced even before 1150. Here, then, the austere beauty of the Early Romanesque form and disposition of the interior continued to prevail, though not without its modification in certain details. Often the compound piers were more elaborate, with bundles of projecting rectangular or round engaged shafts; the arches were frequently no longer plain but finished off with fillet moldings, so that in cross section they would appear to be a continuation of the compound pier supporting them. Galleries appeared in many regions where no trace of them existed previously: the Lower Rhineland, Lombardy, Tuscany, Apulia. The blind triforium began occasionally to be used in flat-ceilinged buildings as well. Along with the Norman churches and Speyer, other buildings began articulating the upper wall in flat-ceilinged central naves, either with shafts alone or with blind arches or cross-arches, though few of the latter have survived and are therefore objects of dispute. Here again we must mention the Lower Rhine, Lombardy, and Tuscany (for example, San Miniato in Florence and Sant'Antimo).

Articulation of the outside walls also became more general. Though often restricted to simple demarcation of fields by means of pilaster-strips and scalloped friezes or blind arches, there could be more elaborate compositions, often dividing the wall into stories or relief strata.

Without going beyond the tangible, visible facts of architectonic form, we can see that there was a vast number of differences between the art of the twelfth century and that of the eleventh. To some extent, what the earlier century had achieved by its own efforts was now something to be taken for granted: stone vaulting over large spans and at great heights had suddenly become practicable. Though it was not yet practiced everywhere, it was henceforth within the range of possibilities (though wooden ceilings continued to be erected, and not just in isolated examples but in entire categories of buildings and in every region at all times). Even where vaulting ran into the greatest of difficulties, namely in the basilical central nave, it became so frequent that many scholars—wrongly, I think—have not been able to resist the temptation of transposing this backward in time to make of it the conscious goal of earlier periods. Nevertheless, the technique of building in stone—of working it, of erecting firm structures with it, of setting up a double shell, in short, everything men have learned by intuition and experience about architectural construction and statics—had become the common property of a large part of the Western world. The art of vaulting had been able to profit from the experiences and achievements of the Carolingian central-plan church, the southwestern European hall church, and the smaller and for the most part lower secondary chambers in such buildings. However, in mastering the art of working in large dimensions, new forms of vaulting were developed. Vaulting with a continuous support—the barrel vault and cupola—was as much modified as vaulting reposing on separate points, namely the cross vault. The semicircular barrel vault acquired a more pointed profile as well as cross-girding in Burgundy; in the cupola churches of southwestern France, the cupola over a drum came instead to rest on pendentives and cross-springers; the cross-groined vault without girding (the product of interpretation of two barrels at right angles to each other) became a higher, more concise cross vault between cross-springers, as in Speyer, or a cross-ribbed vault as in Durham, Utrecht, and Lombardy. In certain of these transformations the solid, self-supporting shell became itself the structural armature.

The wall went through similar transformations. The homogeneous wall contained between two flat surfaces became a through-structured fabric. Early Romanesque forms of articulation set into the wall surface—pilaster-strips and scalloped friezes—or directly in front of it—engaged shaft, half-columns, blind arches—led to the decomposition of the wall into piers and solid wall (the upper story of Speyer I), into piers and arcades (the galleried churches of Normandy), or even into outer wall, inner wall, and colonnette arcading (as in the dwarf gallery, tribunes, and the like).

The replacement of the Antique column by the pier became so much a matter of course (with exceptions in Italy) that it eventually became possible to re-admit the Classical support without disturbing the Romanesque stylistic unity, although almost always only in subordinate roles in a building of more than one story, as in the choir ambulatory supports in Cluny or the aedicule columns in Speyer Cathedral. Antique capitals and cornices likewise offered forms to enrich the architectonic vocabulary, the contradiction between their former and present contexts seeming to matter little.

Above all, however, the frugal simplicity and abstract quality of the Early Romanesque was now often a thing of the past, giving way to a kind of

beauty that appeared to have an inner life of its own, despite the fact that it was still expressed through predominantly abstract forms. The use of architectural sculpture and ornamentation became increasingly widespread, though its primary function as an aid in articulation of the wall was seldom forgotten or superseded—a change that would come about only in the Late Romanesque.

The change in style that took place between 1060 and 1080 can also be observed in the vaulted hall church. Like the basilica, it had a clearly definable geographic distribution. Engaged columns and transverse arches introduced into the overall scheme a system that strikes one as more rigorously articulated. Arcades and vault zones were brought into close relationship, and the bay became an essential element of architectonic organization, countering the continuous flow of the barrel vault in the longitudinal axis of the interior. In the cupola church, southwestern France devised the most effective means conceivable to make in clear that the interior was composed additively, through a succession of individual bays. There also the wall was through-organized by shafts and blind arcades indoors and out, and in the Aquitanian cupola churches it was opened up into strata and hollowed out by gallery passages. A large number of elaborate

105. Caen, Sainte-Trinité ("Abbaye aux Dames"), interior looking east
106. Ouistreham, Saint-Samson, interior looking northwest

articulating elements were utilized to define the story levels on the apses and within the contours of the simple gabled façades.

In Western architecture, a great diversity of cultural regions and architectural systems coexist in peace and equality. Viewed in terms of history, this corresponds to the multiplicity of territories in the days when nations as such had not yet taken shape. The kings in reality were scarcely more than *primi inter pares,* and even the German king had difficulty enforcing his claim to supremacy—then only by insisting on his dignity as Holy Roman Emperor.

The late eleventh century saw imperial power enmeshed in the disorders involving the issue of investiture. The territorial powers rose up against the central authority. An ecclesiastical reform party combated the abuses that, in their eyes, arose from the position of the Church as an official arm of Ottonian imperial power (bishops and abbots were heavily involved in secular functions). Emperor Henry IV's submission to the pope at Canossa in 1077 marked a turning point. With the Concordat of Worms in 1122, Henry V put an end to the conflict that had stirred all of Europe. It is debatable whether that conflict expressed itself in architecture as well. The great new church of the Burgundian monastery at Cluny, a chief center of ecclesiastical reform, was anything but in line with the new principles proposed. In dimensions and splendor it vies for primacy with the new imperial cathedral at Speyer, but reveals nothing that might suggest its association with a reform movement. Among German supporters of the reform party, the lead was taken in the diocese of Speyer by the clerics of the monastery at Hirsau, who held out for the Swabian "anti-king." Was their new church of Sankt Peter und Paul—a flat-ceiling basilica with columns—designed as an antithesis to the cathedral at Speyer? Or was it simply built in the old tradition that had remained active into the late twelfth and even the thirteenth century?

Despite che struggle over investiture and the beginning of the decline of the Empire and of the imperial office, despite the perpetuation and even the reinforcement of the disintegrating powers of feudalism, the West in this period seems if anything more secure than in the past. For the moment, its external enemies posed no great threat and had been repulsed at various frontiers. The Reconquista was making considerable progress in Spain (this was the time of El Cid), and soon half of the Iberian Peninsula would be Christian again. In southern Italy, Norman knights acting as mercenaries in the pay of Byzantium had gained a foothold and would soon seize power in Apulia; before the middle of the twelfth century, they would extend their reign throughout southern Italy and Sicily. At the eastern border of the Empire, on the Elbe and Saale rivers, the Ottonian emperor returned to the charge, and this time successfully. In the territory between the German kingdom and Poland, marches and bishoprics were instituted with lavish support. The First Crusade to win back the Holy Land and the cities dear to Christendom was driving into the very heart of the Arab lands.

THE VAULTED BASILICA

One of the clearest signs of a stylistic revolution during the last third of the eleventh century is the vaulting over of the high nave in the basilica. The question can be raised as to whether this should be viewed only as an advance in engineering skill. However, seen in the perspective of time, there can be no doubt that it truly represented a development, since vaults had been limited to quite modest spans until around the middle of the eleventh century. When they began to cover larger areas, special safeguards had to be adopted, notably buttressing through vaults of equal height in hall churches or through towers or the like—as in the chancel at Speyer, where a barrel vault fifty-two and one-half feet wide is buttressed by two towers. Eventually, wide-spanned vaults were hazarded over the transept and the basilical central nave without any special buttressing (though, in a few outstanding buildings, with exceptionally thick and strong walls). It remains to be investigated whether Speyer was unique in having both visible and concealed wooden mooring in its vaults. This technique became widespread in the twelfth century, and in the second half of the century (even more so in the thirteenth) it became so generalized that wood-ceilinged churches became more or less exceptions in Late Romanesque architecture, to say nothing of the Gothic.

As for the inception of the technique, it is characteristic that a considerable number of vaulting systems were developed that to a greater or lesser extent—according to how one looks at them—seem as independent of each other as were the regions where they were devised. Furthermore, the shapes of vaults themselves are markedly differentiated in construction and form. Thus, we can distinguish the so-called bound system with cross-groined vault, with rectangular profiled band ribbing and with round profiled ribbing, as well as with sexpartite vaulting. In all these cases, there are two bays in the side naves to every one in the central nave, and the length and breadth of the bays maintain the relationship of one (the side nave) to two (the central nave). This explains the rigorous "binding" of the system. There is also the system with transverse oblong vaults in the central nave, where the number of bays in all three naves is the same. Here too the vaults can be either groined or ribbed. There are mixtures of these two systems—in Durham Cathedral, for example—and there is, besides, a separate group in Burgundy with pointed barrel vaults in the central nave.

All these vaulting systems are accompanied by correspondingly diversified systems of wall articulation. Common to all is the vertical division into bays by means of projecting engaged shafts, and often with horizontal divisions into stories by means of blind arcades, galleries, triforia, or even merely cornices. This articulation, however, was not confined to the central nave but was used in the most varied ways for the walls of the transept, chancels (the apses in particular), and other areas. The exterior of the building was equally subject to this sort of enrichment. Because all parts

of the building were involved in this decorative process—including the exterior and always without exception flat-ceilinged interiors—we can be sure there was a connection with the change in formal vocabulary attendant upon the stylistic conception of the High Romanesque. From this standpoint, construction may be seen as only one factor among many. Whether or not one of these factors had a predominant and causative function is one of the problems of architectural research on which agreement will quite likely never be reached.

Norman and Anglo-Norman Architecture

In 1066 Duke William of Normandy conquered the English kingdom, thereby vastly increasing his territory. For many years thereafter, the political center of gravity of the Norman kingdom continued to be England, and the arts too, though with a slight time lag, reflected this change. In the course of the late eleventh and twelfth centuries, many large and even gigantic buildings went up, replacing those of the former Anglo-Saxon powers and differing greatly from them. Although the Norman element came to predominate, regional differences did exist, so that one can distinguish between Anglo-Norman and Continental Norman churches.

During the decades around 1100, some large vaults were erected in England and Normandy, thus giving rise to several entirely vaulted buildings of significance for all of Europe—most notably the cathedral at Durham, the church of the Benedictine abbey at Lessay in Normandy, and the two great abbey churches at Caen. The majority of the large new constructions, however, remained faithful to the wooden ceiling until far along in the twelfth century, though side by side with them were a few with barrel vaulting, notably the crossarms at Mont-Saint-Michel, or with cross-groined vaulting, specifically in the longitudinal choir of Sainte-Trinité (the "Abbaye aux Dames") in Caen.

The great English cathedrals and abbey churches are characterized by their extraordinary length, which makes their markedly articulated upper walls extremely effective. The vertical shafts, the long continuous horizontals of the pier arcades, the gallery arcades and passageways in front of the windows, and the open timberwork ceilings all conspire to create a unique and unmistakable architectural style. In almost every instance, unfortunately, the buildings have been considerably altered by Gothic vaulting and other changes, as is so often the case on the Continent also.

In Norman architecture the vaulting of the main area was almost exclusively of the cross-vault type. The rich articulation of the walls carries over into the vault, so that the ribbing seems to the eye to be a continuation of the engaged half-column support. The significance of all this is clear in the cathedral begun in 1093 at Durham in northern England, where full use was made of rib vaulting—a fact that earns it a prominent place in the history of High Romanesque vaulted architecture, alongside Speyer II and Cluny II. In England it remained at first as isolated an example as Speyer

II was in the Rhineland, indeed even more so since the German innovations were quickly taken up at Mainz and, soon thereafter, in other vaulted churches on the Lower and Upper Rhine. The spatial plan of Durham is based on the "bound" system: every second support is a large, round, dressed-stone pillar incised with geometric spirals and other such patterns. The main piers are articulated into compound forms with shafts extending to the ribbed vaults, which in the side naves are square in plan; in the central nave, however, the double bays and markedly longitudinal oblong forms of an original and remarkable character: between two strong transverse arches there are two transverse oblong vaults having in common the same central lozenge-shaped cap. This is a unique alternative to the sexpartite vault that was to appear somewhat later, though it strikes one as not very mature as a formal solution. With its twin-towered west façade and large square crossing tower, Durham is highly impressive on the outside too, an impression further enhanced by its situation on a hill almost entirely surrounded by a loop in the river.

To match Durham, there is the abbey church at Lessay, the first fully vaulted building in Normandy. Especially impressive is the way the stone ceiling binds together powerful pillars, secure walls, and a clearly demarcated interior space. As in Durham too, an inner passageway runs in front of the windows of the clerestory. The vaulting system, however, is different. The cross-ribbed vaults over transverse oblong bays arise from pillars of the same form. In the reconstruction done after World War II, it was observed that the ribbed vaults were not added later, as one would suppose, because the ribs do not correspond precisely to the shafts, having been set up "inorganically." Since we are so accustomed from Early Gothic buildings to find the vault ribbings "organically" integrated into the system of supporting shafts, we have almost taken this for granted as the norm. Lessay and the contemporary Norman churches, however, teach us that precisely this organic correspondence was lacking from the start and had to be arrived at through a long process of development. What is already clear in Lessay, on the other hand, is that the wall shafts and vault ribbings can have the same plastic form, with the same projections and moldings. It was not until thirty or forty years later and in the northern part of the Ile-de-France—in the abbey church of Saint-Germer-de-Fly and in Saint-Etienne at Beauvais— that the organic relationship between both of those forms was ultimately developed.

Saint-Etienne and Sainte-Trinité in Caen utilize the third Norman vaulting system, as does Saint-Samson in Ouistreham. Saint-Etienne had engaged shafts on all of its piers as early as its original building, but they were of two types—either plain and single or compound with a bundle of three, a consequence of the system of alternating supports. When the church was vaulted a few decades later, the architect showed considerable sensitivity in taking into account the elements already present. He did not put up cross-groined vaults such as existed in the choir of Sainte-Trinité and in the side naves, since this would have meant superimposing large-surfaced vaults on the already richly articulated walls of the middle nave; instead, he provided the groins of the vaults with convex moldings that continue the form of the supporting shafts and, moreover, are aligned with them. Thus, each engaged shaft carries over, so to speak, into another projection that cuts across the room either transversely as a cross-springer or diagonally as a rib. In this way, the ribbed vault assumes its form as the natural consequence of both the supporting shafts and the elaborately articulated wall system; it does this, furthermore, in the innovatory form of the sexpartite cross vault.

Examined more closely, neither in Durham, Lessay, nor in Saint-Etienne in Caen is there a truly organic connection between shaft and rib at their point of connection. As for Sainte-Trinité in Caen, there too it is assumed that the sexpartite central-nave vaulting was done later, but it remains to be proved whether the central nave itself belongs mainly to a second or third stage of building.

In Normandy as in England in the late eleventh and the entire twelfth century, there existed side by side vaulted and unvaulted churches and even vaulted and unvaulted areas within a single church. In Anglo-Norman architecture, even most of the vast middle naves were deliberately not vaulted over for an entire century, which tells us that we should not interpret vaulting as a modern and progressive conception, despite the fact that it is one of the roots from which the Gothic would later grow. The Norman churches of the late eleventh and twelfth centuries are neither "Gothic" nor even "proto-Gothic" or "crypto-Gothic." Those are terms belonging to a teleological conception that is out of place here. However, the unique and regionally determined character of the churches was responsible for creating the preconditions that, a half or even full century later, were the starting point for further developments in other regions. Yet the consequences drawn from them in those other regions were simply not drawn in Normandy itself. What is more, the Gothic architecture that arose on the bases of those consequences—as well as from entirely different preconditions—certainly had an effect in its turn on Normandy. What arose then, however, was an entirely different architecture: Norman Early and High Gothic and the so-called Early English Gothic.

Scholars have invented all sorts of legends concerning the origins of rib vaulting, proceeding more or less consciously from the notion that vaulting had, from the start, been the secret goal for which medieval architecture yearned: if medieval architects nevertheless built churches with flat ceilings or unconcealed timberwork, the explanation given was a lack of technical skill or of appropriate materials. True as that may be in individual cases, it is untenable as a generalization. The wooden-ceilinged building has its own implicit laws and a clearly marked character. Because in our time we have come to understand and appreciate the abstract beauty and austere grandeur of the Early Romanesque boxlike interior, we can no longer credit

114. Maria Laach, Benedictine abbey
church, exterior from the north
115. Maria Laach, Benedictine abbey
church, interior looking northeast

the notion that it owes its existence solely to the fact that its builders were incapable of constructing a vault.

These observations are particularly pertinent with reference to Norman buildings, where one has tangible evidence of how a flat wall surface was first pierced by openings, then given plastic relief by three-dimensional elements, and finally hollowed out by passageways and galleries. Out of the smooth expance of the so-called Ottonian wall in the church at Bernay (Liess called it a *Tafel,* a flat panel) there developed the central-nave wall in Jumièges—which is dynamically activated by articulating elements and half-columns—and ultimately the system based on supports, arches, and half-columns used in Saint-Etienne in Caen. These developments have little to do with vaulting: when vaulting was added to them, it had to fit into the wall below because the ribs were conceived as conforming with the Norman system of compound piers.

Thus, vault ribbing has an articulating function in the first place, or—in other words—an aesthetic significance. Is it also an important factor in construction? One is inclined to deny this when one learns that ribbed vaults of the twelfth and even the thirteenth centuries continued to be built like Romanesque vaults with a thickness of from twelve to sixteen inches, and that the mass of the vault was composed in the same way as the walls, out of rubblework (gravel in a rich base of mortar). The ribbing seems, in fact, to be no more than a garnish added afterward, as P. Abraham pointed out in 1934. However, it can certainly have a constructional significance if it serves as centering during the building of the vault, compelling its form to be determined no longer by the surface of the dome but by the groin lines. As a result, when the ribs are schematically projected down to the floor, there are straight diagonal lines rather than imprecise and fluctuating groins.

It has been pointed out that the plastic shaping of the groin lines by the ribs creates an additional effect, in that the shafts imitate the diagonal course of the ribs and thereby break through the frontality, as it were, of the Romanesque wall—an idea stressed by P. Frankl when he said that ribbing "contaminates" the Romanesque interior.

Here, then, is another kernel out of which the Gothic was to develop. There is also a third: in the diagonal ribbing there is doubtless an urge to emphasize the other arch lines of the vault plastically, and thus to produce something like a supplementary blind arcade wherein the vault meets the wall. The concave segments of the vault thereby become more and more simply fillers in the spaces between the components of a supporting armature. All of these are consequences, however, that were realized only over a stretch of time.

The Upper Rhineland

The Early Romanesque cathedral at Speyer was consecrated in 1061, though probably only the interior was in fact completed. Twenty years later, Henry IV ordered work on it to be resumed. The general plan as well as the crypt,

crossing, nave, and west front were left to stand as they were, but the apse and crossarms were entirely rebuilt, the central nave was vaulted over, and the upper parts of the six towers were added. There were astounding innovations, among which the vaulting of the main nave was only one. Only the chancel had been vaulted in the first phase of building, and this was by a huge barrel buttressed by the towers at the corners of the transept. It seems likely that vault exerted excessive pressure on the walls east of the transept, making rebuilding and reconsolidation inevitable, though the flooding of the Rhine adduced as a reason at the time does not strike me as convincing.

The tall blind arcading of the central nave was carried over to the exterior of the apse, which was crowned with a dwarf gallery, a passageway open to the outside through a slender arcade and running under the eaves around the building at the level where the vault joins the wall. In the interior too the wall is composed of two shells enclosing an open space; the main area is encircled at ground level with chapels and, in the apse, with a wreath of niches. This articulation carries over into the transept but in much larger dimension, both inside and out. In front of the transept apses there is an aedicule-like structure strikingly suggestive of the Renaissance, and the capitals as well as the roof cornice on the north side of the building display Antique forms. Above all, the architectonic decoration is markedly emphasized in this stage of building, particularly in the ornamental surrounds of the transept windows.

In the central nave, cross-groined vaults were devised in such a way that each encompasses two arches of the colossal arcades of the original nave. The walls are given rhythm by an alternation of strong and weak projections corresponding to the succession of bays created by the vaults above them. The bays of the vault units in the side naves, left from the original building, and the new enlarged vaulted bays of the main nave produce here for the first time the "bound" system that in the twelfth century became obligatory for vaulted basilicas in a great many regions. Here it was carried through more clearly and more thoroughly than in Norman churches.

The bound system, the vaulting, the more marked relief articulation of the walls, the slicing of the wall into two shells, the architectonic decoration—all of these are elements of the mature Romanesque style, which more and more determined the character of architecture in the twelfth century. Speyer Cathedral is the apex of that development, an imperial edifice erected with the most lavish outlay imaginable in its time. In many respects, it remains unique and unmatched. Its rebuilding permits us to observe how many bases of future architectural developments had already been formulated in the Early Romanesque, but also how many were new creations worked out at Speyer.

The second imperial cathedral on the Upper Rhine, that at Mainz, likewise still conserves certain portions from Early Romanesque times, though not to the same extent as at Speyer. Although the central-nave articulation at Mainz need not have come to terms with the colossal order

of the walls, as was the case at Speyer, it did in fact do so, quite likely because of the imposing articulation of the walls with their emphatic relief elements. As it worked out, however, the elements were all recast, reduced, and made shallower. The buildings erected immediately afterward entirely rejected any articulation of the central-nave wall not directly connected with the vault supports. This is the case throughout the Rhineland, so much so that the architecture of the Upper and Lower Rhine valleys appears virtually indistinguishable. One really hesitates to say in which geographic category the former Cistercian abbey church at Eberbach in the Rheingau district should be classed.

Around the middle of the twelfth century, an especially notable and handsome group of churches arose in Alsace—at Saint-Jean-Saverne (Sankt Johann Zobern), Rosheim, and Sélestat (Schlettstadt)—as well as across the Vosges in Lorraine, at Étival and Saint-Dié. Most significant is the parish church in the small former imperial town of Rosheim. It is the best preserved of this group of vaulted basilicas using the bound system. Everything in it is compact and sturdy, with walls and piers of exceptional weightiness and with columns whose bases, shafts, and capitals are capable of bearing such a manifold burden. Bulky engaged shafts give rise to thick ribs, which make even the vault zone participate in the three-dimensional physical heaviness of the whole.

With few exceptions, the bound system founded in Speyer II became the

*121. Saint-Benoît-sur-Loire,
Benedictine abbey church, interior of
the choir looking southeast*

rule throughout the Upper Rhine region from Basel to Mainz, at least wherever the flat-ceilinged basilical form was not still in use. Both types reflect a conservative attitude going even beyond that of the Lower Rhine area, and one that was to remain basic until around the middle of the thirteenth century.

Along with this group should be mentioned certain Romanesque buildings of which only portions survive, namely the former abbey churches at Murbach and Marmoutier (Mauresmünster) in Alsace. Characteristic of architecture along the Upper Rhine is the use of yellow and red sandstone, and nowhere is it more effective than in these powerfully walled twelfth-century churches. At Murbach, all that survives is the east end with a very high transept of staggered levels, almost exactly as in the Auvergne, and three flat-backed choirs. The narrow and steep interior is interesting for the flat band-ribbed vault of a type that, in the middle decades of the century, appeared along the entire Rhine as well as in Lombardy and, after 1159, also in the crossarms of Speyer Cathedral. At Marmoutier, the west front has the fortress-like solidity of Speyer Cathedral, but is more elaborately and more delicately articulated—an early demonstration of the art of varying fewer motifs. A three-arched porch opens in the middle, and the entire structure is crowned by three towers somewhat removed from each other, this too recalling Speyer. Both of these Alsatian churches, though otherwise quite different from each other, are vaulted throughout.

The Lower Rhine and Meuse Valleys

In this region the large, important, and famous churches were almost always vaulted in the twelfth century, yet by and large the beginnings of vaulted constructions date from somewhat later here than on the Upper Rhine and in Normandy. Here again there are three very different systems of nave vaulting, though they all emphasize the clear gradations in space typical of the basilica. The most important and also the earliest vaulted building here was in Utrecht: the Mariakerk founded by Emperor Henry IV in 1083 and consecrated in 1097. Although it was demolished in the nineteenth century, we have many detailed views of it painted by Pieter Saenredam. In the central nave, it had band-ribbed vaults supported on diagonally disposed shafts engaged in complicated compound piers.

The galleries above the side naves were also vaulted, and they carried over into a short transept in the middle of the church. In the west there was a second transept and in the east a third, but only the latter was fully developed and supported a crossing tower. With its well-defined articulation, shafts, and vaults and its large gallery openings, the Mariakerk had much in common with the Norman style. However, there were even more closely related churches in Lombardy, but since the early cathedrals of Novara, Vercelli, and Pavia have not survived one cannot be absolutely certain of the resemblance. What is more, it is difficult to date it precisely. Gall dated the nave at no earlier than around 1170, but it could just as well

have been erected in conjunction with the eastern portions built around 1120-30. The Onze Lieve Vrouwekerk in Maastricht and Sankt Clemens in Wissel near Xanten give us some idea of the architecture of this vaulting system.

A more extensive group of churches came into being in the 1130s: the former Premonstratensian abbey church in Knechtsteden near Cologne is the finest to have survived, but the church of the abbey of Rolduc (Klosterrath) in Dutch Limburg is no less important. Its three transepts reveal links with the first group; its vaults are constructed without exception with groins rather than ribs, and the system of supports is simpler and more strongly engaged in the walls. This is the solution arrived at in Speyer II, and the roots for it are certainly to be sought there. However, at Rolduc all its consequences were carried through, something not feasible in Speyer, where so much of the earlier building was retained. To list only a few of its chief modifications, there is a clearer alternation of pillars and columns, there are large open surfaces between the wall shafts and in the vaults, and the windows in the clerestory are grouped in pairs under the wall arches. The result is a thoroughly clear, restful, harmonious architecture in which High Romanesque vault construction finds its classical expression.

The third solution is found in Maria Laach near Coblenz. This Benedictine abbey was founded by the palatine counts in 1093, and building of the church went on for more than a century. It is probable that the nave was begun in the first period of building and was planned as a flat-ceilinged basilica with articulation of the central-nave wall. When it was consecrated in 1156, the eastern parts were certainly completed and probably the nave as well, though the west front and west atrium were not finished until around 1200. The interior owes its character to its double-choir plan and to the clear cruciform organization of its eastern parts. The nave does not follow the bound system, and instead of a rhythmic alternation of supports there is a regular sequence of piers and engaged shafts. Consequently, there are short oblong—not square—bays in the central nave, and they are covered by cross-groined vaults that, because of the basket-handle or elliptical cross-arches, appear stilted longitudinally, a problem for which vaulting technique was already equipped (as indeed it had been in the eleventh-century vaults over the side naves of Speyer Cathedral). As for form, however, the problem was not sufficiently mastered to provide for the bound system. Perhaps this was so because a flat ceiling was intended at first, which meant that the division of the ground plan and the disposition of the piers would not have mattered, but what remains an open question is whether the beams (whose existence is not in doubt) were needed only for a provisional ceiling or for the definitive covering—in short, whether the vaulting was executed only as an afterthought or as a consequence of a specific change in plan. These problems, however, have nothing to do with the noble beauty of the exterior of Maria Laach, in which two differently conceived groups of three towers each, one at either end, balance each other and crown the structure spanning

the poles formed by the west front and the east transept.

The cathedrals of Speyer and Mainz unquestionably set the style here, and the architectural forms and decoration point to a connection in time as well. In Maria Laach too the plan went through several modifications, which accounts for the fact that the Lower Rhenish element already came to the fore before the middle of the twelfth century, as is clearly visible in the east apse, the west towers, and the atrium—all belonging to the Late Romanesque.

Lombardy

From excavations made at Sant'Ambrogio in Milan, we can visualize the preceding church there as an elongated three-naved building with columns—a basilica of the traditional type. There survive, from that earlier construction, not only the base of one of its columns in the present central nave but also, and more important, the entire east end to its full height. As in the North, a full quarter of the apse, together with its cross-groined vault, protrudes beyond the near wall, so that the three apses do not lie in a row as previously, but are powerfully staggered in position. Beneath the eaves of the apse there is a row of deep niches—a form that anticipates the dwarf gallery, as we have seen.

126. Ely, cathedral, interior, the
central nave looking southwest
127. Ely, cathedral, interior, the east
transept

In the twelfth century, a virtually new building went up, including the entire nave with an open octagonal tower above the easternmost bay of the central nave. Only the apses and the tower on the southwest side of the building were preserved from the previous edifice. A new tower was erected, as a counterpoise, on the northwest side. Such towers are perfectly symmetrical with relation to the church itself, but they are set so far to the sides that the result is not a genuine twin-towered façade. In front of the church and in its longitudinal axis there is a very long atrium surrounded by vaulted passages. This forecourt, like similar constructions in the Rhineland, marks a return to the axiality of Roman buildings and the atria of Early Christian architecture. Its far end is closed off most impressively by the powerful broad façade of the church proper, with its entire breadth spanned by a single gable. The east wing of the atrium is here developed into two stories, and its upper story—with its arches of varying heights—is set into the gable like a huge loggia.

This façade makes us anticipate a hall interior, which in fact we find: galleries repeat the arcades of the side naves, and no clerestory rises above them. It is reminiscent of the galleried interiors of southwestern Europe, but entirely transformed in breadth and weightiness. In addition, the vaulting system is entirely different, composed exclusively of cross vaults and following the basic plan of the bound system.

This can be seen in the grandiose wall of the central nave with its succession of bays, where two side-nave arches topped by two gallery arches are subsumed each time under a single wall arch directly involved with the vault; this pattern is emphasized by the alternation of stronger and weaker articulated piers. The framing of the arcades by means of half-columns and arch friezes continues exactly the articulation of the atrium arcade and emphasizes the relationship between the forecourt and the nave. As in so many Italian churches, there is no transept, but over the easternmost bay of the central nave there is a vaulted octagonal cupola tower that admits light. It does not mark the crossing but the *chorus,* the choir area.

The entire building is in handsome, gleaming red brick, and only the bases, shafts, and capitals of the columns are in light-colored hewn stone, as are the ribs of the vaults. The splendid northwest bell tower, the *torre dei canonici,* ornamented on every story with pilaster-strips and a frieze of blind arcades, was built in 1128. The nave was evidently added to it, though probably not long after. With its characteristic vaulting system, bound sequence of bays, and ribbing arising from shafts placed diagonally to the piers, Sant'Ambrogio is the most important surviving building of an extensive group known only through old illustrations: it included, among others, the old cathedrals of Pavia, Novara, and Vercelli, the latter consecrated in 1132.

Related traits were to be found in the no longer extant Mariakerk at Utrecht in the Lower Rhine region. However, unlike Sant'Ambrogio, all these now-destroyed churches were built in basilical form.

Cross vaulting chiefly with band ribbing, apses with galleries, façades with large gables, and tribunes—these are a few of the features with which architecture now concerned itself, in northern Italy in particular. The bound system in pure form can be seen in San Sigismondo at Rivolta d'Adda in the Cremona area, and good examples in smaller buildings are San Savino in Piacenza and Santi Pietro e Paolo in Bologna. There are tribunes in San Michele in Pavia, San Fedele in Como, and San Giulio on the island of the same name in the Lago d'Orta, the latter two considerably redone in Baroque style. San Fedele in Como is particularly noteworthy for the broad trilobate plan of its eastern half, its polygonal chief apse, and its double-shelled walls with a passageway indoors and galleries outdoors. Here, as in San Giulio at Orta, the original architecture of the nave can be deciphered beneath the Baroque stuccowork. (San Giulio has a famous pulpit with sculptural decorations that reveal close affinities with those in the transept at Speyer.)

Unfortunately, the interiors of the two large churches in Pavia—San Michele and San Pietro in Ciel d'Oro—have suffered somewhat from alterations. In both, the façade is simply a screen in front of a basilical nave and is articulated by slender half-columns, by the portal, reliefs, and a gallery following the triangular contour of the gable. This represents the fully developed form of Lombard screen-façade that was first conceived at Sant'Ambrogio in Milan as a façade consistent with a galleried hall and that was to remain the model even in the fourteenth and fifteenth centuries.

The articulated apses with highly developed dwarf galleries that are so

130. *Alpirsbach, former Benedictine abbey church, interior looking east*

131. *Niederlahnstein, Sankt Johannes Baptist, interior looking east*
132. *Lillers, collegiate church, interior, central nave looking southeast*

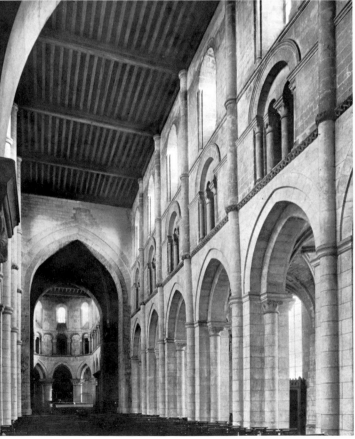

numerous in Lombardy and the Upper Rhineland were thought earlier to be North Italian creations. However, the earliest securely datable example in that region, and also the finest, would appear to be Santa Maria Maggiore in Bergamo. It dates from 1137, which means that Speyer preceded it by a half-century.

Burgundy

Another variety of vaulted basilica is found in Burgundy, and it appeared shortly before 1100 in a group comprising Paray-le-Monial and Cluny III. These buildings are obviously connected with the preceding barrel-vaulted basilicas we know chiefly from the abbey church at Payerne, which may itself have been preceded by Cluny II. The barrel-vaulted basilica form was used as early as around 1000 in the upper story of the narthex of Saint-Philibert at Tournus. In these examples, however, the barrel is still fully round-arched, and the way in which the windows at Payerne cut into the vault with parabolic lunette-like arches can be thought of as still Early Romanesque: moreover, there is no division into stories.

It is not in Burgundy but in its neighbor to the west, Berry, that one finds the next step, in the choir of Saint-Benoît-sur-Loire: here the barrel vault is set off from the wall and the windows are in the vertical plane of the wall. A middle zone with a blind triforium is interposed conspicuously between the nave arcades and the clerestory to make three clearly defined stories. farther south, in Nevers, in the church of Saint-Etienne, begun in 1063, there is a similar clear relationship between wall and vaulting. There, the cross ribs and shafts (lacking in Saint-Benoît) clearly demarcate the bays. However, the three-storied elevation is realized not by a blind triforium but by genuine galleries that are covered by quarter-barrel vaults and therefore require no special place for their roofs on the central-nave wall.

At Paray-le-Monial and Cluny, a further step was taken when the wall and vault were even more evidently separated by a cornice. Here again the windows are set in the vertical part of the wall and, consequently, are very small. The barrel vault is decidedly pointed, which can be ascribed to engineering considerations, since the steeper the pressure line falls and the lower it reaches the wall of the central nave, the more favorable will be the static relationshps. The pointed arcades, for their part, can be explained as an attempt to fit in with the lines of the vault. Whatever the case, the pointed arch lends the narrow and steep interior a certain elasticity.

The middle story, consisting of a blind triforium as in Saint-Benoît, is now closely involved in the articulation of the wall. Fluted pilasters are superimposed on the fronts of the central nave piers and are themselves surmounted by a second series of similar pilasters; together with a cornice, these make an oblong frame for the pointed-arched arcades. A third series of fluted pilasters is located in the triforium story, where they are smaller and alternate with the blind arches. Cornices separate these blind triforia from the clerestory and the latter from the vault. The result is an entire

133. Hildesheim, Sankt Godehard,
exterior, the east end
134. Quedlinburg, Sankt Servatius,
interior looking east

system of vertical and horizontal elements, which seems intimately incorporated into the surface planes. One gets an impression of controlled exuberance and sumptuousness that has little in common with either the energy-laden Norman style or with that of the Lower Rhine, where the aim is to enclose space. The difference between the regions could scarcely be made more plain.

The mature stage of the Romanesque is characterized in Burgundy by a group of buildings generally associated with Cluny III and including—besides Paray-le-Monial—the cathedral at Autun, Notre-Dame in Beaune, Saint-Andoche in Saulieu, the cathedral at Chalon-sur-Saône, and the Benedictine abbey church at La Charité-sur-Loire, a group extending in time to the middle of the twelfth century. These are large and magnificent edifices of classical beauty but with a character all their own. The clarification of the relationships is evident: the central-nave windows lie unambiguously in the wall of the clerestory and no longer cut into the barrel vault. Even more important is the system of articulation in which piers and walls are provided with pilasters and cornices, creating a pattern of verticals and horizontals in more perfect equilibrium than anything before or since in Romanesque architecture. It is quite certainly an Antique system, and in this case we can propose the origin with considerable certainty: the two surviving Roman city gates in Autun, known now as the Porte d'Arroux and the Porte Saint-André, display the system in all its essentials. Fluted pilasters frame arches and support cornices on a number of stories. The open archway and the blind articulation of the upper story of the city gates are matched almost exactly by the pier arches and triforium zone in the Romanesque cathedral. No more would be needed than to repeat the second story on the third, adjust the piers to the proportions of the basilica, and provide the barrel vault with ribs.

As in a few other regions also, the system of the central nave is carried over into the transept and the choir, thereby achieving a unity in the high walls that anticipates the Gothic cathedral. Here too we see how splendidly the flat surfaces of the walls and their articulation complement the smooth surfaces of the vaults. The nave is nevertheless relatively narrow and steep, since, despite the pointed form of the vault, the strong outward thrust of the barrel made it impossible, when utilized at such heights, for the nave to have the breadth and spaciousness it has in the lower churches on the Rhine and in Lombardy.

It must be remembered that this Burgundian group does not represent the first time we have encountered multi-storied articulation. It had noteworthy forerunners in the Carolingian gatehouse at Lorsch, in the columns disposed in front of the central-nave piers at Sant Pere de Roda, in the three-storied choir walls of Sankt Luzius in Werden, and in the west façade of Trier Cathedral.

Like other regions, Burgundy was not content with a single architectural system. Along with the barrel-vaulted basilica, we find the hall church typical

97

of southern France: examples are Saint-Pierre-de-Clages in Switzerland, Saint-Martin d'Ainay in Lyons, and the later Saint-Jean-Baptiste in Grandson, a citadel town in Upper Burgundy (today Switzerland).

A third Burgundian architectural system recognizable in the abbey church at Anzy-le-Duc is closely related to that of the Rhineland and Lombardy in which cross-groined vaulting is used, though like Maria Laach it rejects the bound system in favor of a rapid succession of narrow oblong bays, and the walls are not articulated into stories. This is a plan followed decades later in the great abbey church at Vézelay. Its beauty lies in its balanced proportions and the plastic relationships consequent upon the harmonious division of the central-nave wall by a conspicuous stringcourse, as well as in the architectonic sculpture of its portals and capitals, which—like that of Autun—is wonderfully rich and of truly high quality. Among small buildings with the same architectural system, there are the churches at Issy l'Evêque and Pontaubert, while Semur-en-Brionnais with its genuine triforium is somewhat exceptional.

In this context, we should mention another very famous building, the church of the Cistercian abbey of Fontenay. Although related to the barrel-vaulted single-naved churches of the South, here the blind arcades of the longitudinal walls are deepened into chapels covered with transverse barrel vaults and the dividing walls are opened up to make passageways rather like side naves. The result, once again, is something like a hall-plan interior, but in its static weight and its method of lighting it is quite different from anything existing previously in the North. One thinks of it as a hall plan because there is no clerestory to admit light from above and because the side naves are not conspicuously subordinate to the central nave. In any event, it is uncertain whether one should speak here of side naves or of rows of chapels, and so it is difficult to say if Fontenay should be categorized as a barrel-vaulted single-naved church or as something resembling a hall church.

Westphalia

In the twelfth century, vaulting was finally introduced into Westphalia as well—always and without exception in basilicas utilizing the bound system. The earliest example is the former Premonstratensian nunnery at Kappel, which shows the same marked austerity and cubic rigor observed in other Westphalian churches of that century. The older single-naved church of Sankt Patroklus in Soest was at that time expanded by the addition of lateral naves and was vaulted over in the central nave. These lateral modifications are easy to read there, but what is especially characteristic is the hugeness and heaviness with which everything was conceived. Powerful shafts in front of the piers support the cross-arches, and at their corners (to support the longitudinal arches) there are strong round engaged elements with neither base nor capital. The system is fully worked out though extremely limited, and it is remarkable how many smaller churches in the area subsequently imitated it. The ex-convent church at Lippoldsberg on the Weser River in Hesse and a group of related churches with vaults in the bound system should also be mentioned here, for their vocabulary is purely Westphalian.

THE FLAT-CEILINGED BASILICA

In the introduction to this chapter it was pointed out that, alongside the "avant-garde" vaulted basilica, churches of more conservative character continued to be built, and in numbers far exceeding the more advanced ones. In view of the special nature of medieval sources of information, we cannot expect to find explicit reasons for this conservative position. Nevertheless, it may well have been deliberate, either as the simple expression of attachment to tradition or for reasons related, in some degree, to those that modern aesthetics might adduce. In many cases we can assume that there was an unthinking adherence to centuries-old habits, and there may well have been a lack of architects and artisans familiar with the constructional and technical demands of erecting large-scale vaults. Whether, along with this and under particular conditions, the architectural system may have been considered the expression of some precise attitude toward life or politics is a question much discussed of late, but one must keep in mind the danger of anachronistic interpretation.

In all the regions examined in the first chapter, flat-ceilinged construction continued to be practiced, though to very different degrees and with very different effect on subsequent stylistic developments. Elsewhere, however, it was the flat-ceilinged basilica that predominated almost exclusively during the twelfth century as well, and we must now examine this type briefly—though it means returning to regions already discussed in connection with the vaulted basilica.

England, Normandy, and Brittany

The Norman Conquest of England in 1066 was followed by a rash of new construction. With the single exception of Durham Cathedral, these were all wooden-ceilinged basilicas. During the century between 1080 and 1180 English architecture derived its character from those churches, and—in England as on the Continent—a church often took many decades to build. Most were added to and modified in the Gothic period, and only a few still give an unequivocal picture of their original appearance, though in many cases it can be reconstructed.

A great work stands at the beginning of this period: the cathedral of St. Albans (Hertfordshire), begun in 1077. Although virtually still Early Romanesque in style, with great flat stretches of central-nave walls, it nonetheless shows many traits of future English architecture, most notably in that the church is exceptionally long, as is the transept, thereby forming a genuine Latin-cross plan. The crossing, of the "isolated" type, is topped by an open tall square tower, the only such accent on the building. The upper

found in Saint-Etienne at Caen have been replaced by openings divided in the middle, as at Cérisy-la-Forêt. The gigantic walls, almost like a uniform lattice of architectural members, are unforgettable, and the pattern is carried over into their great transepts; the latter, however, are for the most part single-naved, so that the half-columns and arches are set blind into the wall and are not involved in the spatial disposition. These elements are often superimposed in as many as four or five stories, most notably in Winchester and Ely.

Besides these cathedrals in southern, central, and eastern England, there are special developments in the west and north in particular. The cathedral at Gloucester, begun in 1089, resembles Saint-Philibert in Tournus and Sant'Abbondio in Como in having high cylindrical pillars and high side naves. In this powerful and broad interior, the massive round pillars have their share in creating a grandiose effect. Nonetheless, the builders did not refrain from employing galleries and passageways in front of the windows. Portions of a similar architecture survive in the abbey church at Tewkesbury in Gloucestershire and in Hereford Cathedral; because of their four-storied wall elevation with gallery and triforium in the transept, they have been claimed by J. Bony as important predecessors of the Early Gothic wall system.

Other buildings dispense entirely with vertical articulation by means of responds, an element already markedly in retreat at Gloucester. In them the three stories create the effect of a longitudinal sequence of superimposed round-arched arcades, as in the surviving nave from mid-twelfth century in the abbey church of Dunfermline in Scotland or, in Nottinghamshire, in the minster at Southwell of about 1100 and the remains of the priory at Worksop. Something similar is found on the Continent in Tournai Cathedral—where, however, a blind triforium creates a third story between the gallery and the fourth-story windows. Besides this, there is often no subdivision of the gallery arches: this is evident in the late eleventh-century priory church at Blyth (Nottinghamshire) and in the ruined St. Botolph's Priory in Colchester (Essex).

All of the churches named thus far originally had wooden ceilings—most likely open timberwork—but have not preserved them. A few, Ely for one, have wooden plank ceilings today or else barrel vaults, but most have Gothic vaults. In this too, then, England proved conservative, though this does not hold true for Durham Cathedral, as we have seen.

Beginning with the second quarter of the twelfth century, Continental Normandy retreated markely from its onetime advanced position. There too, the wooden ceiling persisted along with vaulting. In their present state, the abbey church at Mont-Saint-Michel and Saint-Vigor at Cérisy-la-Forêt come closest to their original appearance, whereas other churches—Saint-Georges at Saint-Martin-de-Boscherville among them—were subsequently vaulted over. In Normandy as elsewhere, along with the great cathedrals and abbey churches with their three-storied elevations there are simple

walls are laid out in three stories of almost equal importance: the lateral naves as well as the galleries have large undivided round arches on many-stepped cruciform piers, while in front of the clerestory windows runs the typical Norman gallery—likewise opening each time in a single arch only. Flat rectangular engaged shafts divide the wall into narrow bays. In the transept too the walls are three-storied, with a wall passageway instead of galleries but with the usual sort of twinned arches. All this, together with the crossing with its four great piers and arches and its high tower, makes the cathedral of St. Albans one of the greatest architectural marvels of medieval Europe. The church is built in plastered-over rubble stone with considerable use of bricks from the site of the old Roman town of Verulamium. This may explain the rather flat style, which differs from everything we know in Continental Normandy, especially in the piers and shafts.

In any case, the next church to be built already followed the Continental model. The wall system used in the cathedral of Norwich (Norfolk), begun in 1096, and in Waltham Abbey near London is closer to that of Saint-Etienne in Caen than to St. Albans. There is also a similar rhythmic alternation in the arrangement of the round responds and piers articulated with engaged columns. Unlike Saint-Etienne, however, the clerestory passageway is entirely related to the narrow bay and opens in a graduated triple arch that enhances the solemn triumphal character even more. At Ely the cathedral was begun in 1090, at Winchester in 1079 (only the transept survives from the Norman period), at Peterborough in 1118, and at Chichester in 1186. In all these later buildings, the widely opened galleries

XIII. Southwell, minster, exterior

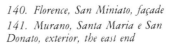

basilicas with walls articulated by no more than half-columns, as in the church of Saint-Gervais in Falaise. There are equally good examples of this in the neighboring region of Brittany, at Quimper, Locmaria, Yvignac, Redon, and Loctudy. Throughout northern France, until fair into the twelfth century the flat-ceiling pillared basilica of the simplest form predominated, scarcely exceeding the stylistic limits of the eleventh century. The collegiate church at Lillers in Artois, the church at Chivy in the Ile-de-France, and the cathedral of Tournai on the Schelde in Belgium are by far the most elaborate buildings, with three- or even four-storied walls beneath a wooden ceiling.

The Rhineland

Throughout the twelfth century on the Upper Rhine, not only vaulted churches were built, but also traditional simple flat-ceilinged basilicas with plain smooth walls above arcades supported on columns or piers or both in alternation. The churches in Hirsau (Sankt Peter und Paul, which is in ruins, and Sankt Aurelius, preserved in part), Gengenbach, Alpirsbach, Schaffhausen in Switzerland, and Lautenbach in Alsace are the most important of these, followed at the start of the thirteenth century by those at Schwarzach and Haguenau. In other regions too the Roman-style flat-ceilinged basilica lived on into the thirteenth century. For this reason, the theory that it was associated on the Upper Rhine with an anti-imperial current of monastic reform seems not very convincing—chiefly because the most outstanding example of that orientation, the abbey church at Limburg on the Haardt, was itself an imperial foundation.

A transept with isolated crossing was the rule, and tripartite choirs and twin-towered façades were frequent, though they have survived only in rare instances. Other types of west front, such as were evidenced already in Early Romanesque times in the choir-tower at Mittelzell on Reichenau and the transverse fronts of Speyer and Mainz cathedrals are better documented.

143. Sant'Antimo, Benedictine abbey
church, exterior from the northeast
144. Gropina, San Pietro, interior
looking east

While the monastic rule of the Hirsau reform movement was perhaps inclined to adopt the kind of tripartite choir used in Cluny II (since it was associated with the reform effected at Cluny), the church at Hirsau—except for this purely functionally determined architectural plan—had absolutely nothing in common with either Cluny II (which Conant claims was barrel-vaulted) or with Cluny III, despite certain scholarly opinions to the contrary. Indeed, the rich architecture of Cluny III, whose chief aim was to create an overwhelming splendor, provides the greatest contrast imaginable with Hirsau. The connection between the monastic reform at Hirsau and the new rule at Cluny is a historical fact. However, on the basis of our present knowledge and an objective evaluation of the data, the oft-proposed link in architecture is entirely improbable.

Likewise along the Lower Rhine and the Meuse, the flat-ceilinged basilica of the early Romanesque lingered on tenaciously into the thirteenth century. Even in a metropolis such as Cologne, churches of this type were still being built at the end of the twelfth century, notably Sankt Cäcilia and the new nave of Sankt Pantaleon—a sign that people still appreciated the austere, clear, and simple architecture of earlier times. There was also a group of flat-ceilinged basilicas with longitudinal galleries, especially in and around Coblenz, at Niederlahnstein, Ems, and Dietkirchen, though there is also an important example in Cologne: the church of Sankt Ursula. In a third group the central nave wall is articulated with blind elements: examples are at Orp-le-Grand in Belgian Brabant and Saint-Séverin-en-Condroz near Liège. A subject of repeated discussion is whether vaulting was planned for these churches but never executed. In a few cases, notably Sankt Matthias in Trier and Sankt Vitus in Hochelten near Düsseldorf, there is evidence that there were once vaults, but there are others where this was certainly not so—Saint-Vincent in Chérain (Belgian Ardennes) and Sankt Ursula in Cologne, for instance. Their articulation is exactly what it appears to be, as in Speyer I and in the Early Romanesque Norman churches, but elsewhere it takes the form of a diversified alternation of supports and double bays.

East of the Rhine

As along the Rhine, so too in many German regions east of the Rhine—Swabia, Franconia, Thuringia, Lower Saxony—handsome examples can be found of flat-ceilinged basilicas of a simpler type, with columns or also with piers. Justly renowed are, for example, the ruins of the monastery at Paulinzella in Thuringia and, especially because of its good architectonic sculpture, the abbey church at Königslutter in Lower Saxony. In the latter region there is a group of important buildings, virtually all of which have the doubled alternation of supports—pier-column—column—introduced at Sankt Michael in Hildesheim around 1000. They also, quite naturally, have an isolated crossing. The architectonic effect is more severe than in Sankt Michael, not because the central nave is steeper but because the side naves are narrower, adhering to the "classical" High Romanesque relationship

of 1:2 between the central and side naves. All forms are clear, concise, and exact. It is precisely in these Lower Saxon buildings that one can see why the second phase of the style can be taken as a period of fulfillment and maturity, as a "High Romanesque" and, to some extent, the norm.

At the outset there is the collegiate church of Sankt Servatius in Quedlinburg, the burial place of Emperor Henry the Fowler, set on a cliff and commanding a view of the city. In the crypt, portions of the original structure can still be seen. The church as it stands now was built between 1070 and 1129. The crypt extends as far forward as the crossing, whose form, therefore, does not emerge at its purest. The west towers on the exterior are to be discounted, since they date from 1880.

Sankt Godehard in Hildesheim, built between 1133 and 1172, has a double-choir plan with two west towers and a crossing tower; it displays in pure form the elements we have mentioned. The choir with its ambulatory is very handsome, especially on the exterior, even though quite unusual. The latest restoration has divested the church of a large part of its excessively obtrusive modern painted decoration. This sequence of churches is rounded out by the mid-thirteenth-century final state of the convent church at Fischbeck.

Scandinavia

In Denmark and the southern Swedish territory of Scania (held by Denmark at the time), stone architecture on a monumental scale began with the cathedral in Lund and with the related church in nearby Dalby. The former is often mentioned in connection with Speyer II, but essentially that connection applies only to the strikingly rich and beautiful architectonic decoration and to a few portions of the building such as the transept and the plan of the crypt, taken as a whole, however, it has little to do with Speyer. The east apse, with its three-storied blind articulation and dwarf gallery, very much recalls the Lower Rhenish style. After some hesitations as to the plan, the nave was carried through as a vaulted basilica but suffered much in the nineteenth century through excessive restoration. In examining the Late Romanesque, we shall encounter even more often churches in which the builders hesitated between flat ceilings and vaults indeed, as we shall see, this can be taken as a characteristic sign in considerable areas of eastern and northern Europe. In Denmark, the cathedral at Viborg and the Benedictine church at Ringsted are also heavily restored but still show the original plan of a flat-ceilinged basilica.

Northern Italy

In Lombardy and the neighboring regions of northern Italy—Piedmont in the west, Emilia and Veneto to the east—the mature phase of Romanesque architecture was ushered in by Sant'Abbondio in Como, whose single-naved vaulted choir with apse is flanked by two slender towers rising at the east end of the side naves. The cathedral at Ivrea preceded it with a similar pair

of towers firmly linked to the main structure, and Aosta Cathedral is not unrelated to this. If it is often insisted, quite rightly, that the tendency in the northern pre-Alpine regions to adopt a simple basilica plan with three apses but no transept suggests a transalpine relationship with the South, one must also acknowledge the reverse: that it is almost only along the southern edge of the Alps that there are such groupings of towers, except for the special case of the Norman territories in southern Italy. The thorough-going articulation of the exterior wall is fully realized in Sant'Abbondio, with pilaster-strips and small-arched friezes all around the building. To these are added ornamental elements, notably richly decorated flat frames around the windows such as had previously been used only indoors on shrines and altars. Around 1100, in various regions, architectonic ornamentation and sculpture began to appear in much more elaborate form. The age of relief decoration and great sculptured portals was dawning.

The nave at Sant'Abbondio is five-aisled, narrow and steep, and has a gloomy majesty. The contrast between the high cylindrical pillars in the central nave and the columns between the side naves shows the kind of graduation in size that in five-naved churches often poses difficult problems. As in Pisa Cathedral and Saint-Sernin in Toulouse also, five naves are an obvious indication of an especially high claim to importance on the part of a church, and the double graduation works out handsomely in the otherwise quite flat and plain west façade.

The cathedral of Modena and San Zeno in Verona are large-scale buildings going well beyond the achievements of Sant'Abbondio. Both were originally flat-ceilinged with alternating supports and cross-arches between which Gothic vaults were later inserted (in Modena), and then a cloverleaf-arched wooden barrel vault (San Zeno). We cannot be at all sure what the cross-arches and the original ceiling were like in Modena. Both churches have basilical façades of graduated heights with imposing bell towers standing in isolation off to one side. Modena Cathedral is especially noteworthy for the arched gallery that runs around it, continuing across the façade and crowning the lateral naves and three apses at the east end. Only on the east is it a genuinely practicable dwarf gallery, whereas along the nave, though the columns stand out from the back wall, the tall intervening piers remain engaged, quite certainly because the wall itself was not strong enough to permit more than this. Thus, we have an interesting initial phase of development in this cathedral. In both churches the crossarms are low, and a large hall-crypt extends beneath them and the east bay of the central nave, so that there is no crossing.

The interior of Modena Cathedral is entirely of brick and reveals a mature mastery of the technique. In addition, it is notable for its floorless false galleries affording interesting vistas. The portals and façade are richly decorated with carved reliefs, and such ornamentation was also used at San Zeno to set off the famous bronze doors. There are a number of still unsolved chronological problems concerning the activity in these churches

of the celebrated masters Wiligelmus, Guglielmo, and Niccolò.

Though the great cathedrals of Parma and Piacenza go back to the first half of the twelfth century, they are best considered Late Romanesque works. Piacenza also has a wealth of smaller Romanesque churches—among them San Savino, Sant'Antonino, Santa Brigida, and Sant'Eufemia—and in Verona, besides San Zeno and the cathedral, there is the galleried church of San Lorenzo, which (like Sant'Ambrogio in Milan) has no clerestory and therefore has a hall-like interior but without vaulting in the central nave.

The church of Santa Maria e San Donato in Murano in the Venetian lagoon was dedicated in 1140. It is a wooden-ceilinged cruciform construction of basilical type, with great emphasis on its eastern "false façade," which connects the apse and side portions by means of a rich articulation of galleries. It is a church that goes its own way, so to speak, but that belongs to the overall North Italian context, from Venice to Piedmont.

Tuscany

The cathedral (Duomo) of Pisa must be counted among the largest and most extraordinary buildings of Europe. It leaves an indelible impression on its stream of visitors because of the splendor of its polychrome marble, its ensemble of cathedral, bell tower, baptistery, and *composanto,* and the spacious greensward on which they are situated. Like Speyer and many English cathedrals, it lies at the edge of the old city. The Duomo is the largest Romanesque church in Tuscany. For a century after the Pisans defeated the Saracens in a sea battle off Palermo in 1063, their port city was the leading power in the western Mediterranean. The cathedral at Pisa, begun promptly after that victory, testifies to the city's past greatness. As a five-naved construction with galleries and a three-naved transept, as well as by reason of its great size, its octagonal cupola over the crossing, and its three apses to the east, north, and south, the cathedral conveys an effect of great dignity.

These various elements are linked together in an interesting fashion. The nave is a steeply proportioned colonnaded basilica rising to a sixteenth-century coffered ceiling that is decidedly too heavy for the thin-walled basic structure; the original was quite likely in open timberwork. The large columns are of uniform size and regularly spaced. The galleries, as is usual, have alternating supports: columns between cruciform piers linked by biforate arches. The upper story is without articulation, and because of the narrow interior one scarcely notices that the windows are not aligned with the arcades.

Four stronger pillars support a large cupola, but there is no crossing. The crossarms hardly make any effect on the interior space, since the central-nave wall continues under the cupola. This is not the product of a later alteration but is already apparent in the ground plan. The crossarms are narrower than the nave, and their own central aisle is narrower and lower. Each virtually constitutes an accessory church in itself, since the galleries are separated from

150. Segovia, San Millán, exterior
from the southeast
151. Ávila, San Vicente, interior, the
central nave

the cupola area through "bridges." Highly diversified vistas result from the variously positioned arches and columns. We have here certainly the greatest difference from the art of Central Europe, which in that period never failed to make clear the cross-shape of its churches by means of an isolated crossing. Italy is a case in itself, and one should not apply to it the standards of the North, as H. Thümmler made convincingly clear when he countered the opinion of P. Frankl.

This also explains the outer appearance of the cupola. Thought of without the large blind arches and Gothic gallery, the octagonal form of the drum becomes more apparent, and the cupola itself is seen to follow the pointed oval form that it has inside. But since the crossarms are lower than the nave, it also does not create the full effect that we are accustomed to in the crossing towers of the North.

The multi-storied exterior articulation is extraordinarily rich. Pilasters support blind arches and architraves that stand out from the wall on the main apse and the later west façade, forming galleries on the upper stories. This articulation circles the entire building, continuing over the side naves, clerestory, crossarms, and apses, only the latter being further emphasized by columns. Lozenge-shaped relief elements and rich decoration on capitals, the edges of arches, and cornices provide an almost incalculable abundance of individual forms, which are nevertheless still clearly framed.

The name of the architect—cited in an inscription as Busketos—must be mentioned whenever the question is raised of the important architects of the Middle Ages. Yet like almost all of the others, he remains a shadowy figure, unlike the painters and sculptors of the South, and the unsolved questions of the history of the edifice do not really permit him to emerge from anonymity.

It was not before the fourteenth and fifteenth centuries that the city of Florence disputed Pisa's artistic lead, and by then it was Gothic and Renaissance churches that set the tone. Its Romanesque cathedral, Santa Reparata, has recently been excavated, and its few vestiges can be seen in an artificially constructed cellar. Despite a relatively elaborate plan with a staggered choir, the old cathedral must certainly always have been eclipsed by its own baptistery.

The church of Santi Apostoli is a simple columnar basilica of the eleventh century. The Romanesque portions of Santa Trinita are known only through vestiges, on the basis of which H. Saalmann has recently made a hypothetical reconstruction. More interesting was San Piero Scheraggio, parts of which were incorporated into the Uffizi. It should be thought of as a church with transverse arches. Some idea of it can be gotten from San Miniato, the church of a Benedictine monastery built on the edge of a hill outside the old city. The relaxed system of the columnar basilica with open timberwork ceiling was consolidated here to the maximum by alternating columns and quatrefoil piers, with each of the latter supporting a cross-arch. The result is a powerful division into bays, even if it does not follow the rhythm of

the bound system. One bay makes up the choir and apse, which are elevated high above the crypt. The church, which in part goes back to the eleventh century, is a plain rough stone building, as can be seen in the side naves and outdoors. However, the impression it makes is due to the marble inlays (some of which are only painted) that cover the interior as well as the façade, overlooking the city and the Arno. Every detail of the façade aims at harmony and beauty, and while it is said that it too is not a unified single conception but the product of various periods, this is difficult to prove, since its constituent parts—the distinct stories of the central nave, the side naves, the gable—are certainly conceived in close relation to each other and scarcely can be isolated as individual forms. Similar inlaid façades are found at the Badia of Fiesole and the collegiate church of Empoli.

Marble is an important factor in Romanesque architecture from Carrara to Florence (that is, in western Tuscany), affecting above all the exterior appearances of churches. Its cold smooth surface can be cut to leave almost no trace of the craftsman's hand, which is why these buildings often lack something of the vitality that comes precisely through minor imperfections. The aim here is an immaculate appearance, and it is almost as if all architectonic problems are sidestepped in favor of a single pre-existing scheme.

On the other hand, there is a surprising multiplicity of forms, within a quite similar basic plan, in the churches scattered throughout the Tuscan countryside. The plan is that of the most simple timberwork-roofed basilica, with neither transept nor towers and with relatively thin walls on columns or piers, and is typified by San Pietro in the village of Gropina. Only a few churches depart from this scheme, among them the Benedictine abbey church of Sant'Antimo in the province of Siena, which is of interest for its galleries and choir ambulatory. A worthwhile scholarly project would be to study the regional differences in Central Italian architecture, since even at a glance one recognizes formal differences between Tuscany, Umbria, the Marches, and Lazio: one need only think of the churches of Spoleto and its environs, of Ancona, Tuscania, Viterbo, and Tarquinia, to name only the best known.

Apulia

In Apulia, on the Adriatic coast of southern Italy, two groups of buildings were constructed beginning with the end of the eleventh century, and a greater contrast is scarcely imaginable than that which exists between these flat-ceilinged galleried basilicas and hall churches with cupolas and barrel vaults. The difference between them is strictly according to type, since geographically one finds both varieties intermingled.

The point of departure for the first group was San Nicola in Bari. When the body of that saint was brought to Bari in 1087, work was begun immediately on a new church. At its east end there is a huge continuous transept of imposing magnitude both as an interior and as a great

154. Le Dorat, collegiate church,
exterior from the northwest
155. Le Dorat, collegiate church,
interior looking southeast

architectonic cube—a magnitude heightened by three tall apses. A somewhat earlier building of the same sort is the cathedral at Salerno in Campania,
but even it seems to have been preceded by the now-destroyed abbey church
at Montecassino, generally held to be its prototype and perhaps going back
to Early Christian models. In Bari the simple plan was modified by
concealing the apses behind an outer wall and by erecting towers at the
corners of the rectangular block of masonry that resulted from this
procedure. This was something entirely new, as was the refashioning of the
traditional flat-ceilinged basilica form. The broad lateral naves were covered
with cross-groined vaults indoors, and outdoors were opened into deep
niches, thus acquiring simultaneously both reinforcement and a form all their
own. The nave itself is not very long and is divided into two spatial areas
by a compound pier in the middle. It would not be incorrect to speak of
bays here. Above the side naves run galleries with three-light arched
openings, and above these in turn are the clerestory with round-arched
windows and the open timberwork ceiling (replaced by a richly carved,
gilded, and painted flat ceiling in the seventeenth century), which here too,
as everywhere south of the Alps, remained the standard form.

No earlier example in the South is known for the galleries, so that it
remains uncertain whether they should be viewed as a direct throwback to
such fourth-century Roman churches as Sant'Agnese and San Lorenzo fuori
le Mura, or whether one should postulate some hypothetical missing link
or connection with architecture north of the Alps. The latter is most likely
the case, because the Norman knights, who first appeared here as
mercenaries in the service of the Byzantine emperor, seized power for
themselves around 1060 and, in the course of the late eleventh and the
twelfth centuries, subjected southern Italy and Sicily to their rule.

Comparing San Nicola in Bari with older or contemporary churches in
Normandy, one finds at first more differences than similarities. However,
precisely those elements that we find strange or even innovatory in the South
point to the North. This applies especially to the towers: at the west corners
of the nave rise two large square towers seemingly intended to enclose a
porch or atrium between them; together with the two towers at the east,
they create an ensemble that dominates the entire church and firmly braces
it at all corners. A fifth tower over the middle of the transept was added
later. Had it been completed indoors also, it would have marked off a distinct
crossing and crowned it with an octagonal cupola. A blind arcade runs
around the building. On the transept walls and the eastern towers it appears
as a flat row of blind arches but is much deepened along the nave, so much
so that one can even speak of them as buttress piers with transverse barrel
vaults between them. The front of the arcade continues on the upper level
and covers the nave galleries. Here there is a kind of external gallery
opening to the outdoors through arches (like a Rhenish or Lombard dwarf
gallery), though it is connected with the indoor gallery by a shed roof and
therefore has a different spatial and structural arrangement.

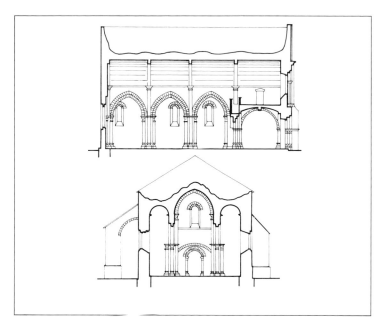

156. *Sainte-Gemme-la-Plaine, church, the nave in longitudinal and transverse section (from Crozet, 1971)*

157. *Saintes, Saint-Eutrope, axonometric projection of the choir (from Crozet, 1971)*

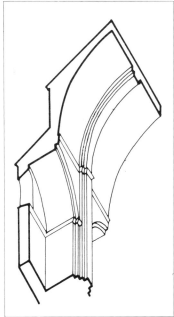

158. *Orange, cathedral, axonometric projection of a detail of the nave (from Choisy, 1964)*

159. *Châtel Montagne, priory church, interior looking east*

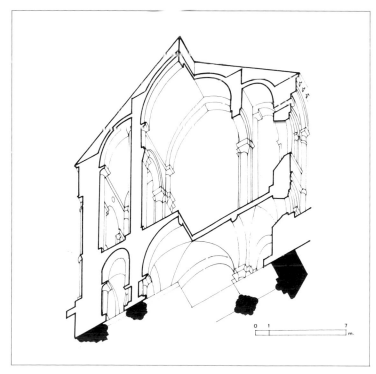

109

What has been described here does not entirely match what one sees. As so often happens in the course of a long period of building, the west towers are not symmetrical. A crossing cupola was planned but never executed, which explains why the transept is interrupted by two longitudinal arches, though these were obviously added later and there never was a fully developed clearly demarcated crossing. Finally, in the fourteenth century, the thin central-nave walls—already weakened by the gallery arches above—gave way to pressure from the lateral nave walls. To counteract this, cross-arches were introduced halfway up the central-nave walls, thereby creating interesting intersection but confusing the picture of the originally severe interior (though it is not difficult to imagine the original effect; compare the cathedral of Bari). In addition, a crypt running under the entire transept as well as the three apses gives us an idea of the original undivided transept (without isolated crossing) with its rows of slender columns.

The history of the building of San Nicola is controversial. We have pointed out a few basic traits and interconnections as defined by R. Krautheimer, but these too remain in part merely presumptions. However, the more recent interpretation of the architect F. Schettini, the restorer of the building, appears dubious, since he attempts to explain certain key features as holdovers from the rebuilding of a Byzantine viceroy's palace.

San Nicola provided the inspiration for a half-dozen large churches in Apulia. The cathedrals of Bari and Bitonto are most closely related to it and are the best preserved of these. Variations are found at Bitetto, Troia, Giovinazzo, Trani, and Ruvo. The latest such building, with Late Romanesque (and in part Gothic) details, is the cathedral of Altamura, though it has suffered much from its nineteenth-century restoration.

The vaulted churches of Apulia belong to a later style, and will be discussed in the chapter on the Late Romanesque.

*162. San Leonardo di Siponto,
exterior, north flank with portal*
*163. Cavagnolo Po, Santa Fede,
interior, the nave looking southeast*

Wooden-Ceilinged Churches in Southwestern Europe

Single-naved churches with barrel vaults and cupolas as well as barrel-vaulted hall churches (to be discussed in the next chapter) were the predominant forms in southwestern Europe to either side of the Pyrenees. However, it would be an inadmissible oversimplification to pretend that there were not also wooden-ceilinged interiors. Larger single-naved aisleless churches often furnished the core for subsequent rebuilding with vaults. Since they had only thin walls, they must be thought of as extremely simple in form and with an open timberwork ceiling, something like the churches of the Italian mendicant orders of the thirteenth and fourteenth centuries. The three-naved hall with open timberwork ceiling is another type that has as yet scarcely been studied in this context. The ruined church at Sant Pere de Burgal is a very early example, and at Saint-Pierre in Vienne pier arcades were introduced as early as the tenth or eleventh century into an even older, Late Roman aisleless building. Sant Climent in Tahull (famed for its frescoes, now in the museum at Barcelona) is of the same architectural type, with round pillars, but dates entirely from the twelfth century. However, there were also basilicas of traditional type, the oldest known example being the cathedral of Jaca. Its eastern portions were consecrated in 1063, while the nave (with alternating supports) is somewhat more recent and, despite subsequent vaulting, still affords us a view of the interior much as it was. The early eleventh-century San Sadurní de Tabérnoles is notewothy for its horseshoe-shaped arcades.

The important churches of San Vicente in Ávila and San Isidoro in León, the latter consecrated in 1149, are likewise basilicas, but were intended from the first to carry vaulting (which, however, was only added later). In the present overall picture of Romanesque architecture in southwestern Europe, these wooden-ceilinged buildings play no conspicuous role. Nevertheless, they have some historical importance as a secondary trend and therefore deserve at least some attention.

MATURE FORMS IN SOUTHWESTERN EUROPE

By southwestern Europe we mean the area between the Loire and the Duero and comprising southern France and northern Spain. In the Middle Ages the Pyrenees constituted no real barrier. Were we not so conditioned today by national and linguistic frontiers, the unity of these lands would be more evident. The Romanesque architecture of the entire region assumes its character from a few constructional types that exist in hundreds of examples throughout this territory, yet nowhere else do they exist in such dense concentration. Southwestern Europe is, in short, the homeland of the Romanesque vaulted hall and single-naved types, and the forms of vaulting preferred here were the barrel and the cupola.

As elsewhere, the key role was played by different regional centers at

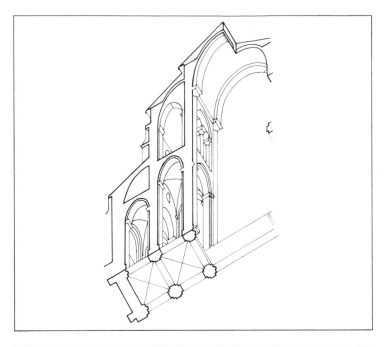

164. Toulouse, Saint-Sernin,
axonometric projection of the nave
(from Choisy, 1964)
165. Toulouse, Saint-Sernin, interior,
detail of the transept

different times. We have already considered the Pre-Romanesque and Early Romanesque architecture of Catalonia, but aside from that one area in southwestern Europe, scarcely any significant buildings survive intact from earlier than, roughly, the middle of the eleventh century. Thereafter, however, in the later part of that century and in the twelfth, a great number of churches arose throughout the lands between the Mediterranean and the Atlantic, among the many celebrated in the history of architecture and surviving into the present.

In complete contrast to the regions considered hitherto, total vaulting of the church interior occurred in southwestern Europe as early as the eleventh century but was the rule in the twelfth. This has to do not only with the architectural system employed but also with a new relationship between man, building, and space. The difference is striking if one looks, north of the Loire, at such extremely simple flat-ceilinged basilicas as Saint-Pierre in Chartres or Saint-Genest in Lavardin, and at vaulted basilicas whose central naves are markedly divided into stories by a blind triforium, as in the cathedral of Le Mans or in Saint-Nicolas, the church of the former abbey of Saint-Laumer in Blois. On the south bank of the Loire, one is aware of it again when one comes upon a cupola church in Fontevrault, a barrel-vaulted aisleless interior in Notre-Dame-de-Nantilly in Saumur, and barrel-vaulted hall churches in Beaulieu-les-Loches or Cunault. However, it is not only in vaulting and certain forms of interiors that we find specifically southwestern European traits, but also in such other outstanding creations as the polygonal apse with rich and often many-storied exterior articulation, or the gable façade found on hall churches throughout this vast region.

Following closely upon the successful reconquest of large parts of the Iberian Peninsula, the prevailing forms of religious and civil architecture spread farther and farther south. By the mid-eleventh century they had reached the Ebro and Duero, and at the start of the twelfth century the Tagus. Naturally, however, there was a certain time lag between these military events and the new building projects, just as there was after the Normans conquered England and southern Italy or after the Germans pushed into eastern Europe.

Hall Churches

The hall church, found in several hundred examples throughout southwestern Europe, is the most frequent and most homogeneous architectural type in that region. The general traits indicated for the Early Romanesque hall church also hold true for its successor: it it often a squat and compact structure covered by a single large saddle roof from which the central nave does not project. The side walls almost always have buttressing piers, though these do not have the slender tapering shape familiar in Gothic architecture, and the walls are often entirely unarticulated heavy blocks of masonry with a shed roof ending below the crown of the wall. Sometimes the piers are linked by arches parallel to the longitudinal wall—an arrangement used on

166. *Orcival, former Benedictine priory church of Notre-Dame, interior the crossing looking northwest*

167. *Orcival, former Benedictine priory church of Notre-Dame, interior, view from the south crossarm into the crossing tower and the north crossarm*

168. *Saint-Nectaire, priory church, exterior from the south*

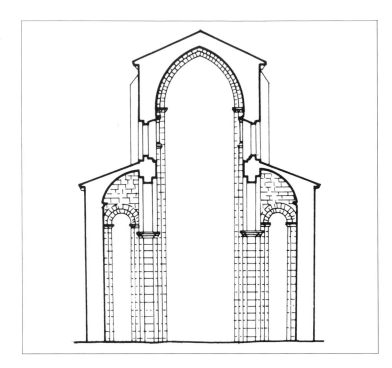

169. Arles, Saint-Trophime,
transverse section (from Koepf, 1954)
170. Lugnano in Teverina, Santa
Maria Assunta, interior looking east

occasion to make a defensive passageway, which (together with battlements) lends a military character to the exterior, as in Saint-Pons-de-Thomières in Languedoc and Champdieu in the Lyonnais district. The west front reflects the cross section of the interior and is usually a simple façade wall with a large gable. Here too there is often a division by means of vertical shafts corresponding to the naves inside. However, it is just such façade walls that invite articulation, and, as we shall see, many are in fact divided by blind arcades into distinct stories.

Smaller and simpler constructions often have the same sort of gabled wall at the east end with three apses annexed to it, as at Verdun (Ariège) in the Pyrenees. Transepts, more or less projecting, are frequently present, often juxtaposed to a choir with an ambulatory and crown of chapels. Despite the fact that the crossing tower is frequent, it seldom assumes the dominant character it has in basilical churches, and very often there are no other towers—though there are some very impressive exceptions, especially in the Limousin area, where a west tower may balance a crossing tower, as at Le Dorat, and where occasionally too there is a separate tower isolated at one side, as in Saint-Léonard-de-Noblat.

As in the Early Romanesque, the interior assumes its character from the approximately equal height of the three naves, so that light enters only through the walls of the side naves, façade, and choir—as, for instance, in Sainte-Gemme-la-Plaine. Because of this, many Romanesque hall churches are plunged into a mysterious gloom, often so much so that it is difficult to make out the architectural forms with any precision.

A semicircular barrel vault over the central nave is virtually the rule, with only isolated exceptions in which it is replaced by a cloister vault over cross-arches—Saint-Hilaire-le Grand in Poitiers and the Benedictine priory church in Champagne (Ardèche) come to mind, and one can compare the cathedral of Le Puy-en-Velay, likewise in the Languedoc—or else by steep octagonal pyramid vaults, as in Saint-Ours in Loches (Touraine). The heavy, lidlike, hermetically sealed form of the barrel vault is extremely characteristic of the numerous Romanesque hall churches and accounts for the homogeneous impression they impart, no matter how extensive their variants. Toward the end of the eleventh century, the continuous barrel vault was generally replaced by the barrel divided off by cross-arches, though these had been known previously. This meant that supports and ceiling were more intimately related but also, and more importantly, that in this form too, just as in vaulted basilicas, the bay was introduced as an element of spatial articulation. We have already met with cross-girding on barrel vaults as far back as Carolingian time, notably at Monte Naranco, but it did not become widespread and characteristic in the central nave of hall churches until the second phase of the Romanesque. What is more important, as we shall see, is whether and how the cross-arches were connected with the supports or projecting shafts.

The principal elements subject to variation in the hall-church plan are

171. Poitiers, Saint-Hilaire-le-Grand,
interior, nave looking southeast

172. Fontevrault, abbey church,
interior of the choir

173. Fontevrault, abbey church,
interior looking southeast

the proportions of the interior, the forms of supports utilized, and the vaults over the side naves. Short and long, low and high, narrow and broad interiors are to be found in hall churches just as in basilicas. For supports there are plain round or square piers, as at Saint-Nazaire in Carcassonne and Saint-Rambert near Lyons, or round or square piers with semicircular engaged shafts, as at Chauvigny and Saint-Savin-sur-Gartempe in the Poitou region, and these latter are by far the most frequent. As we said, it is important also whether and how the supports, as well as the engaged buttresses of the outside walls, are connected with the vault. The Pre- and Early Romanesque barrel vault seems as a rule to soar freely above the arcades, as at Naranco—where the connection by means of vertical bands strikes one as more ornamental than structural.

Only in the late eleventh century was genuine architectonic linkage established between vault and supports, this becoming virtually the rule in the twelfth century. It took two forms: either the half-column shafts on the central-nave piers continue over the pier imposts to take the weight of the transverse arches directly on their own capitals, or else another element is interposed. P. Frankl has attempted to establish some chronological order for the various arrangements existing side by side in Saint-Savin, for example, and to interpret them in terms of a progressive development from the unarticulated to the articulated, from the block mass to the functional structure. While this sort of approach is certainly correct as a generalization, it is inclined to break down when the attempt is made to apply it to a specific building.

The combination of the same or different vault forms in the three naves opens up further possibilities for variation. Three parallel barrel vaults were the normal form in the Early Romanesque, characterized by simple juxtaposition with no connecting elements and by their marked division of the interior into separate areas. This is often still found in the twelfth century, sometimes modified by the use of quarter-circle barrel vaults in the side naves or even the remarkable form of the single-hipped barrel whose abutment line lies lower on the outer wall than over the central-nave arcades. The latter form looks by no means as odd in reality as might be expected from the drawing of its cross section, for one thing because the vault zone is plunged into darkness and so its exact form is often difficult to discern with precision.

Cross-groined vaults over the side naves appear to be the most recent stage in the development of the Romanesque. They are found in Saint-Savin from as early as the end of the eleventh century, and there the absence of cross-arches and even of genuine pier arches is an indication of their chronological position. Finally, there are hall churches with transverse barrel arches over the side naves, but all of these belong to the Late Romanesque period.

The hall church in the various forms outlined here is found throughout the territory between the Loire and the Duero, between the Atlantic and

the Mediterranean. It is peculiar to Aquitaine—the Poitou and Saintonge areas especially—with such representative buildings as Notre-Dame-la-Grande in Poitiers, the ruined Benedictine priory in Montierneuf, the churches in Lesterps, Saint-Savin-sur-Gartempe, Chauvigny, Preuilly, Melle, and Aulnay. In Limousin, the hall developed a special form, with a cupola over the westernmost bay (which is counterpoised to the open crossing tower), as in Le Dorat, Saint-Léonard-de-Noblat, La Souterraine, Saint-Junien, and Beaulieu-sur-Dordogne. North of the Pyrenees, the hall church appears everywhere from Bordeaux across the Languedoc region to Roussillon, and it suffices to name Saint-Gaudens, Saint-Lizier, Unac, Fontfroide, Verdun (Ariège), Saint-Aventin, Carcassonne, and Elne. It extends also into the Massif Central and vicinity and as far as the Rhône, with outstanding examples at Champdieu, Saint-Rambert, Le Thoronet, Chauriat, and Valence. Going up the Rhône, it is found as far as the Upper Burgundy region in Swizerland, and in particular at Grandson (Vaud) and Saint-Pierre-de-Clages (Valais). As for Provence, to mention only a few examples, it can be seen at Tarascon, Silvacane, in the church of Saint-Victor in Marseilles, and in the Dauphiné region at Embrun.

South of the Pyrenees, hall churches abound in Catalonia, where they directly continued the Early Romanesque style. There are examples elsewhere too: in Aragon, León, Galicia, and as far as Castile, among them churches at Frómista, Ávila (San Andrés), and Santiago de Compostela (Santa María la Real de Sar). The upper church of San Salvador de Leyre in Navarre is an interesting special case.

The hall church as a form was to spread far beyond southwestern Europe in the Late Romanesque period, but even more in the Gothic. The various groups found in Westphalia, the Upper Palatinate, Piedmont, Lombardy, the Marches, Apulia, and Sicily are discussed in a later chapter. However, isolated examples appeared here and there before the middle of the twelfth century and therefore deserve brief mention at this point.

Galleried Hall Churches

Among the hall churches of southwestern Europe, there are two important and well-known groups with vaults inserted halfway up the side naves, thereby imparting a very effective supplementary reinforcement to the structure. As in galleried basilicas in Italy and the North, this produces an upper-story room above the side nave. On the other hand, one wonders if the longitudinal galleries were not the point of departure, but this is an old question whose answer is not known. Naturally enough, architects are inclined to explain it in terms of structure, the adherents of cultural-historical phenomena by other interpretations.

Similarly, it is difficult to establish any sure chronology on the basis of construction dates. Three large and important churches vie in claiming priority: Sainte-Foy in Conques, Saint-Sernin in Toulouse, and Santiago de Compostela, to which can be added the church of Saint-Martial in Limoges

176. Agen, cathedral of Saint-Caprais, exterior, the east end

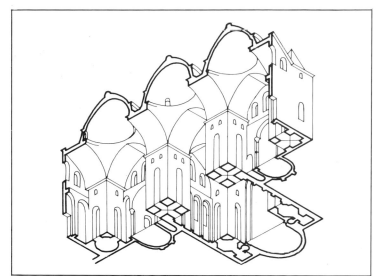

177. Périgueux, Saint-Front, axonometric projection (from Choisy, 1964)

178. Echillais, church, west façade

(destroyed). All of them repeat the system of the nave in the transept, which therefore results in a three-naved hall church with lateral nave galleries. At the east end, the side naves continue around the chancel and apse in the form of an ambulatory and are accordingly supplied with the usual minor apses. The latter, however, are conceived as isolated one-storied chambers, so that the galleries are broken off at this point. As in other Romanesque hall churches, here too the apse is laid out in basilical fashion (as is also, frequently, the crossing). At Toulouse, the lateral naves are duplicated to make a total of five naves across, but there is no gallery over the outermost nave. As in Santiago de Compostela and Limoges, here too the nave is very long. In Conques, however, it is shorter; only here the galleries are not continued around the rear of the transept.

These three churches have open crossing towers, though they were modified and heightened later. This made it necessary in Toulouse to reinforce the crossing pier, with the result that the interior appears markedly divided. Finally, they are alike in having important sculptured portals and in having west towers added later—in Toulouse they are Late Romanesque, in Santiago Baroque, in Conques nineteenth-century.

Their interior elevations are almost identical. There are slender square piers studded with four half-columns, and high round-arched arcades surmounted by double openings of the galleries, which are themselves

covered with quarter-barrel vaults. In the central nave, the engaged half-column shafts rise all the way to the abutments of the barrel vaults, and each shaft supports a cross-arch. The narrow proportions of the interior and the close intervals in the repetition of half-columns and cross-arches have much to do with the impression made. The constructional advantage of the hall system is fully exploited: the vaults over the central nave and galleries run side by side to provide mutual support, permitting the piers and shafts to be relatively thin and the openings broad and high—so much so that even from ground level one can look up into the galleries, which as a result play a part in the overall spatial picture. Though the central-nave walls are two-storied, and therefore recall the walls of the basilical central nave, the impression persists of a hall with naves of equal height. This impression is furthered by a lighting system in which the central nave has no openings for light in its own upper story and so must depend on the windows in the west front, on the crossing towers where present, and on the indirect sources in the side naves and galleries. The result is almost contradictory: on the one hand, an elegant articulation with a strong tendency to height, together

with a rapid succession of bays at the lower level; on the other hand, an oppressive heaviness in the dim interior.

The way the side naves and galleries encircle the transept is decidedly imposing. They were planned to do so in Conques also, but were never executed there. In Toulouse, the impression is somewhat blocked by the reinforcement of the crossing piers, but the full splendor of the design can still be appreciated in Santiago de Compostela.

That great church in the northwestern corner of the Iberian peninsula became famous through its possession of the relics of the apostle St. James. Pilgrimages from Spain, southern France, and even beyond became numerous and seem to have followed specific routes (Conques, Toulouse, and Limoges all lay along those pilgrimage roads), which has led to the widespread supposition that the close affinity between the churches along these routes was determined by this fact. I do not believe this to be justifiable on strictly historical grounds, since there are innumerable Romanesque churches along the pilgrimage roads that have a quite different aspect. And there are churches of the Santiago type—at Alet in Brittany and Marcilhac near Cahors in Quercy (both now in ruins), and at Orense south of Santiago and Coimbra in Portugal—that are scarcely considered in this question, presumably because they happen not to lie on the pilgrimage routes. What is involved, therefore, is nothing more than a romantic modern "legend" like those that have arisen about so-called Cluniac architecture, about what used to be known as the Hirsau school of architecture, or about the fabled itinerant Cistercian builders' workshops.

The second group of galleried hall churches lies in a circumscribed area, the French Massif Central. Something like eight churches make up the Auvergne group: Notre-Dame-du-Port in Clermont-Ferrand, Notre-Dame in Orcival, Saint-Austremoine (now Saint-Paul) in Issoire, the former abbey church of Saint-Amable in Riom, Saint-Nectaire, Saint-Saturnin, Ennezat, and the collegiate church of Saint-Julien in Brioude. Some of these are virtually isolated in the majestically wild mountains, others are in densely built-up cities. Today we have rejected the early dating proposed by many older scholars and consider the entire group as belonging to the twelfth century; all display well-developed Romanesque forms alongside decided reminiscences of the Pre-Romanesque.

The naves are laid out in much the same fashion as in the preceding group, but they are shorter and of a quite different aesthetic character, due above all to the fact that the galleries and their openings are lower and that there are no cross-arches for the central-nave barrel vault (or only in isolated cases). At the west end there is usually a transept, whose original form and function do not seem to have been investigated as yet. A second and higher transept lies at the east, between the nave and the choir, the latter having the usual form, with ambulatory and minor apses. The east transept, crowned by an octagonal crossing tower, is the most unique feature of hall churches in the Auvergne, different from all types of transepts that we have seen

elsewhere. The bays are graduated in height from the outside to the middle, and enriched by diverse arrangements of vaults. Semicircular and quarter-circle barrels lead upward to an octagonal cloister vault that sits on squinches over the crossing. This graduation is repeated on the outside in an admirable manner. The transepts form powerful blocks, and in front of their east walls the ambulatory chapels unfold in a sumptuous procession to create an impression virtually unmatched in Romanesque architecture.

In the interior, between the bays of the transept and crossing and between the latter and the nave, lower transverse arches are intercalated, with additional arcades opening in the walls above them. The graduated spaces with their perspective vistas seen through the arcades lend to this basically rigorously organized interior an architectonic richness and mysterious solemnity, intensified even more by the glimpses afforded into the nave and the choir.

Similar in its spatial design—a hall church with side-nave galleries—is Sant'Ambrogio in Milan. If this majestic building, discussed above in connection with Lombardy, is so different in its effect from the architecture of southwestern Europe, it is due principally to the cross-vaulting and the bound system. It is, however, worthy of note that even with these entirely different elements of conception and construction it was possible to design and build a galleried hall.

Just how much the major regions of Europe are defined and differentiated by the characteristic and widespread contrast between hall church and basilica becomes clear only when we see what exceptions there are: in all of northern France there is only one, the barrel-vaulted hall of the priory church at Saint-Loup-de-Naud in the Ile-de-France; in the entire Lower Rhine and Meuse valleys again only one, the Early Romanesque (and still flat-ceilinged) hall church at Theux near Liège. In Lombardy there are a number of partial attempts at hall planning, among them the west bay of San Pietro in Ciel d'Oro in Pavia and the east end of the church at Rivolta d'Adda, but only one fully valid and monumental realization: Sant'Ambrogio in Milan. While the latter is thought of as the highest achievement in Lombard architecture, this may not be so true historically, because if the now-destroyed churches at Novara, Vercelli, and Pavia still existed and if the two main surviving churches in the latter city were still in their original state, we would more readily recognize Sant'Ambrogio to be an exception to the rule.

Barrel-Vaulted Basilicas

We have met with the barrel-vaulted basilica on several occasions in the course of this study: in the Carolingian Asturias at Valdediós, in Early Romanesque Catalonia at Cardona, in Burgundy both in Early Romanesque times—in the ante-church at Tournus—and on the threshold of the High Romanesque, at Payerne. Saint-Etienne in Nevers represents the type enriched by galleries, the group at Paray-le-Monial and Cluny III the type

with three-storied wall articulation in the central nave. Having pointed out the connection between Burgundy and the lower Rhône area, we can now, along with barrel-vaulted hall churches, list a number of barrel-vaulted basilicas in the south of France and in northern Spain. They are especially numerous in Provence, but there is a scattering of them in Languedoc and elsewhere. Most notable are Saint-Trophime at Arles in Provence and the churches at Saint-Paul-Trois-Châteaux (Dauphiné), Bourg-Saint-Andéol, Saint-Guilhem-le-Désert, Quarante—all three in Languedoc—and Chama-lières-sur-Loire (Velay), Châtel-Montagne in Bourbonnais, and Mauriac (Auvergne). These few examples suffice also to show that the form extended in time from Early to Late Romanesque. Examples are found in

Central Italy as well, in the Umbrian village of Lugnano in Teverina, for instance. Often there is some indecision about the form, which is not so north of the Loire: there are no windows despite the marked basilical heightening of the central nave in the churches at Carennac (Quercy) and Cruas (Velay); the windows are disposed in an irregular and scattered order in the abbey church at Sénanque (Provence); they are present on only one side of the central nave at Seo de Urgel across the Pyrenees in Lérida. For such reasons, these buildings must be understood as occupying an intermediate position in which certain traits of the hall plan are plain to see.

Barrel-Vaulted Single-Naved Churches

Barrel-vaulted single-naved churches are also found in great numbers south of the Loire: important examples are Santa María de Naranco, the cathedral at Orange, Sant Jaume de Frontanyá, Sant Ponç de Corbera de Llobregat, and the fortified church at Royat. Whereas single-naved churches with cupolas can be exceptionally large, those with barrel vaults are, as a rule, restricted in scale, because the stone vault exerts a strong outward thrust that imperils the walls supporting it. Often one can see that, even with greater strength and thickness, the walls have at one time or another had to be buttressed by piers added later. If the longitudinal walls are pushed outward beyond a certain point, the crown of the vault sinks, fissures appear at the flanks, and finally the middle third of the vault collapses. This can be seen in the famous picturesque ruin at Val-des-Nymphes near La Garde-Adhémar in southern Dauphiné.

There are two effective means of counteracting this outward thrust, both of them known from early times: either the wall must be strengthened, or the barrel vault made more pointed. The longitudinal walls can be reinforced both indoors and out by buttressing shafts that are then linked by blind arches to the same result as in hall churches: a very effective articulation and consolidation of the structure. Similarly, the barrel vault can be reinforced at points of strain by underpinning it with cross-arches. If the elements projecting from the piers are profiled or if there are engaged half-columns, obviously they can be linked with the cross-arches. The result is a succession of bays in place of a continuous and unarticulated interior, and this is the form frequently assumed by the barrel-vaulted aisleless church in Spain and in France south of the Loire during the High Romanesque period.

More surprisingly, it was possible in exceptional cases to cover very broad interiors with pointed barrel vaults; an impressive example of this is in Saint-Paulien near Le Puy-en-Velay. An early building, Saint-Pierre in Montmajour (Provence), shows that the system was already fully worked out in the tenth century, but still with a round-arched barrel vault (which was, accordingly, small and had a modest span). There are, however, a great many examples from the eleventh and twelfth centuries, extending from the Loire—Notre-Dame-de-Nantilly in Saumur—to the Tagus, from Provence

to the Basque country and into Galicia. Famous examples include the ex
cathedrals at Agde in Languedoc and Digne in Provence, the abbey church
of Montmajour, Saint-Gabriel near Arles, and Saint-Pons-de-Thomières in
Languedoc. The Romanesque portions of the cathedrals at Cavaillon and
Avignon are less well preserved, but to one familiar with the system it can
still be recognized there.

The spatial plan is very simple as a rule, but can be enriched by crossarms
and an octagonal tower over the crossing. As in the Early Romanesque, this
type of cruciform barrel-vaulted aisleless interior was frequent also in the
twelfth century, and it was one of the points of departure for a further
development (to be discussed in the chapter on the Late Romanesque in
connection with Fontenay and the early Cistercian churches).

Like the hall church, in this type too the external buttresses, when linked
by arches, make possible a defensive passageway, and there are instances
of this at Les Saintes-Maries-de-la-Mer and at Royat.

Churches with Cupolas
There are sixty single-naved Romanesque churches with cupolas in the
southwestern quarter of France, among them cathedrals and abbey churches
of large dimensions—at Périgueux, Cahors, Solignac, Souillac—as well as
many small village churches. Compact solid longitudinal walls are linked
by broad cross-arches, and these are crowned by circular cupolas of
semicircular cross section resting on spherical pendentives. Bays in vaulted
churches are most emphatically marked in this form, and the Romanesque
organization of space reaches one of its high points here.

The interior walls are often two-storied: below, there are blind arcades
on pilasters; above, windows beneath wall arches that match the cross-arches.
In many churches the wall with windows is set back toward the outside and
thereby gives rise to an inner passageway broken through by the cupola
piers, which means that the cupola church belongs to the typological groups
with double-shelled walls. However, unlike the practice in most regions,
the passageway is not shut off from the interior by an arcade of columns
but remains open, as it were, and this is in line with the large form and spatial
breadth of these churches.

Only a few of the largest churches have a transept, notably those at
Solignac, Souillac, and Périgueux. In them the crossarms are designed
exactly like, or similar to, the bays of the nave. The crossing is covered by
a cupola, as are all the other bays. The east end is closed off by an apse with
a half-cupola, and in some of the large churches this is likewise articulated
into two stories with absidioles below (but no choir ambulatory).

From the exterior, most of the cupola churches look like great cubes of
masonry separated by broad bands of wall and crowned by the free-lying
cupolas, most of which were roofed over only later. Some have been exposed
again in modern times, notably at Saint-Front in Périgueux (with extensive
Neo-Romanesque additions) and Sainte-Marie in Souillac.

Cupola churches seldom have towers, and the gigantic single tower of Saint-Front is an exception, as are also the two towers originally planned to stand at either end of the transept of Angoulême Cathedral (only the north one actually exists); at Cahors Cathedral, a Gothic transverse structure was added in front of the west side.

The development of the architectural form can be read in the onetime cathedral of Saint-Etienne at Périgueux. Originally, there were four bays and cupolas. Two were destroyed, though one can still see where they were joined. The surviving west bay is the older, displaying the concise, clear forms of the High Romanesque. The east bay was added a few decades later, and with richer plastic forms and many columns. The earlier stages of development—the west bay—are related somewhat to Cahors, Solignac, and Souillac, whereas the more recent ones—the east bay—may be compared with Angoulême Cathedral and the abbey church of Fontevrault, the latter lying just south of the Loire, near Saumur, and representing the northernmost point of diffusion of this form.

Between these two stages belongs the present cathedral of Périgueux, Saint-Front, by far the best known example of the form but also the most problematic. Around 1850, it was "restored" much too extensively by the architect Abadie, who added a choir entirely of his own invention—though he rebuilt the west tower and the exterior of the cupolas in what seems essentially acceptable fashion. The overall result, however, strikes one as inauthentic because of its fatal glossy smoothness and blatantly conspicuous forms. Nevertheless, even the critical observer cannot remain insensitive to the impressive effect of the interior: five cupolas set very high and in cruciform arrangement make for an extraordinary composition. In addition, the massive piers supporting these cupolas are themselves hollowed out, so to speak, each articulated into four sub-piers linked among themselves by arches and vaults. The system is familiar from the somewhat earlier church of San Marco in Venice and is known to go back ultimately to Emperor Justinian's Church of the Apostles in Constantinople. Had the latter survived, we would no doubt have found the sort of differences between it and Saint-Front that we recognize exist between San Vitale in Ravenna and the Palatine Chapel in Aachen. It is often discussed whether Saint-Front may not be the cupola church from which all others in Aquitaine derive, a supposition that would make the lines of connection clear. This, however, is unlikely, since we know a number of important examples of earlier date than Saint-Front: foremost among them are the former cathedral of Saint-Etienne in Périgueux itself and the cathedral of the same name in Cahors. Therefore, the question of the orgin of the type remains open.

If we compare Saint-Front with San Marco in Venice, once again we see to what a great extent the character of a church interior depends on its decorative concomitants, primarily the treatment of its walls and ceiling. Mosaics make the Venetian church appear non-European, whereas Saint-Front—despite its nineteenth-century Neo-Romanesque modifications—

belongs completely within the range of types under discussion here.

Formerly numbered among cupola churches were also Sainte-Marie-des-Dames in Saintes and the abbey church of Saint-Pierre in Moissac, which is justly renowned for its sculptured portal (today, however, only the vestiges of the earlier system tell us that cupolas existed before the present Gothic rib vaulting).

Three churches—Saint-Hilaire-le-Grand in Poitiers, the cathedral of Le Puy-en-Velay, and the Benedictine priory church in Champagne (Ardèche)—combine the hall form with cupola vaulting over the central nave, though they utilize octagonal cloister vaults instead of the circular cupola. This is the only feature these three otherwise very different churches have in common.

Under the heading of Romanesque cupola churches, one thinks chiefly of the twelfth-century group from Aquitaine in southwestern France, certainly the largest and most significant ensemble of churches in which the cupola plays a dominant role. There are also a number of other groups, however—which offers further proof of the diversity of the Romanesque. In Apulia there are hall churches with cupolas over the central nave, the most important being the old cathedral at Molfetta. Conspicuous in Salamanca and its environs are great round crossing towers with elaborate Late Romanesque articulation. San Marco in Venice is a unique case, but it had a late follower in Sant'Antonio in Padua. Finally, one must not forget the Rhine and Meuse valleys, where cupolas play an important role, especially in the west ends of churches; in Sainte-Gertrude at Nivelles there are no less than eight in a single multi-storied edifice.

Façades

It is not surprising that the hall church and the vaulted aisleless church, as distinct and autonomous organisms with their own interior configurations, should find special formal solutions for the façade and also, in part, for the plan of the east end of the building. This is especially striking as far as the façade is concerned. It is often treated as an articulated wall more or less conforming to the cross section of the interior but not always closed off with a gable corresponding to the saddle roof of the nave. Especially favored was the upright or horizontal oblong with a horizontal upper line. By these means the façade was made somewhat independent, becoming a kind of screen in front of the building and, like that type when it reached maturity, obeying its own rules of articulation with various stories of blind arcades. There is even an isolated example of a screen-façade with galleries at Arezzo.

The autonomy of façade wall and its articulation was increased when, as often happened, the westernmost pair of lateral buttress piers of the nave were incorporated into it. This meant that the proportions of the façade differed even more from those of the interior, so that one is often uncertain whether a cupola church, a barrel-vaulted aisleless church, or a hall church lies behind it. When a façade of this type is further combined with small

189. Mainz, chapel of Sankt Gothard, interior looking east

flanking towers and with an ensemble of three portals, the monumental effect is enhanced, as can be seen in a number of examples in southwestern France: at Cadouin, Civray, Gensac, Ruffec, Pons, Surgères, Maillezais, Petit-Palais, Melle, Saint-Amant-de-Boixe, Saint-Jouin-de-Marnes, and Sainte-Marie-des-Dames in Saintes. The cathedral at Angoulême has one of the finest of these façades, though it is marred by Neo-Romanesque tower bases.

As their main articulatory elements, the hall façades of southwestern France developed the engaged half-column or shaft, the horizontal cornice, and the blind arcade—a small number of basic elements with an astounding range of possibilities. Viewed generally, the development began from the simple vertical division of the façade into sections often corresponding to the naves of a hall church, or conversely from a marked horizontal division into stories by means of cornices and blind arcades. These elements could then be combined in a great variety of ways, as one sees at Echillais and Echebrune. Individual decorative elements and even figurative sculpture in smaller dimensions were increasingly added to these components, so that by the mid-twelfth century occasional façades were virtually covered with a web of intricately detailed elements, as at Notre-Dame-la-Grande in Poitiers.

Scholars such as H. Christ, P. Frankl, and L. Schürenberg have tried to discern some developmental law behind this articulation of the façade, but none of their explanations succeed in covering the multiplicity of phenomena involved, and so remain unsatisfactory.

This rich invention and development is primarily centered in southwestern France, but there are façades of the same type throughout the southwest of Europe, from Santo Domingo in Soria to Champagne (Ardèche). There is also a specific type of façade on hall churches with galleries, exemplified in the transept-like fronts of great churches of the Santiago de Compostela type. In the Auvergne, to the contrary, there are often western transverse structures with multi-storied interiors but these have as yet been little studied. Barrel-vaulted basilicas most often have plain façades echoing the cross section of the nave, and these are enhanced by richly sculptured large portals, as at Arles and Saint-Gilles-du-Gard.

East Ends

It was not only in the nave and the façade, but in the eastern portion as well, that the hall church reached a culmination, and this in two distinct forms: one, the large three-naved transept as found in Santiago de Compostela, with galleries and with a corresponding ambulatory around the choir; the other, the transepts of the Auvergne, which are staggered in height and have a kind of lattice of arcades. On the other hand, in "normal" hall churches the plan of the eastern portions plays a lesser role; the problem of the crossing is not as crucial as it is in the basilicas of the north, nor is the transept so markedly related to the nave. Even when its barrel-vaulted arms are of some length, they often remain lower than the nave (in Saint-Hilaire at Poitiers, for example), in which case the crossing seems sunken in, so to speak. The crossing is almost always delimited by four similar arches, as in the North also, and almost always too it is square in ground plan and crowned by a cupola-like vault set on squinches at the corners. The vault assumes a great variety of types: octagonal cloister vault, circular cupola, depressed cupola, and so on. For the most part, these crossing cupolas are dark inside, virtually or entirely without windows, even when they are raised externally into octagonal crossing towers. Indoors, their crown often scarcely reaches the height of that of the central-nave barrel vault, and it is precisely this that is responsible for the impression that the crossing is "sunken in" rather than a central climax to the entire interior. This is true also of barrel-vaulted basilicas—for example, Saint-Philibert in Tournus, Saint-Trophime in Arles—as well as of many single-naved churches. The few cupola churches that are cruciform in plan do have, on the contrary, fully developed crossarms, but their crossings too are not markedly elevated above the roof level. In the Jura region there are transitional forms in which one often cannot be sure whether the higher central nave originally had windows and was in fact conceived as a basilica; typical of these is the former priory church at Saint-Lupicin. In these respects too, therefore, the architecture of southwestern Europe is essentially unlike that of the North.

As for the plan of the choir, the two chief types—the choir with ambulatory and the choir composed of units of different height—are the norm in southwestern Europe. The elaborate though still severe articulation and the staggered heights of the chapels around the choir ambulatory with respect to the choir, transept, and crossing tower make many examples of these famous: one need only think of Conques in the Aveyron, Beaulieu-sur-Dordogne in the Limousin, Saint-Savin-sur-Gartempe in Poitou, Valence in the Dauphiné, Fontgombault in Berry, Saint-Menoux in the Bourbonnais, among others. The differentiation of the eastern portions from the nave, mentioned above, is seen also in the fact that the choir with ambulatory is often laid out on the basilical plan. Indeed, one might even say that instances of such choirs designed according the hall plan are less frequent, though there are examples in Poitiers—in both Saint-Hilaire and Notre-Dame-la-Grande. The choirs of a few cupola churches (for instance, at Solignac and Souillac) are distinguished by a single huge apse that corresponds to the vast cupola-bays of the nave and that has lower chapels issuing from it directly, and this is so at Agen as well. The basic form may be either semicircular or polygonal. With their diversity of ground plans articulation, especially on the exterior, the apses in particular constitute the chief claim to fame of southwestern Romanesque architecture. Outside of the Lower Rhine and Meuse valleys, no other region experimented with such an abundance of possibilities and arrived at such fine solutions. In this Aquitaine holds the lead, but Languedoc, Provence, and Castile also have many to their credit, and we need name only a few examples: in southwestern France at

Bégadan in the Gironde and at Geay, Rétaud, Rioux, and Saintes in
Charente-Maritime; in Aveyron at Perse; in Provence at Cavaillon,
Montmajour, and Saint-Ruf near Avignon; in Spain at Cervatos (Santander)
and Vallejo de Mena (Burgos); and again there is even an isolated example
in Italy, at Arezzo.

As already stressed in our introduction, towers and west fronts do not
have the same importance in the hall churches as they do in the North,
though their contribution is certainly often grossly underestimated. There
are towers of outstanding size and beauty at Saint-Front in Périgueux, at
the abbey church in Brantôme, at Saint-Aubin in Angers, and isolated bell
towers of truly unique architectural fantasy, such as that of the cathedral at
Le Puy-en-Velay. There are even groups of towers. As in Early Romanesque
times at Cuxá, so too in the High Romanesque at Angoulême two large
towers were erected on the stern side of the transept and even had a part
in the plan of the interior—though there, as at Cuxá, one of the towers has
unfortunately not survived. More often we encounter the combination of
a tower in front of the façade with a tower over the crossing, as at Le Dorat
and elsewhere in the Limousin or at Cruas (Ardèche) on the Rhône; these
are, however, exceptions in the overall picture, and plans involving a
number of towers remain the prerogative of the North.

The Central Plan

Except for the Palatine Chapel in Aachen, the most renowned and largest
Romanesque central-plan churches belong to the mature and late stages of
the style. All the various architectural types are found among them, but they
have been transformed in wholly individual fashion. The simple octagon
without accessory chambers (other than chapels and passages within the
thickness of the walls) is typified by San Giovanni, the baptistery of Florence.
The Greek-cross central plan with ambulatory is well represented in a
number of regions: in northern Italy, in the baptistery of San Pietro in the
Piedmontese town of Asti and San Tomè outside the Lombard village of
Almenno San Bartolomeo; in southern France, in the former abbey church
at Charroux in Poitou and the parish church at Neuvy-Saint-Sépulcre in
Berry; in Brittany, in the ruined church at Lanleff; in Westphalia, in the
chapel at Drüggelte; in the Rhineland, in the church of Sankt Martin in Bonn
(destroyed); its unrivaled masterworks are San Marco in Venice and
Saint-Front in Périgueux. The square plan with four interpolated supports
was favored for chapels in San Satiro in Milan and the Palatine Chapel at
Germigny-des-Prés—and in the twelfth century was consolidated into a
distinct type of two-storied castle chapel, especially in imperial territory.
Along with a few other buildings, San Claudio al Chienti in the Marches
of Central Italy shows this plan in a variant.

The third phase, most often termed "Late Romanesque," began around 1140/50. The term is acceptable as long as "Late" is understood purely factually, as chronologically the latest of the three main phases. An interpretation in a biological sense, with any implication of "old age" or senescence, is out of the question, as are also any laudatory or deprecatory associations. What is true is that, in a few places around the middle of the twelfth century, certain signs of changes began to be evident that make the term "Late Romanesque" acceptable not only as a chronological division, handy in marking off phases in a long development, but also as the designation for a stylistic period. Looking backward, it is obvious that this is the last period in which the concept of "Romanesque" is still relevant. Many qualities characteristic of the Early and High Romanesque now disappear, sometimes even the compelling simplicity and clarity or even the highly impressive massiveness of their interior and exterior structures. Yet no one can deny that this late phase brought together and enhanced many—not all—of the existing possibilities, nor that it mastered new formal and conceptual ones. The breadth that could be spanned by vaulting was extraordinarily increased. There are edifices replete with tranquil beauty and "classical" harmony, others that reveal an enormous inner dynamic and movement, still others approaching the bizarre, the "Baroque," even the "Mannerist."

Late Romanesque architecture, like that of its predecessors, has many extremely diverse faces. As a rule, the differences are once again regional. However, general common characteristics are not lacking. The structure as a whole becomes more complex: the closed half-cylinder of the apse is broken up into a polygon; towers are no longer square but octagonal or round; roofs are made steeper and thereby acquire a more impressive shape, particularly evident in the gables; the roofs of apses and helms of towers become many-sided pyramids, may be placed on the bias, and may be covered with lozenge-shaped roofage over the gables, resulting in varied animated effects and a picturesque enrichment as compared with the elementary pyramid form of the Early and High Romanesque tentlike roof.

Most of all, however, the articulating elements were increased and emphasized. Plain flat surfaces became rare, and where present mostly provide a contrast to broad or numerous openings in a wall. Blind arches and niches lend the wall surfaces a spatial plasticity all their own. Pilasters and columns project from the walls in differing thicknesses, making up various strata covering the surface with something almost like a scaffolding of diverse forms. All in all, both indoors and out the walls took on highly differentiated relief.

Simple columns and square or oblong piers became less usual, and even where these basic forms can still be detected, they are nevertheless subjected to complications. Round forms such as billet moldings and corner colonnettes transform the sharp angles of supports, arches, and shafts. Elements that, by preference, are contoured or at least rounded off project from walls and vaults. There are decidedly more horizontal cornices and vertical engaged shafts. All this is most striking where the wall itself is opened up, made less solid, stratified in various ways so that wall and space interlock—a process that takes place on both interior and exterior walls in the most varied treatment of passages in front of windows, triforium passageways, and dwarf galleries.

Many of these changes were anticipated in the preceding periods. In a number of regions they can be detected decades or even a century earlier than in others. This is especially evident in the articulation of the basilical central-nave wall and the apse, as well as in the development of passageways and the simultaneous opening up of the walls. Nevertheless, these forerunners seldom achieved a fully developed form and scarcely ever are to be found together in a single building as they are in the most characteristic Late Romanesque churches.

Because the arch is semicircular in the Early and High Romanesque, an impression was created that it was the dominant form—so much so, in fact, that in earlier years architectural historians spoke of this as a "round-arch style." Occasional exceptions—pointed arches in Provence and in twelfth-century Burgundy—prove the rule. In the Late Romanesque, the arch is frequently broken at the crown to create a pointed arch or broken twice at its hips to constitute a trefoil. The lobed arch (also called cusped or multifoil) is found in a few regions—the Lower Rhine, southern France, and northern Spain—while the sharp-pointed, so-called lancet arch appears in Norman and Anglo-Norman churches, where also there are often overlapping intersecting arches. At this time too the arches of the window openings take on a diversity of forms: palmetto, fan, and keylike shapes are common along the Lower Rhine.

The same process took place with vaulting. The flat-ceilinged church with its simple boxlike interior became much less frequent. While it did not wholly disappear, it lingered on as scarcely more than a relic of the first and second phases of the Romanesque style. Vaulting became the rule almost everywhere, though it too was altered. The use of the barrel vault with its large, quiet, uniform surfaces declined. Like the walls, the cross-groined vault was provided with round elements that can legitimately be called "ribs." Builders were partial not only to laying in these ribs along the groins, but also to underlaying the crowns of the vault segments with them and on occasion to using them to make even smaller subdivisions of the vault surfaces. The basic form of the cross vault was modified in many regions by domelike concavities. Similarly, the hemispherical cupola of the apse was often divided by ribs and blown outward like a sail, so to speak, by means of concave segments, and this is found even where the apse does not have a polygonal ground plan.

The pure circular cupola too was more and more superseded by the ribbed cupola, or at least basically altered by means of ribs. Intermediate forms developed, including the so-called domical or cloister vault, which

can be interpreted as a suspended cupola with four ribs underlaid or as a bulging cross vault with arched crown ribs.

Where the vault segments meet the wall, they delineate wall arches. The transverse arches are often ornamentally profiled or contoured. The crown of the vault is emphasized by a keystone, but this is not as natural as it may seem: from the keystone one can decipher the evolution of the cross-groined vault, especially that in which the ribs have a rectangular bandlike profile. In these, during the Early Romanesque, one rib runs all the way across to create an uninterrupted half-circle, which means that the other rib, bisecting it at a right angle, must be made up of two equal pieces. In the High Romanesque, a square and then a cross-shaped keystone was formed. Only in time did the keystone take on a disklike form of its own. Already in the second phase, there were attempts at this (some even go back to the Early Romanesque); however, by the middle of the twelfth century, the tendency became more widespread. In fact, in many regions it was remarkably reinforced, though the extent to which such new developments forged ahead differed very much from one region to another.

Comparable developments took place with regard to the smallest details. The round torus on the base of a column is now flatter, the scotia (or neck groove) more deeply undercut, and the toelike projections at the corners of the base are replaced by smoothly juxtaposed leaflike forms. By and large, it is only in places of minor importance that the capitals still use the abstract forms of the cube or cushion, the goblet-block, and the pipe-bowl. Predominant was the goblet form, covered organically with stems, buds, and leaves leading smoothly to the shaft. Many round elements—cornices and ribs, for example—were elaborately contoured and undercut. Mitering was done not only where obligatory—on bases, cornices, stringcourses, and the like—but even for its own sake on elements such as shaft rings. There was an almost incalculable increase in the number of individual forms in ornamental architectonic sculpture, and anyone who has traveled much and beheld the profusion of forms that exist *in situ* will greet with skepticism the self-assured claims of many scholars to perceive concrete and specific relationships between them.

If many previously important regions became less prominent in this period, it may be because they reached a saturation point or for such reasons as economic decline, wars, and so forth. Normandy, for one, falls behind considerably in the second half of the twelfth century. Burgundy, previously outstanding for its sumptuousness, reverts to architectural systems of puritanical rigor and plainness. This is often said to be associated with the foundation and flourishing of the Cistercian order, but it is a tendency also found in churches not connected with that order. In the vast stretch of southern France, almost all areas south of the Loire continue to prefer the hall and aisleless forms to the basilical one that, with few exceptions, predominated north and south of the Alps. If the hall and aisleless forms were, like the others, vastly altered by the introduction of the cross-ribbed

195. Nivelles, Sainte-Gertrude,
transverse section of the west front
(from Lemaire, 1942)
196. Cologne, Sankt Aposteln,
interior of the east end

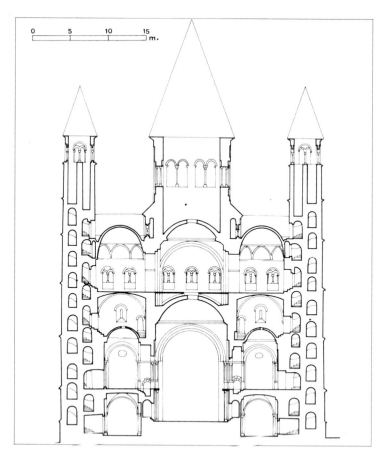

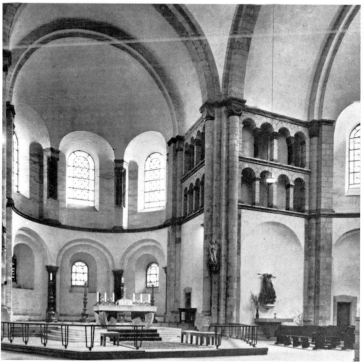

vault, fundamental traits were nevertheless preserved in both the interior and the exterior.

In any case, the distinguishing characteristics of each geographic region remained much as they had been in the High Romanesque. The central regions, those that around 1100 had taken the lead in vaulting the basilical portions of the church, continued to be innovators by devising ever richer interior plans and ever more logical articulation of all the walls; this is also true of England. While the hall and aisleless plans remained the norm south of the Loire, cross vaults with ribs superseded barrel vaults and cupolas, which meant that there too the general appearance was essentially different. Westphalia and a small group of buildings in Piedmont favored the hall plan, for which Apulia and Sicily found new solutions by the use of cupolas. Northern Italy, northern Spain, and the lands east of the Rhine preferred to vault their basilical interiors. In many respects, however, the High Romanesque style remained the norm in those regions and made possible the development of factors leading directly to the diversified local forms German writers group under the term *Sondergotik*. In many regions, the tradition of the flat-ceilinged basilica lived on simultaneously, though it was only in Sicily that it brought about uniquely impressive new solutions.

If one looks at regions where Late Romanesque art had a full and especially exuberant career—the Rhineland, for instance—it becomes evident that this phase covered a full century, until around the middle of the thirteenth century and, here and there, went even beyond. This coincides largely with the period in political history when the Hohenstaufen dynasty held power in the Holy Roman Empire, an era of such vitality and realism as far as the history of culture in general (and of literature in particular) is concerned that it is only natural to think of the entire period as the "Hohenstaufen era." Similarly, the architecture of the time also often directly evokes notions of the reality of life in the here-and-now, as we find so strikingly personified in the chivalric epics of the time, in the poetry of the Minnesingers, and in the personalities of Walther von der Vogelweide and Frederick I Barbarossa. It is surely not by chance that, in the architectonic sculpture of the Hohenstaufen era, demonic and grotesquely threatening depictions tend to give way to scenes of living, active human beings, nude as in Antique art, who bustle about in the midst of organically verdant foliage. If alongside quite natural-looking animals we still find fabulous beasts, nonetheless even the latter are imbued with a more realistic and friendlier expression. We find this same natural and easy delight in the heritage of antiquity in another outstanding personality of the time, Emperor Frederick II. This brilliant and "human" side of Hohenstaufen art has been explored in the remarkable studies by W. Pinder.

The use of dynastic names to designate art epochs admittedly has its disadvantages, especially when we are dealing with Europe as a whole, as has already been remarked in connection with so-called Ottonian art. This brings us, however, to an especially difficult problem, which has plagued

art history since the invention of that discipline: it is what Pinder called the "uncontemporaneity of the contemporaneous" (or, more simply, the "cultural lag"). In the preceding periods, the Early and High Romanesque, we can observe by and large a certain simultaneity in art throughout Europe. Around the middle of the twelfth century, however, a greater differentiation arises between one region and another, and in the first half of the thirteenth century—even as early as 1200—those differences reach a climax, so that one can no longer speak of "Late Romanesque" in connection with the French crown lands, where the new (in many respects quite different and even quite opposing) Gothic style had already affirmed itself.

Here, then, is a phenomenon much like that of the fifteenth century when, alongside the rich and exuberant flowering of an energetically active Late Gothic art, there suddenly arose in Tuscany an entirely opposed orientation, the Early Renaissance. The diffusion of both the Tuscan Early Renaissance and the northern French High Gothic has been penetratingly studied, but not without such errors as viewing their developments in too linear a fashion and attributing all merit to one or the other side. The result has been that scholars have come up with almost as many sub-varieties of Gothic (for which they had to coin the name *Sondergothik*) and almost as many aberrant currents in the Renaissance (which have had to be attributed to Mannerism or the Early Baroque) as, earlier, there had been distinct regional stylistic centers in the Romanesque.

In the French crown lands, the *domaine royal,* the end of the Late Romanesque can be dated precisely by the year in which the present cathedral was begun at Chartres: 1194. But everyone will agree when I claim the northern French "Early Gothic"—from the building of Sens and Saint-Denis around 1140 to that of the south crossarm at Soissons and the choir of Saint-Remi in Reims around 1190—to be, instead, Late Romanesque. Ernest Gall had already made a point of this, though with some circumspection, and recently, in 1970, the description of the Late Romanesque and Early Gothic by H. G. Franz likewise made much of this possibility. In any case, the architecture of the French crown lands undeniably has two faces: along with traits related to the Late Romanesque, there are clear lines of development that in those lands, and only there, lead to the High Gothic. Beginning with the end of the twelfth century, the architectural style that eventually became the High Gothic can be considered representative of the French monarchy, which in the thirteenth century undertook decisive steps toward its goal of conquering many territories and assimilating them into what would one day be France. During the reigns of Philip Augustus and Saint Louis, major advances were made in the creation of a national state.

In a number of large regions with their own tradition, the Late Romanesque lived on for many decades more than in the French crown lands. This is graphically illustrated in the Lower Rhineland: Sankt Salvator in Werden was rebuilt between 1250 and 1275 in full Romanesque style.

198. *Maastricht, Sint Servatius, imperial hall on the upper story of the west front, interior looking south*

199. *Schwarzrheindorf, Sankt Klemens (double chapel), transverse section in reconstruction of the first phase of building, plan of the ground floor, longitudinal section in reconstruction of the first phase of building, plan of the upper story*

This fact is all the more notewothy since, in the immediate vicinity of Werden, major buildings testifying to the eastward spread of French High Gothic had been erected as far back as 1248-55, namely the cathedrals of Cologne and Utrecht and the abbey church at Altenberg. The problem, however, is that in these exactly contemporary but quite different buildings, we are faced with systems that the unprejudiced observer will be sure are quite lacking in the chief traits of the High Gothic, though he may well doubt whether they represent the regional *Sondergothik* or a Late Romanesque stylistic development incorporating occasional Gothic formal elements. This applies particularly to the so-called Burgundian Early Gothic seen in the Cistercian abbey churches at Noirlac (Berry), Fossanova (Lazio), and Ebrach (Bavaria), but also to the many edifices that went up in Spain at the end of the twelfth and the beginning of the thirteenth century.

THE REGIONS IN THE HEARTLAND OF EUROPE

Among the many regions that remained faithful to the basilica form even in Late Romanesque and Early Gothic times, those between the Loire and the Rhine are of particular note. There, interiors and especially wall elevations were subjected to elaborate subdivision, with galleries and triforia being particularly favored. The wall surfaces were broken up by vertical and horizontal elements along with blind arches and niches, but they were also literally hollowed out, and the double-shelled wall enclosing a cavity became a widely diffused and important factor in architectural technique and design. In these regions too we are confronted with a number of more complex conceptions whose origins and development have been of great interest to art historians, though most often the focus has been on the origins and rise of the Gothic alone. By contrast, the question of the real essence of Late Romanesque architecture and the laws governing its creative processes has been raised all too seldom.

Cologne, the Lower Rhine, and the Meuse Valley

If we turn first to this region, it is because many distinctive traits of Late Romanesque architecture are found here in particularly clear form, and because it possesses an especially large number of important buildings and an entirely unique formal vocabulary that can be detected early and that persisted recognizably for a very long time despite a great many transformations. Researches took to studying it quite early, and it has been a point of concentration ever since.

The Late Romanesque style persisted for over a century in the Lower Rhine and Meuse valleys. It initiated around the middle of the twelfth century in a number of major churches, among them Sankt Klemens in Schwarzrheindorf, the nave in the former Benedictine abbey church at Brauweiler, the triple-conch choir of Gross Sankt Martin in Cologne, and

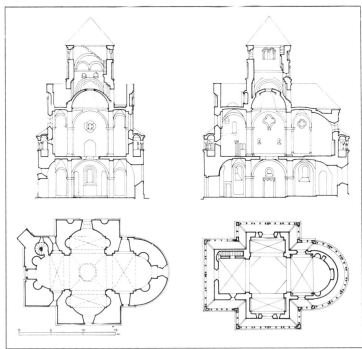

200. *Limburg-an-der-Lahn, cathedral of Sankt Georg, interior looking into the crossing tower and the vaults of the central nave*

201. *Limburg-an-der-Lahn, cathedral of Sankt George, interior looking southeast into the transept*
202. *Limburg-an-der-Lahn, cathedral of Sankt Georg, west front*

XIX. *Cologne, Sankt Aposteln, exterior*

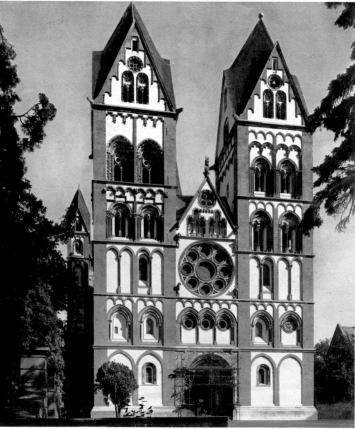

other three-storied apses with dwarf galleries. At the other extreme, the abbey church of Sankt Salvator in Werden was built as late as the third quarter of the thirteenth century—at the same time as work began on the High Gothic choir of Cologne Cathedral—and in forms one would expect instead to date from around 1220. Thus, the style spanned at least three or four generations, and its manifestations are correspondingly diversified, though a few decisive traits remain the norm, precisely those we recognize as Late Romanesque.

The new stylistic era began with the trefoil-shaped choir of Gross Sankt Martin, which—together with the Gothic cathedral—today still dominates the city from the banks of the Rhine. However, the earliest plan did not call for the present high square crossing tower with four small turrets at the corners, but for a cupola presumably like that on the church of Sankt Aposteln in the same city. The three apses at the east end all follow the same pattern, with two stories of blind arches topped by a gallery. This trefoil structure beneath the stair-turrets locks tightly into the rest of the building, which made for a smooth transition to the high middle tower when it was added somewhat later. Here, right from the start, a classical formula was found for the trefoil east end, the articulation of the apses, and the galleries with their coffered frieze on the parapets. Much of this was repeated almost exactly around 1200 at Sankt Aposteln a few streets away, though in even more mature and harmonious form.

In its interior as well, Sankt Martin displays the typical features of Late Romanesque apses, with niches hollowed out of a massive wall, over these a passageway with slender columns, and above the arches a semi-cupola. This pattern is used for all three apses; the corner bays act as huge piers supporting the tower and are linked by barrel vaults. Instead of a higher octagonal cupola, a hanging dome was erected over the crossing.

Alongside Gross Sankt Martin and Sankt Aposteln, which were followed by Unsere Liebe Frau at Andernach, Sankt Castor at Karden, and other churches with this sort of apse, there is a second group somewhat more graceful in aspect and typified by the minster in Bonn, Sankt Kastor in Coblenz, Sankt Gereon in Cologne, and Sint Servatius in Maastricht. In all of these, the apses are flanked by towers and give the impression of an ornamental façade from which the round apse projects. Inside, niches and articulation into stories are the principal features.

Besides these churches with their central-plan concept, façade-like articulation, and opened-up walls, there are several groups of churches with new types of west fronts. At Sainte-Gertrude in Nivelles, as a hundred years earlier in the cathedral at Trier, a crosswise structure was combined with an apse and stair-turrets in a silhouette like that of the west front at Maria Laach and with a square middle tower above the cross-building. Inside, however, Sainte-Gertrude offers a rich ensemble of spatial areas: fore-halls and gallery chapels, a west choir, a large three-bay cupola-covered aisleless chamber high above the roof-ridge of the church. This is one of the major

achievements of Late Romanesque architecture, although much harmed by the renovation of the tower in the seventeenth century and by the demolition of the apse; a thoroughgoing restoration was necessary after years of neglect and a fire during World War II.

In another group, west choirs figure in a specific architectural conception in which they are treated as three-bay transepts. In their interiors, markedly projecting wall piers and arches support the cross vaults and take the weight of the corner towers, as in Saint-Jacques in Liège and, somewhat later, Sint Germanus in Tirlemont (Tienen). Other "west-choir halls," to use the term of Albert Verbeek, are further distinguished by a system of niches and passageways between the vault piers, as in Saint-Barthélemy in Liège, Sint Servatius in Maastricht, and the severely damaged former collegiate church in Xanten.

Here we see that the niche hollowed out of the wall and the passageway resulting from breaking through it are interchangeable and structurally related. Very likely this represents a return to traits found in the mid-eleventh century, to something like the west front of Trier Cathedral. Whether or not, other than this, there was some influence from Norman architecture and its derivatives (such as Tournai Cathedral) is difficult to ascertain and evaluate. The more refined graduation of the structural blocks by towers over the apse and west choir seems as characteristic here as the marked articulation of the outer and inner walls.

The system was open to modification. At Sankt Georg in Cologne, it was restricted to a square west choir originally planned to be crowned by towers, as in the castle chapel at Schwarzrheindorf (later expanded to become a Benedictine nunnery) and its small sister-church of Saint-Nicolas-en-Glain near Liège (no longer extant), both of which date from 1151.

No less diversified are certain churches built in the first half of the thirteenth century. Sankt Quirinus at Neuss in the North Rhineland and the minster at Roermond in the Dutch Limburg continue the series of cloverleaf apses with dwarf galleries and open crossing towers, but infuse the previously quietly balanced structural mass and articulation with a new, stronger movement. The west fronts become increasingly complicated. In Sankt Andreas in Cologne, the crosswise transept-like main chamber is, so to speak, raised to the upper story, while below it lies the famous corridor with dentated arches on its cross girders—a structure that is both the ground floor of the west front and the east wing of the cloister (no longer existing), the latter here, as in Sankt Gereon in the same city, having lain in front of the church and been interlocked with the west front. In the churches at Andernach and Limburg-an-der-Lahn, the general plan of the west front approaches that of the two-towered façade but still suggests a cross-building with low towers so that, from the outside as well, one is conscious of a transverse hall in the upper story. In the Meuse region, Sint Germanus in Tirlemont (Tienen) has another of the so-called westchoir halls, and the Roermond minster transforms the simple crosswise plan into a large hall-like

structure with a U-shaped gallery.

The naves, though always of different heights as in the basilica plan, are for the most part short. The simpler ones retain the bound system with smooth walls, as in the parish church at Moselweiss on the outskirts of Coblenz, while the more important ones have longitudinal galleries over the side naves, as at Andernach, Neuss, Sinzig, or Roermond; or else have central-nave walls articulated with blind arches or niches in the manner of a triforium, as at Brauweiler (after 1141) and in the Cologne churches of Sankt Andreas, Sankt Aposteln, and Sankt Kunibert. The splitting of the wall into two layers had previously been worked out only in apses and west fronts, but was now applied to naves as well. In this manner, in the Bonn minster, Sankt Margaretha in Gerresheim, and Gross Sankt Martin in Cologne a genuine triforium was achieved that seems closely related to that of northern French Early Gothic and that certainly came into being as a result of that influence. In the Bonn minster, it is combined with a passageway in front of the clerestory windows and thus arrives at a fully realized double-shelled articulation of the central-nave clerestory like that in the contemporary cathedrals of Geneva and Lausanne, though these are in more "progressive" Early Gothic forms.

On the other hand, at Sankt Georg in Limburg-an-der-Lahn in Hesse, galleries, triforia, and an external passageway in front of the clerestory were combined in the central nave into a four-storied system whose affinity with the cathedrals of Laon and Noyon has long been recognized. There can be no doubt that the builder of the church at Limburg knew those cathedrals, which makes it all the more surprising that he was able to translate the dynamic articulated structure of those northern French edifices into his quite different, heavier, more massive stylistic conception. The transition occurred almost without a break, and so this church—exceptional in its landscape setting as well—can still be thought of as a masterpiece of Lower Rhenish Late Romanesque architecture. With its closely packed group of towers rising above the cliffs over the Lahn River, it realized architectural ideas that were no more than embryonic in Laon and other churches. Especially fine also is the way the four-storied arcaded elevation is carried out in the transept and choir.

Similarly, the architect of Sankt Gereon in Cologne also combined Late Romanesque and early Gothic forms as he wished, fusing them into a four-storied elevation—though an entirely unconventional one—in which all the bay walls are set at angles to conform to the plan of a pre-existing Late Antique oval church with deep niches, which had been incorporated into the new design. The great ten-sided ribbed cupola with pendant keystone has nothing of that almost arrogantly playful character found in many other buildings; instead, it forms a noble crown for the solemn central-plan structure beneath it.

It has long been stressed, and rightly, that scarcely another region cultivated the central plan in Romanesque times as assiduously as the Lower

Rhine. The cloverleaf ground plans of the eleventh, twelfth, and thirteenth centuries fuse three-quarters of a central-plan structure with a nave. As well as relatively centralizing plans in which, for instance, there may be short crossarms with a continuous ambulatory as at Sankt Peter in Sinzig or Sankt Kunibert in Cologne, there are genuine polygonal central-plan structures with ambulatories running entirely around them, notably the citadel chapels at Kobern in the Rhineland and at Vianden in Luxembourg. Besides these, there are smaller constructions such as the chapter house in Sankt Pantaleon in Cologne as well as certain quite exceptional hall plans. The chapel from Ramersdorf, which was later transplanted to the cemetery in Bonn, may be numbered among them, but also—on a vastly larger scale—the Late Romanesque vaulted interior of Trier Cathedral. There, as is so often the case, the double-choir plan is an inheritance from an earlier phase of construction, but insofar as it was preserved in subsequent rebuilding and even architectonically emphasized, it would also seem a characteristic of Late Romanesque architecture on the Lower Rhine. With their two choirs, two transepts (or, at any rate, an eastern transept), and a transverse west front, many of the large churches mentioned here can be assigned to this category.

With their three-storied exterior articulation, the decorative band of coffered frieze, and the opening of the wall into a dwarf gallery, the above-mentioned apses show what concern there was with beauty and ornamentation in the art of the Lower Rhine. This is corroborated in their interiors by the use of niches and passageways to lessen the austerity of the wall. Along with this, a plump roundness in the body of the building both inside and out remained the norm until around 1200, after which apses were increasingly built on angular, many-sided ground plans. It is evident that this too was done as an aid in diversifying the form and should not be interpreted as a breakthrough of the new Gothic style. Both indoors and out, the standard remained an elevation with stratified stories marked off by cornices and crowned by a gallery. Uninterrupted buttressing piers and shafts, so characteristic of the Gothic, are either entirely lacking or are present only in a subordinate role. The wall continues to be a solid closure, pierced in order to admit light but not itself a web of Gothic windows with tracery. The Lower Rhenish polygonal apse of the sort found in the transepts at Bonn and Roermond and at Sinzig, Boppard, Münstermaifeld, and Sankt Severin in Cologne breaks down the Romanesque half-vault into segments between ribbing, fans the vault out like an umbrella, and correspondingly hollows out the wall into niches. Unlike the Gothic absidal vault, it never stresses the separateness of the segments through sharp angles.

The polygonal apse had Early Romanesque forerunners in the Lower Rhine region, notably in Sint Lebuinius in Deventer and Sankt Georg in Cologne, but quite certainly did not derive from these. Rather, we can observe how, in the long course of its construction during the latter half of the twelfth century, the east apse of Trier Cathedral more and more modified the prototypes borrowed from Lorraine—the cathedral of Verdun-sur-Meuse and the church in Mont-devant-Sassey—to bring them more into line with the forms current in the Lower Rhine region. For its part, Lorraine may well have derived the polygonal ground plan from Provence, or at least from southern France, rather than from specifically Early Gothic sources.

There was a considerable proliferation of small details in the Lower Rhenish Late Romanesque. Much effort has been invested (by R. Hamann above all) in establishing their exact origin—Normandy, Burgundy, Provence, Languedoc, or Lombardy—and in determining the roads followed by builders, journeymen, and workshops. Often, however, this procedure runs the risk of explaining one unknown factor by another, thus merely perpetuating the problem. In discussing these origins, it seems of

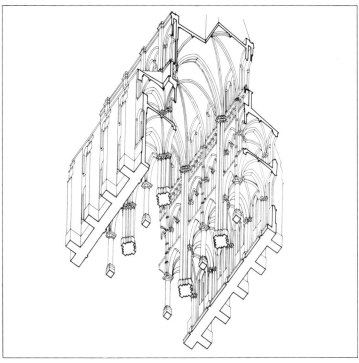

209. Heisterbach, ruins of the Cistercian abbey church, vestiges of the choir ambulatory vaults
210. Noyon, cathedral of Notre-Dame, axonometric projection of the nave (from Gall, 1925)

paramount importance to me not to overlook the creative power that summoned forth all these forms and synthesized them into a whole. Among such individual forms, those that emphasize the decorative rather than the structural character are most striking: pendant keystones, dentated arches (set with a frieze of blind scalloped forms), trefoil arches, fan windows. All of these serve to conceal the fact that arches and vaults are built up out of numerous elements joined together and make them appear, to the contrary, sculpural, as if carved out of solid matter. Pointed gables and lozenge and hipped roofs similarly transform solid blocklike structures and shapes into more irregular and diversified ones. Bases and cornices are often bent around vertical elements, free or engaged columns are interrupted by rings around their shafts, even—in fact, precisely—where there is no architectonic reason for it. The ribs increase in number in the vaults, and not only in cross vaults but also in barrel cupolas and half-cupolas so that the segments fan out like an umbrella and in certain cases, just as in England, produce forms that seem direct anticipations of Late Gothic figurations, notably at Sinzig and Heisterbach.

For long now, the fact that color played a part in this Rhenish architecture has been a matter for study, and in recent decades a number of buildings have been restored both inside and outside—no longer, however, in the color of the natural stone (the grayish yellow of tufa, the bluish black of trachyte and slate), but in lively contrasts of whitewashed surfaces with red, yellow, and black architecural members. Figurative painting was not lacking in the interiors, though it was generally restricted to the surfaces left free by the articulation. Stained glass also had its place, yet it did not play the major role it would in the High Gothic cathedrals. By contrast, Lower Rhenish and Mosan architecture lacked the sculptured portal altogether, nor was there room elsewhere either within or without the building for any sculpture that would detract from the architectonic elements.

The Late Romanesque constructions of the Cistercians are, as a rule, uniformly in the style of the particular region where they are located. Nothing is more revealing in this connection than the contrast between two roughly contemporary Cistercian churches, one at Otterberg in the Palatinate, the other at Heisterbach in the Rhineland; the latter is now a ruin in which only the head of the choir survives. The rich openwork articulation at Heisterbach is wholly unlike the massiveness at Otterberg. At Heisterbach, two transepts interrupt the long nave. In the surviving east end, there is a semicircular apse with ambulatory on elegant doubled columns, and an inner passageway in front of the upper-story windows. The ambulatory is enhanced by a wreath of deep semicircular niches. The vaults are richly ornamented and divided into segments by profiled projections that can scarcely be called ribs, creating forms anticipatory of the Late Gothic star and fan vaults found in Anjou and in the Early English style. In the choir bay, a genuine triforium corresponds to the openings that articulate the horizontal stretch of nave wall between the arcades and the clerestory. With such an abundance of ornamental forms (and we have mentioned only the chief ones), Heisterbach constitutes a high point, even within the rich repertory of forms known and used along the Lower Rhine. Otterberg, conversely, has a simple cruciform plan with the use of the typically High Romanesque bound system in the nave.

Following the example of Heisterbach, the Onze Lieve Vrouwekerk in Maastricht had multiple transepts—three, in fact—as early as around 1170; with its high lateral naves and two-storied choir ambulatory, it displayed a richly animated interior design.

The French Crown Lands: Ile-de-France

Beginning around 1130/40, attempts were made at vaulting over the upper reaches of churches in the *domaine royal,* as had already been done in the surrounding regions. However, what was used was neither the Burgundian formula with pointed barrel vaults, nor the Rhenish bound system with cross-groined vaulting; neither the cross-groined vaulting in short bays in such isolated attempts as at Maria Laach and Vézelay, nor the solution found in the great galleried churches in Utrecht and Lombardy, where the bound system was combined with band-ribbed vaults and obliquely set engaged half-columns. Obviously, the builders looked here instead to their Norman predecessors, who had utilized sexpartite (and at times rectangular) vaults and round profiled ribs.

The system of the auxiliary engaged shaft also derived from Norman practice: it was precisely this form of vault that developed out of the vertical half-columns with which the Normans articulated their high central-nave walls even before they conceived of vaulting. In other ways too the link with Norman prototypes is close. The same possibilities for spatial and wall design that we recognized in the Norman early Romanesque are brought into play once again: the zones beyond the side-nave roofs are articulated with blind triforia, notably at Saint Nicolas in Blois and in the cathedral at Le Mans, though more often there are rows of openings onto the timberwork roofs of the side naves that create "false galleries," as in Saint-Etienne in Beauvais and the cathedral of Sens. Or there are fully built upper stories over the side naves, constituting genuine longitudinal tribunes as in the Early Romanesque buildings of Champagne and Normandy. Both elements were combined quite early: the genuine gallery as fully built upper story and the false gallery as an element of articulation with openings onto the roof area. Saint-Germer-de-Fly (Oise) shows this in an early stage, and Notre-Dame in Paris and Chartres Cathedral have round openings. Then there is a fully constructed four-story elevation in the cathedrals of Noyon, Laon, Châlons-sur-Marne, the new choir of Saint-Remi in Reims, the south crossarm of the cathedral at Soissons, and finally in Notre-Dame at Mouzon (Champagne). Where unified new buildings went up, as in Noyon and Laon, this system was also extended to the transept. Such unification of the interior was already a concern of Norman architecture in the eleventh century—in Sainte-Trinité

213. Pontigny, Cistercian abbey
church, interior looking east
214. Perrecy-les-Forges, church, west
front, elevation and plan of the
ground floor (from Klingenberg,
1910)

in Caen, for instance. In the buildings of the second half of the century, the triforium too was taken up again, no longer as a blind arcade but as a passageway that looks as if it lies within the wall. Again there is a connection here with Normandy. True enough, the passageways within the thickness of the walls—first in the transept, then in the middle nave in front of the clerestory windows, in the apse, and in the crossing tower—was not adopted, but the basic conception had something to do with disengaging the blind arches of the triforium from the wall and converting them into a freely open arcade as was done here. Like the window passageways of Normandy, the triforium passages do not truly lie within the full thickness of the wall: their outer wall rests on special blind arches, which in Norman churches are visible but are here concealed behind the vaults of the tribune. The blind triforium was already known in the form of a blind arcade in Burgundy, in choirs with ambulatories south of the Loire (in Berry especially), and with troughlike niches on the Lower Rhine. There was thus no need to look to Normandy for the form in itself, though the enhanced spatiality certainly perpetuates Norman notions.

The four-storied elevation of the central-nave wall is one of the paramount features of architecture in the French crown lands in the latter half of the twelfth century. It is responsible for many interiors of radiant splendor and beauty, which are further enhanced through the elegance of the workmanship. Probably, however, this combination too is an invention, if we may use that word, of the neighboring and border lands. In Saint-Germer (on the border of Normandy) we find a hint of it, but the first consistent and full realization took place in Tournai Cathedral in the Walloon-speaking zone of the Schelde Valley (as well as in the Flemish zone of nearby Picardy) in the form of a flat-ceilinged building without engaged supports.

The choir ambulatory—another element current in Normandy, specifically in Rouen, Jumièges, and Fécamp—became especially important in this context, since it permitted the three- or four-storied wall system to be carried through in the apse as well. While this was possible even without an ambulatory, as in the transept-apses in Noyon, the articulation does not follow the natural logic that it does in the three-storied basilical interior. The involvement of the apse in the double-shelled articulation is another feature clearly anticipated in Normandy at Sainte-Trinité in Caen and at Cérisy-la-Forêt.

Finally, the twin-towered façade was known both in and even beyond all the regions where the flat-ceilinged design was followed. Judging by the surviving examples, however, it was doubtless worked out in purest form in Normandy—in Saint-Etienne in Caen above all. Two towers terminating the side naves on the west and linked by a structure similarly terminating the central nave, with three portals either joined directly to the interior or set off from it by a narthex with transverse tribune above it: this was the normal solution and was to remain so for the High Gothic period as well.

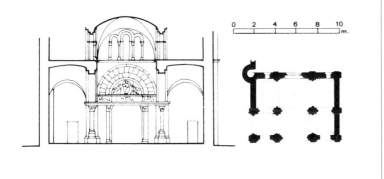

The twin-towered façade of the northern French early Gothic is one of the great creations of medieval architecture. The bodies of the towers are sculpturally articulated by buttress piers at the corners and in front of the sides, and the added support makes possible the large openings in the several stories. Furthermore, with their stories of the same height, there can be a more consistent linkage to the central portion, and this results in a genuinely unified structure deserving the name of "façade." Arcades on the outside duplicate the elevation of the central-nave wall. All this is displayed in purest fashion at Noyon and Paris, whereas at Chartres, Sens, Senlis, and Saint-Denis later alterations must be taken into account. At Laon, the spatial depth—particularly that of the arches of the narthex—creates agglomerations of shadows, and the intensive splitting up of the masses results in an extraordinarily animated overall impression, while the baldachin-like structures at the corners of the upper story perpetuate the traditional idea of towers (albeit transformed into something fantastic).

From 1140 to 1190, the architecture of the crown lands visibly aimed at ever more vigorous articulation, at refining and thinning down the forms, and at rendering interiors more transparent and better illuminated. However, it arrived at these ends by means that remained by and large within the canon of Romanesque forms and the Romanesque stylistic approach. If art historians always designate this architecture as "Early Gothic," it is because they view it almost exclusively in terms of its historical development. Insofar as both the forms and the techniques of the High Gothic were prepared for here, the designation is justified. Yet since the decisive break represented by the cathedrals of Chartres, Soissons, and Bourges did not take place until the 1190s, it might be more accurate to speak of a "Proto-Gothic" or a "Pre-Gothic" architecture.

Noyon, Paris, and Saint-Remi in Reims still have round windows and, in part, round choir ambulatory chapels. A considerable proportion of the arches in Laon Cathedral are round, and even where they appear to be broken or pointed they almost never have the unequivocally sharp form of the High Gothic arch. The buttressing system now exposed on the exterior, masking over the clear cubic elevation of what is still a Romanesque structure, likewise dates only from the 1190s. Such buttressing was, in fact, usually a later addition to buildings begun in the Early Gothic period. The seemingly new profiles of the arches still reveal their origins in the Romanesque arch with its rectangular stepped cross section, now made less harsh only by cable molding. Not before the High Gothic would the arch be composed entirely of round elements. The choir of Saint-Martin-des-Champs in Paris is an exemplary instance of how the Late Romanesque, well before the Gothic, could infuse movement into an interior.

Many writers credit the abbey church of Saint-Denis near Paris with initiating the new Gothic style. How right are they? In 1137–40 Abbot Suger added a twin-towered façade to an existing Carolingian church, thereby creating a blocklike mass that is entirely Romanesque in effect. The

217. Ely, cathedral, reconstruction of the original west front (from Conant, 1959)

218. Lincoln, cathedral, reconstruction of the original west front (from Escher, 1929)

three sculptured portals have been renovated but still do not really go much beyond the Romanesque columnar figure. The interior is covered with exceptionally strong ribbed vaults that quite obviously struggle with the difficulties involved in harmonizing the lines of the arches and imposts. The result is an almost Baroque impression of Late Romanesque exuberance. At the east end, over the Carolingian crypt and around the old apse, a new choir was built in 1140–43 but apparently never completed. What survives is the choir ambulatory and a wreath of semicircular chapels that are more intimately related spatially than was previously the custom. The light pointed-arch rib vaults are now managed with sureness and elegance. The outer walls are pierced with numerous and quite large windows. What we have here, then, is an older building enlarged through relatively limited means, perhaps already with the aim of eventually redoing it entirely—though that was not initiated until 1231, when it was carried through in entirely progressive High Gothic forms.

The high esteem in which Saint-Denis is held is tantamount to a legend. It derives in the first place from its connection with an outstanding personality, Abbot Suger, and from his writings, which (unfortunately with an all too rare wealth of details) tell us about the decision to build the church and about its planning and execution. Yet what he says seems more typical of the high point of the Romanesque, the twelfth century, than of any decisive change in style. Whether Suger really intended to carry the work further is unknown, nor do we know how it would have looked. Attempts at reconstruction have been based on buildings actually executed and surviving—the cathedral at Sens in particular—and show little beyond what can be seen in that church. Nevertheless, even Saint-Denis is best understood as a Late Romanesque creation.

The High Gothic

When the decisive break came after 1190 it did away with the galleries, raised the side naves, lowered the triforium, and lenghtened and enlarged the clerestory windows until they filled the entire field of the wall arches. Only then were the wall and its surface really radically opened up. The continuous wall was replaced by a succession of buttressing piers protruding to the exterior; the combination of a number of windows resulted in the Gothic tracery window; the cutting away of the solid wall to make place for triforia and windows made it necessary to divert the outward thrust of the vaults to arches falling onto buttressing piers that were now much extended upward. The bound system, despite the fact that it had a decided influence on the sexpartite vault, was given up in favor of short bays with rectangular vault fields. Even the tower was broken down into its basic components of corner piers and arches. All of this together made up a unified system that was very carefully worked out in all respects, which had never before been the case.

Nor do these constitute all the variations from the so-called Early Gothic.

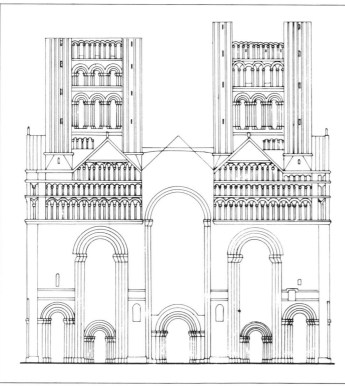

219. *Tournai, cathedral, exterior from the northwest showing transept, transept and crossing towers, north portal, and nave*

220. *Tournai, cathedral, interior of the south crossarm*

221. *Eberbach, former Cistercian abbey church, interior looking east*

For the first time the entire edifice was unconditionally unified, meaning that the differentiation of bay, vault, and wall systems in different parts of the building was virtually abandoned. So too, for the first time, wall masses, wall surfaces, and individual elements took such a secondary place as compared to the totality that we are justified in speaking of a "diaphanous structure" or "latticework walls." For the first time too the window assumed decisive importance as part of the whole, and this was due to the concomitance of a number of processes: the opening was so enlarged as to virtually take up all the wall surface; the stone lacework of the tracery made it easier to fill the entire space with glass; a distinct iconographical program was worked out for each window, thus filling the architectural setting with huge deeply colored (but self-illuminating) surfaces. Conversely, the building itself came to be considered a secondary matter, at most a frame for the stained-glass images, and this was because the architectonic structure of the interior grew increasingly difficult to perceive in this darkly gleaming light. Furthermore, on the exterior, the solid block of wall was transformed (and even concealed) by the buttressing, whose chief purpose there in the first place was to make it possible to dissect and open up the stone shell around the interior in this extreme fashion. Aside from such technical exigencies, the new style early acquired an expressiveness of its own and almost took on the purely nonfunctional beauty that finely engineered structures sometimes reveal.

In addition, the High Gothic cathedral displayed greatly enlarged portals, which were adorned with an extraordinary proliferation of statues (these were found in increasing numbers elsewhere as well, both inside and out). The extensive iconographical programs for the northern French portals are certainly inconceivable without the precedent of southern French Romanesque sculpture, whatever turn that art may have taken by then. Like the High Gothic stained-glass images in the interior, this sculpture led to a total transformation of the exterior. In some of the most important cathedrals it went so far as to engulf the architecture in its finely detailed forms; the objective observer frequently finds himself looking at it almost as an inversion of the respective roles of architecture and sculpture, a phenomenon analogous to the Hindu temple.

High Gothic cathedral architecture, with the characteristics just noted, remained confined to a relatively small territory whose borders were Orléans and Tours in the south, Arras and Tournai in the north, Reims and Bourges in the east, Amiens and Saint-Quentin in the west. Normandy and Picardy modified the system in significant details. Along the Rhine, south of the Loire, and south of the Pyrenees it obtained a foothold only sporadically, south of the Alps generally not at all, east of the Rhine again only in isolated instances (and then very much modified). The French High Gothic, often thought of as an internationally diffused style, is in fact no more than a thin net spread across a dense stratum of buildings, each still very characteristic of their own regions. While these may show certain

141

affinities with the Gothic vocabulary, local Romanesque traditions remain rather clearly at the base of their conception. This holds true for the wooden-ceilinged single-naved churches of the Italian mendicant orders, for the deliberately simple architecture of those same orders wherever German was spoken, for the type of aisleless interior with chapels widely diffused to either side of the Pyrenees, and finally—most especially—for the type of church often recognized as the counter-form to the High Gothic cathedral, namely the hall church. The latter is found almost everywhere in Europe, in some cases in clearly delimited areas, in others widely dispersed.

While thorough presentation and evaluation of Gothic architecture is not our aim in this volume, it is indispensable to allude here—however briefly—to the new manifestations that appeared virtually at the close of the Late Romanesque period. Up to about 1200, even the architecture of the French royal domain remained confined to the Late Romanesque style, and there continued to be a great deal of mutual influence among the various artistic regions. This was followed, however, by a nearly contradictory development: the wonderfully diversified beauty of Late Romanesque architecture yielded to the High Gothic cathedral style arising from a single small territory—the Ile-de-France. A general impression of the new style can scarcely be gleaned anywhere outside that limited region before the second quarter of the thirteenth century.

Late Romanesque and Early Gothic in Burgundy
The three basic architectural systems of the Burgundian High Romanesque were described above, and they continued without significant changes in the Late Romanesque until around 1200. The most marked differences occurred in the group of churches typified by Cluny, but only a single building needs mention in that connection—the cathedral of Langres (Champagne). There the wall elevation was still carried out in the earlier manner, but the central nave was covered with cross-ribbed vaults instead of a pointed barrel vault. The cross-ribbed vaults fit in with surprising ease, because the columnar shafts already used in Autun in conjunction with the pilasters were adopted in Langres to support the diagonal ribs. The contradiction between the austerely flat and frontal wall elevation and the diagonals of the ribs reaching out into space is more theoretical than visible. In any event, the ribbed vault made it possible to design a powerful and broad interior quite unlike the narrow and steep one of earlier buildings. This was certainly the reason behind the change, and is consistent with the Late Romanesque.

To a great degree, the group represented by Fontenay (which expands the barrel-vaulted aisleless form to include chapels) takes on the character of southern French or, better, southwestern European architecture. At this point, setting aside our geographical arrangement for the moment, we must refer the reader to the section on hall and single-naved churches later in this chapter, which offers further proof of the fact that Burgundy more than any other region had two sources of influence, one in the North, the other in the South.

A third group is connected with the tradition exemplified by Anzy-le-Duc and the nave of Vézelay, and leads more directly to the Cistercian abbey church at Pontigny and the Hospitaler church at Pontaubert (both in the Auxerrois) and to Saint-Philibert in Dijon. These churches transform the system of Vézelay into something simpler and, in certain cases, also more rigid. If we examine the late medieval architectural systems (entirely aside from their factual connections) in search of the one most in line with the spirit of Cistercian reforms, inevitably we must opt for this one.

As in the French crown lands, in Burgundy too Late Romanesque art comes to an end in the decades around 1200. The entire formal apparatus of the Early Gothic was suddenly and most energetically taken over from Champagne at the Burgundian west border (though it must be remembered that this was the Early Gothic and not at all the High Gothic of Chartres, Reims, and Amiens). The new choir in Vézelay, Notre-Dame in Dijon, the cathedrals of Auxerre, Chalon-sur-Saône, Geneva, and Lausanne, the church at Auxonne, and the choir of the cathedral at Nevers all evolve a new system that would seem to be specifically Burgundian. This is most easily distinguished in such motifs as the large open three-naved porch that is two bays in length: in Notre-Dame in Dijon and in Auxonne and Perrecy-les-Forges, it follows the lead of Autun and Vézelay, while in the interior the chief characteristic is the marked lightness of the structural framework and the consistent treatment of the double-shelled wall—the latter almost always conceived with genuine triforia and inner passageways in front of the clerestory windows.

The most impressive work as a whole is certainly Lausanne Cathedral, whose open crossing tower and two very transparent west towers loom high over Lake Geneva. South of Burgundy, we find the earlier parts of the cathedral of Lyons to be connected with this group (which R. Banner has treated exhaustively).

With these buildings, Burgundian architecture in the first half of the thirteenth century assumed an important intermediate position between the conservative regions still utilizing the Late Romanesque style and those that were adopting the High Gothic of the French crown lands. Not a single church in Burgundy adhered to the High Gothic architectural system in the same way that, after 1250, occasionally happened along the Rhine and in southern France.

Normandy and England
Extraordinarily active in the eleventh and early twelfth centuries, Normandy begins in the second quarter of the twelfth century to stagnate in its building activity. We have seen that the line of development was taken up and carried further virtually unbroken in the regions to the west, that is, in Picardy and

226. Otterberg, former Cistercian
abbey church, transverse section of the
transept, plan of the east end (from
Eckardt and Gebhard, 1942)

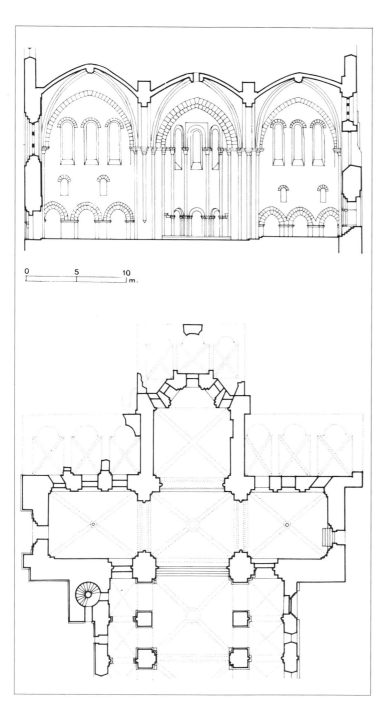

throughout the French crown lands. Certainly this did not occur without some decisive modifications aimed at a consistent further development of the structural framework. In any case, the abbey church at Fécamp, the only important late twelfth-century building in Normandy, fits neatly into this development, as is seen by leafing through the chronological tales in E. Gall's invaluable book on northern French Gothic architecture (published in 1925). Nevertheless, the three-storied elevation of its central-nave wall, its fully built up galleries, and especially the inner passageway in front of the clerestory windows all prove Fécamp to be still entirely Norman in character.

For its part, however, England remained faithful to the basic existing patterns in a good number of the largest churches built in the late twelfth century, and did so without excessive modifications. What is more surprising, though, is that until around the end of the century it continued to erect wooden-ceilinged interiors, all probably in open timberwork. With the wall articulation as a basis, three main groups of interior can be distinguished.

One perpetuated the complete articulation of the wall as it had already been developed at the start of the twelfth century: piers with round-arched arcades, galleries mostly with biforate openings, high clerestories with inner passageways often emphasized in the middle, bay and bay, by graduated tripartite arches—the latter a motif found also in Lower Rhenish and Mosan architecture where it was used, however, in an entirely different spatial context, as in the west choir hall of Sint Servatius at Maastricht. Engaged shafts in front of each pier—a good example is Peterborough Cathedral, whose nave was completed in 1194/97—impart an exceptional dynamism to these walls. Yet despite the fact that the forms are more substantial and massive, no less is achieved here in activating the walls than in northern France.

The second group—this type was diffused by the choir of Hereford Cathedral, dating from around 1100, and the earlier nave of the abbey church at Romsey (Hampshire)—has a quite unique interlocking of nave arcades and gallery arches: the side-nave piers are extended upward as blind articulation; the nave arches are so high that they frame the gallery openings, whereas a second row of such arches (the only ones actually to exercise their function) is set below between the piers. The small cathedral of Oxford and the abbey churches at Glastonbury (Somerset) and Jedburgh (Scotland) show the same arrangement, which is somewhat arbitrary and therefore accords well with Late Romanesque conceptions on the Continent. Perhaps what we have here is a combination of the large round pier, as found in Durham and Gloucester, with the gallery.

Like the other two groups, the third type of interior utilized a system already established around 1100, one in which three stories are super-imposed as rigorously separated horizontal layers running the entire length of the nave, but without vertical accents or connections. What survives (the

227. Piacenza, cathedral, façade
228. Morimondo, Cistercian abbey church of Santa Maria, façade (with 18th-century porch)

229. Morimondo, Cistercian abbey church of Santa Maria, interior looking northeast

nave and nineteenth-century choir) in the ruined priory church at Worksop (Nottinghamshire) and in the abbey church at Dunfermline (Scotland) offer characteristic examples of this sort of nave. One would not expect to find so much wall surface in an Norman building, though even here it is effectively hollowed out by the large continuous arches of the gallery and passageways. Also relevant in this context is Rochester Cathedral (Kent), built around the middle of the twelfth century, in which the shafts of the ground floor break off at the cornice at the foot of the gallery; the ruins at Kelso in Scotland have this same layered structure. It was in this group as a whole that the tendency toward insistent horizontals typical of the English Early Gothic began to manifest itself.

Another striking though not frequent peculiarity of English architecture is the so-called screen-façade, which is placed in front of the nave in such a way as to conceal it as if behind a wall when viewed from the west (in this it is similar to the façade walls of Lombardy and Aquitaine). Here, however, no gable crowns the wall, though it is richly articulated with blind arcades on multiple stories—as, for example, on the ruined Cluniac priory church at Castle Acre (Norfolk). At Rochester Cathedral, turrets divide the façade into three sections, thus making it rather like the Continental transverse west fronts exemplified in the original powerful Romanesque front at Lincoln Cathedral. The latter was enlarged into a kind of Early Gothic screen-façade toward the end of the twelfth century by vertical construction on its towers and by the addition of arcaded walls to its sides. The broad west front of Ely Cathedral has a huge central tower (itself studded with four corner turrets) that looms over transept-like wings (the north wing has survived only in fragments), which in turn end in paired towers, while blind arcades divide the entire front into several stories.

In the first half of the thirteenth century, Early Gothic cathedrals in England—in the style known as "Early English"—continued to receive this sort of screen-façade, notably Peterborough (begun in 1201), Wells (in 1220), and then Salisbury. Though all have their individual variations, they have in common a decided rejection of the twin-towered façade, which scholars so often wrongly think of as the normal solution.

Around the end of the twelfth century and in the first half of the thirteenth, we find the first Gothic buildings on the Continent as well as in the British Isles. They are related to the so-called Early Gothic of the French crown lands, but when viewed from that standpoint are very arbitrary modifications or reinterpretations of that style. Along with some buildings in Burgundy and a few along the Rhine and the Meuse, we come upon further groups in the *domaine royal* that are significantly influenced by northern French Early Gothic, particularly as exemplified by Sens Cathedral.

The Norman ex-cathedral of Lisieux and the English cathedral of Canterbury (begun in 1174), which must be mentioned first, are the closest in character to the new church of the Ile-de-France. Their three-storied elevation is harmonious as in Sens, even if the clerestory is already somewhat

230. Piacenza, cathedral, interior,
the cupola of the crossing tower viewed
from below
231. Piacenza, cathedral, interior
looking northeast

lower (though, by way of compensation, fitted out with an interior passageway). Both features subsequently remained virtually the absolute rule, as they did also in the major Norman constructions of the following period—the choirs of Saint-Etienne in Caen and of the cathedral in Bayeux. Whereas part of the effect in Canterbury is due to the lively note of color struck by the numerous black marble column shafts, the Continental churches mentioned put greater emphasis on their special Norman character by using such typical elements as lancet arches and rosettes set deeply into the upper wall surfaces.

One of the truly unique achievements in all medieval architecture is the looplike form given the walls of Canterbury's choir. It is clear how this came about: the choir was enlarged by a few narrower bays that were connected to the vestiges of the original semicircular apse. The resulting S-curve is Late Romanesque in conception, not Gothic. The English version of Early Gothic (as previously mentioned, often called Early English) also contrasts vigorously with the so-called classical Early Gothic of the French crown lands, and even more decidedly with the style of the High Gothic cathedrals. The long continuous horizontal rows of arches in the nave arcades, galleries, and passageways impart a predominantly horizontal character to the English interiors, while the verticals of the shafts are reduced or even suppressed, as in the ruins of the abbey at Rievaulx.

Entirely unlike the structural rationale of the northern French edifices, the introduction of tiercerons and ridge-ribs into the vaults created a rich decorative impression, clearly exemplified in St. Hugh's Choir in Lincoln Cathedral (begun in 1192). Here, in addition, the builders even dared to use asymmetrical ribbing—Frankl called the results "crazy vaults." Similar echoes, or anticipations, of Late Gothic vaulting can also be observed in the Lower Rhine area, in the side nave at Heisterbach and the galleries of Sankt Peter in Sinzig.

The transformation of the wall system in Normandy involved a comparable radical negation of the laws of the "classical" Gothic as found, for example, in the nave of Rouen Cathedral, the collegiate church in Eu, and the cathedral in Coutances. While those buildings do not properly belong in a discussion of Romanesque architecture, it is important to note the persistence of various regional traditions, even if modifications are introduced. The Late Romanesque of many regions appears in another light when one realizes that, in England also, it was only around 1245–50 that the first buildings presupposing the High Gothic system—notably Westminster Abbey and York Minster—went up, and that this was more or less contemporary with developments in the Rhineland.

The Schelde Valley and Lorraine
Between such large and well-known artistic regions as Burgundy, the French crown lands, Normandy, and England to one side and the Upper and Lower Rhineland and the Meuse Valley to the other, there are areas that cannot

boast of so many edifices dating from the early period or that have not
preserved them, and so are not commonly thought of as truly autonomous
artistic centers, though in fact they deserve to be. Among them are Lorraine,
the area to the south around the upper course of the Meuse and the Moselle,
and the region to the north along the Schelde. Their intermediate position
between more important cultural regions is quite evident. However, in both
cases, whether these areas should be classified as either German or French
is not the essential question, since the stylistic quality of all artistic endeavors
between the Loire and the Rhine is homogeneous.

Along the Schelde, the most important edifice after the monumental
Early Romanesque collegiate church of Saint-Vincent in Soignies is the Late
Romanesque cathedral of Tournai. With its originally wooden-ceilinged
nave of around 1140, the latter is among the earliest churches to realize
the four-storied wall elevation with galleries and blind triforia. The trefoil
plan of its eastern portions follows the earlier examples of Sankt Marien im
Kapitol in Cologne, which dates from the middle of the eleventh century,
and of the early twelfth-century Saint-Lucien in Beauvais. Its four closely
juxtaposed square towers, gathered around a similarly square crossing
tower, constitute one of the unforgettable sights in all architecture and give
us an idea of what the architects of the Early Gothic cathedrals (and to some
extent even those of the High Gothic) really had in mind when they planned
and began (but in not a single case ever completed) the tower groups.

Furthermore, because of its transept apses, the cathedral of Tournai
played an important part in the development of the two-shelled wall. Its
solution takes an intermediate position between a two-storied ambulatory
(with side naves continuing around the choir) and a gallery hollowed out
of the wall. Other churches in Tournai, Ghent, Bruges, Mons, and Lissewege
(on the North Sea) carry this further in a Late Romanesque-Early Gothic
synthesis that, when compared with English and Norman architecture, has
an identity of its own.

In Lorraine, in the cathedral of Verdun-sur-Meuse, one can still detect
the double-choired flat-ceilinged basilica of the Early Romanesque behind
the Baroque modifications. Its new east choir with polygonal apse and
multi-storied accessory chambers, built in the middle of the twelfth century,
was unfortunately destroyed, though the east apse survives (its upper portion
was completed according to a modified plan and in a wholly Lower Rhenish
manner). Several related buildings in Trier are also still standing, among
them Sankt Simon: only a fragmentary ruined choir, its steep apse survives
with the dominating verticals of its buttress piers and crowning dwarf
gallery. Between the Vosges and the Meuse there is a whole group of related
apses with many isolated towers, yet no large-scale building is still standing.
The chief churches of the other seats of bishoprics, namely Metz and Toul,
were renovated in the Gothic style, while smaller buildings often show a
notable affinity with the hall-plan interior.

In speaking of Romanesque architecture in Lorraine, one cannot help

mentioning the architectonic decoration, which usually consists of frilled or cloudlike bands, omega-friezes, and the like. Its character is entirely personal, and its unforgettable richness and animation are virtually Baroque in feeling.

If we pause here to reflect for a moment, it strikes us that the territory between the Rhine and the Loire reveals an architectural conception seldom found elsewhere. Therefore, despite all regional and stylistic differentiations, these regions ought to be discussed in unison. In the following pages, we shall see that, quite in line with this, traits predominating there are absent elsewhere, or at least are of lesser significance.

THE LATE ROMANESQUE-EARLY GOTHIC "SIMPLE" VAULTED BASILICA AND THE FLAT-CEILINGED INTERIOR

Broad areas of Europe continued to prefer simpler types of construction to the elaborate and highly varied styles favored along the Lower Rhine, in the French crown lands, Burgundy, Normandy, the Anglo-Norman regions, and to some extent in the intervening areas as well. In the face of the extraordinary diversity of that more elaborate style and its deliberately restless, dynamic, and energetically progressive manner, this simpler one seems stubbornly conservative.

Here too we can single out certain geographical centers and the regions associated with them. They include the Upper Rhenish plain from Basel to Mainz, the entire German-speaking area east of the Rhine except for Westphalia, the Nordic countries, the stretch of land from the Baltic to the Adriatic that we think of as East-Central Europe, and even Lombardy and a good part of the Iberian Peninsula. All these regions possess an abundance of buildings, many of great artistic beauty and superb craftsmanship.

Flat-ceilinged churches were still being built in the thirteenth century, and they exemplify the conservative orientation even more than do the simpler types of vaulted churches. Isolated examples are found even in the areas between the Loire and the Rhine—not only in small humble country churches but also in edifices of considerable dignity, as in the flat-ceilinged basilicas of Saint-Georges in Haguenau (Alsace) and the former abbey church at Schwarzach (Baden). Even in a metropolis such as Cologne the trend is found far into the late twelfth century in Sankt Cäcilien and Sankt Pantaleon.

In Italy, the conservative approach was the norm south of Emilia, and chiefly in Tuscany and Apulia. Vaulted buildings, especially those built by the Cistercians, are entirely alien there and, where found, are immediately recognizable as importations. Anyone who has visited San Galgano in Tuscany or San Martino al Cimino, Fossanova, and Casamari in Lazio cannot escape this impression. The cathedrals at Cefalù and Monreale in Sicily provide the most convincing proof of the role the flat-ceilinged basilica could

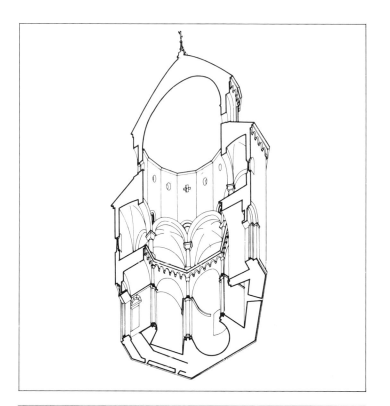

236. Arsago Seprio, baptistery, axonometric projection (from Reggiori, 1935)

237. Zamora, cathedral, interior looking across the central nave

still play in the late twelfth century and of what could still be achieved through the use of that form.

If we were proceeding by some rigorous system, this theme would require a long chapter of its own, due to the lengthy list of significant buildings to be cited. However, the relevant churches are discussed in these pages in other contexts, since only a few of them did in fact open up new possibilities. Essentially, the great majority of flat-ceilinged basilicas merely perpetuated the traditions of the High Romanesque, and it is only in such details as profiles and capitals or in the articulation of individual building parts (apses and towers, for example) that one can recognize when they originated. By and large, the High Romanesque can be said to continue into the thirteenth century in Italy.

The Upper Rhine

The entire architecture of the Upper Rhenish lowlands is overshadowed—figuratively speaking—by the great imperial cathedrals of Worms and Mainz. Both structures, the former entirely and the latter in large part, owe their present appearance to Late Romanesque forms. Even an older cathedral such as the one at Speyer betrays the influence of the Late Romanesque, albeit remotely, in the helm roofs of its towers. The vaulting system at Speyer, however (created around 1100), exerted its own influence for almost one and a half centuries. Thus, the simpler type of the bound system continued to be used in the large constructions of the late twelfth and early thirteenth centuries: the cathedral and the churches of Sankt Martin and Sankt Andreas in Worms; the Cistercian abbey churches at Eusserthal and Otterberg and the former Premonstratensian abbey church at Enkenbach, all in the Palatinate; the former abbey church at Fritzlar in Hesse; Saint-Léger at Guebwiller in Upper Alsace and the former Benedictine abbey churches at Altorf and Neuwiller-lès-Saverne in Lower Alsace; and the minster in Breisach in South Baden. The powerful rhythm of the simple bound system was well suited to its aim of achieving an imposing form and a weighty monumentality. For this reason, we need not look here for what we find so easily in the Lower Rhineland—elegant relaxation in forms and such embellishments as three or four stories in the central-nave wall and inner passageways opening up the apse wall—but instead for a throughgoing massiveness and severity that are further emphasized by the material used: the splendid sandstone (usually red) of the nearby mountains. Here too, dressed-stone construction was brought to extraordinary perfection. The minster at Basel represents a certain exception in that it is the only church on the Upper Rhine to have galleries; the minster at Freiburg-im Breisgau, which should have followed this plan, had to wait until the High Gothic period for the erection of its nave. In contrast to the art of Cologne and the Lower Rhine, based on a wealth of forms and at times a playful lightness, all these Upper Rhenish churches preserve the ponderous weight characteristic of Rosheim (or even accentu-

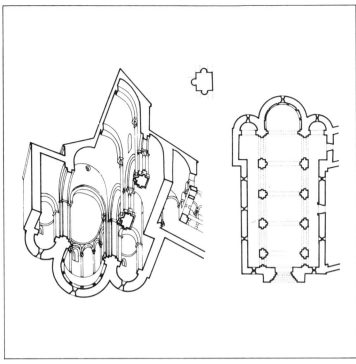

238. *Santa María de Vilabertrán, collegiate church and cloister, axonometric projection and plan (from Palol and Hirmer, 1966)*

239. *Salamanca, Catedral vieja, exterior of the apses with the lantern dome known as the Torre del Gallo to the right*

ate it, as at Otterberg). Their piers and walls are almost greater in volume than the space in the side nave or the opening of the nave arcades.

If Upper Rhenish architecture reveals a conservative attitude by maintaining the bound vaulting system of the nave until around the middle of the thirteenth century, it often shows the same attitude by persisting in the double-choir plan, as at Worms and Mainz. It is in the choirs, however, that it displays a wealth of impressive inventions. The two choirs of the cathedral at Worms create an unforgettable impression. The imposing exterior structure at the east choir, with its flat straight wall and gable locked between plump round turrets, follows a transept crowned by an octagonal tower. This is an excellent illustration of the way the mature Romanesque contrast of pure cubes is heightened by the plastic articulation of framed fields and by colonnaded galleries. As for the slender tower-like polygon of the west choir, both inside and out its horizontals are broken up and staggered to create a restless movement that can be interpreted as the translation of a spiritually agitated era into architectural form. Rudolf Kautzsch has written an absorbing analysis of this building.

Unfortunately, because of alterations and partial demolition, we can appreciate two other significant interiors only through hypothetical reconstructions: the choirs of the minster at Basel and the onetime Cistercian church at Otterberg. Both modified the plan of choir-plus-ambulatory in a unique manner, though each in its own way. In Basel the crypt, ambulatory, apse, and surrounding gallery made up four stories staggered in relation to each other and opening in quite different fashions so as to create a fantastic spatial sequence, though this can be deduced now only with difficulty because of the Late Gothic alterations. In Otterberg the polygonal apse, covered with a vault in the form of a cross section of a sphere, was set into a ring of rectangular chapels that made up a thick-walled rectangle below and formed an ambulatory through narrow passages.

The polygonal form of the apse was finally uniquely transformed in the trefoil plan of the west choir of Mainz Cathedral, where there are heavy staggered buttressing piers, a dwarf gallery recalling those in the Lower Rhine area, and a huge octagonal tower over the crossing. If one is tempted to speak of a Late Romanesque "Baroque" here, this is more than a rhetorical flourish: the Baroque upper parts and crowns that Franz Ignaz Neumann added after 1767 justify that expression

In the cathedrals at Worms and Mainz, but also in the smaller polygonal choir of the collegiate church in Pfaffen-Schwabenheim near Mainz and that of the church in Pfaffenheim in Upper Alsace, the specifically Upper Rhenish character of this art becomes clear, as it does also in the former Benedictine abbey churches at Sponheim and Offenbach-am-Glan and in the Marienkirche at Gelnhausen (Hesse), this style shows its capacity to adapt to its own purposes elements of the Burgundian Early Gothic as well as of the Lower Rhenish Late Romanesque, and this is evident too in the Cistercian refectory surviving at Schönau near Heidelberg.

A conservative perpetuation of earlier architectural conceptions is displayed especially in certain flat-ceilinged basilicas that, to a lesser extent than on the Lower Rhine, took on Late Romanesque characteristics. These include the Cistercian abbey church at Maulbronn in North Württemberg (less famed for its church than for its well-preserved ensemble of monastic buildings), Saint-Georges at Haguenau in Lower Alsace, and the Benedictine abbey church at Schwarzach in Baden, the latter being one of the rare brick buildings on the Upper Rhine and recently the object of a very successful restoration in which, among other things, its original color was revived.

After the cathedrals already mentioned, the minster at Strasbourg also underwent rebuilding in the Late Romanesque style. As usual, this began in the east portions with the transformation of the Early Romanesque apse. In the transept, the huge open space of its flat-ceilinged Ottonian predecessor was preserved, but for its vaulting a solution of typical Late Romanesque fantasy was devised: four high slender pillars were inserted into it, and each crossarm was covered with four cross-rib vaults of the same height. The result was an entirely unconventional two-naved transept-hall fully in accord with the double-portal plan (with the famous sculptures) as well as with the so-called Angels' Pillar adorned with statues in three tiers. Furthermore, its contrapuntally rotating organization urges the visitor to experience the interior in terms of its spatiality. Here, as in the minster at Freiburg, from the west crossing piers one can read what the Late Romanesque plan of the nave was before it was replaced with a High Gothic plan.

Northern Italy

In the late twelfth century, vaulting became common in northern Italy. There, as north of the Alps, it was very often still associated with the classical formula of the bound system. Brick was used most, and its vigorous red color went well with the massiveness of the piers and articulation and with the taste for broad planar surfaces, seen above all in the large screenlike façades typical of this region. While engaged supports, ribs, pointed arches, and sexpartite vaults were by no means rare here in the thirteenth century, they never produced the kind of autonomously dynamic articulated structure with which those elements were associated in northern France. The east ends of churches were built mostly on a simple spatial plan, though regulation crossarms with isolated crossings became more frequent, especially in churches built by the Cistercians—who, in fact, were responsible for most of the new and larger undertakings aside from cathedrals. Once again, it is characteristic that in not a single case were their churches built according to the Burgundian formula of southern French character, with a barrel-vaulted aisleless hall having rows of chapels as in Fontenay. Instead, the design of the vaulted basilica with bound system, traditional in this region, remained in force. The assumption by H. Hahn and R. Wagner-Rieger that

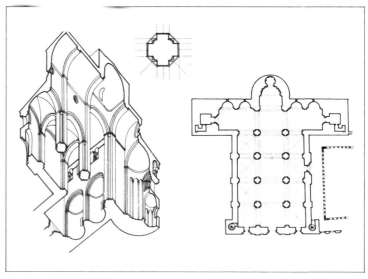

some of these churches were begun on the pattern of Fontenay is not strictly verifiable, though it cannot be rejected categorically. Perhaps its most likely evidence is in the abbey church of Staffarda in Piedmont.

The Cistercian ban on towers, continued subsequently by the mendicant orders, was quite in accord with the general Italian tendency to conceive the body of the church without such appendages and to erect alongside the church an entirely separate and isolated bell tower. However, this did not apply to choir and crossing towers, examples of which we have already noted in Milan and Pavia. The Cistercian abbey church at Chiaravalle Milanese has a high and conspicuous multistoried octagonal crossing tower, and in the cathedral of Piacenza the crossing tower opens into the interior like a huge cupola.

Chiaravalle Milanese, no doubt the best known of the Late Romanesque Cistercian churches in northern Italy, has powerful, thick, squat round pillars. The round-arched arcades are grouped into pairs by the pier shafts and central-nave vaults, the bay walls are broad and stratified, the interior heavy and full.

Noteworthy too are the abbey churches at Staffarda and Rivolta Scrivia in Piedmont and Chiaravalle della Colomba in Emilia. Another Lombard abbey church, Morimondo, dispenses with the bound system in favor of a simple non-rhythmic succession of bays with transverse rectangular vaults. However, the so-called Gothic travée has nothing more than the "system" in common with the authentic Gothic. Piers, walls, and vaults continue to convey a predominant impression of mass. Here, as in Germany, anyone who investigates such buildings in terms of their reception of the new Gothic style inevitably comes up with a negative answer, which then makes the building itself seem of less value. To do justice to this art, one must view the persistence of certain stylistic aspects as the basis for everything else. These churches must be interpreted in terms of the late phase of the Romanesque, not as Gothic. This fact still holds true even for Sant'Andrea in Vercelli, where the pointed arch prevails, the interior becomes narrower, and the members thinner, but where the unarticulated wall between central-nave arcades and clerestory, the continuous dwarf gallery, and the screen-façade are all such decidedly retardataire features that—as in the case of many buildings north of the Alps—one is inclined to think of it more as a direct transition from the Late Romanesque to the peripheral local idiom of the *Sondergothik* than as a reduced version of the fully developed Gothic style of the French cathedrals.

While these buildings constitute a norm or at least something very like a basic type, a few special achievements stand out that place Lombardy in the foremost rank of the European Late Romanesque.

The cathedral of Piacenza is in many respects indebted to its Lombard predecessors, and its west screen-façade is among the most important examples of the type. The nave and choir modify the bound system by introducing sexpartite vaults together with their appropriate type of

244. Goslar, church of the former
Cistercian nunnery of Neuwerk,
exterior from the southeast

245. Goslar, church of the former
Cistercian nunnery of Neuwerk,
interior looking east

supporting shafts. Innovations consist of the high side naves and the
powerful round pillars (which almost remind one of those in Gloucester
Cathedral). Only a few of the latter have engaged supporting shafts, and
only one pair of pillars, those east of what can be called the crossing, have
four of them in the standard arrangement. The powerful cylinders of the
pillars and the high arcades are highly effective and make the interior almost
resemble a hall church. Triple-arched low galleries and simple clerestory
windows break up the expanse of the upper half of the central-nave walls.
In the next to last double bay there is no vault over the central nave: instead,
we find the opening of the huge tower that begins with three superimposed
and graduated drums and ends as an octagon. In this double bay and in the
half-bay immediately to the west of it, the galleries are lacking and the
central-nave arcades rise higher and open into a transept that, quite uniquely,
is conceived on the hall plan. It has three naves and three bays and at both
the north and south ends is closed off by three apses of staggered height.
Each crossarm constitutes a huge hall of two times three bays with
freestanding pillars but does not attain the height of the central nave, ending
instead just below its windows. As in the cathedral of Pisa, the central nave
here runs through under the high tower and the crossarms have a certain
degree of autonomy. By displacement in the ground plan—three transept
bays as against two crossing bays—as well as in the elevation, an interplay
of spatial areas results, disclosing its uniqueness at the point where the
basilical nave matches up with the hall-form crossarms. Words can only
suggest the effect at Piacenza, just as that of the equally unconventional
hall-transept of Strasbourg Cathedral cannot be communicated in either
words or pictures: on the exterior, the vast design was never completed,
and must be imagined from assembling and completing its various
components.

If in Piacenza the harmony of basilical nave, hall-transept, and high
crossing tower is elevated to an extraordinary and complex level, in the
cathedral of Casale Monferrato in Piedmont we find a narthex of even more
surprising novelty. The main body of the church, as we see it today, is a
hall with five naves staggered in height and with rows of chapels on the
long sides. The narrow naves and the close juxtaposition of the piers make
it difficult to appreciate fully the gloomy hall. This is further complicated
by the fact that a restoration unified all the elements and so makes it unclear
now what the original architecture is and what was added in the nineteenth
century. What is unique, however, is the narthex stretching across the entire
width of the five-naved cathedral: seen from outside, it acts as a great
screen-façade between two slender towers. Inside, it is a huge room, some
sixty-five feet wide, under a single vault and surrounded on three sides by
two-storied accessory areas. The lateral naves on the long sides are high,
but still leave room for an upper story with windows, and there are rows
of chapels with gallery-like passageways above them. On the west side, on
the back of the façade wall, these galleries are carried over as an insertion

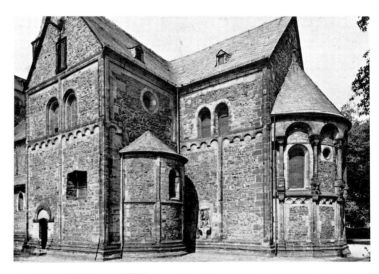

into the main room so that beneath them there is a low narthex and above a tribune that is fully open.

The main room itself is almost square in ground plan and is equivalent to three times three bays of the nave. However, it is vaulted without any intermediary supports and in a truly unique manner. Paired band-arches stretch the entire great span from east to west and from north to south, intersecting at right angles. Over them rise thin walls liked in part by barrel vaults, in part by cross-ribbed vaults. Thus, there is a higher vaulted zone above the grid of parallel ribs. The whole scheme recalls Islamic star-ribbed vaults and may be remotely inspired by them, but the application of vaults of this type to such a high and broad room, hemmed in by adjoining rooms, creates a highly fanciful impression. Here the ancient architectural idea of the westwork lives again in a manner that in many respects recalls the Rhenish and Mosan west choir halls but that is, in fact, unique. Something related is found in Gravedona in Lombardy, where the bell tower projects from the center of the west front and incorporates the portal.

The third building that can be considered a special achievement of the Lombard Late Romanesque is the baptistery of Parma in Emilia. Its octagonal mass, set diagonally across the piazza from the cathedral façade, resembles a steep tower with its six stories girdled by colonnaded galleries with passageways. Considering the technical means available at the time, this was the greatest height to which it was possible to carry a double-shelled wall. Actually, it is three-shelled, since inside also there are several superimposed passageways set in front of the thin wall; this facilitates the transition from the exterior octagon to the interior sixteen-sided polygon. Sixteen extremely slender engaged columns lead to the same number of ribs in the pointed-arched cupola. Famous for its sculpture and portals by Benedetto Antelami, the baptistery at Parma deserves equal praise as a brilliant technical-architectonic feat, though the technical bravura does surpass its architectonic and formal merits (unlike Sankt Gereon in Cologne, where the latter take precedence). A look back to the baptistery in Florence reveals where its roots lie, but also the thoroughgoing opposition between the styles of Lombardy and Tuscany. Another precursor of the remarkable building in Parma may have been the baptistery of Cremona, built some two hundred years earlier.

The overall picture of Late Romanesque architecture in northern Italy would hardly be complete if we did not take into account phenomena somewhat peripheral to the main developments. Beyond the Apennines, in Genoa, architecture was more strongly oriented toward Tuscan examples. Indeed, that city's cathedral (wooden-ceilinged), galleried, and basilical in form) recalls its counterpart in Pisa. In terms of both geography and art history, Liguria is in fact more open to the west (Provence) than to the north (the Po Valley). In earlier chapters, we found clear reminiscences of northern architecture in the Alpine valleys of Italia, notably at Aosta and Ivrea, and we see something similar in this later period—at the cathedral

248. Jerichow, Premonstratensian
abbey church, drawing of the interior
showing elevated choir and crypt (from
Sesselberg, 1897)

249. Wechselburg, church of the
former Augustinian priory, plans of
the stages of building of the east end,
projection of the east end (from Küas
and Krause, 1968)

of Trent, for instance, and in several Romanesque churches in Susa. In Piedmont, there is even an entire group of smaller Late Romanesque churches in hall form (a special case that we shall have occasion to mention again later), and throughout northern Italy there are many interesting small central-plan buildings: typical, if little-known, examples are at Mariano Comense, Agrate Conturbia, and Arsago Seprio.

Spain and Portugal

What we observed in connection with High Romanesque architecture in the Iberian Peninsula repeated itself in this later stylistic phase. The borders between Christian lands and the realm of the Almohades were pushed farther south—as far as the Guadiana River at the start of the thirteenth century. The cities of Tarragona, Saragossa, and Coimbra, liberated for decades, then entered into Romanesque architectural history, and other cities (Cuenca, Toledo, Mérida, and later Seville) were won back that were to play a role in the High Gothic.

Purely in terms of architectural history, the same phenomenon recurred: new types of buildings appeared having no connection with the Catalan tradition, even if they arose in that region. Among them were the cathedral of Tarragona, begun in 1171; that of Lérida, begun in 1203; and, in Huesca, the church of San Pedro el Viejo. These can be grouped with the cathedral of Ciudad Rodrigo in the province of Salamanca and with three churches in closely neighboring towns: the old cathedral of Salamanca, begun in 1152; the cathedral of Zamora, built between 1151 and 1174; the collegiate church at Toro, begun in 1160; and the cathedral of Tudela, built between 1194 and 1234. Because all of these are cruciform basilicas with cross-ribbed vaulting, French scholars tend to claim them as Early Gothic works, whereas the Spaniards (quite rightly, to my mind) emphasize their Late Romanesque traits. The forms are extremely powerful and heavy. Huge drum- or cross-shaped bases support thickset and squat compound piers with engaged shafts of various thicknesses. With large pointed arcades opening widely between the lateral and central naves, there is something almost like a hall-plan linkage of the separate spaces. The splendid capitals with Late Romanesque foliage and figures are full of plastic energy. Above the arcades, which reveal a considerable thickness of wall, the central-nave and side-nave walls are unarticulated and flat, pierced only by pointed-arched windows. The cross-arches, ribs, and keystones are all as appropriately robust as one would expect. If one clings to the traditional definition of the Gothic, the pointed arches and ribbed vaults can be taken as significant elements of that style. However, if one thinks of the decisive modifications in the so-called Early Gothic churches of the Ile-de-France with their four-storied wall elevation, and later in the High Gothic cathedrals having a three-storied elevation, a large three-naved transept, a uniform wall system in all parts of the building, and, above all, a diaphanous wall structure, then the Spanish churches built between 1150 and 1220 appear almost as pronouncedly Late

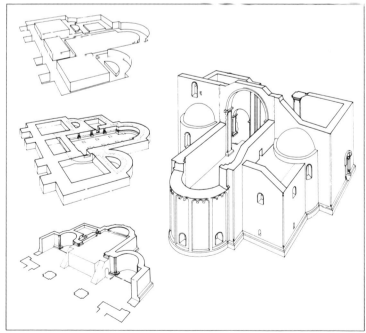

Romanesque in style as the cathedrals of Worms, Bamberg, and Naumburg.

Connected with this group, though in part aberrant, are many other churches in northern and central Spain, among them the cathedral of Orense in Galicia and the church of Santiago del Burgo at Zamora in León with its cross-groined vaulting, but also a few of the Cistercian foundations upon which churches were built or renovated in the late twelfth and early thirteenth centuries—those, for example, in Fitero and La Oliva (both in Navarre), Valdediós in Asturias, and Veruela in Aragon.

It is fully consistent with this approach that the splendid façade of the south arm of the transept of Zamora Cathedral, the so-called Puerta del Obispo, should be entirely composed of stories and stratified walls and have a wealth of lively details, but especially that the crossings in the above-mentioned churches at Salamanca, Zamora, and Toro are crowned by the famous round cupola towers with their profusion of plastic forms. Wealth of imagination, not a rigorously executed system, is what counts here. These crossing towers in Salamanca, especially the Torre del Gallo of the old cathedral, are high-points of the Late Romanesque in western Europe and recall—though with the differences to be expected from their geographical remoteness—the famous Hohenstaufen creations in Cologne and the Rhineland. The capitulary hall in the cathedral of Plasencia in Estremadura should be mentioned in connection with these crossing towers.

In all of French architecture there is only one small group of buildings—including the Burgundian Cistercian church at Pontigny and a few smaller buildings in related systems—that could possibly be described as akin to these Spanish churches. However, they are comparable in neither their overall plan nor in the character of their architecture (which is entirely lacking in plastic weight), but only in a certain similarity of the wall system. For this reason, the Spanish buildings must be deemed a special group and even a special Late Romanesque achievement.

The above-mentioned churches constitute the most important and most characteristic group in northern Spain. Their architectural system is related to that of Pontigny in principle, but is decidedly different in weight and volume, and in this respect is unlike everything we know in northern France. The relationships pointed out by scholars such as E. Lambert apply above all to isolated forms, though one exception should not be ignored: the choir of Ávila Cathedral anticipates that of Vézelay. On the exterior, however, the choir ambulatory with its ring of chapels is assimilated into a single round block of wall that protrudes like a bastion from the city wall. This was done for defensive purposes, but nonetheless reveals a desire for closed mass form like that we observed in the group discussed above.

Deserving of special mention is the much-visited abbey church of Santes Creus in the vicinity of Tarragona, which is striking because of its crude square pillars and powerful broad cross-arches between the bays. The same system was adopted in the cathedrals of Cuenca and Sigüenza in Old Castile and in the monastery church of Santa María de Huerta in Old Castile, but

251. Bamberg, cathedral, exterior,
the east end with the apse of St.
George's choir

252. Prague, Svatý Jan, plan and
reconstruction of the exterior of the
west apse (from Mencl, 1948)

with more progressive forms that led to an outright Gothic style. San Isidoro
in León and San Vicente in Ávila were given cross-ribbed vaults not initially
provided for in the plan of their central naves.

In addition to the vaulted basilicas with cross-ribbed vaulting there is
another type more rooted in tradition. Thus, the early Catalan barrel-vaulted
hall churches have successors in the Late Romanesque—at Vilabertrán and
Besalú, for example—though in these the later style asserts itself only in
details, while the general plan of the interior differs little from that of its
predecessors. The Romanesque hall church is generally seen in too limited
a context, as typical of south western France. The fact is, as we have stressed,
that the plan is important in all of southern France and, during the High
Romanesque phase, south of the Pyrenees as well. This is also the case in
the Late Romanesque period, in which we again find both the barrel-vaulted
hall church high articulated piers and the galleried hall of the type seen at
Santiago de Compostela. Among the former we may mention the collegiate
church at La Coruña and the abbey church of Santa María del Cambre, both
in Galicia, and among the latter the cathedral of Coimbra in Portugal. The
same holds true for the barrel-vaulted churches with basilical upper stories
having windows, though these are often on only one side. The most
important church of this sort on Spanish soil is the cathedral of Seo de Urgel,
which has a west screen façade flanked by towers (completed in modern
times) and a huge apse with dwarf gallery.

A few Cistercian churches also belong to the tradition of south-western
European barrel-vaulted churches, notably those at Meira and Armenteira
in Galicia, Poblet in Catalonia, and Moreruela in León. The Benedictine
abbey church at Oya in Galicia is the only building to follow the plan of
Fontenay: it is single-naved interior lined with chapels.

As elsewhere during the heyday of the Late Romanesque, in Spain too
we find broad range of small churches, from cross-vaulted and barrel-vaulted
aisleless types to wooden-ceilinged buildings. Among the latter, San Juan
de Duero, a church of the Knights of St. John in Soria (Old Castile), is
especially remarkable: to either side of the entrance to its barrel-vaulted
choir (already much narrower than the broad nave) there is a kind of
baldachin, a stone vault on pillars, that gives a striking architectonic emphasis
to the side altar it surmounts. The splendid cloister, now roofless, is famed
for its stilted intertwining arches of decidedly Islamic appearance. Elaborately developed apses, either polygonal or round and with blind arcades above
columns, are frequent, and the most pretentious of them—at Cervatos in
the province of Santander and Vallejo de Mena and San Vincentejo in that
of Burgos—are rather like those in Aquitaine.

In Spain too it is characteristic of the Late Romanesque that there are
buildings of highly individual character that do not fit into the established
types. Thus, the simple octagonal central-plan church of the Santo Sepulcro
at Torres del Río in Navarre diverges from what one might expect by its
star vault with flat band ribbing, and in the same region San Miguel at Estella

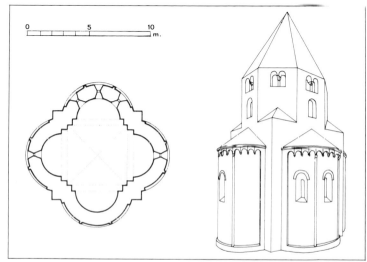

253. Ellwangen, Sankt Veit, exterior
from the southeast
254. Zwettl, Cistercian abbey,
interior of the chapter house

has an exterior ambulatory. If, more often than north of the Pyrenees, we encounter forms here that immediately suggest their Islamic origins, we nevertheless cannot help but wonder why there are not many more of them and in many more places. Horseshoe arches, scalloped arches, and star-ribbed vaults are, in fact, almost the only forms in which the Islamic influence appears, and the way they are integrated with more usual forms can be seen in Eunate and San Juan de las Abadesas.

The task of sorting out the rich treasure of historical monuments in Spain according to regions has so far scarcely been attempted. As in many other countries, it has been considered enough to connect obvious groupings with areas defined by the history of a territory, and in these few pages we simply cannot make up for such superficial treatment.

East of the Rhine

With the exception of Westphalia and Friesland, the lands east of the Rhine present a uniform picture by and large. Throughout the entire century of Hohenstaufen rule their architecture remained conservative. Changes based on specific Late Romanesque forms took shape only on their periphery, and then chiefly in the smaller individual forms. The vaulted basilica of the bound system and sometimes also the flat-ceilinged basilica continued in use for cathedrals and for the larger abbey and collegiate churches.

The standard cruciform plan with isolated crossing remained the rule almost everywhere. West fronts with spacious interiors, which played so great a role along the Rhine, were rare east of it. Often, however, there were twin-towered façades and west transepts, mostly without any increased emphasis on the development of the interior. Crossing towers were virtually absent, though occasionally there were two flanking turrets to the east; together with the west towers, these formed an elaborate complex of towers, as in Bamberg and Naumburg. Inside, there was almost always the simple form of basilica, without galleries and triforia. Where galleries or similar structures did exist—as can be seen at Ribe in Denmark, Freyburg-an-der-Unstrut in Thuringia, and in the church of Sankt Sebald at Nuremberg—there is reason to suspect (and not on these grounds alone) Rhenish connections. Simple interior plans, cubic masses on the exterior, strong walls, and energetic articulation—these dominate the picture. When it comes to details, however, there is again a great diversity that makes possible the recognition of regional characteristics (at least in embryonic form), though here too we can only single out the most significant general characteristics. For lack of space, it is not possible to do justice to the multiplicity of relevant buildings, nor to do more than suggest the complex relationships involved among them.

A notable phenomenon east of the Rhine is the ambivalent attitude toward vaulting. This seems as yet largely unrecognized by scholars and accounts for a certain tentativeness in their judgments. It can be said that, outside of Wespthalia where it was encouraged, the idea of vaulting the main

255. Murrhardt, Walterichskapelle
adjoining the city church, exterior
from the east

areas of churches—including the central nave—was considered, though without recognizing the consequences. Thus here, more than anywhere in the West, one perceives a vacillation in the builders' intentions. This has recently been conclusively demonstrated by D. von Winterfeld with regard to Bamberg Cathedral, and many parallel examples can be singled out. Main piers with engaged shafts and accessory piers were built to support vaulting in the bound system. In the uppermost story, however, windows were inserted where shafts and vaulting allowed no place for them. Did this indicate (as it still does today) that the parties involved—patron and architect—did not see eye to eye on what should be done? This notion is difficult to reconcile with the usual manner in which a church was built. Nonetheless, the evidence at Bamberg is convincing, and can be explained by the desire to preserve intact in the new building major features of the pre-existing Early Romanesque cathedral dating back to Emperor Henry II. However, in many other buildings where a similar uncertainty persists in matters of vaulting, no such concrete evidence has been forthcoming.

A genuine Late Romanesque profusion and enrichment of forms is rare in this entire region. Isolated exceptions are found in the cathedral of Bremen and in the former Cistercian nunnery church (the Neuwerk) in Goslar.

Northern Germany and Northern Europe

Around the middle of the twelfth century, the process that in Spain, southern Italy, and Scandinavia had already brought about the spread of Western power and its cultural manifestations (notably Christian thought and Romanesque art) now reached the northeastern borders of the Empire. As was the case with the Arabs and their Islamic faith and the Byzantines' loyalty to the Eastern Church, here too the neighboring peoples and their pagan beliefs were in part suppressed, in part assimilated. It was not only a matter of military conquest, however: in equal measure, and concurrently, the new forms were at least to some extent introduced through peace treaties in the course of the occupation and settlement of these territories. This process, which spanned several centuries and only much later led to secure national links, was abetted by economic ties and the establishment of cities. The result was abetted by economic ties and the establishment of cities. The result was the incorporation of east-central Europe into the political and cultural orbit of the West as far as the Elbe, Oder, and Vistula rivers. Once this opening to the West had been accepted by Jutland, Scania, and the Baltic islands in the North and by Bohemia, Moravia, Hungary, and Slovenia in the South, they were joined by the lands between the Elbe and the Saale rivers in one direction, by Little Poland and Great Poland in the other. Until well into the twelfth century, the two latter regions remained devoid of political unions and of the impact of Christianity.

Beginning with the middle of the twelfth century, a considerable number of Romanesque churches were built in a zone east of the Elbe—particularly

256. Třebíč, abbey church of Svatý
Prokop, interior looking west
257. Třebíč, abbey church of Svatý
Prokop, the crypt

in the Altmark and western Brandenburg, but also farther south in Lausitz and farther north along the Baltic as far as the mouth of the Oder River. Several waves of building activity can be identified here. The earliest large construction was the church of the Premonstratensian monastery at Jerichow on the Elbe, a flat-ceilinged basilica of great beauty and great precision in its treatment of forms, and one that is outstandingly well preserved. A two-aisled crypt fills the space under the square choir and apse and extends out beneath the isolated crossing. The barrel-vaulted auxiliary choirs open onto the square crossarms. In the west two high square towers rise in front of the side naves, while a third and lower tower stands somewhat to the fore. Thus, we have here a twin-towered façade combined with a three-towered west front. The entire building is constructed of glowing red brick, a new material handled here with fully mature technique. The question arises whether both the idea of using brick and the architectural forms themselves may have come from churches in Lombardy. Many scholars consider this to be the case, though others claim indigenous origins for building in brick. If the matter is not considered too rigidly, it must be conceded that entirely different architectonic forms in brick were developed in a number of regions at various times, specifically in Languedoc, the Bavarian highlands, Flanders, the Netherlands, and the Lower Rhine. A. Kamphausen has pointed out preconditions that are often overlooked: bricks removed from Roman ruins were habitually re-used as raw material by builders west and south of the old Roman fortified frontiers (called the Limes). It was a long established custom to use brick as an accessory reinforcing material in fortresses, city walls, and foundations. To be fully exploited it had only to be utilized as an independent material, one that could be left visible from the outside. Rhenish tufa (a porous rock) was hewn into bricklike shape and exported to considerable distances, Denmark for one.

Finally, Jerichow has little that is Lombard in its spatial plan. Neither the regulation cross-form of its eastern portion nor the firmly incorporated and conspicuous towers of the group on the west are characteristic there. Only the crypt opening on the central nave can be considered related, but even that feature could be found north of the Alps—in the first construction at Speyer, for instance. At the same time as Jerichow, or soon after, large flat-ceilinged basilicas were built at Havelberg and Brandenburg. Both were subsequently altered by Gothic vaults and additions.

In the north of Germany and Europe as a whole, Late Romanesque vaulted construction appeared in astonishingly mature form by the late twelfth century. The bound system, first introduced in Speyer and Mainz around 1100, had spread along the entire Rhine in its fully developed Romanesque form by around the middle of the twelfth century, but scarcely anywhere east of the Rhineland did it have sophisticated successors. Even as late as around 1170, the cathedral of Braunschweig was built in an old-fashioned manner, due to the native preference of Saxon architects for vaults without cross-ribs. On the other hand, churches being built at that

time east of the Rhine were visibly indebted to Rhenish forms. The most important of these are at Lehnin, thirty-odd miles east of Jerichow between Brandenburg and Berlin, at Ratzeburg, and at Lübeck, with smaller ones in the Altmark at Diesdorf and Arendsee and in Holstein at Altenkrempe and Bad Segeberg.

In Lehnin a Cistercian abbey was founded around 1180, and it took almost a century before it could be consecrated (in 1262), yet the effect of such a protracted building period can be observed only in certain details. The system was in fact preserved virtually without alterations. The clear, bold, and methodical organization of the bound-system vaulting is rendered exceptionally effective here by the contrast between the red bricks and the light plaster surfaces. If there are any Cistercian traits it may be the lack of towers and— a lesser factor—the way the engaged shafts in the central nave begin not at floor level but at some place above the bracket consoles. Not even the transept chapels maintain the arrangement of cells in rows that is so characteristic elsewhere: each is conceived instead as a large chamber with its own central supports. The apse with its three-storied blind articulation recalls those on the Lower Rhine. The Cistercian churches at Doberlug (old name Dobrilugk) and Zinna are the most important Romanesque vaulted buildings of the thirteenth century in the Mark Brandenburg (East Germany). The cathedral of Ratzeburg, on an island in the lake of the same name, is somewhat simpler, and that of Lübeck is much altered by Gothic rebuilding.

In Denmark, the cathedral erected in the middle of the twelfth century at Viborg in Jutland is a truly significant example of the flat-ceilinged basilica with piers, and there is another with an elaborately developed east end at Ringsted on the island of Zealand. Among vaulted basilicas should be mentioned the Cistercian church at Sorø and the somewhat later abbey at Løgum. In Ribe the spacious rib-vaulted galleried basilica with towers and articulated apse gives one the illusion of being transplanted to the Lower Rhineland, so closely is it related to the church in Roermond.

Like east-central Europe, the North too had a noteworthy preference for the central plan. Its round churches, often vaulted over four interpolated supports, are well known. There are no less than four on the island of Bornholm in the Baltic. The monumental church at Kalundborg on Zealand recalls the destroyed church on the Harlungerberg near Brandenburg. Four apses are attached to the Greek cross of the main interior, and an octagonal tower emphasizes the middle. Together with four corner turrets, they make a truly impressive ensemble that is densely concentrated in a manner matched only by Tournai Cathedral.

The cathedral at Roskilde near Copehagen was erected as a royal burial place and therefore conceived with appropriate sumptuousness. In its plan involving choir ambulatory and gallery, four-storied wall elevation, and a group of towers, it is connected with the great churches of the Early Gothic in the French crown lands, though its true nature is that of a Late

Romanesque massive construction that was simplified in the nave and covered with Gothic vaults. Here too we find the typical difficulties in relation to vaulting.

The entire northern German plain up to the North Sea and the Baltic, the Jutland Peninsula and the Danish islands, and southern and central Sweden all have, along with cathedrals and abbey churches, innumerable and often well-preserved smaller churches whose study is both rewarding and fascinating. In Norway they are fewer in number. While on the Continental mainland and along the Baltic the links to northern Germany are apparent, on the Norwegian coasts one can at times perceive Anglo-Norman connections, as in the transept of Trondheim Cathedral.

Central, Southern, and East-Central Europe

Comprised under this heading are the following present-day political divisions: Bavaria, the southern part of East Germany, the eastern half—Swabia—of the federal state of Baden-Württemberg, all of Austria, Poland, Czechoslovakia (created from the territories of Bohemia, Moravia, and Slovakia), and the western part of Hungary and Slovenia. Until the end of World War II, the largest part was a German region where German was spoken: Thuringia, Swabia, Bavaria, Austria, Pomerania, West Prussia, East Brandenburg, Silesia, and the Bohemian border regions. The core of Poland and Bohemia had always been essentially Polish or Czech.

In all these areas there were Late Romanesque buildings, though not in the same proportions. There were fewest along the middle stretches of the Oder River, the lower Warta River, and the Bohemian mountains bordering on the plateau, and east of the Vistula River there were practically none. For all these regions, what was said at the start of the preceding section concerning their distinctive traits is equally valid. This has virtually nothing to do with national or ethnic differences, past or present, even if that simple statement may offend the civic pride of the various interested parties. Nor—though it would yield intriguing results—can we go into too great detail here concerning the artistic-geographical diffusion of the various types and forms found in these regions. Suffice it to say that in these eastern zones also small single-naved churches exist in the hundreds all the way from the Baltic to the Adriatic. In the western Slavic territories there are a great many small cruciform central-plan buildings, especially in Slovenia and Bohemia; three are in Prague alone.

The simple flat-ceilinged basilica, usually with square pillars, is widely diffused, though many were vaulted over in Gothic or Baroque times. There are well-known examples at Maulbronn and Schwäbisch-Gmünd in Swabia; Wechselburg in Saxony; Sankt Jakob at Regensburg in Bavaria; Gurk, Seckau, and Sankt Paul in Lavanttal in Austria; Kruszwica in the Warta area of Poland; and Bélapátfalva in Hungary. It is noteworthy that only one such church has galleries, that at Kościelec in Poland. Most of these buildings are cross-shaped, and only a few have such peculiarities as the trefoil

arrangement of transept and apse found in Poland at Plock and Tum.

Alternating supports, though they do exist in Czerwińsk in Poland, are rare, as are columns. The example at Strzelno in Polish Pomerania has the unique distinction, found nowhere else, of having one of its columns carved with relief figures under blind arcades. In Swabia we find a group of churches with elaborate architectonic decoration; these have been specially designated as "ornamental churches."

Though they are the rule in Rhenish areas, Late Romanesque vaulted basilicas are rare east of the Rhine. The most famous large examples are the cathedrals at Bamberg and Naumburg, both of which are double-choired and vaulted in the bound system. By and large, that system made its way into the east only with the introduction of Late Romanesque ribbed vaulting, and the cross-groined vaults in Naumburg are exceptional. Moreover, the examples are not very numerous and consist principally of the most famous buildings from the decades around 1200: at Bronnbach in Franconia, Ellwangen in Swabia, Arnstadt in Thuringia, and, in the Bavarian population area, the Franziskanerkirche in Salzburg of later date. The easternmost examples are at Heiligenkreuz in Austria, Pannonhalma in Hungary, Kammin at the mouth of the Oder, Trebnitz in Silesia (like Pannonhalma, with sexpartite vaults), and Alba Iulia (Gyulafehérvár) in Romanian Transylvania. Along with these must be mentioned Třebíč in Czechoslovakian Moravia, a double-choired building with extremely odd vaulting (octagonal ribbed cupolas over the apse and long choir, cross-groined vaults with plaitwork ribbing over the central nave). An entirely isolated case is Viktring in Austria, which follows the interior and vaulting plan of Fontenay, with longitudinal barrel vaults in the main nave and transverse barrel vault in a sequence of chapels rather than side naves.

Besides the buildings that lay out the nave in the powerful rhythm of the bound system, there are a few with oblong transverse vaults in simple succession, in particular Sankt Sebald in Nuremberg, which has a kind of triforium, and Altenstadt bei Schongau in Upper Bavaria, as well as a few in Poland—Wachock for instance—and in Hungary, at Ják, though it was not vaulted until the nineteenth century, the ruined church at Zsámbek, and the abbey church at Bélapátfalva.

We have already referred to the round churches as a special category, and to these should be added the more elaborate central plan structures of the castle or fortress chapels at Landsberg near Halle (Saale), Freyburg-an-der-Unstrut, Nuremberg, Landshut, and Cheb in Czechoslovakia, as well as the Walterichskapelle in Murrhardt and such outstanding capitulary halls as those at Bronnbach and Zwettl.

A great number of more important and more interesting churches that play a role in art history are not included in this enumeration, among them some whose still intact Romanesque exteriors enclose a completely transformed interior: in Thuringia the collegiate church at Freyburg-an-der-Unstrut, in Franconia the Neumünster in Würzburg and the former Benedictine abbey church at Gross-Comburg, in Bohemia the abbey church at Doksany, in Hungary the one at Lébény. To these can be added almost all the Romanesque churches in the Bavarian and Swabian Alpine and pre-Alpine regions.

Late Romanesque and Regional Gothic

In our discussion of the Late Romanesque in the Upper Rhineland, Lombardy, Spain, and the lands east of the Rhine, we mentioned many churches often treated as early manifestations of the Gothic style, as was the case recently in R. Wagner-Rieger's illuminating book on the beginnings of the Gothic in Italy. While that approach may involve a significant art historical phenomenon, it often leaves one with the unsatisfying impression

262. Aulnay-de-Saintonge, Saint-
Pierre-de-la 'Tour, interior looking
northeast

263. Asnières, ruins of the abbey
church, drawing of the interior of the
east portion with vault and roof
structures exposed (from Mussat,
1963)

of not doing justice to the buildings in and for themselves. When it comes
to the implantation of individual forms or even to what can be called systems,
what is uniquely creative in this architecture gets overlooked. For this
reason, therefore, it is a matter of prime importance, in justifying this section,
to emphasize precisely those too-often ignored relationships.

Since the publication in 1914 of Kurt Gerstenberg's pathbreaking book
Die deutsche Sondergotik, it has come to be widely undertood that there is not
a single Gothic style typified by the northern French cathedrals, but instead
a considerable diversity of stylistic manifestations. Earlier research was still
by and large under the sway of a nationalistic approach to history and
regarded such varied forms as nationally conditioned transformations,
especially in Germany and Italy. Raymond Rey's *L'Art gothique du midi de
la France* (1928) aimed at a similar revaluation of the architecture of southern
France and Spain. The book's lesson was not, however, sufficiently heeded,
though more recent general studies on Gothic architecture have paid some
attention to this phenomenon: K. H. Clasen speaks of "southern Gothic,"
and P. Frankl and H. Jantzen point out the divergent aspects the style
assumed.

Despite this, the overwhelming impact of the northern French High
Gothic cathedrals has so intimidated almost all writers that they continue
to view southern French, Spanish, Italian, and even German Gothic of the
thirteenth and fourteenth centuries as more or less "reductions" of a "true"
style. The buildings of the mendicant orders (Franciscans and Dominicans),
in which many aspects of this so-called Special or Regional Gothic are
especially pronounced, have also been overshadowed.

If it seems out of place to discuss the Regional Gothic in a book on
Romanesque architecture, the justification is that the Late Romanesque itself
was often defined and treated as a transitional style in earlier studies, an
approach occasionally still found today.

We must keep in mind above all the "grammar" of the forms. The fact
is that in many regions it was the Late Romanesque itself that introduced
the ribbed vault, the pointed arch, the buttressing pier, and the flying
buttress, though admittedly in very simple forms. From time to time it also
made use of other elements considered Gothic, such as tracery windows (or
at least their embryonic forms), the crocketed goblet capital, the engaged
supporting shaft, the shaft ring, and so on. In the so-called Transitional Style,
however, these elements were not incorporated into a superordinate and
essentially structural context that could be considered innately Gothic, but
instead were utilized as embellishments and variations for an essentially Late
Romanesque system of continuing massiveness and solidity.

Basically, the Regional Gothic of the thirteenth century, and often that
of the fourteenth as well, had more in common with the simple stylistic forms
of the Late Romanesque than with the mature High Gothic of northern
France. It was by no means committed to such High Gothic traits as a
twin-towered west end, a three-naved transept, and a five-naved longitudinal

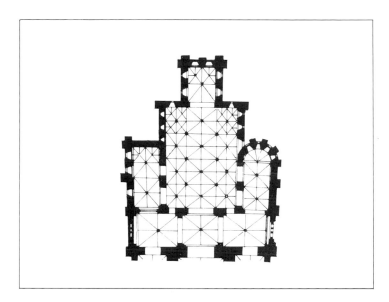

choir with ambulatory and wreath of chapels, nor to the three-storied elevation with genuine triforium and large tracery windows reaching quite low down, or even to that transformation of the wall and its relations to space and light defined by H. Jantzen as a "diaphanous structure." The Regional Gothic either uses wholly different plans for its interiors—the hall or the aisleless plan—or conceives the basilica form in a way that reveals a conception of the architectural structure other than that found in northern French cathedrals. In examples of the Regional Gothic, we generally find a simple transept with a single choir area or three apses at the most. There is also a simple west tower, but most significant are the large plain wall surfaces with small windows but without multi-storied elevations and without any predominance of the vertical elements—in short, quite simple and immediately apprehensible relationships. Very often there is neither a sculptured portal nor dark stained-glass windows. Because of such traits, the vaulted basilica of the Regional Gothic is entirely and directly related to the Late Romanesque and Early Gothic, simply bypassing the High Gothic of the northern French cathedrals. The stylistic transitions between the cathedral of Tarragona and that of Lérida, between the nave at Neiderzissen and that at Münstermaifeld in the Rhineland, between Sant'Andrea in Vercelli and San Francesco in Bologna, all seem fluid. The profiles are more sharply undercut, the horizontals become less prominent, the pointed arch is somewhat more accentuated, but the dominant trait remains the intact surfaces of the walls, and one is scarcely aware of any attempt to break them down, let alone dissolve them.

Thus, in many cases, Late Romanesque architecture simply evolves into the Regional Gothic without a break; when portions of a church are conceived in these separate styles, therefore, they usually connect up smoothly and without discrepancies. On the other hand, where northern French High Gothic churches incorporated older portions of existing buildings, as a rule there is a harsh contrast, as we see in Beauvais and Le Mans. This contrast is also evident in certain other churches that reveal close connections with the High Gothic, notably in Cambrai (destroyed), Tournai, Strasbourg, or even Bordeaux and Toulouse. There is a similar disparity between the choir of Magdeburg Cathedral with its four-storied elevation and the nave, which was added later and lacks the gallery and triforium zones. The Liebfrauenkirche in Trier and the Elisabethkirche in Marburg both have much in common with the Early Gothic style of Champagne, and in their interior dispositions they display characteristic variants with preferences for the hall and central plans, as scholars have long recognized.

HALL CHURCHES AND SINGLE-NAVED CHURCHES

In the Late Romanesque period, the antithesis between the basilica and the hall form continued to be a fundamental fact of architectural history. To understand what follows, the reader must refer to those other chapters where

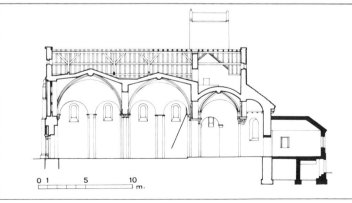

we discuss the earlier bases of the forms to be treated here, notably the hall-crypt and exterior crypt, the double-chapel, such typical monastery components as the multi-naved cloister, capitulary hall, refectory, and dormitory, and, finally, such central-plan churches as Santa Sofia in Benevento, where the chief emphasis is on ambulatories.

We have seen that the hall church made triumphal progress in southwestern Europe from the late tenth century on. Beginning in Catalonia (and Roussillon), the form took over in Languedoc and Aquitaine, and in the twelfth century prevailed throughout the entire region between the Duero and the Loire, including the Rhône Valley from Provence to Burgundy. In these regions it exhibited a number of variations, either with three parallel barrel vaults or with barrel vaults in the central nave and cross-vaults or quarter-barrels in the side naves; in isolated cases there were even cupolas (though transverse barrel vaults in the side naves were limited to the lower church at Tournus). Galleries in the side naves change the picture of the interior, though without decisively effacing the hall-form character, as in Auvergne (at Clermont-Ferrand, Orcival, and Issoire) and elsewhere.

The area in which the Romanesque hall church prevailed was penetrated also by other types: barrel-vaulted aisleless churches with cupolas in the Aquitaine in particular, barrel-vaulted basilicas especially in Provence and neighboring parts of the Languedoc. The hall form itself invaded regions favoring the basilica form: in Lombardy there are various examples, among others at Pavia and Rivolta d'Adda, and the famous Sant'Ambrogio in Milan, which is a galleried hall with ribbed vaulting. Along the middle Danube in the Upper Palatinate there is a scattered group of hall churches that soon abandoned the barrel vault for the cross-vault.

In Westphalia there are also numerous early efforts, including the chapel of Sankt Bartholomäus (1017) in Paderborn with its pendant cupolas on columns and, from the middle of the twelfth century, the two-naved chapel of Sankt Nikolaus in Soest and the central-plan chapel at Drüggelte. There too the ground-floor hall of the westwork—the so-called westwork crypt—was developed further, notably in Sankt Patroklus and Sankt Thomae in Soest. In the Meuse Valley, in present-day Belgium, there is an entirely isolated example in the flat-ceilinged pillared hall at Theux near Liège.

With few exceptions, the Early and High Romanesque hall church derives its character from the barrel vaulting over the central nave, and this is especially so in southwestern Europe. It was precisely this feature that was suddenly changed around 1150: the cross-ribbed vault replaced the barrel vault, and the naves were much more widely opened up to each other; because of the cross-ribs the bays were more emphasized than had ever been the case with the barrel-vault transverse springers. Viewed in terms of the Gothic, and specifically of the Late Gothic hall form, it was only then that the key traits of the hall character assumed their full significance: equal value was accorded to all orientations, whether west-to-east, north-to-south, or

268. *Loches, Saint-Ours, exterior from the north*

269. *Candes, Saint-Martin, interior looking northwest*

oblique; space itself assumed greater importance than the stone supports, ceiling, and walls; all portions of the interior became freely linked, affording a multiplicity of vistas and an interplay of overlappings and intersections.

The structural element, made conspicuous by the combination of articulated piers and ribbed vaults, becomes drastically reduced in the Late Romanesque-Early Gothic hall church as a consequence of the greater concavity of the vault and the increase in number of its ribs.

There is a group of important hall churches in Aquitaine. The cathedral of Poitiers and others like it have articulated piers, ribbed vaults, and a two-storied elevation, while smaller hall churches have cloister vaults on exceptionally slender columns. Something similar appears in the Early English style (though there one does not find the hall plan applied to the entire interior) in the retrochoirs of the cathedrals.

Though the hall church in this transformed guise is an extremely impressive creation, taken as a whole its popularity declined in southwestern Europe. In southern France and northern Spain it was more and more replaced by the single-naved plan. It should be remembered that High and Late Gothic hall churches are rare in Languedoc, though there are such significant exceptions as Saint-Michel-des-Lions in Limoges and the priory church of La Chaise-Dieu. Conversely, Spain became one of the principal centers of that form in the Late Gothic period.

A certain Westphalian group, with examples at Paderborn, Lippstadt, and Herford, would appear to be closely related to these Aquitanian halls. Beginning with the late twelfth century, the hall became the characteristic form in this region, giving rise to several other systems, one quite different from the other. Thus again, in the thirteenth century, Westphalia would seem to have been a chief source for the numerous hall churches in Hesse and along the middle Rhine. The form had an extraordinarily great diffusion in the fourteenth, fifteenth, and sixteenth centuries almost everywhere in the Germanic linguistic regions, in the northwest and northeast, in Thuringia and Saxony, in Swabia, Franconia, Bavaria, and in the southeast far into east-central Europe.

In the wake of the Late Romanesque relaxation of forms, isolated hall-like structures (among them the west front at Roermond and the western portion of the church at Oberpleis) began to appear, even in the heart of the territory favoring the basilica. While at Ramersdorf near Bonn and Niederweisel near Frankfurt-am-Main small churches were conceived with hall interiors, they certainly are not to be viewed as of prime importance in themselves, but rather as more likely related to the structures typical of monastery refectories and dormitories.

Alongside the two principal centers of diffusion of the Late Romanesque hall church—Aquitaine and Westphalia—there are a number of smaller groups elsewhere. In Lorraine and Piedmont there are halls in the bound system comparable to those in Westphalia. Quite unlike these, however, are the halls of the Upper Palatinate with their cross-vaulting, not to mention

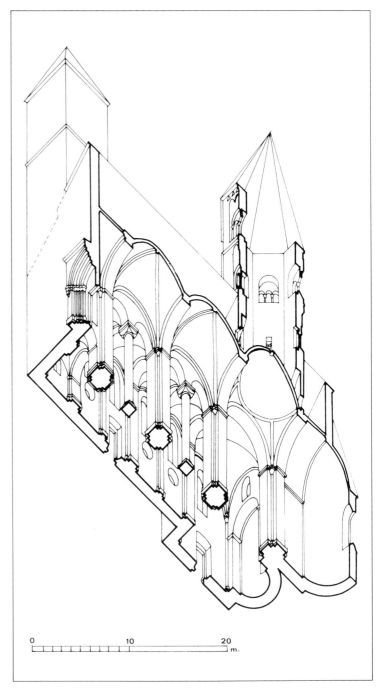

270. *Soest, Sankt Patroklus, west front*

271. *Münster, cathedral, interior looking northeast*

272. *Minden, cathedral, interior showing detail of choir wall*

273. *Münster, collegiate church of Sankt Ludgeri, axonometric projection reconstructing the original state (from Thümmler, 1958, drawn by Preis)*

XXI. *Cologne, Sankt Gereon, exterior*

274. Vercelli, San Bernardo, interior
looking east
275. Trent, San Lorenzo,
axonometric projection (from
Thümmler, 1958, drawn by Nones)

those in central Italy, which for the most part continued to be barrel-vaulted.
Finally, in southern Italy we find three-naved churches with cupolas over the
central nave and with high vaulted side naves: the best known are the
ex-cathedral at Molfetta in Apulia, which takes a foremost place among the
non-basilical interior designs; and a few churches in Sicily, notably San Cataldo
in Palermo, which have a similar plan though with unvaulted side aisles.

In the High Romanesque period, the predominant form in southwestern
Europe was the vaulted single-naved interior, often of monumental proportions. Though the cupola church was restricted to the western half of southern
France, the barrel-vaulted aisleless church is found everywhere south of the
Loire, from the Alps to the Atlantic. These two types were transformed in the
second half of the twelfth century, with the cross-ribbed vault replacing the
barrel vault and cupola (otherwise, however, the essential traits of the plan
were preserved). The fewest variations took place in single naved, often
cruciform edifices, of which the cathedral at Angers is the largest and best
known. There the bay and wall system of the cupola church is still used, but
in place of the circular cupola over pendentives there is a ribbed cupola that
eliminates the crowning cornice, unifies the crown of the vault and the
pendentives, and weaves a net of ribbing over the whole. In Provence and the
Languedoc heavy wall projections were still used both indoors and out,
though now as buttresses and supports for cross-ribbed vaults.

In a third group, the blind arches between the interior wall projections
were deepened into chapel-like accessory areas. The first steps toward this
had already been taken in such a barrel-vaulted aisleless High Romanesque
construction as the cathedral in Orange. When the shafts were interrupted
by arches and the chapels linked with each other, passageways resembling
side naves resulted. This type is to be seen in extremely diverse transformations, and some of the most popular (and largest) examples were built by
the Cistercian order. With Fontenay, the group reaches far into northern
Burgundy and spreads westward into Upper Burgundy, then eastward into
Lorraine.

The Holy Land

As a consequence of the Crusades, Palestine and its neighboring regions
became a very remote province of southern French architecture. As early
as the eleventh century and even before, Christian pilgrims either
individually or in large groups visited the holy places and consecrated sites
of Palestine. In the First Crusade (1097-99), Frankish knights conquered
the land that was to remain in their possession for two centuries thereafter
and that was divided into four separately ruled domains. Knights from many
different European lands took part in the following crusades, but warriors
and ecclesiastics from the territory of present-day France were in the
majority (a number of German emperors and kings also played a part). Great
fortresses, among them the famed Krak-des-Chevaliers, secured the land
against the Arabs.

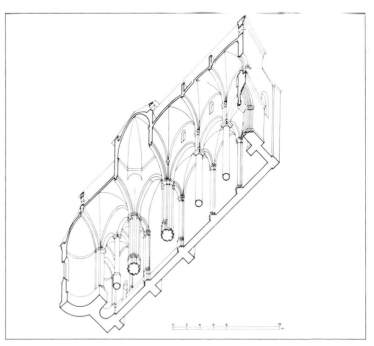

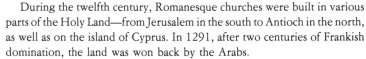

During the twelfth century, Romanesque churches were built in various parts of the Holy Land—from Jerusalem in the south to Antioch in the north, as well as on the island of Cyprus. In 1291, after two centuries of Frankish domination, the land was won back by the Arabs.

The architecture of the citadels and churches in the Holy Land belong unequivocally to the style of southern France. It is worth noting that here—quite unlike what occurred at times in Spain—scarcely any Islamic influence can be detected. The chapel in the Krak-des-Chevaliers has a single-naved interior with apse, and is covered by pointed barrel vaults divided by cross-arches and resting on engaged shafts. It is in no way different from the countless barrel-vaulted aisleless churches in southern France and Spain. In the citadel at Margat, the chapel is covered by two cross-groined vaults without a middle cross-arch.

The more important churches confirm this impression. In the south, there are cross-vaulted basilicas (St. Anne in Jerusalem, the church at Abu Ghôsh) that also resemble those in southern France. This is even clearer in the hall churches of the northern areas—the cathedral at Gibelet (Byblos), the church at Tortosa (Tartus), and St. Phocas at Amyūn.

On the whole, the Crusaders seem to have been decidedly conservative in clinging to twelfth-century church types, and one can note little that reflects the above-mentioned transformations in the Late Romanesque and/or Early Gothic manner.

Aquitaine

It has become customary to view hall churches such as the cathedral of Poitiers as a collateral line of Early Gothic development. The piers and pilasters hold supporting shafts that are differentiated according to their function. The vaults have ribs, the arch contours are increasingly pointed, and if the windows only rarely and not until later have tracery, they too are nonetheless pointed. All of these are parallels to the Early Gothic development in the French crown lands. But most important, the piers and related members become more slender, and the functional relationship to the vault ribbing is obvious.

There is also another, and quite different, aspect to this architecture. First of all, there is the matter of the interior plan. The three naves are of equal height and even tend to assume the same breadth. The central nave does not surpass the others in height (is not, in other words, basilica), and so has no direct illumination from outside. By contrast, in the cathedral of Poitiers—despite the fact that the westernmost and somewhat later bay of the central nave has a slightly elevated vault—there is a zone of darkness in the upper part of the central nave just as in any Late Gothic hall church of graduated height.

Looking rather closer, we find that the vaults are so markedly concave as to suggest the shape of a cupola. Consequently, the upper delimitation of the interior takes on a rather undulating character. Vaults are for the most

part divided into eight segments, rather than four or six. There are ribs along
the crown of the vaults in both directions, but these apical ribs do not extend
the length and breadth of the interior in the form of long straight lines;
instead they espouse and emphasize the concave undulating vault form. At
the same time, by means of ornamental fields they convey a certain
playfulness that counters the impression that they are a purely structural
armature.

Thus, many essential peculiarities of the Romanesque hall church were
retained in Aquitaine. Indeed, in many respects the hall character now
emerges in purer form, because parallel barrel vaults no longer cover the
interior and thereby demarcate the three naves; instead, there are cross
vaults opening to all sides in their full height and width. In large
buildings—those at Poitiers or in Notre-Dame at Le Puy-en-Velay—it is
precisely this free-flowing spatiality that is responsible for a felicitous
impression further reinforced by the light that pours in through the outer
walls, and this must have been so at Asnières as well.

In smaller constructions, such as the choir of Saint-Serge in Angers or
the narthex of Saint-Martin at Candes, very thin monolithic columns
substitute for piers, so that the hall achieves a refined lightness and
transparency.

The elevation of the interior wall involves only two stories, not three
or four as in the northern Early Gothic. It is highly reminiscent of the wall
articulation of cupola churches in Aquitaine, where there is a sequence of
blind arches on the lower story and, on the upper one, the wall is set back
in front of the window wall. Here too a passageway breaks through the
pilasters. Thus, the well-developed two-shelled wall already found in
Romanesque cupola churches is retained here.

As a hall, the church does without buttressing elements, and the exterior
impresses one as squat and closed in. A single large saddle roof encompasses
all three naves and terminates at both east and west by a large gable. The
outside is conceived primarily as a large block with uniform roof, and is
therefore quite opposed to the multipartite organism of the northern French
cathedrals.

In its overall plan as well, the cathedral of Poitiers takes advantage of
certain consequences that had previously rarely been carried through in
Romanesque hall churches. Nave and choir are virtually unified, whereas
the transept is separated off as an independent component. The result is the
plan that has been described as the "choirless hall." In its ground plan, the
entire building forms a single rectangle out of which there project only two
west towers and two symmetrical chapel-like bays midway along the sides
of the nave. The latter can be viewed as a vestigial transept, but in terms
of the total interior it has only minor significance.

The southwestern French hall church, which is well described in the book
by A. Mussat, may appear as a collateral development when viewed in the
context of Early Gothic architecture in France. However, considered in the

larger European context, it proves to be an extremely significant creation,
having equal status and value with the many other forms in Late Romanesque
architecture.

Westphalia

Westphalia is considered the land of hall churches. It achieved this
distinction, however, only in the late twelfth and the thirteenth centuries.
Before then there were isolated forerunners of this type in the chapel of
Sankt Bartholomäus in Paderborn (1017) and the two-naved chapel of Sankt
Nikolaus in Soest, dating from the middle of the twelfth century. Along
with the very frequent hall-crypts, the so-called westwork crypts and similar
plans are especially emphasized in this region. Though none of these plans
leads directly to the hall church, they cannot be omitted from our
consideration.

279. L'Escaldieu, former Cistercian
abbey church, interior looking west
280. Lescar, former cathedral of
Notre-Dame, interior looking northeast

From the end of the twelfth century on, the hall church became established throughout Westphalia. However, Lower Saxony in the east and the Rhenish regions (both Upper and Lower Rhinelands) in the northwest and southwest reveal only isolated examples of the form. The sudden and extensive development in Westphalia proved of considerable richness, with no less than five distinct types, each having its main concentration in a different part of the region.

Most of the churches in the mountainous southern part of Westphalia— Sauerland and Siegerland—are small, with stout walls and thick piers, such as we see in the parish churches at Balve and Plettenberg. There are various vaulting systems: barrel, cross-groined, and single-hipped. The well-known and very characteristic church of Sankt Maria zur Höhe (known also as the Hohnekirche) in Soest is exceptionally broad, short, and low, with conch vaults over the side naves. A similar emphasis on breadth is found in the larger cross-groined vaulted hall churches at Lippstadt, in the Marienkirche at Herford, Paderborn Cathedral, and the Liebfrauenkirche in Bremen. The cathedral at Minden, with its decidedly Gothic forms and huge tracery windows, is connected with these and demonstrates how stylistic differentiations became negligible in these thirteenth-century hall churches. Rather more pronounced Late Romanesque elements are to be seen in the group to the northwest—primarily at Billerbeck and Legden, along with Ootmarsum in neighboring Holland—where there is a Late Romanesque alternation of supports and variation of heights in the interior, but no loss of the hall-form character.

Evidence of great independence in architectural thinking is provided in the numerous vaulting systems developed in Westphalian hall churches well before the so-called Early Gothic hall churches at Paderborn and elsewhere in the region. The much-discussed question as to how to explain the correspondences with the Poitiers style cannot be solved so conclusively as to permit assuming any influence from Aquitaine. The group in the vicinity of Münster, and notably Sankt Ludgeri in that city, shows parallels with northern Italian buildings, as Thümmler has pointed out, and another comparison might be with the hall churches in Lorraine using the bound system—for example, Mont-Saint-Martin and Sainte-Marie-au-Bois.

Two of the largest Late Romanesque churches in this region are not in hall form. They are the basilical cathedrals of Osnabrück and Münster, which have a good many reminiscences, in their galleries and other details, of the styles along the Lower Rhine, as does the choir of the cathedral at Minden. The cathedral at Münster goes back to an eleventh-century double-choir plan with two transepts. Inside we experience one of the most unique impressions in all medieval architecture: the broad expanses of individual areas blend into a hall-like whole, an effect created by the fact that the side naves open high and wide onto the central nave. This unusual appearance was achieved by omitting the middle support of the bound system.

In the north of Westphalia, as well as in neighboring Friesland, in the

western (Netherlandish) part as much as in the east, there are many single-naved churches, often in brick, whose unmistakable character is attributable to their high-swelling, deeply concave vaults with cross and crown ribbing. Many of them have transepts, and therefore a cruciform plan. Thus, here too there is a reminiscence of Aquitaine.

Northern and Central Italy

Though the hall church was not cultivated in northern Italy with the same persistence as in southwestern Europe, there is significant evidence of it there in the early twelfth century. Besides Santa Fede in Cavagnolo Po, certain other smaller Late Romanesque churches belong to this tradition, among them San Pietro in Robbio, the east portion of San Lorenzo in Trent, and San Bernardo and San Marco in Vercelli. H. Thümmler, who was the first to appreciate the importance of these latter buildings, dated the first three in the last quarter of the twelfth century and the fourth after the middle of the thirteenth. All of them have cross-ribbed vaulting. A few have alternating supports in the bound system and therefore are very close to the Westphalian churches of the Legden and Billerbeck group: one can compare San Marco in Vercelli with the convent church at Metelen near Münster, though the others too can be compared directly with churches in Westphalia (for example, San Bernardo in Vercelli with the parish church in Plettenberg). One must ask, with Thümmler, if there were direct relationships here.

Among Late Romanesque churches in central Italy, especially in the Marches, Umbria, and the Abruzzi, there are also a number of hall churches. These have been studied as a group by W. Krönig. Except for those with dark barrel-vaulted interiors and based on centralizing plans, they remain stylistically conservative. Worth mentioning are the cathedral of San Leo in the Marches, San Michele Arcangelo and San Silvestro in Bevagna in Umbria, and San Sisto in Viterbo in Lazio.

Apulia

Like other important centers of Romanesque architecture, Apulia is not restricted to a single type of church. Alongside galleried basilicas with open timberwork ceilings, there are smaller simple basilicas that tend to repeat the arrangement of San Nicola in Bari, among them San Gregorio in the same city. Of special interest, however, is a group of vaulted hall churches, the largest and most important being the ex-cathedral of Molfetta, though it also includes the church of Ognissanti near Valenzano and a few small buildings in Trani. In the ex-cathedral at Molfetta, articulated piers support broad round arches that divide the interior into two or three square bays in the central nave, with narrowed bays in the side naves. Above the crowns of the nave arcades there are quarter-barrel vaults curving inward from the outside walls. In the central nave, handsome circular cupolas either sit on

pendentives immediately above the arch spandrels or are lifted up by a drum. The result is a unified vaulted ceiling over the entire interior, rising to the middle like a cloverleaf arch but still giving the impression of a perfectly delimited stone vault. The cupolas dominate, and the quarter-barrel vaults are decidedly subordinate, almost like a kind of buttressing extended into the interior. The hall church and the cupola church are combined here into a system that is "closed" both constructively and spatially, something known nowhere else—not even in southwestern Europe, where this combination of cupola and barrel vault was never exploited for the innumerable hall churches of that region. While the two regions have in common buildings of an emphatically closed character (their interiors being, as it were, concealed), their systems are different.

The exteriors of these Apulian churches are usually plain, consisting of a stone block with shed roofs over the side naves and surmounted by cupolas that are sometimes concealed behind octagonal brickwork structures crowned by similarly octagonal pyramidal roofs. The ex-cathedral at Molfetta has a twin-towered east front like that of Bari.

Neither inside nor outside is there anything "Oriental" about these cupola-halls. They are entirely Western in their rigorous application of a system and entirely Romanesque in their organization and massiveness. Despite this, writers persist in associating them with Byzantium. This seems only natural, since here, on the southeastern coast of Italy facing the Ionian Sea, we have the shortest sea route to Istanbul: Brindisi, Otranto, and Taranto are only some 620 miles away, and the old historic ties have not been forgotten. Nevertheless, we must insist on the obvious autonomy of the churches involved.

The group centering around Molfetta is Late Romanesque, dating from after 1150. During that period, builders everywhere attained maturity in dealing with the materials and techniques involved in erecting vaulted buildings, which makes it doubly difficult to answer questions as to the origins of this style, though they cannot be sidestepped. For one thing, the Normans maintained links with their homeland at that time as they had before. One must also remember the dynastic connections with Aquitaine through the Plantagenets. A direct artistic connection with southwestern France cannot be discerned, but the possibility of some sort of relationship is difficult to rule out, especially when we look at further groups.

To begin with, there is San Benedetto in Brindisi—a handsome and perfectly pure hall church with large columns, having not cupolas but cross vaults with band ribs. Then one must mention vaulted basilicas, especially Santo Sepolcro in Barletta, for which W. Krönig postulated connections with northern France because of the passageway within the central-nave wall supported by projecting consoles. The twelfth-century choirs with deambulatory found in southern Italy—at Venosa and Acerenza in Basilicata, at Aversa in Campania—show that this area was not isolated, but had numerous links with the North.

284. Bonmont, former Cistercian abbey church, transverse section of the nave (from Bucher, 1957)

285. Fontenay, former Cistercian abbey, axonometric projection of the church and monastic buildings (from Bucher, 1957)

To return, however, to the cupola church, it should be remembered that within the region itself there are some buildings and groups of buildings that would seem to be linked in one way or another with the Molfetta group. First there is San Leonardo di Siponto in northern Apulia, which constitutes a direct initial step toward the system. Closely related to it is Santa Maria di Siponto, a square central-plan building with crypt, the authenticity of whose vault is open to suspicion but must nevertheless be taken into account. Then there is the remarkable tower with rich interior articulation and oval cupola known as the Tomb of Rotari in Monte Sant'Angelo. Furthermore, *trulli* are found throughout the region. These are small cupola-like construction serving in part as huts in vineyards but also as dwellings going back to prehistoric and protohistoric times and possibly connected with small Mediterranean pre-Christian cupola buildings. Certainly the use of stone, vaulting, and the cupola go back to a very ancient tradition, but just how much can be attributed to this remains an open question. The cupola churches of Sicily (which, like San Cataldo in Palermo, have hall-like interiors) will be discussed later, together with other manifestations of Sicilian art. The aesthetic interconnections between those buildings, despite the fact that they belong to very different architectural systems, are so obvious that for once we can let aesthetic appearance and character take precedence over a systematic approach. However, we should not overlook such Apulian churches as Santo Sepolcro in Barletta or San Giovanni Battista in Matera, which refuse to fit into any of our structural categories.

Southwestern Europe: Single-Naved Churches

As in High Romanesque times, so too in the late twelfth century and after there were a great many single-naved churches of monumental dimensions. We have already mentioned that they too replaced the barrel vault and cupola by the cross-ribbed vault. In southwestern France, many churches of this sort were laid out in the cruciform plan with transepts of some importance. The best known and largest of these is the cathedral of Angers. If we admit that the hall churches of the late twelfth century are connected with those of the Romanesque, then here too we can take the step of classifying the innumerable churches of the Angers type as a continuation of the cupola churches of Aquitaine. The cruciform ground plan, the two storied elevation with inner passageway, the division into square bays with cupola vaults—all these are the same. Only the vault form differs, with hyperconcave cross-ribbed vaulting instead of circular cupolas on pendentives. Here again, as a rule, eight ribs are used and disposed so as to make clear the marked concavity. The resultant form is known as a domical or cloister vault. Walls are double-shelled but somewhat thinner than in the first half of the twelfth century, and shafts are likewise thinner and more thoroughly articulated.

In both cases—the hall church and the single-naved cruciform church—

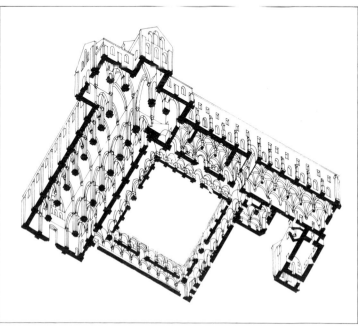

175

passageways and no arbitrary crown or ornamental ribs. Everything here is monumental, though not exaggeratedly so. A basilical choir with ambulatory of the northern French cathedral type was added to the cathedral's east end in the late thirteenth century. It was obviously planned to replace the nave by one in the newer style, since the choir was built off-center; the newer style, however, was not implemented. The result is a unique construction of entirely heterogeneous components aligned on wholly different axes. Something of this sort happened also, though less crudely, in the cathedral of Bordeaux. There too there is an aisleless nave that was subsequently altered by cross-ribbed vaults and then enlarged by a large High Gothic east end with transept and choir-ambulatory.

In the southeast, in Provence, the church at Le Thor exemplifies the introduction of the cross-ribbed vault into the single-naved interior, which before then had always been barrel-vaulted. Here still the Romanesque massiveness of walls and pilasters is maintained.

The three churches at Toulouse, Bordeaux, and Le Thor are not the only examples we may cite, but they do show with special clarity the continuing taste in southern France for the single-naved church, a form not fundamentally altered by cross-ribbed vaulting.

The Single-Naved Church with Rows of Chapels

It was not, however, the simple type of aisleless church that was to become significant for Gothic architecture in southern France and northern Spain, but rather the type represented by the famed abbey church of Fontenay in northern Burgundy—a broad and decidedly elongated structure with a large saddle roof, no towers, and little articulation. Were it not for the transept and the altar area protruding on the east, it would scarcely differ from the monastic buildings usually disposed around a cloister. Its squat shape makes one anticipate a hall church based on the southern French model, but on passing through the west portal, one's impression is that it is much more a huge barrel-vaulted single-naved interior stretching away at the rear. The proportions of the rather low pointed arches suggest a comfortable spaciousness, and the twilight gloom of the compact interior is lightened only through variously sized groups of windows in the east and west. Cross-arches at narrow intervals divide the barrel vault of the main nave into short bays, and the division is effected along the walls by half-columns. Between the latter there are again pointed arches to either side, which here open onto chapel-like collateral chambers running along the entire nave on both sides. These too are covered with pointed arched barrel vaults, but these vaults are perpendicular to the nave and their crowns barely reach the height of the impost line of the longitudinal barrel vaults. The walls on which they rest are likewise at right angles to the nave and separate the chapels from each other. Those walls in turn are pierced by pointed-arched openings, so that one almost has the impression of longitudinal side naves. One may say that the effect of chapels in a row—the consequence of the

the transition from barrel vault and cupola to hyper-concave ribbed vaulting is difficult to grasp—and unexpectedly so, since there are not even any transitional forms. The changeover came abruptly, which is all the more reason to be surprised that the cross-ribbed vault could be adapted so effortlessly to completely different interior plans.

Southern France

Hall churches related to the cathedral of Poitiers and single-naved churches related to that of Angers are concentrated in the area of Poitou and Anjou, but in the south too there are parallel developments. In Languedoc, the nave of the cathedral of Toulouse is aisleless and of great breadth. Cross vaults with wide-spanned band ribs mask three huge, almost square bays; the longitudinal walls are articulated by powerful pilasters and only the west wall has a story with blind arcades above the portal. There are no

287. *Itala, San Pietro, axonometric projection (from Di Stefano, 1955)*
288. *Monreale, cathedral, axonometric projection of the east end (from Choisy, 1964)*
289. *Monreale, cathedral, sanctuary*

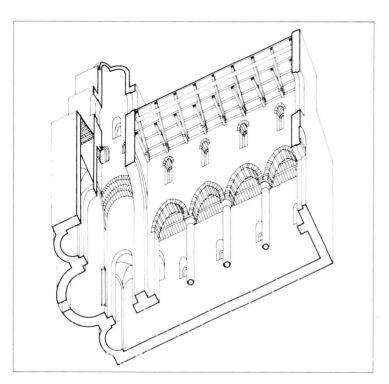

287. *Itala, San Pietro, axonometric projection (from Di Stefano, 1955)*
288. *Monreale, cathedral, axonometric projection of the east end (from Choisy, 1964)*

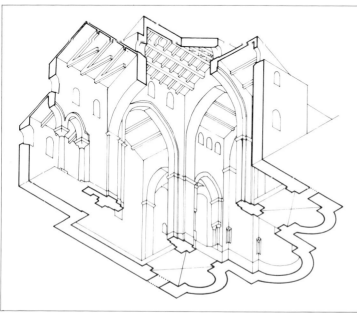

289. *Monreale, cathedral, sanctuary*

transverse barrel vaults and the impression of side naves echoed by the linking arches—was the determining factor. From the standpoint of construction, what is decisive is that the separating walls and the transverse barrel vaults very efficiently shore up and buttress the longitudinal vault, thereby making an extremely tight architectural structure in which the vaulting is virtually immune to static damage. The crossarms were devised as larger chapels that are broader, higher, and longer than those along the nave. However, they too do not attain the height of the crown of the nave vault and therefore create nothing that can be called a crossing. The central nave runs through to the eastern stern wall, which opens into the oblong altar area by way of a pointed arch. The arches of the altar area and the crossarms are of equal height. Thus, the old motif in which the crossarms

to establish a step-by-step genesis of this motif from one church to the next, one finds instead the precise opposite: the close linkage of the chapels in Fontenay became increasingly weaker in the churches at Bénévent-l'Abbaye, Silvacane, L'Escaldieu, Flaran, and Lescar. Nevertheless, one must insist that Fontenay was a northern forerunner of this southern type.

In Burgundy, and even in Upper Burgundy (present-day western Switzerland), there is a group of related buildings. If their barrel vaults were replaced by cross-ribbed vaults, as in the simple churches of the single-naved type described above, then we would have the form of aisleless church (but with chapels along its nave) that is found in innumerable examples throughout southwestern Europe, most particularly at Perpignan, Carcassonne, Gerona, Manresa, and Barcelona. Characteristic of these Burgundian churches is the partly ruined and deconsecrated Cistercian church at Bonmont in Switzerland.

Sicily and Southwestern Italy

Here, under Norman domination and essentially within the twelfth century, a type of architecture was developed that is among the strangest in the Western world. The Normans—first dukes and then, under Roger II (1130–54), kings—in no respect perpetuated here the architecture of their earlier realm in southeastern Italy. There are all too few points of contact between the buildings of Apulia and those of Sicily, though in the western part of the mainland, in Calabria, occasional buildings—Santa Maria della Roccella ("La Roccelletta") near Catanzaro, for one—are related to those in Sicily. In the north this formal approach reached as far as Campania, where the cathedral of Caserta Vecchia, northeast of Naples, is somewhat related. We may also mention the atrium of Salerno Cathedral and Amalfi Cathedral with its much restored cloisters.

The largest and most important church to be discussed here is the cathedral of Monreale. Beginning in 1183, King William II built a huge ensemble there comprising a royal palace, an archiepiscopal palace, and a monastery, along with a church that had to serve for all three and also as a royal burial place. The façade lies behind a porch with three large arched openings and flanked by two square and scarcely articulated towers—a plan that is remarkably un-Italian and that recalls buildings north of the Alps. The nave is basilical, with tall columns, broad arcades, thin walls, and an elaborate open timber-work ceiling. This is entirely in the Italian tradition, and the broad pointed arcades give evidence of the building's date.

The most interesting component is the eastern portion, which opens into an extraordinarily broad but short transept. The crossarms are of the same height as the central nave but lower than the crossing itself. The latter, viewed from outside, looks like the structure over the stage area of some large nineteenth-century opera house, with its flattish saddle roof projecting above all the other parts of the building. This connects with a tripartite sanctuary linked to the interior by large pointed arches, and the east end

are low and so do not isolate out the crossing lives on in this Late Romanesque vaulted building. More concretely, it can be understood as being in the southwestern European tradition of the so-called sunken crossing.

The conception of the interior is quite typical of what we find in southern France. Even if it is not an authentic hall form, it differs fundamentally from the Rhenish and Norman approaches because of the lack of graduation in height, the elongated central nave, and the dynamic effect of the light entering from above. The basis of this kind of interior is without doubt the barrel-vaulted single-naved form existing in innumerable examples throughout southern France and northern Spain. Many churches of this type have blind arches on the side walls, often deepened to the point of becoming side chapels. Similarly, one finds elsewhere that the separating wall between the chapels is pierced, though on a lesser scale. The fact is that if one attempts

terminates in three tall apses. More than anything the Late Romanesque
produced elsewhere, the general plan of Monreale resembles that of Early
Romanesque churches in the North (the cathedral at Gerace is likewise
reminiscent of the collegiate church at Nivelles). Thus, the crossing is not
isolated, as was virtually the case throughout Europe ever since the decades
around 1100 at the latest. The east end is made especially prominent by
means of mosaics with large figures on the inside and, on the outside, by
rich articulation with tall, pointed, overlapping blind arches that are further
enhanced by minutely detailed patterns inlaid in various colored stones.
Although stylistically translated into the Romanesque, the mosaics bear
Greek inscriptions suggesting their Byzantine origin; moreover, their
shimmering gold backgrounds are entirely alien to the West. On the other
hand, the geometric designs on the exterior of the building permit us to
assume that Arabian craftsmen had a part in the work at Monreale. These
foreign elements are thoroughly fused in an overall creation whose greatness
is undeniable. The cathedral's carefully selected site in the Conca d'Oro,
with its magnificent sweep of park descending to the city of Palermo far
below and affording a panoramic view of sea and bay, constitutes a heroic
landscape like those envisaged by Classical painters, but one that is lush with
semi-tropical vegetation.

The churches that preceded the cathedral of Monreale in time had already
paved the way for its unusual plan. The most important of them is the
cathedral at Cefalù, where there is a similar façade with two somewhat
projecting corner towers flanking an open portico and where the nave is
likewise a columned basilica. Also comparable is the superelevation of the
transept and choir, though everything is narrower and steeper in Cefalù.
We can probably get some idea of the genesis of the type there: as usual,
work began with the east portion, which was planned as a tall flat-ceilinged
structure with ambulatories inside and out. Those passageways still exist,
though they are in part walled up. Had they been completed as originally
intended, the result would have been a bold piece of architecture with the
Norman element very conspicuous, albeit transformed. It can be assumed
that the construction of the nave was lower than originally intended,
adjusted to a modified and markedly reduced plan in which it became a
simple traditional colonnaded basilica almost without articulation. This is
the genesis first proposed by H. M. Schwarz and later accepted by Italian
scholars. If it is correct, then it provides the key to Monreale's plan, which
elevated into a much more significant conception a design that at Cefalù
was largely the product of accident and compromise.

The simple colonnaded basilica with stilted arcades, transept, and three
immediately contiguous apses is found also in a few more poorly preserved
examples in Catania, Mazara del Vallo, Itala, and Messina. At the close of
the twelfth century, the cathedral of Palermo introduced the idea of building
on a grandiose scale. Today, only the exterior gives us a true picture of the
cathedral's former aspect (the interior has been transformed in Neoclassical

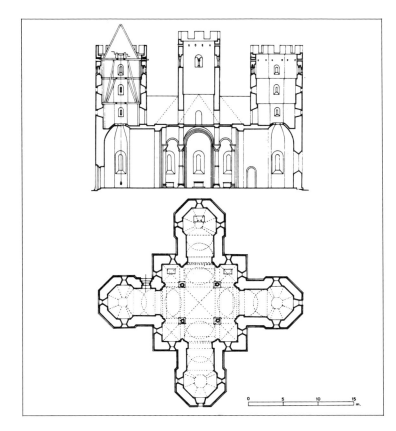

and wooden-ceilinged interiors, or the high and often stilted and pointed arcades on columns. The uniqueness of this architecture is emphasized even more by the exteriors, whose basic contours are those of a closed box on which the cupolas appear to rest directly; there is very shallow articulation, often with pointed arches that may or may not overlap. Islamic elements (stalactite cupolas and star-ribbed vaults) are certainly recognizable, but it is easy to overestimate their significance. In any case, these, like other forms of a different character, are well integrated into the overall ornamental picture.

Beginning with the middle of the twelfth century, there is no mistaking the signs of the Late Romanesque phase in Sicilian architecture: rich and often exaggerated articulation (especially on the exterior, and in particular on the apses); powerful graduation and expansion of the interior from the low nave to the high transepts; a tendency to centralizing forms of interiors and to a seemingly Eastern type of cupola vaulting; and, finally, a delight in such maneristic forms of decoration as stone inlays and stalactite vaults. Similar effects were striven for in the Cologne and Lower Rhine regions, though in an entirely different fashion and with wholly different means.

It is noteworthy that these Sicilian churches were furnished with Byzantine forms of mosaics, Islamic decorative elements, Catalan-Provençal sculpture (in the capitals of the cloister at Monreale), and bronze doors with reliefs by masters from Pisa and Apulia. Nevertheless, the eclectic traits present in the courtly art of Palermo do not predominate exclusively.

A very important part is played by civil architecture in the overall picture of the Late Romanesque in Sicily. The Norman royal city palace in Palermo (the Torre Pisana in the present Palazzo Reale) and the pleasure palace of La Zisa and La Cuba in the surrounding countryside have their rooms disposed axially and symmetrically in cube-shaped buildings, a feature new to Europe and undoubtedly developed out of the Islamic tradition, but with an effect on Western architecture virtually comparable to that of the Renaissance. This trend was especially fostered by the Hohenstaufens, to whom the Norman kingdom in southern Italy fell through marriage in 1195. The Castello Maniace in Siracusa and the Castello Ursino in Catania have the regulation square shape with round towers, a formula that in turn influenced the Apulian castles of Emperor Frederick II.

In the thirteenth century, church building declined in Sicily. It took on such Gothic elements as ribbed vaulting and polygonal apses, though it promptly modified them in the direction of a regional Gothic, with no reminiscences whatsoever of the northern French High Gothic. This was notably the case at Badiazza near Messina and in San Francesco d'Assisi (or dell'Immacolata) in the city itself.

Architecture of the Cistercian Order
An exposition of Late Romanesque architecture would be incomplete if it did not consider that of the Cistercian order. Even in terms of numbers

style). The long nave links a three-towered west front with a broad transept, creating a richly articulated and shieldlike wall. It stretches between two small turrets and serves as a foil for the three apses, making a most impressive architectonic effect.

Smaller churches in this style, a number of which survive in Palermo itself, are striking for their high domes completely exposed on the exterior. Often the domes crown only the crossing, as in San Giovanni degli Eremiti, Santo Spirito, Santa Trinità ("La Magione"), and the Palatine Chapel (all in Palermo); or they may be repeated in the middle, as at Forza d'Agrò near Messina, or in the western part of the nave, as in San Giovanni dei Lebbrosi, or even in various bays of the central nave of a hall-like interior, as in Santa Maria dell'Ammiraglio ("La Martorana") and San Cataldo—the latter three also in Palermo or its environs. While these churches may be assigned to one or another of the categories standard in Europe—simple and cruciform aisleless churches, basilicas, hall churches—those types seem of less significance here than such unique traits as cupolas, the alternation of vaulted

293. Regensburg, Allerheiligenkapelle
in the cathedral cloister, section and
elevation (from Ostendorf, 1922)

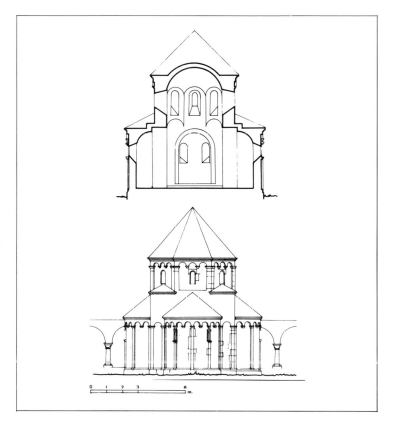

alone, their churches and abbeys made an essential contribution to European architecture of the time. More than other orders, the Cistercians infused their buildings with an unmistakably spiritual atmosphere. In spite of this, architectural historians are faced with a question: aside from that atmosphere, was there a specifically Cistercian architecture with its own types of ground plans, its own architectural system, specific forms, and its own builders and workshops? In older as well as in more recent research, the answer has very often been in the affirmative.

Implicit in the preceding pages has been a denial. We have discussed a number of important Cistercian churches according to their geographic locations and along with other architecture in the same region: Heisterbach with the Lower Rhine, Fontenay with southwestern Europe, Pontigny with Burgundy, Otterberg with the Upper Rhine, and still others with Lombardy and Spain.

Let us return to the historical facts. The Cistercian order was founded in 1098 in Cîteaux, near Dijon in northern Burgundy. After Bernard of Clairvaux joined it in 1113, the order made extraordinary progress; he left Cîteaux in 1115 to found the monastery at Clairvaux. Cistercian abbeys, both those newly founded and those converted from existing ones, could be counted in the hundreds throughout Europe and constituted a major part of all architectural activity until around the middle of the thirteenth century.

The order proclaimed a reform of monastic life that can be summed up in modern terms as a return to Early Christian simplicity. During the first century of its existence, its churches conformed to this ideal, being without towers, architectonic sculpture, or figurative decoration. In these ascetic negations, Cistercian architecture would seem to have been following the prescription of St. Bernard himself. An attempt has been made recently (by H. Hahn, R. Wagner-Rieger, and K. H. Esser) to prove that the saint had a preference for a specific type of church—that of Fontenay. We do, in fact, find a few Cistercian churches of this type in widely separated places: Alvastra in Sweden, Viktring in Austria, and Agrigento in Sicily. However, it is not irrelevant that they all lie in peripheral regions of Europe where an architectural tradition was not firmly established. The proof that such a system was worked out initially (such as has been sought in connection with many other buildings) cannot be taken for a fact. As so often is the case, it is especially the beginnings that remain obscure. The important Cistercian churches that survive—predominantly vaulted basilicas—date only from the late twelfth and early thirteenth centuries. Some were laid out in the bound system, among them that at Eberbach in the Rheingau and Chiaravalle Milanese and Chiaravalle della Colomba in northern Italy. In the thirteenth century, the plan with transverse rectangular bays—the so-called Gothic bay—became more and more frequent, and there are well-known examples of it at Ebrach near Bamberg (Upper Franconia), Walkenried in the Harz Mountains, Morimondo in Lombardy, San Galgano in Tuscany, and Fossanova and Casamari in Lazio. Scholars tend to think of these as related to the diffusion of the so-called Burgundian Early Gothic, with Pontigny and Acey (in the Jura Mountains) in mind. However, this style too is not limited to the Cistercians, as a glance at Sant'Andrea in Vercelli or Santo Sepolcro in Barletta shows, while Heisterbach belongs entirely to the Lower Rhenish style.

THE CENTRAL-PLAN CHURCH

Earlier we considered central-plan buildings of Pre-Romanesque times, notably the minster at Aachen and its successors, and noticed that to some extent the westwork likewise involved concepts related to the central plan. No period of the Romanesque was without important examples of this form. It was often used in connection with specific functions, most frequently for baptisteries, which in Italy especially—one need only think of those in Florence, Cremona, Parma, and Pisa—assumed a truly monumental scale. Besides these, there were central-plan churches modeled after the Holy

Sepulcher in Jerusalem, well-preserved examples being the Knights Templars' church of La Vera Cruz in Segovia, the round church of the Holy Sepulcher in Cambridge, and the parish church at Neuvy-Saint-Sépulcre in Berry. Furthermore, there are centrally planned double-chapels with two stories, such as were favored for citadels and palaces in the twelfth and thirteenth centuries, especially in imperial territories. Isolated examples elsewhere include one at Hereford in England (it has not survived) and another at Montefiascone near Viterbo. From a later time there are also Knights Templars' chapels such as the one in Laon.

Numerous examples of each type of plan exist, many being concentrated in specific geographic areas. In east-central Europe, with its core in Bohemia, we find the simple round chapel with apse. In Jutland and the Baltic islands there are many round chapels with four intercalated supports and sometimes with two stories. Related to these are the more complex square plans with four apses and four (sometimes five) towers; these plans were used in the church on the Harlungerberg near Brandenburg, which has been destroyed, and in Kalundborg in Denmark.

From the ancient territory of Gallia Cisalpina (in northern Italy, above the Apennines) to Provence, one often finds octagonal forms with niches, and these date from Late Antique times to the Early Romanesque. Central-plan churches with an ambulatory are relatively rare, existing mostly in northern Italy—Santo Sepolcro within Santo Stefano in Bologna, the Rotonda San Lorenzo in Mantua, San Tomè in Almenno San Bartolomeo, and San Pietro in Asti are examples. Nevertheless, they are also found north of the Alps at Drüggelte in Westphalia, at Senones in Lorraine, and at Bonn (Sankt Martin) and Worms (Sankt Johannes) in the Rhineland (the latter three have not been preserved). To these may be added the citadel chapels at Kobern, also in the Rhineland, and at Vianden in Luxembourg, along with the choir-crown rotunda crypt from the early eleventh century in Saint-Bénigne in Dijon. At Kobern, Vianden, and Dijon only the lower story has survived, in the guise of a crypt. In Sint Pieter at Louvain a related structure, possibly dating from around 1100, has been excavated and can be seen under the Gothic choir. Other similar structures are found in Saint-Germain at Auxerre and Sankt Michael at Fulda, both from the ninth century.

The Greek cross is also found as a ground plan, more conspicuously in chapels dedicated to the Holy Cross, as in the case in the Heiligkreuz chapel in Trier (destroyed in World War II but since reconstructed), the Chapelle Sainte-Croix in Montmajour in Provence, and the reconstructed abbey church of Sainte-Croix in Quimperlé in Brittany. The related four-leaf clover form was used in characteristic fashion in two small buildings dating from around 1150 (corresponding to the early Hohenstaufen period, which was marked by a taste for classically harmonious relationships): the double-chapel (now the parish church of Sankt Klemens) in Schwarzrheindorf near Bonn and the Allerheiligenkapelle in the cloister of the cathedral at Regensburg in Bavaria. There is an important ninth-century example at Zadar in Yugoslavia, Svaty Donat (the church of St. Donatus), a smaller Early Romanesque baptistery in Biella in Piedmont, and a special form in the baptistery at Galliano near Cantù in Lombardy.

The double-choir plans, originating primarily in the region of the medieval empire and from as early as Ottonian or even Carolingian times, transformed the oblong basilical form in a way that has been described—certainly not entirely without reason—as "centralizing." Another combination is the triple-conch plan whereby the transept and choir of a basilica were united in a single composition. These are found in Cologne and the Lower Rhine, as well as in Picardy and, especially, northwestern France and such neighboring regions as Tournai. With the exception of the Early Romanesque churches of Sankt Marien im Kapitol and Sankt Georg, both in Cologne, they number among the great achievements of the Late Romanesque and the so-called Early Gothic, along with the special four-storied examples of Sankt Gereon or the baptistery in Parma.

Chapter Five

DOMESTIC AND MILITARY ARCHITECTURE

The church building is the most outstanding artistic creation of the Middle Ages. In it the spiritual, religious, and artistic forces of the period were realized in their most permanent form. Almost every European city or village has an ancient nucleus still apparent in its present appearance. Though that nucleus may have been transformed and often virtually wiped out, it can usually still be identified by the presence of one old church in thousands of settlements.

Viewed strictly as architecture, the church represents artistic expression at its purest. And, despite all the prerequisites it was expected to fulfill, the church was the freest expression of the creative forces of the past. The number of churches to have survived so far outweighs civil architecture in importance that the ensuing discussion of domestic and military buildings will necessarily be brief.

The City

The Roman cities of the Late Antique period were reduced to ruins by barbarian invasions. Life was not completely extinguished in them, but frequently it survived only at a very low level. The Christian communities often merely took over such available buildings as were still habitable or capable of repair. If this was an expression of continuity with the past, as scholars have often argued, what was involved was a continuity of place, and not of artistic form. Towns in the Romanesque age often were founded on the debris of Roman settlements, but theory obeyed new laws of development and growth. Their most visible hallmark is their surrounding wall, set up not only as an indispensable protection but also because of an overpowering psycho-social compulsion.

The town of Pre-Romanesque and Romanesque times has disappeared from sight as completely as that of ancient civilizations. While the medieval city still lives on today almost everywhere in Europe, it is as a rule only in the form of a network of streets and occasionally walls, having been rebuilt over and over again. Fires, destruction through wars, and ever-increasing demands for domestic comfort, together with changing social and economic relationships, have left little of the medieval fabric still standing. Thus, in no city does the totality of High Medieval urban architecture survive. A number of smaller places in the Mediterranean region do, however, still look much as they once did: Viviers-sur-Rhône in southern France, Saint-Guilhem-le-Désert in Languedoc, San Gimignano in Tuscany, and many other towns in southern France and central Italy. The only way we can get an idea of the appearance of the villages and farmsteads of Romanesque times is by searching for the earliest vestiges of them in remote places. However, the architectural form of most cities can be reconstructed through the basic traits in their overall plans, and that form reveals a gradual growth under the pressure of the need to fortify and protect the city by a girdle of walls, so that the inhabited areas extend outward in bulges and circles but do not radiate along the existing roads.

In most old cities we can still decipher the plan of the earliest nucleus (often Roman). The rectangular, round, or semicircular line of walls of the oldest nucleus is still reflected in the network of streets. Similarly, one can recognize subsequent extensions that often reached out to other directions and that only later themselves coalesced into a new overall form. The city grew in rings, seldom fanning out as it does today because of the fortified protection that the social and political factors of the age made so necessary. Cologne serves as an example of this sort of development.

Often within the plan of a city there are special nuclei in which monasteries or cathedral chapters form a ring of their own. In Trier the fortified cathedral close constitutes a city within the city; this is still plain to see today.

The early medieval town as we perceive it today has a closed form, usually circular even in those instances where it developed out of a rectangular Roman nucleus. It has an irregular network of narrowly winding streets that we think of as fascinatingly picturesque. The streets often broaden into something like a square and then narrow down again, have twisting courses with frequent detours, or fork and tend to make triangular open places. Decidedly rare are right-angled intersections of straight streets as well as axial alignments of streets, square, and monuments. All of this we know from the Late Gothic city, but in its essentials the Romanesque town must have been no different.

Streets, and frequently entire neighborhoods, were reserved for particular categories of inhabitants. Merchants and craftsmen had their special districts or streets, often still reflected in their present-day names. Then as now, wealth and social position were mirrored in the size, material, and form of houses. Community buildings, churches and chapels, the town hall and mint, were all situated in rows or blocks of houses or in squares. There was no rule for this, however. The main church can lie amid a tangle of narrow lanes and be accessible only through blind alleys or side streets, as is still the case in Orange, or else be on the outskirts of the town on large but vaguely defined open plots of gound, as in Pisa or Speyer or, more often, England. There was a special preference for setting the cathedral or an important abbey or collegiate church in a high commanding position—often at the center of an entire upper town, as in Laon, Langres, Lincoln, Quedlinburg, San Giminiano, and Gerona.

When there were fortifications, they were often no more than a wall and moat in early times, later expanded to a ring of walls. Their few openings were guarded by special towers and gates. If a feudal lord, or even a bishop, had his castle within the town walls, it was usually in a corner, surrounded by its own walls, and often on the highest point of the terrain or encircled by water. In Gothic times, but even before, citadels lying close to the town but outside its walls could be linked to it by long stretches of wall, as in Jaén or Bacharach. The fortifications consisted of a circular wall with a defensive battlement inside and a moat outside, though often simply of a wall, palisade, and moat. Rectangular or round towers projected to the exterior and made it possible to protect the walls against invaders by raking fire.

The crenellated battlement was by and large the only strictly functional form, though it too provided a very effective crown to a wall. Towers contained or flanked the few gates. In the Late Romanesque defenses of Cologne, they took the form of regulation gatehouses on symmetrical ground plans. Like so many cities, Cologne demolished its Romanesque fortifications down to a few vestiges, though they had stood, well-preserved, until as late as 1880. Ávila, in Castile, is unique for still having an intact circle of Romanesque walls with towers and gates. That such an opulent system should have been built so early is understandable when one remembers that the town lay close to the border, in a region recaptured from the Arabs not long before.

The Romanesque Dwelling

The overwhelming majority of Romanesque dwellings, whether peasant or urban, were built of wood. If this is only an assumption, it is amply justified by the fact that no trace whatsoever survives of them. Even monastic buildings and knightly residences within the feudal strongholds would appear to have been frequently wooden. We cannot, however, hope to close this gap in our knowledge, since not even drawings supply the details for this early period, at least as far as wooden buildings are concerned. The result is paradoxical: thanks to extensive excavations, we know more about prehistoric and protohistoric dwellings than about those early medieval ones built in wood. We can presume that the types and the construction of the early hallform house, the house on stilts, and the like continued into the Early Middle Ages. This can be demonstrated for a special category, the monumental wooden granaries of abbeys, a few of which have survived—at Ter Doest in Flanders, for example. Only in recent years has the research of Walter Horn and others brought out the facts about this evolution and shifted the romantically tinged earlier interpretations into a clear historical light. Similar connections should be sought in relation to dwellings.

When we speak today of the Romanesque dwelling, we think of the stone houses of the eleventh and twelfth centuries that have survived in many places throughout Europe. Nowhere have such dwellings survived as large ensembles, but virtually only as isolated examples in such places as Saint-Gilles-du-Gard in Provence, Cluny in Burgundy, Rosheim in Alsace, Winkel in the Rheingau, as well as in Trier, Coblenz, Karden, Boppard, and Münstereifel in the Lower Rhineland, Ghent in Flanders and Tournai on the Schelde, Ascoli Piceno and elsewhere in Italy, and in Prague. Rounding out our list of surviving buildings with others that can be traced from a methodical combing of old pictorial sources, we find that many places—Cologne for one—had many more stone houses than survive today.

The common characteristic of the façade is a quite consistent lack of plastic articulation, with the main emphasis placed instead on the shape of the windows. In addition, in Rhenish and Flemish gabled houses there are often corbiestepped gables, whereas elsewhere they generally terminate horizontally with gutters. With only a few Late Romanesque exceptions, one must think of the ground plan as very simple, with two or three rooms, as a rule opening directly into each other without any corridors. The so-called *appartement simple* is often met with—even in palaces—from the start of modern times.

One peculiarity of the medieval city, visible today only in a very few places, was the dwelling tower. The earliest surviving example seems to be the so-called Frankenturm (the Tower of the Knight Franco) in Trier from the middle of the eleventh century, while the well-known examples in Regensburg date only from Gothic times. There were many such towers once, but their effect on the overall town picture can be seen now only in San Gimignano in Tuscany, where several have been preserved and where the other houses scarcely exceed the medieval average in height. Isolated dwelling towers, once occupied by an entire family and its retainers, have survived elsewhere, most notably in Bologna and Florence.

It can be seen from these selected examples that there were also marked regional differences in domestic architecture. Along with residential housing one must mention the town hall and administrative buildings such as have survived in Bragança in Portugal and Lérida in Spain, as well as in Saint-Antonin-Nobleval (Tarn-et-Garonne) and Gelnhausen (Hesse). The *palazzo comunale* of the Italian Gothic represents a continuation of the tradition.

The Monastery

The monastery was the expression of a form of life steeped in spirituality. It takes its place along with the citadel and the town as a key aspect of civil architecture during the Middle Ages, and like them covered all of medieval Europe with a dense network of examples.

In its most significant traits, the architectonic form of the monastery remained much the same, if not identical, throughout the Middle Ages and in every country. When it comes to details, however, the differences are innumerable. The early Irish monasteries merely grouped a few huts freely around a small church within an oval ring of wall. But by around 820—the date of a drawing showing the plan of the monastery of Sankt Gallen (preserved in the library there)—the ideal scheme that would remain in force into Late Gothic times was established: the residential buildings lie on three sides of an oblong or square court; on its fourth side, to either the north or the south, lies the church. A passageway runs around all four sides of the court and constitutes a covered connection between all the buildings. As a rule, the ground floor of the east wing had, adjacent to the church, small rooms serving as sacristy and armarium (the latter a storeroom for liturgical objects), followed by the chapter house—a hall set aside for the

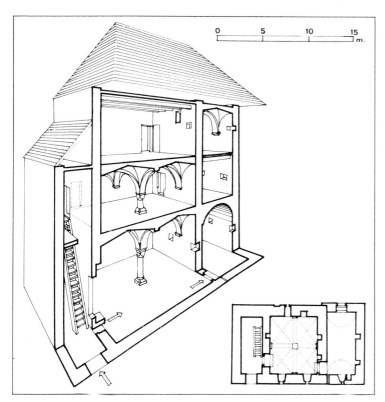

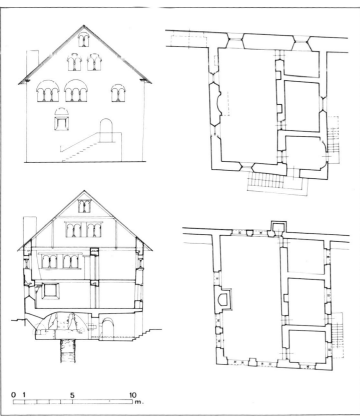

community's frequent gatherings, at which all matters concerning their monastery were dealt with under the presiding abbot or prior. In High Romanesque times the chapter house usually took the form of a vaulted hall with two or four columns, stone benches all around the walls, and often an apse. Access to the cloister was through a door almost always flanked by two groups of windows (a symmetrical grouping of openings such as this is helpful to keep in mind when trying to orient oneself in a ruined building). The *dormitorium* where the monks slept was usually upstairs in the east wing and was directly connected by a staircase with the transept of the church, where the frequent offices were held, even at night. Thus, it was not far from the sleeping area to the crossing. The dormitory was often vaulted: in southwestern Europe it was a barrel-vaulted aisleless chamber, elsewhere a cross-vaulted hall on one or two rows of supports; in some regions, however, there were simply wooden ceilings.

The refectory and kitchens were usually in the buildings opposite the church, with the other outhouses and the monastery gate in the west wing. There was little set aside for convenience and comfort, scarcely more than a well for washing in the cloister and a room to warm oneself in, the *calefactorium*. A circular wall, more or less fortified, surrounded the whole. Larger monasteries had a special courtyard set aside outside the *clausura* for the various crafts and housekeeping activities. Architecturally, it is chiefly the rooms used for the monastic community as a whole that are interesting, especially the chapter house, dormitory, refectory, and cloisters.

In the many cloisters that survive, a patch of garden or at least a bit of vegetation combines with the architecture (and with our romantic view of the past) to create an atmosphere of serene isolation from the busy world outside. The cloister assumes its character from the long procession of identical or rhythmically alternating arches that open onto the courtyard from the ambulatory corridors. While the general design is much the same throughout Europe, there are some regional differences. The Italian cloisters with their openwork roofs are visibly different from the usually barrel-vaulted corridors in southwestern Europe and the cross-vaulted one north of the Alps. Not only was the prescribed basic form open to such modifications but, in larger monasteries, it was made considerably more elaborate—in some cases even with additional cloister walks.

Besides the plan of the monastery at Sankt Gallen, we have another invaluable document that serves to round out what we have learned from the many surviving cloisters: a drawing of Canterbury Cathedral showing the new Gothic part together with the monastery buildings. Unlike that of Sankt Gallen, this is not a mere ground plan in plain line drawing, though neither is it a perspective or even isometric depiction. It is, rather, a combination of ground plan and elevation in which the two planes are telescoped and from which, because portions taken from another vantage point are inserted here and there, the modern viewer gets the impression of perspective, however faulty. This drawing is of fundamental importance insofar as it confirms what we gather from a few other rare sources, mostly manuscript miniatures, namely that what the builders of early medieval times produced in the way of architectural drawings and plans was quite different from those done today.

Very prominently displayed in the drawing is an ingenious system of water conduits, which helps us to understand that conditions in a medieval monastery were by no means as primitive as we imagine today, there being such conveniences as a bath house, extensive toilet facilities, and both a reservoir for rain water and a draw-well.

Cathedral schools and similar secular institutions involving communal existence had much the same overall plan as the early medieval monasteries, and their cloisters and community rooms scarcely differed in any respect.

The Burg

It is not only the countless churches and monasteries that characterize all of medieval Europe from Estonia to Portugal and from Ireland to Sicily, but also the burgs, the feudal castles, citadels, and strongholds. Just as the houses of worship were expressions of the universal Church, so too the burgs testified to a fundamentally similar conception on the level of secular society. They provided military protection for frontiers and roads and were the administrative seats for feudal territories and residences for the nobility.

As a general phenomenon, the burgs were the expression of the early medieval conception of the state, an institution characterized by extensive and increasing decentralization, which was in turn a consequence of the natural economy. The German king governed to the extent that he moved about from monastery to monastery, castle to castle, or fortress to fortress, Early documents and chronicles permit us to reconstruct those travels, which took rulers to the most far-flung parts of their domains, where they could always fall back on the local seats and burgs of their allies and vassals. Their territory was parceled out in both large and small portions as fiefs for the knights, who were bound to perform certain tasks in return, among them to provide military support. The knights generally built their own burgs, from which they could administer and govern their fiefs. Often there was a hierarchy of obligations in which a great feudal lord had other lords as his vassals. This explains the extraordinary number of fortified citadels.

As long as economic and social relationships required such strongholds, they continued to function, and they were in fact one of the powerful forces that held together the medieval West. With the appearance of the fortified castle in late medieval and early modern times, and with the decline of the burg, the Middle Ages waned and the modern world began.

In contrast with the burg—in which everything was determined by purpose and function—a church building seems almost a "free" work of art, one in which, furthermore, creative talents were allowed to flourish in countless ways in its interior. And though churches too have often been rebuilt and modified to suit altered circumstances, their original conception can usually still be deciphered. This is much more difficult in the case of burgs. Almost all of them, especially on the Continent, have in the course of centuries been repeatedly altered to keep pace with developments in fortification techniques and with demands for greater comfort on the part of the residents. With the exception of a few fortified dwelling towers— donjons and keeps—in England and northwestern France, there is scarcely a burg in all of Europe that has preserved its Romanesque character. For this reason, the Romanesque burg by no means permits the sort of clear and definable concept that the Romanesque church does for us. Its specific traits have tended to become assimilated into the Gothic additions, providing a picture that is best referred to by the general name of the "medieval" burg. Even for the specialist it is often difficult, sometimes impossible, to distinguish between the various periods of building and get down to the original appearance.

In the wake of the widespread social changes that made themselves felt most clearly in the fifteenth and sixteenth centuries, the burgs declined in importance. After being destroyed by fire or war, they were no longer rebuilt as had been the practice earlier. Therefore, the majority are now only roofless ruins, grown over by vegetation. Even when they are being carefully maintained or lived in today, one almost never sees them as they looked in the eleventh and twelfth centuries but rather with the much different aspect acquired in late medieval times.

These condistions are no different in many neighboring countries that do not adhere to the Roman religion: in Arab lands and in the Byzantine provinces of the Balkans, the burgs look much the same as in western Europe, whereas the religious edifices of Islam and the Eastern Church certainly do not.

All of this explains why research into these citadels is so often neglected by art historians and represents virtually a separate branch of study. Knowledge of local and territorial history and of the martial arts in all their detail, right down to armor and costumes, are auxiliary studies that must be mastered for purposes of research into this kind of architecture.

From the standpoint of construction, we find wood and earthwork as basic materials—supplemented by palisades, bastions, and moats—in the early period; then, especially with the High Romanesque and thereafter, stone buildings predominate. In many regions we find a transitional phase between the protohistoric ramparts, used as a refuge in emergencies, and the stone-built dynastic burg. Only modern medieval archaeology and its extensive excavations have made us really aware of the importance of one of these, the motte, in which a manmade mound was surrounded by a bailey and an enclosure ditch, with a wooden tower-like building standing at the peak of the cone. This is the basic form of the motte castle we know from numerous Romanesque stone burgs, though for the most part only the mounds of earth, and not the wooden towers, of this primitive form have come down to us.

The motte introduced two important prototypical forms of the high medieval stone burg: the circumambient wall and the tower. This holds true for the burg set on a natural rise of land as well as for the burg on level land. The latter, in its best-known form, the water burg, dispenses with the mound but fills its moats with water and thereby incorporates them into the system of defenses.

Besides the basic components of the Romanesque burg—fortified tower, donjon, and ring walls—there are often dwellings. While the tower often stands free within the circle of walls, it can also be connected with them. As a rule, it has exceptionally thick walls, which—in Hohenstaufen architecture—are made even stronger in fact and in appearance through the use of boss-cut stone. Because of the thickness of the walls they can be hollowed out to make rooms and stairways—an interesting though purely functional analogy to the hollowing out of walls in churches.

The basic form of the tower is usually perfectly simple, of uniform diameter from the ground up without any tapering; it can be square, oblong, octagonal (Steinsberg), or round (Münzenberg in Hesse). The Hohenstaufens favored five-sided towers with a spur projecting on the side that was open to attack (Altenwied bei Neustadt in the Rhineland). In northwestern France—in the Norman territories in particular and, indeed, almost only there—one finds more elaborate forms such as octagonal towers with corner turrets added, or round towers with four three-quarter round projecting

298. Rüdesheim, reconstruction of the
original state of the Upper Burg (from
Tuulse, 1958)

299. Wildenburg, castle,
reconstruction of the north wing of the
"palas" (from Hotz, 1963)

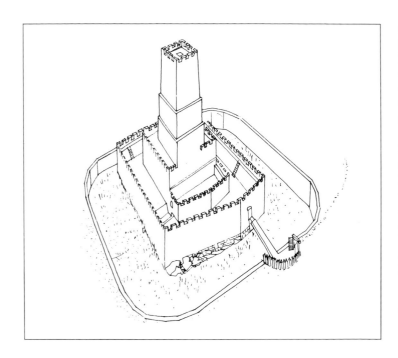

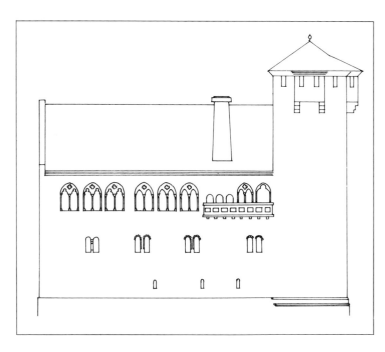

turrets such as are found at Houdan and elsewhere. The tower generally has no entrance at ground level. The door lies high and can be reached only by a ladder or wooden footbridge. The upper stories have wooden ceilings or vaults and are often connected with each other by stairs in the wall. On the ground floor there is a room whose only access is through a hole in the vault. In the popular imagination, this was equivalent to a donjon, but it may in reality have been only a storeroom for provisions.

The Norman keep or donjon is designed rather more as a dwelling, being larger in diameter and often having several rooms on one floor. The Tower of London even contains a two-storied chapel. The exteriors of these Norman keeps have tall strips of masonry that divide the large surfaces into vertical fields and give the buildings a lordly and forbidding appearance. Among major examples in France, there are Loches, Niort, and Beaugency in the Loire region, Château-Gaillard near Les Andelys in Normandy, and Pons in the southwest; in England, Hedingham and Middleham; in Sicily, Adrano; the same type is found in the burgs of the Crusaders in the Holy Land, at Sâfithâ and Margat in Syria.

The outer ring of walls in burgs and citadels is made even more monumental in effect by the towers generally projecting from its corners. These are so constructed as to facilitate strafing the wall with firepower, though this was something that really developed only in Gothic times. If, when we visit such strongholds today, we get the impression of great complexity, it is only because of the addition in the Late Middle Ages of barbicans, outworks, and courtyards for kitchen and other domestic activities.

The outer (curtain) wall has much to do with the general form and external appearance of the burg, as far as both the terrain and the ground plan are concerned. It is striking that often a uniform plan, especially a rectangle, was forcibly imposed on a terrain decidedly unsuited for such a shape. The upper and lower burgs at Rüdesheim on the Rhine, the burg at Neuleiningen in the Palatinate, and the Wildenburg in the Odenwald are instances of this. Very often, however, the course of the outer ring of walls is made to conform to the shape of the terrain, so that there are irregular ground plans that strike our eyes as some strange sort of natural growth. Yet even in these, certain typical forms can be distinguished. A specific form of curtain wall is the English shell-keep, an often circular structure with high walls surrounding an open place. Buildings of impermanent materials leaned against the inside of the wall. As ruins, the impression they give is of an empty shell, as at Restormel in Cornwall.

Burgs set high on the slopes or peaks of hills or mountains frequently have reinforced stretches of wall on the side open to attack. Together with a ring moat, these shield walls protect the access from the side of the mountain. When compared with town walls, the gate is usually not very prominent.

The ring of wall, along with the projecting donjon, is what most affects

the outward appearance and overall plan of the burg. If it is uniformly rectangular, as is mostly the case with strongholds in the plains but also at times with those in the mountains, the whole reminds one of the Roman forts, which undoubtedly were an important point of departure for the medieval burg. At Portchester on the southern coast of England, a Norman castle was built in a corner of a Roman fort, just as town castles frequently were sited within the town walls—for example the 's-Gravensteen in Ghent. Along with these, oval, circular, and irregular plans are frequent.

The majority of medieval burgs served their owners and defenders as living quarters also, so buildings for domestic activities were likewise necessary. Because the latter were often built of impermanent materials, they have rarely survived. For living purposes, either the main tower was used or a special building, the hall (or *palas*), which in large installations included a spacious chamber on the upper story. In Late Romanesque times, this building became the object of special attention, its façade decorated with elaborate architectural forms and arrangements, most often decorated portals, windows and groups of windows with columns and frames, and oriels and balconies. Notable examples of the *palas* can be seen at Vianden in Luxembourg, Münzenberg in Hesse, Wildenburg in the Odenwald, the Wartburg in Thuringia, and Andlau in Alsace.

The transition from the burg to the imperial palace (*Pfalz*) and then to the castle was fluid. The palaces of kings, emperors, and bishops generally put no great emphasis on the defensive structure of even dispensed with them. The large and usually rectangular multi-storied residential building has an impressive hall in the upper story, distinguishable by its window arcades, an apselike bay for the chapel, and often also by an exterior staircase. The best known of these that still preserve some Romanesque portions are at Braunschweig, Goslar, Wimpfen, Seligenstadt, Gelnhausen, and Nuremberg in Germany, and Cheb in Czechoslovakia. Romanesque bishops' palaces are known almost only through old pictures, as is the case at Cologne, Speyer, and Liège, though in Mainz the chapel of Sankt Gothard at least has survived alongside the north wall of the cathedral. Within the framework of Ottonian policy, some of these ecclesiastical palaces developed out of royal palaces, notably at Speyer. The large hall of the Wartburg in Thuringia

shows how much the various basic forms came to resemble each other in the later period.

The castles of the Normans and of the Hohenstaufen emperors in Italy constitute a special high point. In some—at Melfi in Basilicata and Lucera in Apulia, for instance—new and very interesting ideas in fortification were worked out; other examples displayed such new architectonic conceptions as the regular square—in Prato outside Florence and in Catania and Siracusa in Sicily—or the octagon, as the Castel del Monte in Apulia. A few of the Sicilian palaces (La Zisa and La Cuba in the environs of Palermo) simply do not fit into what we expect of the Romanesque burg, what with their exterior articulation and the more elaborate and often symmetrical layout of their rooms. As in Sicilian church architecture, here too Arabic and Byzantine factors must be taken into account.

In the Hohenstaufen period more elaborate architectural forms were used in the interior also, among them vaulted chambers on rows of supports, fireplace, portals flanked by columns, and elaborate window arcatures. The burg chapels often followed the type prevalent among churches in the region. South of the Loire, this meant chiefly a barrel-vaulted single nave with apse, a form that, like the hall church, was then transplanted to the Holy Land. North of the Alps, a two-storied square with four supports was developed for larger installations, as at Goslar, Mainz, Nuremberg, Landsberg near Halle, and Cheb (Eger); an English example is documented for Hereford. The double-chapel from the end of the eleventh century in Speyer was probably originally the chapter house and shows that this type was not restricted to a single function. Smaller burg chapels can consist of a single chamber in Germany too, and even the one in the imperial burg at Trifels bei Anweiler in the Palatinate was so conceived. In Spain there is an example in the two-storied aisleless castle chapel at Loarre in Aragon, dating from the late eleventh and early twelfth centuries.

In smaller burgs and fortified residences, the parish church was the personal church of the lord of the castle and so was often built inside the dwelling tower and provided with a west gallery, as has been demonstrated by L. Genicot for Hamerenne near Rochefort in Belgium and by V. Mencl for an entire group of Bohemian chapels.

Chapter Six

THE CHURCH BUILDING AND ITS ENVIRONMENT

Construction and Function

The furnishings and arrangements in large early medieval churches were entirely unlike those to which we are accustomed, and it made no differences if these were bishopric churches (cathedrals and minsters) or abbey churches (monasteries, priories, collegiate churches). In only a few buildings today can we get an idea of those furnishings and arrangements so essential to the overall impression of the architecture and, indeed, even to the understanding of the time in which it was born.

As early as the Carolingian era, the single altar of the Early Christian basilica was replaced by a number of altars. The plan of the monastery at Sankt Gallen shows that these were disposed one behind the other down the central axis of the church. This was so in the following period too, when the high altar stood in the apse and not the crossing. It is for this reason that the apse and the space often left between it and the crossing are together known as the *sanctuarium* (the altar area) or *presbyterium*. This is the area where offices were celebrated for the monks, *patres,* or for the cathedral or collegiate chapter. The altar with the crucifix was in the eastern portion of the central nave, where offices were celebrated for the laity, whose place was in the western portion of the nave.

According to the Sankt Gallen plan additional altars were set up on the nave piers, though without the close architectonic linkage that was to become an important goal of medieval architecture. Functional demands explain the many basic changes in church design in the course of history. Beginning around the year 1000, chapels were constructed around the altar area and made accessible by a passageway, thus constituting a choir ambulatory with crown of chapels, a form that was to continue into the Late Gothic. Altars were also set up in secondary apses on the crossarms. If the latter play such an important role in most large Romanesque and Gothic churches, it is because—obviously for functional purposes—they afford room for two side chapels, each with a place for an altar. Secondary choirs, which replace these transept apses, double or even triple their number, and at the same time augment their area, are likewise nothing other than places for altars. When they were staggered in ground plan it was certainly part of both a formal and functional requirement. The staggered choir and altar fulfill the same demand. This may be one of the reasons leading to the development of large hall-crypts beneath the crossing and transept. If this supposition is correct, then the choir ambulatory, staggered choir, and transept crypt would all be different architectural forms serving the same purpose, which was to increase the number of altars. In those terms, the simple rectangular chapels lined up along the transept arms in Cistercian churches are explainable as an involution of the staggered choir in response to the order's insistence in its earliest phase on simple forms that were less expensive to build.

As for altars in the side naves, not until the High Gothic was a fixed form arrived at: the succession of chapels aligned along the side walls as we see

them mostly now. In addition, the west front and its upper story contained altars in many cases. If the Romanesque altar was intended to play a central role in the church, its form was nevertheless very unassuming, not at all comparable with Gothic altar retables or even with tabernacle altars or the large Baroque superstructures. A block of brick or tiles, a table that was no more than a slab on four stone supports—this was all as a rule. In many cases, stone, wood, or metal reliefs or, in northern Spain above all, wooden panels with painted figuration decorated the front, which was usually visible since the priest stood behind the altar and celebrated the office facing the congregation (this is again the case since the recent liturgical reform).

Besides the altars, an important factor in the appearance of the medieval church was the *pluteus* or *transenna,* a low stone balustrade of even a wall of human height that ran beneath the west-to-east crossing arches and therefore separated the crossarms from the crossing. In the enclosure that resulted, these structures made up the back wall for the choir stalls where the monks or canons sang the service, for which reason this area was called the "chorus" during the High Middle Ages. This, and not the main altar, was the key place in the church, and is often indicated on the exterior by the crossing tower; if open, the latter provides light for the area. "Crossing" is therefore a modern art historical designation for what was called "chorus" in the High Middle Ages, and for that reason they must have called the crossing tower the chorus tower instead. In the thirteenth-century Gothic cathedrals there was a shift in emphasis: the east portion of the church was very much enlarged and thereby made room within the so-called cathedral choir for the chorus. This is why, accordingly, the name "choir" was shifted to that part of the building and tended to be applied to it in earlier buildings as well. All this must be kept clearly in mind to avoid confusion, and especially in order to understand the references in early medieval literary sources.

The chorus in the crossing of Pre-Romanesque and Romanesque churches was also closed off to the west by a screen. This transverse choir screen might project, together with the chorus, into the central nave. This is the explanation of the cross-wall such as is still found in former Cistercian churches. In most churches they were later demolished, but they can often be reconstructed from their remains. This structure too often had architectonic consequences, necessitating at times a different type of easternmost supports in the nave or an interruption in the regular alternation of supports in order to accommodate it.

The transverse choir screen was often associated with the ambos and lecterns in the later twelfth and thirteenth centuries to make a more elaborate structure culminating in Gothic times in the *lectorium,* the jubé, or rood screen.

The screens were frequently articulated architectonically with blind arcades or other framing forms, and sometimes also embellished with ornamental or figurative reliefs. However, even these often very important art works—notably those at Halberstadt and Bamberg—have seldom been left unaltered in their original position.

Many abbey churches, especially those of the Hirsau congregation, separate the chorus of the *patres* (the monks of priestly status) from that of the *fratres* (the brothers), in which case the latter have their place in the minor chorus that usually takes over the eastern portion of the central nave. Longitudinal and transverse screens alike have through-passages, though these scarcely afford a vista through the structure. Thus, the lower zone of medieval churches was interrupted by these walls, and the eye could only take in the total interior on an upper level. In the late Renaissance and Baroque periods, in line with the directives of the Council of Trent, it became imperative to afford the congregation an unobstructed view of the high altar and celebrant, for which reason most choir screens were demolished and replaced (if at all) by openwork grilles that did not block the view. Very often too, the Romanesque arrangement of the interior was altered in later times to conform to changes in liturgy or taste, and today still we frequently find clergy and congregation clamoring for the removal of one of the few surviving choir enclosures.

In front of the transverse screen in the central nave stood the altar with crucifix where mass was said for the laity, and in front of this in turn there was generally the tomb of the patron or founder of the church. The tomb was in the same position occupied originally by those of the earlier Salic rulers in Worms Cathedral and of the emperors in Speyer Cathedral. In the Romanesque church these tombs were kept simple, as a rule with an inscribed plaque and at most a relief with the figure of the deceased, either set in the floor or on a low catafalque. These likewise have seldom been preserved in their original arrangement. During the Middle Ages, burials inside the church increased immoderately, despite the fact that they were limited to certain distinguished persons and their circle: bishops, abbots, and patrons had their place in the church, the members of the chapter and the *patres* in the cloisters, and laymen in the porch.

Besides the tombs, there were often reliquaries of saint and martyrs whose remains had been removed from their graves and laid in altars or shrines. Such reliquaries, richly embellished with goldsmith's work, were a special archievement of the Rhine and Meuse valleys in the Late Romanesque. We must imagine them set on or above the altars, often in such a manner that the faithful could walk around or beneath them.

We must not think of the churches (in all categories) in the Middle Ages as empty and offering only an occasional service as they do today, but instead almost continually full of activity, such as we see now only in certain churches in Latin countries, for example in Santa María del Mar in Barcelona. Procession and pilgrimage groups filled them with movement. The chief offices, especially on holy days, were much richer and more animated than we know them. Choir lofts or tribunes appear to have existed even in Carolingian westworks, and were generally assigned to upper stories in Romanesque interiors. Instrumentalists of all sorts, not just organists, took part in the offices, with more robust music-making than some would have us believe.

The Influence of the Builder: the Private Church

The medieval house of God was not so exclusively devoted to ecclesiastical use as we are accustomed to today. Nor was the Church, as an institution, so isolated in terms of organization. The interweaving of the domain of the secular state with that of the Church led to a great conflict—the dispute over the right of investiture, which was settled only by force of arms. Secular lords founded churches and monasteries, mostly with pious intent but not without an eye to power and to enhanced prestige, and they reserved certain rights in these. The result was a kind of private personal church in which the feudal lord had a regular place of his own choosing, usually the west tribune; he also reserved to himself the right to appoint the clergy in his church. At a higher level, great lords, kings, and emperors installed (and deposed) bishops as they liked. When the secular powers built churches—which meant having them built with their own funds—they certainly were not likely to forego having their say in what the edifice would look like. Obviously, we can scarcely summon up concrete evidence for this, but in a few cases where the written sources are more extensive and eloquent there are grounds to suspect it, as in Speyer Cathedral.

Even today the influence of the man who commissions or pays for a building manifests itself in a great many ways. It can be restricted to the financial sphere or to certain basic demands for space in the building, but he can also go so far as to take over the entire job of planning, leaving to the architect merely the task of technical execution. We know that this was so with patrons in the Renaissance and Baroque, and in the Middle Ages it must have been no different.

The influence of the founder or patron also manifested itself through the use of the building for a variety of non-religious activities. Rooms were set aside as judgment seats, preferably in the fore-hall or narthex. Treaties and charters were signed in ceremonies before the west fronts of churches and halls. Bell towers also served as observation post against enemies and fires and were often the property of the city, which then also had the responsibility of erecting them.

Even defensive purposes were not alien to the church building. The church as fortress is a familiar notion. It was in the nature of things that the Romanesque church, with its secure walls often surrounded by a burial-ground wall as stout as that of a citadel, should have been used as a refuge in times of peril. Its roof and tower provided good defensive positions. Provided with fighting stations, parapets, saliens for catapults, and machicolated galleries, the church could be transformed into a regular burg, and often was. Certain of these contrivances may, in some cases, have even influenced the architectonic conception of the building: blind arches can reinforce the walls and serve as support for the parapet. The church at Royat in Auvergne is a well-known example, and there is another at Saint-Pons-de-Thomières. The cathedral of Albi, dating from the thirteenth and fourteenth centuries, is built in the typical brick of the Gothic in Languedoc and displays a perfect union of monumental conception with defensive function. As one would expect, this combination is most frequent in the churches of villages and small communities, and there are a great many of them in Romanian Transylvania.

Above and beyond this, functionality seems to have influenced the conception of churches far less than the amount of money available and the requirements of space. Indeed, as things worked out, it must have been difficult to distinguish cathedrals, abbey churches of different orders, and collegiate churches purely on the basis of their general plan and architectural form.

As to identity of the architects in the Romanesque period, this is a question that defies answering. Even the most auspicious written sources have proved of no help to researches, as can be seen in the work on Bishop Benno of Osnabrück by I. Hindenberg, whose findings cannot hold water. The studies of W. Haas have made this situation clear.

Architecture as the Vehicle of Meaning: the Iconology of Architecture
A much-noticed book by G. Bandmann reawakened interest around 1951 in a subject of great cultural and historical importance—the doctrine of meaning in architecture (its iconology). The last to write about it comprehensively, in 1924, was J. Sauer, a theologian working in art history. Despite his work, this aspect had very much retreated into the background because architectural scholarship had been devoting itself to other fields, especially that of formalistic analysis. Now the problem has been posed again.

A great many medieval written sources reveal that a meaning that has become foreign to us was attributed to the church building and its various portions. This fact is beyond question. Thus columns, for example, when twelve in number were looked on as symbolizing the Apostles and, simultaneously, as props of the Church. The cruciform ground plan of the church was thought of as a representation of the cross of Christ. The deviated longitudinal axis of many churches symbolizes the bowed head of Christ on the cross.

The question this raises for the historian of art and architecture is whether and where these associations determined or influenced the form of the church building, or whether they were no more than *a posteriori* interpretations on the part of theologians. Put concretely, did the man in charge of the project order the architect to lay out the church with a cruciform ground plan because of its symbolic significance or because he needed plenty of room for chapels with altars? Did he insist that the nave must have twelve columns, thereby making that part of the church quite long, or was the latter a precondition having to do with the distance between the supports? Was it merely that the theologian or patron had the *a posteriori* satisfaction of applying to the new building a time-honored and well-worn analogy, one with the value of a venerable *topos*? Did the bend in the longitudinal axis result from a miscalculation, perhaps because it was necessary to build around an existing or preceding building and this was the only way to evade the difficulties involved? Did the interpretation merely suggest itself or was it a deliberate point in the program set up by the patron? Further: does the rounded and vaulted apse, and indeed even the arch itself, signify majesty and loftiness? If so, why are there flat-ceilinged altar areas? These are only a few problems, selected almost at random. If we have had recourse to so many question marks here, it is not because we doubt that such "meanings" were in fact seen in the church and its components—this is beyond question—but because it remains problematical whether they really did influence the architectonic plan and form of the church building. The two things quite definitely do not go hand in hand. In the final analysis, it may be that one should not attempt an overall general answer to such questions, but instead judge them case by case. Moreover, one should never lose sight of the fact that the nature of awareness and consciousness of medieval man—and above all of the medieval cleric—differed in essential points from that of a present-day researcher into architecture, be he himself architect or art historian.

THE TECHNICAL ASPECT OF CHURCH ARCHITECTURE

Materials
The social and economic structure of the Middle Ages permitted transport of building materials only within a limited radius. When stone was carried over longer stretches, medieval historians made a point of mentioning it, which indicates that it was something out of the ordinary. Columns and other remains from antiquty were procured for Aachen from Ravenna, and shafts of columns in the abbey church at Sint Truiden in northern Belgium came from the Upper Rhine. Tufa stone likewise was shipped by water from the mouth of the Brohl between Cologne and Coblenz, all the way to Jutland but also upriver to Speyer, where it was used for vaulting; for the powerful arches supporting the crossing tower there, a uniquely hard basalt lava was procured from the Eifel Mountains. In these latter cases, the factors at work had to do with construction, not aesthetics. For the most part, the masons used whatever stone was obtainable near the building site, so that the diversity of color one finds in Romanesque churches in different regions was basically due to that simple fact, and indeed in the most literal sense: the color and texture of the stone together determine the character of a building. Fine-grained, smooth, light gray limestone, of the sort found in

nothern France and England, requires very accurate cutting when used for squared-stone masonry with thin joints. In the colored sandstone region, along the Upper Rhine in particular, the material is somewhat coarser but for that reason more powerful in effect, especially because of its vivid coloring, often a pronounced yellow ocher and a deep red. The greenish stone found in many districts of Westphalia set the character for the Romanesque churches at Soest. It is the dark gray coarse-grained basalt lava of the French Massif Central that gives the buildings in Auvergne their austere and gloomy appearance—lightened, however, by the lively articulation of the building block and by the colored patterns on its surfaces. In Tuscany, especially in the northwest where the renowned quarries at Carrara provide the material, the smooth dazzling white marble that is often in used in alternation with green and black marble and cut and polished with consummate skill excites the admiration of even those persons indifferent to art. More unobtrusive effects are produced by the combination of yellowish porous tufa, gray trachite, and black basalt lava in Cologne and along the Lower Rhine. The tufa-like nagelfluh stone gives Upper Bavarian buildings a distinctively coarse and pitted surface. Black purbeck marble lends a special accent to the early Gothic buildings of England.

While the color and texture of the stone play their part in the outward appearance of a building, more basic are questions of resistance to pressure and to damage from bad weather along with other technical factors involving construction and stability; these were certainly matters of note to the Middle Ages, as we have already pointed out in connection with Speyer. In regions such as the Po Valley in northern Italy where there was no usable stone, the ancient technique of baked bricks was adopted. Characteristic of bricks, as of tufa stone also, is the small format and close-fitting joinings as well as a strong red color or, much less often, a clay-yellow, which can be enlivened here and there by other bricks glazed over in black or green. Since the middle of the twelfth century, this has been the dominant building technique in nothern Europe—from Flanders to Friesland, Holstein, and the Baltic countries as well as to the east in northern Lower Saxony, the Altmark, Brandenburg, and in various places throughout Saxony. Before, using brick, builders in this zone had had to depend on granite boulders.

Foundations

Romanesque buildings were as a rule supported on deep foundation walls that also extended under the rows of supporting pillars and, as spanning gross-walls, reinforced the piers of the cross-arches in the crossing and west front. Thus, the foundations formed a lattice of masonry from which the ground plan of the building can be read with some precision, unlike the High Gothic system in which there was usually a separate foundation for each pier. This means that, if their foundations remain, we can make out what destroyed Romanesque buildings were like, and a good deal of the

value and interest of excavations rest on just that point.

From the foundations we can also learn how thick the walls were, though this is no clue to their height as it would be today. Nor are the different floor pressures in consequence of the different heights of various portions of the building reflected by the depth of the foundation. Thus, no sure conclusions can be drawn about the height of the interior from its underpinnings. This is the greatest handicap to research based on excavation, and is not surmountable by even the most advanced techniques. What we can read from the foundations is whether the building had one or three naves, a transept, and a west front, and what the east portions looked like in ground plan. But we cannot conclude with any certainy what the height of the various areas was nor their mutual relationship. In extreme cases, we cannot even recognize from the foundations if the building was a hall or a basilica. Only towers beginning at ground level can be distinguished in general by a greater thickness of wall or a foundation ledge.

Masonry and Stonehewing

The technique of cutting stone as well as that of building walls can be considered uniform throughout Europe in Pre-Romanesque and Romanesque times, differentiated only to the extent that the architecture itself was. As a rule, they can be distinguished from both the Roman and the Gothic techniques. Walls and piers were generally executed as a shell-like construction. For this type of masonry with rubble for filling, the larger and smoother stones were reserved for the outer surfaces, and craggy rocks and fragments (or even old material from earlier buildings) were mixed with a rich mortar and used for filling.

Hewn stones were built up in horizontal strata layer upon layer but also obliquely and on edge, so that, depending on the direction of the oblique stones, the result is either "corn" or "fishbone" masonry. When the stones are roughed into a rectangular format with the mallet, we have what is known as hammer-hewn small stonework. The intermediary stage between these small blocks and much larger ones was effected, according to W. Haas, by rough-hewn stones—one surface of which (the one that was to remain visible in the wall) was hewn into a regular rectangle and continued to bear traces of the coarse work done on it with the pickax. True dressed stone, on the other hand, is characterized by the chipping away of the edges by which the stonecutter shapes a form from the crude block. The resultant boss is then chipped down to form a flat "mirror" or field, which is picked away with the two-pronged pick or flattened with the ax in a final stage of the process. During the Late Romanesque period, surfaces were made to stand out by toothed rills cut into the stone. In many regions we can see stonecutters' signs neatly carved in the flat field, as either simple geometrical figures or letters, along with other signs having to do with where the stone was to be placed. According to a generally accepted hypothesis, the

"signatures" served in reckoning up the amount of work done by a particular mason.

The main varieties of treatment are found simultaneously in all periods considered here. We find finely joined neat work with large blocks dating from around 800 in the minster at Aachen, from the start of the eleventh century in Sankt Pantaleon in Cologne and Sankt Michael in Hildesheim, from around 1050 in Speyer I, from around 1100 in Speyer II, Cluny III, Durham, Bari, Pisa, Toulouse, and Santiago de Compostela, and in the twelfth century everywhere. Coarse masonry with rubble filler, however, is found not only in Catalonian churches of around 1000 and many Tuscan churches of the twelfth century, but even in such a well-conceived building as the collegiate church at Karden in the Rhineland, from around 1200.

Finely worked and well-preserved block surfaces reveal the masterly craftsmanship to whose beauty we are today particularly sensitive. However, we also find the ancient technique of rough stone rubble walls to be aesthetically fascinating and so go to great lengths to expose it on old buildings, even where it was by no means ever intended and was, in fact, plastered over smoothly.

Instead of hewing building stone out of quarries, understandably enough people sometimes took it from the debris of a building that was to be replaced by a larger or handsomer one. This can be recognized on pieces of dressed stone that bear all the signs of having been meant for another use. Ruins too—above all those of Roman buildings—were a good source of raw material, as can be seen in all the regions of the Roman Empire where one frequently comes upon reliefs, inscriptions, and pieces of treated stone in a quite alien context. Often no attempt was made to conceal them, which may on occasion have been with the thought of giving documentary proof of the Church's victory over paganism, though in specific isolated cases it is usually not possible to say if this was so or not.

Roman bricks, recognizable by their flat format, were often reused also. However, it must remain an open question whether bricks of the same type and form were produced later, and if so, when (it was probably in the Carolingian period). Nevertheless, in the eleventh and twelfth centuries in various regions of Europe bricks were made and used in great quantity—notably in Lombardy, the Netherlands, the North German plain, and then east of the Elbe and in the Baltic lands, but also in the Bavarian highlands (at Moosburg) and the Upper Rhine (at Schwarzach). Even in Tuscany, there are Romanesque buildings partly or entirely in brick.

Construction

The arch was the first major problem that Romanesque builders had to grapple with. As a rule, it was erected on a centering (a wooden frame removed once the mortar has set) and called for extensive buttressing, especially with such broader spans as in the crossing. This is even more true for stone vaults. When the vaults do not mutually buttress themselves, as in the hall church, the outward thrust is taken by especially thick walls. This represented no particular drawback to Romanesque architecture, since mass—mass given form—was precisely one of the means by which it achieved its effects, artistic and otherwise. Another possibility was the reinforcement of the wall at specific points by pilasters indoors and buttressing piers outdoors. These were particularly called for where the wall was widely opened up by arches, nave arcades, galleries, and windows. Engaged half-columns and shafts served also to articulate the mass. Rectangular pilasters, round shafts, and blind arches were given many different shapes in the eleventh century. Here a constructional purpose—the reinforcement of the wall—went hand in hand with a conceptual aim, namely dynamic effect, and their indissoluble union was the product of both the intellectual and artistic work of the architect and of a long tradition of craftsmanship on the part of the workers, a union so close that it is difficult, even impossible, to distinguish their respective contributions. This should be recognized, lest art history be set unsolvable and fruitless tasks.

The use of pilasters and engaged shafts led to the wall itself becoming totally organized, and this also had a decisive effect on its constructional aspects. This was true also when it came to hollowing out the wall by means of passageways, a procedure initiated in the eleventh century. When the wall was no longer a compact stone mass but composed instead of strips of masonry, openings, columns, arches, and vaults, a further step in the direction of complication had been taken. Now, within the wall itself, there was an interplay of forces, of downward pressure and outward thrust. With this also began the centuries-long process in which the mass of wall became enriched with articulation that was to end by replacing it.

With stone vaulting new problems arose. Frames, centering, and molds placed high demands on the carpenter's art. The problem of buttressing involved the third dimension. In the eleventh century, in consequence of the complete vaulting of the higher portions of the church, the edifice became to an even greater degree than before a multipartite organism with a play of forces that defies calculation, even for our highly developed modern science of statics.

The Middle Ages made far more extensive use of anchoring than most of us are aware of. Wooden ring anchors were embedded in the masonry and wooden tie beams were stretched across the room. Much damage was done to the stability of buildings when these anchors rotted, burned, or otherwise gave way. In the Gothic churches of Venice and the Netherland one gets a good picture of how much tie beams (as well as open timberwork) influence the appearance of the interior.

The Floor

The floor in Romanesque churches had a much greater importance in the overall picture of the interior than it does today, because it was often not occupied by pews or seats. Nevertheless, it was frequently of puritanical plainness. For all its dignity as an imperial foundation, the greatest Romanesque church, the cathedral of Speyer, had a simple plastered flooring that may have been colored, as traces here and there suggest. There were also floors of stone slabs or of bricks, and these harmonized well with the general architectural character for which they provided a neutral base.

Pattern and inlaid floors composed of either terracotta tiles or marble inlay were likewise quite numerous, ranging from simple geometrical designs to figurative compositions within framed fields. There are instances in many regions, among them the crypt of Sankt Gereon in Cologne from around 1060, the nave of the twelfth-century cathedral of Lescar in southwestern France, and the large-scale compositions in the cathedral of Acqui in Piedmont and in that of Otranto in Apulia, the latter running down the entire central nave in a single large sweep.

If the floor does not earn attention through its artistic merit, it often becomes the stepchild of architecture. It is certainly prone to become worn out and require replacement. The ignorance of patrons, architects, and craftsmen often explains why a new floor is simply laid over the old one. When this has been done several times, the socles, plinths, and bases of the columns and piers finally disappear beneath them so that the interior looks like a cripple without feet. Other factors too have often had a deleterious effect on floors, such as floods or even a change in the ground-water level

(as happened in the abbey church in Cruas in the Ardèche), while a new feeling for proportions on the part of those responsible for the church has on at least one occasion—in the cathedral of Speyer—led to deliberately raising the floor level as much as two feet. Often enough one's first impression of a medieval church is not satisfying, and only subsequently does one discover that the cause is a raised floor level. Good conservation of monuments should aim at remedying this.

The Ceiling

The ceiling poses a special problem in Early and High Romanesque basilicas and aisleless churches—that is, wherever there is no vault (either originally or of later date). Where the interior is covered over in wood, there are three possibilities:

1. There may be an open timberwork ceiling in which the usually very simple framework and the underside of the roof remain visible. These can be covered over with boards, or else the rafters and roofing can be left visible. While this system is found today throughout Italy and England but seldom north of the Alps, it is very likely that in the latter region as well there were many open timberwoork ceilings in the Middle Ages as is generally claimed for Normandy too, though without any concrete evidence so far.

2. There may be a flat ceiling of boards affixed to the roof beams. If the boards are nailed under them, the result is a smooth surface that can be painted, as in Sankt Michael in Hildesheim and Sankt Martin in Zillis, Switzerland. If the boards are simply set into grooves between the roof beams, a slight relief results. If they are nailed above the roof beams the relief becomes more marked, and we can speak of a beamed ceiling, a form as sympathetic to our modern romantic taste for the rustic as it is appropriate to the Romanesque. Such a ceiling has been imitated in reinforced concrete in the collegiate church at Nivelles.

3. There may be a wooden barrel vault. Here the roof beams are made in the form of an arch, and boards are nailed below them to make a round or pointed wooden barrel vault, which thereby incorporates a large part of the ceiling area into the room below and makes the latter more spacious, as in Mont-Saint-Michel and many churches in the Netherlands. Most of the surviving wooden barrel vaults are from the Gothic period or later. An intermediate solution involves shaping the beams into arches but leaving them uncovered by boards, so that an open, transparent, barrel-like form ensues such as was recently reconstructed at Reichenau-Mittelzell. When linked to the crown of the wall, such wooden trestling provides a cross-anchoring for the upper walls. In wooden barrel vaults, the exposed beams and uprights have a part in the impressive effect of the interior.

For the most part, the original wooden ceilings have been victims of frequent fires. Very often we cannot get an adequate idea of them and so must content ourselves with these general observations.

The Roof

In southern and southwestern Europe the fairly flat roofs are often made of stone slabs that are usually laid on a stratum of masonry covering over the barrel vaults or cupolas, a system that makes wooden roof frames unnecessary.

Sometimes, however, the cupolas were completely exposed, as in San Cataldo in Palermo and, it is thought, in certain cupola churches in Aquitaine that have been or should be so reconstructed, notably at Cahors, Saint-Front in Périgueux, and the churches at Souillac and Solignac.

Otherwise, all other buildings have roofs covered with lead, tiles, or slate resting on a wooden frame. Thin slabs of some stone such as slate or of some metal may have been used as well as wooden shingles. The concave tiles generally had a marked relief ("monks" and "nuns" are the terms for convex and concave tiles, respectively). Romanesque timberwork frames have only rarely survived, though in greater number than is commonly assumed. They are always simple in construction. In a few cases, where large dimensions made them necessary, there were more complicated structures (which, however, cannot be identified with certainty), in particular projecting drain-roofs at Saint-Sernin in Toulouse and Speyer Cathedral or water conduits using roof culverts and simple spouts.

Romanesque roofs correspond in their simple stereometric forms to the overall style: saddle and lean-to roofs make three-sided prisms, tent or pavilion roofs make pyramids, round towers and apses are covered with spherical or hemispherical roofs. It may be concluded that Early Romanesque roofs had a considerable overhang and were without rafter cornices, something that became more and more developed only in the eleventh and twelfth centuries concurrently with the exterior base wall. The slope of the roof changed from the early Romanesque shallow angle of about 30° to a steeper 40° in the twelfth century, but it never reached the steepness of Gothic roofs.

Only here and there do we find folded roofs, with or without gables, in the Late Romanesque, though the church at Bronnbach has one and they are numerous on the Lower Rhine. The characteristic lozenge roof of towers in Cologne and along the Lower Rhine gives them a special accent, as do the cupola roofs of the round crossing towers of Salamanca and vicinity.

Like the floor, the roof is highly perishable and susceptible to accident. Not a single roof has survived that has both the Romanesque framework and its original covering. And, as with floors, later times have by no means respected its form. The tendency to ever steeper roofs is clear and has led to our taking the close association of forms from different chronological periods almost as the natural state of things. Nevertheless, it is a special stroke of luck when we are able to determine with conviction what the original form of the roof was and proceed to reconstruct it. To a certain extent, that is what was done recently in Speyer.

Measure and Proportion

The problems of measure and proportion have been dealt with frequently, though most often in a highly subjective fashion. Writers have proceeded as if it sufficed to be able to inscribe geometrical figures within the ground and elevation plans of old buildings. When this has been done—and it has been often—there is still no proof that the figures and proportions thus arrived at played any part in the initial conception. Different writers have in fact seen different figures and proportions in the same building. For Gothic architecture, in which the possibilities are far more numerous, K. Hecht has made this quite clear—showing, moreover, how easily assertions have been made on the grounds of inaccurate measurements. Wherever there is talk of Roman, Carolingian, and other foot measurements in the literature, one must be cautious. Very often these are based on the presupposition that the foot unit is certain to go smoothly into the given measurements, be they overall or partial. This, however, is an entirely unwarranted assumption.

THE CHURCH BUILDING AND THE ARTS

Sculpture and Architectonic Decoration

Pre-Romanesque and Early Romanesque churches have scarcely any sculpture directly connected with the architecture itself. Except for capitals, it is only such furnishings as altars, ambos, baldachins, and shrines that were so embellished. Even the portal was usually left undecorated. This is why the most eminent expression of Romanesque art seems to us to be the block (or cushion) capital, an entirely abstract form with smooth surfaces. Foliage, Antique forms, and even figurative elements do appear on capitals, but they would seem to be holdovers from an older world. Trapezoid and goblet-block capitals, as well as the Norman scalloped capital, represent parallels to the cushion capital.

Even if all sorts of architectonic sculpture appear in the eleventh century, it was only in the High Romanesque period—and in the most different places—that a wealth of ornamental forms and figurative sculptured tympanum became the rule in many regions. Southwestern Europe— southern France and northern Spain, but also a few churches in Italy— produced great masterworks of figurative sculpture, at once monumental and expressive, and so grandly conceived that they are capable of moving even those who do not fathom Christian pictorial imagery either wholly or in part. During the twelfth century, the sculptural program extended to the walls and columns, and in many instances the portal was expanded into a distinct structure in front of the wall itself, as in Moissac, Carennac, and Oloron-Sainte-Marie. The endless variety of the capitals in the churches and cloisters evoked a world of imagery. As a rule, the law of architecture was respected: only rarely, above all in southwestern France, did sculptural programs cover entire church façades with a flickering network of finely detailed forms, notably in Angoulême Cathedral and in Notre-Dame-la-Grande in Poitiers.

Along with the rise and spread of monumental sculpture went a thoroughgoing articualtion of the entire architectural structure. The wall base and roof cornice were developed and given ever more elaborate profile. In many places cornices were also ornamented—first of all in Speyer II—and windows were provided with ornamental frames, as in Sant'Abbondio in Como and Speyer Cathedral. The boundless admiration that many present-day viewers lavish on these art works often fails to take into account their architectural setting. That they do not harmonize with purer and more spiritually illumined conceptions was something unequivocally proclaimed by Bernard of Clairvaux. The wealth of forms manifested by capitals and architectonic sculpture exceeds description, and one must therefore admire the courage with which many investigators have believed they could unravel stylistic links between them or have even claimed to be able to read the wanderings of masters and itinerant bands of craftsmen from certain forms and details. The closest one can come to this may be the recognition of a few artists in Italy, where—in the arts as well as in other activities—the individual personality was earliest in defining itself. Specific examples are Wiligelmus in Modena and Benedetto Antelami in Parma.

Late Romanesque art added to the wide variety of architectonic sculptural forms. If High Romanesque sculpture had by and large respected the block form, in the late phase the block became more deeply hollowed out and chiaroscuro effects were introduced. Organic forms, vines and leaves, animal and humans were no longer rigorously stylized in an ornamental way, but were instead lifelike and animated. The structurally oriented character of the Early Gothic was best matched by the crocketed goblet capital that originated in the French crown lands and that was taken up and varied in many other regions in the Late Romanesque. With the Early Gothic portals the full-length human figure in monumental form likewise made its entry into architecture. The antecedents of this development go back to the early twelfth century, when the way was paved for the artistic unity of the High Gothic cathedrals of northern France, with their figured portals. In any event, architecture and figurative sculpture remained separate domains in Late Romanesque and Early Gothic buildings.

Plaster, Whitewash, and Paint

In contemporary architecture much is made of the notion of using material "honestly" and "rightly," the architectural theorists of the Cologne Werkbund and their forerunners raising this to virtually a moral principle. The very idea was alien to the Middle Ages. This does not mean that stone and its texture and color played no role. On the contrary, they were viewed merely as serviceable elements, and the fact is that surfaces and colors were altered at will by plaster and whitewash. Raw rubble walls were always plastered over, those with small stones at least smoothed down, but even handsome hewnstone masonry was more de-emphasized by white or colored limewash than was possible with the bare stone. During the restoration of Speyer Cathedral between 1957 and 1970, these became matters of lively controversy, the outcome of which is still visible in the present appearance of the interior. The stones were set in quite arbitrarily in the side naves and on the nave arcades, just as they came from the quarry. This produced a piebald surface entirely contrary to the austere character of Early Romanesque architecture. We know that the cathedral did not look like that in the eleventh century, but instead united the piers, engaged columns, and walls into as system by means of ocher yellow and sandstone red limewash. What is more, even where the various colored stones had already been set in regular alternation, as in the crypt, the west portal, and upper part of the central nave, they were coated over. When this became clear to the restorers, the crypt, transept, and chancel were given a colored wash in subsequent work. However, it was simply not possible to go back over the nave, and finally the arches were deliberately made piebald. Probably in the Middle Ages too the decision as to what should be done were as much tied up with personalities and as much influenced by subjective choices as in the twentieth-century restoration at Speyer.

On the basis of the experience and investigations of architectural historians and conservationists in the course of several decades, it may be concluded that it is ahistorical to expose rough stone walls and to reject the use of colored washes. Nevertheless, this continues to be a fashionable mania. True enough, we must concede that it is now difficult or even impossible to reconstruct what many churches looked like originally in terms of color or even to establish how they were altered in various periods. But there can no longer be any doubt that color was the rule. It varied from light retouching of the stone by means of colored washes in some related tint to contrasts of hewn stone or brick with plastered surfaces, and to overall painting of the entire interior. This often involved a decorative scheme or an extensive program of figurative painting as sumptuous as that in the royal burial chapel in León, where the capitals too are splendidly imaginative. Recent research has again shown that this was just as much the case when brick was used. There can scarcely be said to be such a thing as a building in which the bricks were left raw. The network of joinings was converted into an artistic element by painting along the edges in color. Arch friezes and sawtooth patterns were contrasted and made to stand out by a whitewashed plaster ground. Arches and windows were whitewashed in their undersides and embrasures, but also often painted in different colors or with a pattern such as a checkerboard. As a rule, the vaults were completely plastered over, as has been shown by the exhaustive investigations of D. Ellger concerning the cathedral at Ratzeburg. Numerous parallels from Saxony and Denmark confirm his findings. However, there are other possibilities: A. Haupt found enough in the church at Altenkrempe to justify him in reconstructing a more elaborate and structurally effective color scheme that likewise goes along more emphatically with the plastered surfaces of the walls. In Bergen on the island of Rügen the entire interior of the parish church—piers, arches, walls, vaults—is plastered and then covered with a regular scheme of ornamental and figurative painting.

In recent times the question has been raised as to whether colored architecture has some special significance. Some have gone so far as to relate the frequent use of red to "imperial purple." There is no evidence for this in medieval sources. In any case, the widespread diffusion of that color makes us skeptical. Were the Premonstratensian nuns in Enkenbach and the Cistercian monks in Eusserthal alike imperially minded? In the five stages of building that Ellger was able to show in Ratzeburg did the pro- and anti-Hohenstaufen parties alternate in charge of the church and express their sympathies, respectively, by using red or yellow bricks? Is the real reason not more likely to be the natural color of the stone (yellow and red clay or yellow, red, gray, and white sandstone)? In any case, when they were painted over the color chosen was usually very close to the natural one.

Besides such simple architectural painting, wall painting also played a great role, replacing the mosaics of Early Christian and Byzantine architecture in the Romanesque church. The changeover was exceptionally characteristic. The shimmering of mosaics makes the wall as such unreal, whereas the opaque, matte colors of fresco painting permit it to be present in all its effective reality, which is further evidence of the inner unity of the Romanesque style. However, in this aspect too, many churches and even many regions of Italy proved to be bound to tradition, and mosaic did not fully disappear from them.

Romanesque wall painting generally underscores the main lines of the architecture by means of colored borders and ornamental strips.

Larger surfaces were divided into separate fields by borders within which figurative compositions could unfold whose underlying principles were in accord with those of the architecture. The alignment of the figures in a single plane and all of them of the same height, as well as the waiving of effects of perspective depth—all work toward that same end. The same holds true for painting on glass, which involves the colored glazing of the windows. The first evidence of it goes back to Carolingian times, and a number of examples from the twelfth century (the earliest in Augsburg Cathedral) have survived in good condition. Ornaments, individual figures, and small-figured scenes fit well into the existing architectural form. The color scale is broad and the overall effect bright, in contrast to the darkly glowing windows of the High Gothic that shroud the interior in a deep dusk. Since in any history of architecture one must deal with sculpture and painting as part of an overall architectonic effect, the subject matter, meaning, style, and composition of such works of painting and sculpture cannot be fully discussed here.

SELECTED BIBLIOGRAPHY

Note: *With few exceptions, this bibliography does not list pertinent books and articles in those series and journals chiefly devoted to Romanesque architecture and included here in their own right*

GENERAL

ADAM, E., *Vorromanik und Romanik*, Frankfurt, 1968.

ARGAN, G. C., *L'architettura protocristiana, preromanica e romanica*, Florence, 1936.

BENOIT, F., *L'Occident médiéval. Du romain au roman*, Paris, 1934.

CHOISY, A., *Histoire de l'architecture*, 2 vols., Paris, n.d. [1899]; 2nd ed., 1964.

CLAPHAM, A. W., *Romanesque Architecture in Western Europe*, Oxford, 1936; 2nd ed., 1959; 3rd ed., 1967.

CONANT, K. J., *Carolingian and Romanesque Architecture, 800 to 1200*, Harmondsworth, 1959.

DEHIO, G., and BEZOLD, G. VON, *Die kirchliche Baukunst des Abendlandes*, 2 vols., Stuttgart, 1884–1901; reprinted 1967.

FOCILLON, H., *The Art of the West in the Middle Ages*, 2 vols., Greenwich, Conn., 1963.

FRANKL, P., *Die frühmittelalterliche und romanische Baukunst*, Potsdam, 1926.

FRANZ, H. G., *Spätromanik und Frühgotik*, Baden-Baden, 1969.

HAUTTMANN, M., *Die Kunst des frühen Mittelalters*, Berlin, 1929.

KUBACH, H. E., "Baukunst der Romanik," in H. E. KUBACH and P. BLOCH, *Früh- und Hochromanik*, Baden-Baden, 1964.

———, "Die Architektur zur Zeit der Karolinger und Ottonen," in H. E. KUBACH and V. H. ELBERN, *Das Frühmittelalterliche Imperium*, Baden-Baden, 1968.

PORTER, A. K., *Medieval Architecture: Its Origins and Development*, London and New York, 1909; reprinted 1966.

REY, R., *L'Art roman et ses origines. Archéologie préromane et romane*, Toulouse and Paris, 1945.

SAALMANN, H., *L'Architecture romane, 600–1200*, Paris, 1962.

VERZONE, P., *Werdendes Abendland*, Baden-Baden, 1967.

WAGNER-RIEGER, R., "Architektur," in *Das Mittelalter I* (Propyläen Kunstgeschichte), Frankfurt and Berlin, 1969.

WEIGERT, H., *Baukunst der Romanik in Europa* (Monumente des Abendlandes, ed. H. Busch and B. Lohse), Frankfurt, 1959.

MISCELLANEA, LEXICONS, PERIODICALS

Architectura.

The Art Bulletin, passim.

Arte del primo millennio, Turin, 1953.

Beiträge zur Kunst des Mittelalters, Berlin, 1950.

Beiträge zur Kunstgeschichte und Archäologie des Frühmittelalters, Graz and Cologne, 1961.

Encyclopedia of World Art, New York, 1959–68.

Frühmittelalterliche Kunst in den Alpenländern, Olten and Lausanne, 1954.

Karolingische und Ottonische Kunst, Wiesbaden, 1957.

Neue Ausgrabungen in Deutschland, Berlin, 1958.

Neue Beiträge zur Kunstgeschichte des 1. Jahrtausends, vol. II *(Frühmittelalterliche Kunst)*, Baden-Baden, 1954.

Reallexicon zur deutschen Kunstgeschichte, Stuttgart, in course of publication.

Wandlungen christlicher Kunst im Mittelalter, Baden-Baden, 1953.

Werdendes Abendland an Rhein und Rhur (exhibition catalogue), Essen, 1956.

PRE-ROMANESQUE ARCHITECTURE: GENERAL

BOECKELMANN, W., "Grundformen im frühkarolingischen Kirchenbau des östlichen Frankenreiches," *Wallraf-Richartz-Jahrbuch*, 18, 1956, p. 27.

BRAUNFELS, W., *Die Welt der Karolinger und ihre Kunst*, Munich, 1968.

———, ed., *Karl der Grosse*, 4 vols., Düsseldorf, 1965–67. Includes: A. MANN, "Grossbauten vorkarlischer Zeit und aus der Epoche von Karl der Grosse bis zu Lothar I," vol. III, p. 320; E. LEHMANN, "Die Architektur zur Zeit Karls der Grosse," vol. III, p. 301; and M. VIEILLARD-TROIKOUROFF, "L'Architecture du temps de Charlemagne," vol. III, p. 336.

DEGANI, S., *Medioevo occidentali: L'altomedioevo* (from lectures by L. Crema), n.p., 1958.

ELBERN, V. H., ed., *Das erste Jahrtausend*, 3 vols., Düsseldorf, 1962–64.

HUBERT, J., PORCHER, J., and VOLBACH, W. F., *L'Empire carolingien* (L'Univers des Formes), Paris, 1968.

———, *L'Europe des invasions* (L'Univers des Formes), Paris, 1967.

Karl der Grosse (exhibition catalogue), Aachen, 1965.

"Kirche und Burg in der Archäologie des Rheinlandes," in *Führer des Rhein*, Landesmuseum, Bonn, 1962.

KRAUTHEIMER, R., "The Carolingian Revival of Early Christian Architecture," *Art Bulletin*, 24, 1942, p. 1.

LEHMANN, E., "Die entwicklungsgeschichtliche Stellung der karolingischen Klosterkirche zwischen Kirchenfamilie und Kathedrale," *Wissenschaftliche Zeitschrift der Friedrich-Schiller-Universität*, Jena, 1952–53, p. 131.

———, "Kaisertum und Reform als Bauherren in hochkarolingischer Zeit," in *Festschrift für P. Metz*, Berlin, 1965, p. 74.

———, "Vom neuen Bild frühmittelalterlichen Kirchenbaues," *Wissenschaftliche Zeitschrift der Martin-Luther-Universität*, Halle-Wittenberg, Gesellschafts- und Sprachwissenschaftliche Reihe, 6, 1956, p. 213.

———, "Von der Kirchenfamilie zur Kathedrale, Bemerkungen zu einer Entwicklungslinie der mittelalterlichen Baukunst," in *Festschrift für F. Gerke*, Baden-Baden, 1962, p. 21.

MANN, A., "Doppelchor und Stiftermemorie. Zum kunst- und kulturgeschichtlichen Problem der Westchöre," *Westfälische Zeitschrift*, CXI, 1961, pp. 149–262.

"Pre-Romanesque Schools and Currents," articles by CROZET, VOLBACH, WILSON, DE PALOL, ARSLAN, and HOLMQUIST in *Encyclopedia of World Art*, vol. XI, New York, 1963.

Settimane di studio del Centro italiano di Studi sull'alto medioevo, 13 vols., Spoleto, 1954 ff.

STEIN, F., "In den Jahren 1957 bis 1962 erschienene Werke zur Kunst des frühen Mittelalters, 7–11 Jahrhundert," *Kunstgeschichtliche Anzeigen*, NF 6, 1963–64, p. 105.

SWOBODA, K. M., "Architektur des frühen Mittelalters. Literaturbericht 1950–1956," *Kunstgeschichtliche Anzeigen*, NF 3, 1958, p. 183.

———, "In den Jahren 1950–1957 erschienene Werke zur Kunst der karolingischen Zeit," *Kunstgeschichtliche Anzeigen*, NF 4, 1959, p. 1.

Vorromanische Kunst, intro. by L. GRODECKI (Monumente des Abendlandes, ed. H. Busch and B. Lohse), Frankfurt, 1965.

ZIMMERMANN, W., "Ecclesia lignea und ligneis tabulis fabricata," *Bonner Jahrbuch*, CLVIII, 1958, p. 414.

ROMANESQUE ARCHITECTURE: GENERAL

BANDMANN, G., "Über Pastophorien und verwandte Nebenräume im mittelalterlichen Kirchenbau," *Kunstgeschichtliche Studien für H. Kauffmann*, Berlin, 1956, p. 19.

BEENKEN, H., "Die ausgeschiedene Vierung," *Repertorium für Kunstwissenschaft*, LI, 1930, p. 207.

———, *Die entwicklungsgeschichtliche Stellung der romanischen Baukunst*, *Beiträge zur Kunst des Mittelalters*, Berlin, 1950, p. 47.

BOECKELMANN, W., "Die abgeschnürte Vierung," in *Neue Beiträge: Frühmittelalterliche Kunst*, Baden-Baden, 1954.

DESHOULIÈRES, F., "Essai sur les bases romanes," *Bulletin monumental*, 1911, pp. 77–101.

———, "Essai sur les tailloirs romans," *Bulletin monumental*, 1914, pp. 5–46.

DIMIER, M. A., *Recueil de plans d'églises cisterciennes*, 2 vols., Grignan and Paris, 1949.

FOCILLON, H., *Moyen-âge: Survivances et réveils. Études d'art et d'histoire*, New York, 1943.

FRANKL, P., "Der Beginn der Gothik und das allgemeine Problem des Stilbeginnes," *Festschrift für Heinrich Wölfflin*, Munich, 1924, pp. 107–126.

GALL, E., "Neue Beiträge zur Geschichte 'Vom Werden der Gotik,'" *Monatshefte für Kunstwissenschaft*, IV, 1911, p. 309.

———, "Studien zur Geschichte des Chorumgangs," *Monatshefte für Kunstwissenschaft*, V, 1912, pp. 134, 358, 508.

———, "Zur Frage der Westwerke," *Jahrbuch des Römisch-Germanischen Zentralmuseums Mainz*, I, 1954, p. 245.

GRODECKI, L., "L'Empire ottonien et salien," in L. ———, et al., *Le Siècle de l'An Mil* (L'Univers des Formes), Paris, 1973.

———, "Le 'transept bas' dans le premier art roman et le problème de Cluny," in *À Cluny: Congrès scientifique*, Dijon, 1950, p. 266.

———, "Sur l'origine du plan d'église à transept double," *Urbanisme et Architecture: Mélanges P. Lavedan*, Paris, 1954, p. 153.

HAHN, H., *Die frühe Kirchenbaukunst der Zisterzienser*, Berlin, 1957.

HALLINGER, K., "Neue Fragen der reformgeschichtlichen Forschung," *Archiv für Mittelrheinische Kirchengeschichte*, IX, 1957, p. 9.

HEITZ, C., *Recherches sur les rapports entre architecture et liturgie à l'époque carolingienne*, Paris, 1963.

HÉLIOT, P., *Du Carolingien au Gothique. L'Évolution de la plastique murale dans l'architecture religieuse du nordouest de l'Europe (IXe–XIIIe siècle)*, Paris, 1966.

———, "Le transept cloisonné dans l'architecture du moyen-âge," *Wallraf-Richartz-Jahrbuch*, XXVI, 1964, p. 7.

HERTIG, L., *Entwicklungsgeschichte der Krypta in der Schweiz*, Biel, 1958.

KAHL, G., *Die Zwerggalerie, Herkunft, Entwicklung und Verbreitung*, Würzburg, 1939.

KUBACH, H. E., "Das Triforium. Ein Beitrag zur kunstgeschichtliche Raumkunde Europas im Mittelalter," *Zeitschrift für Kunstgeschichte*, V, 1963, p. 275.

LEHMANN-BROCKHAUS, O., *Schriftquellen der Kunstgeschichte des 11. und 12. Jahrhunderts für Deutschland, Lotharingen und Italien*, Berlin, 1938.

MANN, A., "Doppelchor und Stiftermemorie. Zum kunst- und kulturgeschichtlichen Problem der Westchöre," *Westfälische Zeitschrift*, CXI, 1961, p. 149.

MOBIUS, F., "Westwerk und frühfeudaler Kaiserkult," *Wissenschaftliche Zeitschrift der Friedrich-Schiller-Universität*, Jena, XVI, 1967, p. 55.

PUIG I CADAFALCH, J., *La Géographie et les origines du premier art roman*, Paris, 1935 (Catalan ed., Barcelona, 1930).

RAVE, P. O., *Der Emporenbau in romanischer und frühgotischer Zeit*, Bonn and Leipzig, 1924.

REINHARDT, H., and FELS, E., "Études sur les églises-porches carolingiennes et leur survivance dans l'art roman," *Bulletin monumental*, XCII, 1933, p. 331; XCVI, 1937, p. 425.

ROTHKIRCH, W. VON, *Die Bedeutung des quadratischen Schematismus für die Entwicklung der abendländischen Sakralarchitektur bis zur Mitte des 13. Jahrhunderts*, Altenburg, 1933 (dissertation, Munich, 1930).

SCHAEFER, H., "The Origin of the Two-Tower Façade in Romanesque Architecture," *Art Bulletin*, XXVII, 1945, p. 85.

SCHMOLL, J. A., "Zisterzienser-Romanik. Kritische Gedanken zur jüngsten Literatur: Formositas romanica,"

Festschrift für Joseph Gantner, Frauenfeld, 1959, p. 151.

SCHÜRER, O., *Romanische Doppelkapellen. Eine typengeschichtliche Untersuchung*, Marburg, 1929.

SEDLMAYR, H., *Die Entstehung der Kathedrale*, Zurich, 1950.

THÜMMLER, H., "Nationale Charaktere europäischer Kunst im Spiegel des deutschen und italienischen Sakralbaues," *Die Welt als Geschichte*, 1951, p. 26.

VALLERY-RADOT, J., *Églises romanes. Filiations et échanges d'influence*, Paris [1931].

———, "Notes sur les chapelles hautes dédiées à Saint-Michel," *Bulletin monumental*, 1929, p. 453.

VERBEEK, A., "Die Aussenkrypta. Werden einer Bauform des frühen Mittelalters," *Zeitschrift für Kunstgeschichte*, XIII, 1950, p. 7.

VERDIER, P., "Les transepts de nef," *Mélanges d'archéologie et d'histoire de l'École française de Rome*, LXIV, 1952, p. 179.

———, "L'Origine structurale et liturgique des transepts de nef des cathédrales de Novare et de Pavie," *Arte del primo millennio*, Turin, 1953, p. 354.

WAGNER-RIEGER, R., "Premier Art Roman," *Aachener Kunstblätter*, 41, 1971, pp. 27–36.

FRANCE

AUBERT, M. A., *L'Architecture cistercienne en France*, 2 vols., 2nd ed., Paris, 1947.

———, ed., *L'Art roman en France*, Paris, 1961.

———, *Cathédrales, abbayes, prieurés romanes en France*, Paris, 1963.

BAUM, J., *L'Architecture romane en France*, Paris, 1911.

DEUTLER, C., *Paris und Versailles* (Reclams Kunstführer), Stuttgart, 1970.

BRÉHIER, L., *L'Art en France des invasions barbares à l'époque romane*, Paris, 1930.

BRUTAILS, J. A., *La Géographie monumentale de la France aux époques romane et gothique*, Paris, 1923.

DE LASTEYRIE, R., *L'Architecture religieuse en France à l'époque romane*, 2nd ed., Paris, 1929.

DESHOULIÈRES, F., *Au début de l'art roman. Les églises de l'onzième siècle en France*, Paris, 1929; 2nd ed., 1943.

———, *Éléments datés de l'art roman en France*, Paris, 1936.

———, "La théorie d'Eugène Lefèvre-Pontalis sur les écoles romanes," *Bulletin monumental*, 1925, p. 197.

DIMIER, M. A., *L'Art cistercien, France*, Paris, 1962.

ENLART, C., *Manuel d'archéologie française*. vol. I, 2nd ed., Paris, 1919.

GANTNER, J., and POBE, M., *Romanesque Art in France*, London, 1956.

GIEURE, L., *Les Églises romanes de France*, 2 vols., Paris, 1953–54.

GROMORT, G., *L'Architecture romane*, 3 vols., Paris, 1928–31.

HÉLIOT, P., "Coursières anglo-normandes et rhénanes," *Cahiers de civilisation médiévale*, II, 1959.

——, "Les déambulatoires dotés de niches rayonnantes," *Cahiers de civilisation médiévale*, IV, 1961, pp. 302–322.

——, "L'Ordre colossal et les arcades murales dans les églises romanes," *Bulletin monumental*, CXV, 1957, pp. 141–161.

——, "Remarque sur les voûtes d'arêtes et sur les coupoles dans l'architecture romane," *Revue archéologique*, 1961, pp. 167–190.

HUBERT, J., *L'Architecture religieuse du Haut Moyen-Âge en France*, Paris, 1952.

——, *L'Art préroman*, Paris, 1938.

KELLER, H., *Die Kunstlandschaften Frankreichs*, Wiesbaden, 1963.

MÂLE, E., *La Fin du paganisme en Gaule et les plus anciennes basiliques chrétiennes*, Paris, 1950.

MUSSAT, A., *Le style gothique de l'Ouest de la France*, Paris, 1963.

REY, R., *Les vieilles églises fortifiées du Midi de la France*, Paris, 1925.

SEGERS, H., *Provence, Côte d'Azur, Dauphiné, Rhône-Tal* (Reclams Kunstführer), Stuttgart, 1967.

Series, annuals, periodicals:

Bulletin monumental (Société française d'archéologie), 1834 ff.

Congrès Archéologique (Société française d'archéologie), *passim*.

Dictionnaire des Églises de France, 4 vols., Paris, 1966 ff.

Les Églises de France (Départements de Charente, Cher, Creuse, Paris, Seine), ed. M. AUBERT and J. VERRIER, Paris, 1932 ff.

Petites monographies des Grands édifices de la France, 20 vols., Paris.

NORMANDY AND BRITTANY

ANFRAY, M., *L'Architecture normande. Son Influence dans le Nord de la France aux XIe et XIIe siècles*, Paris, 1939.

BONY, J., "La technique normande du mur épais à l'époque romane," *Bulletin monumental*, XCVIII, 1939, pp. 153–188.

Congrès Archéologique, 1908 (Caen); 1914 (Brest, Vannes); 1926 (Rouen); 1949 (Saint-Brieuc); 1953 (Orne); 1957 (Cornouaille).

GRAND, R., *L'Art roman en Bretagne*, Paris, 1958.

HÉLIOT, P., "La Collégiale de Lillers," *Bulletin de la Société Nationale des Antiquaires de France*, 1954–55, pp. 166–177.

——, "La Normandie et l'architecture romane du Nord de la France," *Revue archéologique*, XXXI, 1951, p. 60.

——, "Les dates de construction de Bernay, Cérisy-la-Forêt et Lessay," *Bulletin de la Société Nationale des Antiquaires de France*, 1959, pp. 188–204.

LAMBERT, E., *Caen roman et gothique*, Caen, 1935.

LIESS, R., *Der frühromanische Kirchenbau des 11. Jahrhunderts in der Normandie*, Munich, 1967.

RUPRICH-ROBERT, V., *L'Architecture normande aux XIe et XIIe siècles en Normandie et en Angleterre*, 2 vols., Paris, 1884–89.

FRENCH CROWN LANDS

AYMARD, O., et al., *Touraine romane* (Zodiaque), La Pierre-qui-Vire, 1957.

Congrès Archéologique, 1902 (Troyes, Provins); 1905 (Beauvais); 1911 (Reims); 1919 (Paris); 1925 (Blois); 1930 (Orléans); 1931 (Bourges); 1934 (Paris); 1936 (Amiens); 1944 (Ile-de-France); 1946 (Paris, Mantes); 1948 (Tours); 1955 (Troyes); 1961 (Maine).

CROZET, R., *L'Art roman en Berry*, Paris, 1932.

DESHOULIÈRES, F., "Les églises romanes du Berry. Caractères indigènes et pénétrations étrangères," *Bulletin monumental*, 1909, pp. 469–492; 1922, pp. 5–27.

ENLART, C., *Monuments religieux de l'architecture romane et de transition dans les anciens diocèses d'Amiens et de Boulogne*, Paris, 1895.

GALL, E., *Die gotische Baukunst in Frankreich und Deutschland. Teil I: Die Vorstufen in Nordfrankreich*, Leipzig, 1925; 2nd ed., Munich, 1955.

HÉLIOT, P., "Remarques sur l'abbaye de Saint-Germer et sur les blocs de façade du XIIe siècle," *Bulletin monumental*, CXIV, 1956, p. 81.

HUBERT, J., "Monuments du XIe siècle entre Loire et Seine," *Bulletin de la Société nationale des antiquaires de France*, 1948–49, p. 253.

LEFÈVRE-PONTALIS, E., *L'Architecture religieuse dans l'ancien diocèse de Soissons au XIe et au XIIe siècle*, 2 vols., Paris, 1894–96.

PLAT, G., *L'Art de bâtir en France des Romains à l'an 1100 d'après les monuments anciens de la Touraine*, Paris, 1939.

——, "La Touraine, berceau des écoles romanes du sud-ouest," *Bulletin monumental*, 1913, p. 365.

BURGUNDY

ANFRAY, M., *L'Architecture religieuse du Nivernais au moyen-âge*, Paris, 1951.

BAUDRY, J., et al., *Bourgogne romane* (Zodiaque), La Pierre-qui-Vire, 1962.

BRANNER, R., *Burgundian Gothic Architecture*, London, 1960.

CONANT, K. J., *Cluny: les églises et la maison du chef d'ordre*, Mâcon, 1968.

Congrès Archéologique, 1907 (Avallon, Auxerre); 1913 (Moulins, Nevers); 1928 (Dijon); 1935 (Lyons, Mâcon); 1952 (Suisse romande); 1958 (Auxerre); 1960 (Franche-Comté).

DICKSON, M., and C., *Les églises romanes de l'ancien diocèse de Chalon: Cluny et sa région*, Mâcon, 1935.

KLINGENBERG, W., *Burgundische Stadt- und Landkirchen*, Berlin, 1910.

MALO, C., "Les églises romanes de l'ancien diocèse de Chalon-sur-Saône," *Bulletin monumental*, XC, 1931, p. 371.

OURSEL, R., *L'Art roman en Bourgogne*, Dijon, 1928.

——, and A. M., *Les églises romanes de l'Autunnois et du Brionnais*, Mâcon, 1956.

PHILIPPE, A., "L'Architecture religieuse au XIe et XIIe siècle dans l'ancien diocèse d'Auxerre," *Bulletin monumental*, 1904, pp. 42–92.

THIOLLIER, F., *L'Art roman à Charlieu et dans le Brionnais*, Paris, 1892.

TOURNIER, R., *Les églises comtoises. Leur architecture des origines au XVIIIe siècle*, Paris, 1954.

VALLERY-RADOT, J., "La limite méridionale de l'école romane de Bourgogne," *Bulletin monumental*, XCV, 1936, pp. 274–316.

VIREY, J., *Les églises romanes de l'ancien diocèse de Mâcon: Cluny et sa région*, Mâcon, 1935.

ZIMMERMANN, W., "Die Gruppenbildung der romanischen Baukunst in der Kunstlandschaft Burgunds," *Rheinische Vierteljahrsblätter*, XXI, 1956, pp. 226–244.

LORRAINE

KUBACH, H. E., "Der Trierer Kunstraum im 11.–13. Jahrhundert," *Trierer Zeitschrift*, XII, 1937, pp. 81–103; XIV, 1939, pp. 58–82.

SANDERSON, W., "Monastic Reform in Lorraine and the Architecture of the Outer Crypt, 950–1100," *Transactions of the American Philosophical Society*, n. s. 61, 1971, pp. 1–36.

POITOU, SAINTONGE, AQUITAINE (SOUTHWESTERN FRANCE)

Congrès Archéologique, 1903 (Poitiers); 1910 (Angers, Saumur); 1912 (Angoulême); 1921 (Limoges, Brive); 1927 (Périgueux); 1939 (Bordeaux, Bayonne); 1951 (Poitiers); 1956 (La Rochelle).

CROZET, R., *L'Art roman en Saintonge*, Paris, 1971.

——, et al., *Poitou roman* (Zodiaque), La Pierre-qui-Vire, 1962.

DARAS, C., *Angoumois roman* (Zodiaque), La Pierre-qui-Vire, 1961.

D'HERBECOURT, P., and PORCHER, J., *Anjou roman* (Zodiaque), La Pierre-qui-Vire, 1959.

GARDELLES, J., "Les vestiges de l'architecture de la fin de l'époque préromane en Gironde (Xe–XIe siècles)," *Revue historique de Bordeaux*, NS VIII, 1959, p. 253.

HÉLIOT, P., "Les portails polylobés de l'Aquitaine et des régions limitrophes," *Bulletin monumental*, 1946, p. 63.

——, "Origines et extension du chevet plat dans l'architecture religieuse de l'Aquitaine," *Les Cahiers techniques de l'Art*, III, 1955, pp. 23–49.

MAURY, J., et al., *Limousin roman* (Zodiaque), La Pierre-qui-Vire, 1960.

ROUX, J., *La basilique Saint-Front de Périgueux*, Périgueux, 1919.

SCHÜRENBERG, L., "Die romanischen Kirchenfassaden Aquitaniens," *Das Münster*, 4, 1951, pp. 259–268.

LANGUEDOC, AUVERGNE

ALLEGRE, V., *L'Art roman dans la région albigeoise*, Albi, 1943.

BEIGBEDER, O., *Forez-Velay roman* (Zodiaque), La Pierre-qui-Vire, 1962.

Congrès Archéologique, 1901 (Agen, Auch); 1904 (Le Puy); 1906 (Carcassonne); 1924 (Clermont-Ferrand); 1929 (Toulouse); 1937 (Figeac, Cahors, Rodez); 1938 (Allier); 1950 (Montpellier); 1954 (Perpignan).

CRAPLET, B., *Auvergne roman* (Zodiaque), La Pierre-qui-Vire, 1962.

REVOIL, H., *L'Architecture romane du Midi de la France*, 3 vols., Paris, 1867–74.

REY, R., *L'Art gothique du Midi de la France*, Paris, 1934.

———, *Les vieilles églises fortifiées du Midi de la France*, Paris, 1925.

THIOLLIER, N., *L'Architecture religieuse à l'époque romane dans l'ancien diocèse du Puy*, Le Puy, 1960.

VALLERY-RADOT, J., "Les églises romanes du Rouergue," *Bulletin monumental*, XCIX, 1940, p. 5.

PROVENCE AND SOUTHEASTERN FRANCE

Congrès Archéologique, 1909 (Avignon); 1923 (Valence, Montélimar); 1932 (Aix, Nice); 1963 (Avignon, Comtat Venaissin).

FORMIGÉ, J., "Remarques diverses sur les baptistères de Provence," *Mélanges F. Martroye*, Paris, 1940, p. 167.

HAMANN, R., *Die Abteikirche von St. Gilles und ihre künstlerische Nachfolge*, 2 vols., Berlin, 1955.

JOLY, M., *L'Architecture des églises romanes du Vivarais*, Paris, 1966.

FRANCE: SPECIFIC LOCALITIES

ACHTER, J., "Zur Rekonstruktion der karolingischen Klosterkirche Centula," *Zeitschrift für Kunstgeschichte*, XIX, 1956, p. 133.

À Cluny: Congrès scientifique, Dijon, 1950.

AURIOL, A., and REY, R., *La basilique Saint-Sernin de Toulouse*, Toulouse and Paris, 1930.

BACHMANN, E., "Die 'Cripte du Pessebre' in Saint-Michel-de-Cuxa und der Sepulchralbau," *Festschrift Swoboda*, Vienna and Wiesbaden, 1959, p. 23.

CROSBY, S. McK., *L'Abbaye royale de Saint-Denis*, Paris, 1953.

EYGUN, F., "Le baptistère Saint-Jean à Poitiers," *Gallia*, XXII, 1964, p. 137.

FELS, E., "Saint-Sever-sur-l'Adour," *Congrès Archéologique*, 1939.

FORMIGÉ, J., *L'Abbaye royale de Saint-Denis*, Paris, 1960.

FORSYTH, G. H., *The Church of St. Martin at Angers*, Princeton, 1953.

GRODECKI, L., "Le 'transept bas' dans le premier art roman et le problème de Cluny," *À Cluny: Congrès scientifique*, Dijon, 1950, pp. 265–269.

HUBERT, J., "L'abbaye de Déols," *Cahiers archéologiques*, IX, 1957, p. 155.

———, "La date des cryptes de Saint-Médard de Soissons," *Bulletin de la Société Nationale des Antiquaires de France*, 1959, p. 123; *Bulletin du Centre International d'études romanes*, 1959, p. 13.

———, "L'église S. Michel-de-Cuxa et l'occidentation des églises au moyen-âge," *Journal of the Society of Architectural Historians*, XXI, 1962, p. 163.

JOUVEN, G., "Fouilles des cryptes et de l'abbatiale de Flavigny," *Les Monuments historiques de la France*, NS VI, 1960, p. 9.

LESUEUR, F., *Les églises de Loir-et-Cher*, Paris, 1969.

———, "Saint-Martin de Tours et les origines de l'art roman," *Bulletin monumental*, 1949, pp. 7–84.

LOUIS, R., *Autessiodurum christianum: les églises d'Auxerre des origines au XIe siècle*, Paris, 1952.

REINHARDT, H., *La cathédrale de Reims*, Paris, 1963.

REY, R., *La cathédrale de Cahors et les origines de l'architecture à coupoles d'Aquitaine*, Paris, 1925.

SALET, F., *La Madeleine de Vézelay*, Melun, 1948.

SAUERLÄNDER, W., "Das 6. Colloquium der Société Française d'Archéologie: Die Skulpturen von Saint-Sernin in Toulouse," *Kunstchronik*, XXIV, 1971, pp. 341–347.

———, "Das 7. Colloquium der Société Française d'Archéologie: Ste-Foy in Conques," *Kunstchronik*, XXVI, 1973, p. 225.

SEDLMAYR, H., "Die Ahnen der dritten Kirche von Cluny," *Festschrift H. Schrade*, Stuttgart, 1960, pp. 49–71.

VALLERY-RADOT, J., *Saint-Philibert de Tournus*, Paris, 1959.

VIEILLARD-TROIKOUROFF, M., "La cathédrale de Clermont du Ve en XIIIe siècle," *Cahiers archéologiques*, XI, 1960, p. 199.

BELGIUM AND HOLLAND

BRIGODE, S., *Les églises romanes de Belgique*, Brussels, 1943.

DEVLIEGHER, L., *Kunstpatrimonium van West-Vlaanderen*, 5 vols. to date, Tielt-Utrecht, 1961 ff.

Dictionnaire des Églises, vol. V: "Belgique, Luxembourg," Paris, 1970.

Inventaris van het Kunstpatrimonium van Oostvlaanderen, 6 vols., Ghent, 1951 ff.

LEMAIRE, R., *De romaanse Bouwkunst in de Nederlanden*, Louvain, 1952.

SCHELDE BASIN

BRIGODE, S., "L'Architecture religieuse dans le sud-ouest de la Belgique," *Bulletin de la commission royale des monuments et des sites*, I, 1949.

De Nederlandse Monumenten van Geschiedenis en Kunst.

DEVLIEGHER, L., "De kerkelijke romaanse Bouwkunst in Frans-Vlaanderen," *Bulletin van de koninklijke commissie voor Monumenten en Landschappen* (Brussels), IX, 1958.

FIRMIN, B., *De romaanse kerkelijke bouwkunst in West-Vlaanderen*, Ghent, 1940.

FOCKEMA ANDREAE, S. J., HEKKER, R. C., and TER KUILE, E. H., *Duizend Jaar Bouwen in Nederland*, vol. I, Amsterdam, 1957.

HÉLIOT, P., "Le chevet de la collégiale de Nesle, l'architecture scaldienne et les influences allemandes en Picardie," *Revue belge d'archéologie et d'histoire de l'art*, XX, 1951, pp. 273–294.

———, "Le chevet roman de Saint-Bertin à Saint-Omer et l'architecture franco-lotharingienne," *Revue belge d'archéologie et d'histoire de l'art*, XXII, 1953, pp. 73–96.

———, "Les parties romanes de la cathédrale de Tournai. Problèmes de date et de filiation," *Revue belge d'archéologie et d'histoire de l'art*, XXV, 1966, pp. 3–76.

HOOTZ, R., *Kunstdenkmäler in den Niederlanden. Ein Bildhandbuch*, Munich, 1971.

Kunstreisboek voor Nederland, Amsterdam, 1965.

LEMAIRE, R., "Les avant-corps de Sainte-Gertrude à Nivelles," *Recueil des travaux du Centre de recherches archéologiques*, vol. III, Antwerp, 1942.

MAERE, R., and DELFERIÈRE L., "La collégiale Saint-Vincent à Soignies," *Revue belge d'archéologie et d'histoire de l'art*, VIII, 1938, pp. 5–48.

MERTENS, J., *Recherches archéologiques dans l'abbaye mérovingienne de Nivelles*, Brussels, 1962.

OZINGA, M. D., *De romaanse kerkelijke Bouwkunst*, Amsterdam, 1949.

ROLLAND, P., "Chronologie de la cathédrale de Tournai," *Revue belge d'archéologie et d'histoire de l'art*, IV, 1934, pp. 103, 225.

———, "La cathédrale de Tournai et les courants architecturaux," *Revue belge d'archéologie et d'histoire de l'art*, VII, 1937, p. 229.

———, "La technique normande du mur évidé et l'architecture scaldienne," *Revue belge d'archéologie et d'histoire de l'art*, X, 1940, pp. 169–188.

———, "Un groupe belge d'églises romanes. Les églises bicéphales à tourelles orientales," *Revue belge d'archéologie et d'histoire de l'art*, XI, 1941, pp. 119–156.

GERMANY

BACHMANN, E., "Kunstlandschaften im romanischen Kleinkirchenbau Deutschlands," *Zeitschrift des deutschen Vereins für Kunstwissenschaft*, VIII, 1941, p. 158.

BUSCH, H., *Germania Romana*, Vienna and Munich, 1963.

DEHIO, G., *Geschichte der deutschen Kunst*, vol. I, Berlin, 1919.

ESSER, K. H., "Über den Kirchenbau des hl. Bernard von Clairvaux," *Archiv für mittelrheinische Kirchengeschichte*, V, 1953, pp. 195–222.

EYDOUX, H. P., *L'Architecture des églises cisterciennes d'Allemagne*, Paris, 1952.

GALL, E., *Karolingische und ottonische Kirchen*, Burg, 1932.

GRODECKI, L., *Au seuil de l'art roman. L'architecture ot-tonienne*, Paris, 1958.

HAMANN, R., *Deutsche und französische Kunst im Mittelalter*. Vol. I: *Südfranzösische Protorenaissance und ihre Ausbreitung*, Marburg, 1923.

HAUPT, A., *Die älteste Kunst, insbesondere die Baukunst der Germanen von der Völkerwanderung bis Karl der Grosse*, Leipzig, 1909.

HOFFMANN, W., *Hirsau und die "Hirsauer Bauschule,"* Munich, 1950.

JANTZEN, H., *Ottonische Kunst*, Munich, 1947; 2nd ed., Hamburg, 1959.

KRÖNIG, W., "Zur Erforschung der Zisterzienser-Architektur," *Zeitschrift für Kunstgeschichte*, 1953, p. 222.

KUBACH, H. E., and VERBEEK, A., "Die vorromanische und romanische Baukunst in Mitteleuropa. Literaturbericht 1938–1950," *Zeitschrift für Kunstgeschichte*, XIV, 1951, pp. 124–148; XVIII, 1955, pp. 157–198.

LEHMANN, E., *Der frühe deutsche Kirchenbau*, Berlin, 1938; 2nd ed., 1949.

———, "Deutsche hochromanische Baukunst," *Zeitschrift für Kunstgeschichte*, VIII, 1939, pp. 223–227.

———, "Über die Bedeutung des Investiturstreits für die deutsche hochromanische Architektur," *Zeitschrift des deutschen Vereins für Kunstwissenschaft*, VII, 1940, p. 75.

———, "Vom Sinn und Wesen der Wandlung in der Raumanordnung der deutschen Kirchen des Mittelalters," *Zeitschrift für Kunst*, I, 1947, pp. 24–43.

MAYER, A., "Investiturstreit und Architektur," *Historische Zeitschrift*, 166, 1942, pp. 90–99.

MOBIUS, F., and H., *Sakrale Baukunst*, Berlin, 1963.

OSTENDORF, F., *Die deutsche Baukunst im Mittelalter*, vol. I, Berlin, 1922.

OSWALD, F., SCHAEFER, L., and SENNHAUSER, H. R., *Vorromanische Kirchenbauten. Katalog der Denkmäler bis zum Ausgang der Ottonen*, Munich, 1966 ff.

REISSMANN, K., *Romanische Portalarchitektur in Deutschland*, Würzburg, 1937.

SESSELBERG, F., *Die frühmittelalterliche Kunst der germanischen Völker*, Berlin, 1897.

ZAHN, W., *Schottenklöster. Die Bauten der irischen Benediktiner in Deutschland*, Freiburg, 1967.

Inventories, guides:

DEHIO, G., *Handbuch der deutschen Kunstdenkmäler*, 5 vols., Berlin, various eds. New edition ed. by E. Gall *et al.*, 9 vols. to date, Berlin and Munich, 1958 ff. Revised ed., 7 vols. to date, 1964 ff.

Die "Kunstdenkmäler" der deutschen Länder und Provinzen.

HOOTZ, R., *Deutsche Kunstdenkmäler. Ein Bildhandbuch*, 13 vols., Berlin and Munich, 1958 ff.

Reclams Kunstführer: Bundesrepublik Deutschland, 5 vols., Stuttgart, 1956–67.

Series, periodicals:

Das Münster; Deutsche Kunst und Denkmalpflege; Deutsche Lande deutsche Kunst; Grosse Baudenkmäler; Kleine Kirchenführer; Kunstchronik; Schrifttum zur deutschen Kunst; Zeitschrift für Kunstgeschichte; Zeitschrift für Kunstwissenschaft.

LOWER RHINE AND MEUSE VALLEYS

BINDING, G., "Bericht über Ausgrabungen in niederrheinischen Kirchen 1964–1966," *Bonner Jahrbuch*, CLXVII, 1967, p. 357.

GALL, E., *Dome und Klosterkirchen am Rhein*, Munich, 1956. Translated and adapted by O. COOK, *Cathedrals and Abbey Churches of the Rhine*, New York [1963].

GENICOT, L. F., *Les églises mosanes du XIe siècle*, Louvain, 1972.

———, *Les églises romanes du pays mosan* (exhibition catalogue), Celles, 1970.

KUBACH, H. E., "Der niederrheinische Kunstraum von der ottonischen bis zur staufischen Zeit," *Zeitschrift des deutschen Vereins für Kunstwissenschaft*, V, 1938, pp. 1–15.

———, "Die frühromanische Baukunst des Maaslandes," *Zeitschrift für Kunstwissenschaft*, VII, 1953, pp. 113–136.

———, "Spätromanische Baukunst des Maaslandes," *Das Münster*, 7, 1954, p. 205.

———, and VERBEEK, A., *Romanische Kirchen an Rhein und Maas*, Neuss, 1971.

LEMAIRE, R., *Les origines du style gothique en Brabant. Vol. I: L'Architecture romane*, Brussels and Paris, 1906.

REINERS, H., and EWALD, W., *Kunstdenkmäler zwischen Maas und Mosel*, Munich, 1921.

TIMMERS, J. J. M., *De Kunst van het Maasland*, Assen, 1971.

ZIMMERMANN, W., "Kunstgeographische Grenzen im Mittelrheingebiet," *Rheinische Vierteljahrsblätter*, XVII, 1952, pp. 89–118.

———, "Zur Grenze des niederrheinischen zum westfälischen Kunstraum," *Rheinische Vierteljahrsblätter*, XV–XVI, 1950–51, pp. 465–494.

UPPER RHINE AND ALSACE

GALL, E., *Dome und Klosterkirchen am Rhein*, Munich, 1956. Translated and adapted by O. COOK, *Cathedrals and Abbey Churches of the Rhine*, New York [1963].

HECHT, J., *Der romanische Kirchenbau des Bodenseegebietes*, vol. I, Basel, 1928.

KAUTZSCH, R., *Der romanische Kirchenbau im Elsass*, Freiburg, 1944.

KNOEPFLI, A., *Kunstgeschichte des Bodenseeraumes*, vol. I, Constance, 1961.

NOTHNAGEL, K., *Staufische Architektur in Gelnhausen und Worms*, ed. F. ARENS, Göppingen, 1971.

RUMPLER, M., *L'Architecture religieuse en Alsace à l'époque romane*, Strasbourg, 1958.

SCHÜRENBERG, L., "Der Anteil der südwestdeutschen Baukunst an der Ausbildung des salischen Stiles," *Zeitschrift für Kunstgeschichte*, VIII, 1939, pp. 249–280.

———, "Die salische Baukunst am Oberrhein," *Deutsche Archiv für Landes- und Volksforschung*, IV, 1940, pp. 185–199.

WILL, R., *Alsace romane* (Zodiaque), La Pierre-qui-Vire, 1965.

———, and HIMLY, F. J., "Les édifices religieux en Alsace à l'époque pré-romane," *Revue d'Alsace*, XCIII, 1954, p. 36.

WESTPHALIA

BURMEISTER, W., *Die westfälischen Dome*, Munich, 1951.

MÜHLEN, F., "Westfälische Baukunst im Überblick," *Bulletin van de Nederlandse Oudheidkundige Bond*, 6th series, XVI, 1963, p. 98.

THÜMMLER, H., "Die Anfänge der monumentalen Gewölbebaukunst in Deutschland und der besondere Anteil Westfalens," *Westfalen*, XXIX, 1951, p. 145.

———, "Die frühromanische Baukunst im Westfalen (Soest, Paderborn, Vreden)," *Westfalen*, XXVII, 1948, p. 177.

———, "Karolingische und ottonische Baukunst in Sachsen," *Das erste Jahrtausend*, Düsseldorf, 1962–64.

———, "Mittelalterliche Baukunst im Weserraum," *Kunst und Kultur im Weserraum, 800–1600* (exhibition catalogue), Corvey, 1966, p. 166.

———, "Westfälische und italienische Hallenkirchen," in *Festschrift für Martin Wackernagel*, Cologne and Graz, 1958, p. 17.

———, and BADENHEUER, F., *Romanik in Westfalen*, Recklinghausen, 1964.

———, and KREFT, H., *Weserbaukunst im Mittelalter*, Hameln, 1970.

FRANCONIA, SWABIA, BAVARIA (SOUTHERN GERMANY)

ECKARDT, A., and GEBHARD, T., *Kunstdenkmäler von Bayern, Pfalz IX, Stadt- und Landkreis Kaiserslautern*, Munich, 1942.

STROBEL, R., *Romanische Architektur in Regensburg*, Nuremberg, 1965.

SILESIA

ŚWIECHOWSKI, Z., *Architektura na slasku do polowy XIII wieku*, Warsaw, 1955.

GERMANY: SPECIFIC LOCALITIES

ACHTER, I., "Die Kölner Petrusreliquien und die Bautätigkeit Erzbischofs Bruno (953–965) am Kölner Dom," in *Das erste Jahrtausend*, vol. II, Düsseldorf, 1963, p. 948.

BADER, W., *Die Benediktinerabtei Brauweiler*, Berlin, 1937.

BANDMANN, G., "Die Vorbilder der Aachener Pfalzkapelle," in *Karl der Grosse*, vol. III, p. 424.

BEENKEN, H., "Die Aachener Pfalzkapelle," in *Aachen zum Jahr 1951* (Rheinischer Verein für Denkmalpflege und Heimatschutz), p. 67.

BEHN, F., *Die karolingische Klosterkirche von Lorsch/Bergstrasse*, Berlin and Leipzig, 1934.

BESELER, H., and ROGGENKAMP, H., *Die Michaeliskirche in Hildesheim*, Berlin, 1954.

BORGER, H., *Xanten. Entstehung und Geschichte eines niederrheinischen Stiftes*, Xanten, 1966.

BRAUNFELS, W., ed., *Karl der Grosse*, 4 vols., Düsseldorf, 1965–67.

CHRIST, H., *Die sechs Münster der Abtei Reichenau*, Reichenau, 1956.

CICHY, B., *Die Kirche von Brenz*, Heidenheim, 1966.

EFFMANN, W., *Die karolingisch-ottonischen Bauten zu Werden*, vol. I, Strasbourg, 1899.

———, *Die Kirche der Abtei Corvey*, Paderborn, 1929.

ESTERHUES, F., "Zur frühen Baugeschichte der Corveyer Abteikirche," *Westfalen*, XXXI, 1953, p. 320.

———, "Zur Rekonstruktion der ersten Corveyer Klosterkirche," *Westfälische Zeitschrift*, CVIII, 1958, p. 387.

FEHRING, G., "Die Ausgrabungen in der Stadtkirche St. Dionys zu Esslingen am Neckar," *Zeitschrift des deutschen Vereins für Kunstwissenschaft*, XIX, 1965, p. 1.

FELDTKELLER, H., "Eine bisher unbekannte karolingische Grosskirche im Hersfelder Stift," *Deutsche Kunst und Denkmalpflege*, 1964, p. 1.

———, "Neue Forschungen zur Baugeschichte der Drübecker Stiftskirche," *Zeitschrift für Kunstwissenschaft*, IV, 1950, p. 105.

GERKE, F., "Die Königshalle in Lorsch und der frühkarolingische Monumentalstil," in *Kultur und Wirtschaft im rheinischen Raum: Festschrift für C. Eckert*, Mainz, 1949.

GROSSMANN, D., "Kloster Fulda und seine Bedeutung für den frühen Deutschen Kirchenbau," in *Das erste Jahrtausend*, vol. I, Düsseldorf, 1962, p. 344.

JURASCHEK, F. VON, "Die Bauten der Königshalle in Lorsch und die Triumphalarchitektur der Spätantike," in *Frühmittelalterliche Kunst*, 1954.

KAUTZSCH, R., *Der Dom zu Worms*, Berlin, 1938.

———, "Zur Baugeschichte des Mainzer Domes," *Zeitschrift für Kunstgeschichte*, VI, 1937, p. 200.

———, and NEEB, E., *Der Dom zu Mainz* (Die Kunstdenkmäler im Freistadt Hessen II/1), Darmstadt, 1919.

KEMP, T. K., "Grundrissenentwicklung und Baugeschichte des Trierer Domes," *Das Münster*, XXI, 1968, p. 1.

KLEINBAUER, E., "Charlemagne's Palace Chapel at Aachen and Its Copies," *Gesta* (International Center of Romanesque Art), IV, 1965, pp. 2–11.

KREUSCH, F., *Aachen. Über Pfalzkapelle und Atrium zur Zeit Karls des Grossen*, Aachen, 1958.

———, *Beobachtungen an der Westanlage der Klosterkirche zu Corvey*, Cologne and Graz, 1963.

———, *Kirche, Atrium und Portikus der Aachener Pfalz*, Düsseldorf, 1965 (reprinted from *Karl der Grosse*, vol. III).

KRUMMWIESE, H. W., and MEYER-BRUCK, H., *Das tausendjährige Stift Fischbeck*, Göttingen, 1964.

KÜAS, H., and KRAUSE, H. J., *Die Stiftskirche zu Wechselburg*, 2 vols., Berlin, 1968, 1972.

KUBACH, H. E., "Saint-Nicolas-en-Glain, ein Schwesterbau von Schwarzrheindorf," *Kunstchronik*, VI, 1953, p. 92.

———, and HAAS, W., *Der Dom zu Speyer* (Kunstdenkmäler von Rheinland-Pfalz), 3 vols., Munich, 1972.

LANG, E., *Ottonische und frühromanische Kirchen in Köln*, Coblenz, 1932.

LEHMANN, E., "Die Bedeutung des antikischen Bauschmucks am Dom zu Speyer," *Zeitschrift für Kunstwissenschaft*, V, 1951, pp. 1–16.

MAGIRIUS, H., *Der Freiberger Dom*, Weimar, 1972.

MILOJCIC, V., "Ergebnisse der Grabungen von 1961–1965 in der Fuldäer Propstei Solnhofen an der Altmühl (Mittelfranken)," *Berichte der Römisch-Germanischen Kommission 1965/66*, Berlin, 1968.

MÜLLER, O., *Die Einhardsbasilika in Steinbach*, Mainz, 1965.

OSWALD, F., and FISCHER, M. F., "Zur Baugeschichte der Fuldäer Klosterkirchen. Literatur und Ausgrabungen in kritischer Sicht," *Beihefte der Bonner Jahrbücher*, 1966.

RAHTGENS, H., *Die Kirche St. Maria im Kapitol zu Köln*, Düsseldorf, 1913.

RAVE, W., *Corvey*, Münster, 1958.

REISSER, E., *Die frühe Baugeschichte des Münsters zu Reichenau (Mittelzell)*, Berlin, 1960.

SANDERSON, W., "Die frühmittelalterlichen Krypten von St. Maximilian in Trier," *Trierer Zeitschrift*, XXXI, 1968.

SCHAEFER, L., *Der Gründungsbau der Stiftskirche St. Martin in Zyfflich*, Essen, 1963.

SCHÖNE, W., "Die künstlerische und liturgische Gestalt der Pfalzkapelle Karls des Grossen in Aachen," *Zeitschrift für Kunstwissenschaft*, XV, 1961, p. 97.

TER KUILE, E. H., "De kerken van bisschop Bernold (Utrecht, Deventer, Emmerich)," *Bulletin van de Nederlandse Oudheidkundige Bond*, 6/12, 1959, pp. 148–163.

VERBEEK, A., "Die architektonische Nachfolge der Aachener Pfalzkapelle," in *Karl der Grosse*, vol. IV, p. 113.

———, *Kölner Kirchen*, Cologne, 1959.

———, *Schwarzrheindorf. Die Doppelkirche und ihre Wandgemälde*, Düsseldorf, 1953.

WEYRES, W., "Zur Baugeschichte der vorgotischen Kölner Kathedralen," *Kölner Domblatt*, 26/27, 1967, p. 7.

WILL, R., *Eschau* (Kleiner Kunstführer), Munich, 1970.

———, "La cathédrale romane," in *La cathédrale de Strasbourg*, Strasbourg, 1957, p. 35.

ZIMMERMANN, W., *Das Münster zu Essen*, Essen, 1956.

———, and BORGER, H., *Die Kirchen zu Essen-Werden*, Essen, 1959.

AUSTRIA

DEHIO, G., *Handbuch der Kunstdenkmäler Österreichs*, 5 vols., Vienna and Munich (numerous editions).

EGGER, R., "Die Martinskirche in Linz," *Österreichische Zeitschrift für Kunst und Denkmalpflege*, XVII, 1963, p. 165.

GINHART, K., *Die Martinskirche in Linz*, Linz, 1968.

———, "Mittelalterliche Bauforschung in Österreich," *Kunstchronik* VI, 1953, pp. 88, 141.

———, et al., *Die bildende Kunst in Österreich. Vorromani-*sche *und romanische Zeit*, Baden (Austria), 1937.

HOOTZ, R., *Kunstdenkmäler in Österreich. Ein Bildhandbuch*, 4 vols., Vienna, 1965 ff.

JURASCHEK, F., and JENNY, W., *Die Martinskirche in Linz. Ein vorkarolingischer Bau in seiner Umbestaltung zur Nischenkirche*, Linz, 1949.

Österreichische Kunsttopographie, 1907 ff.

Österreichische Zeitschrift für Kunst und Denkmalpflege.

PÜHRINGER, R., *Denkmäler früh- und hochromanischer Baukunst in Österreich*, Vienna and Leipzig, 1931.

Reclams Kunstführer: Österreich, 2 vols., Stuttgart, 1961.

Romanische Kunst in Österreich (exhibition catalogue), Krems, 1964.

SWITZERLAND

BOUFFARD, P., et al., *Suisse romane* (Zodiaque), La Pierrequi-Vire, 1958.

Die Kunstdenkmäler der Schweiz, 59 vols. to date.

Frühmittelalterliche Kunst in den Alpenländern, Olten and Lausanne, 1954.

GANTNER, J., *Kunstgeschichte der Schweiz. Vol. I: Von den helvetisch-romischen Anfängen bis zum Ende des romanischen Stils*, Frauenfeld, 1936.

HECHT, J., *Der romanische Kirchenbau des Bodenseegebietes*, vol. I, Basel, 1928.

HOOTZ, R., *Kunstdenkmäler in der Schweiz. Ein Bildhandbuch*, 2 vols., Munich, 1969–70.

Reclams Kunstführer: Schweiz, Stuttgart, 1966.

Zeitschrift für Schweizerische Archäologie und Kunstgeschichte.

SWITZERLAND: SPECIFIC LOCALITIES

BIRCHLER, L., "Zur karolingischen Architektur und Malerei in Münster-Müstair," in *Frühmittelalterliche Kunst in den Alpenländern*, p. 167.

BLONDEL, L., "L'Abbaye de St.-Maurice d'Agaume et ses sanctuaires," *Zeitschrift für Schweizerische Archäologie und Kunstgeschichte*, XXII, 1962, p. 158.

BUCHER, F., *Notre-Dame de Bonmont und die ersten Zisterzienserabteien der Schweiz*, Berne, 1957.

HECHT, K., "Der St. Galler Klosterplan—Schema oder Bauplan?," *Abhandlungen der Braunschweigischen Wissenschaftlichen Gesellschaft*, XVII, 1965, p. 165.

HORN, W., and BORN, E., "The 'dimensional' inconsistencies of the plan of St. Gall and the problem of the scale of the plan," *Art Bulletin*, XLVIII, 1966, p. 285.

LOERTSCHER, G., *Die romanische Stiftskirche von Schönenwerd*, Basel, 1952.

MÜLLER, I., and STEINMANN, O., "Die Disentiner Kirchen," in *Frühmittelalterliche Kunst in den Alpenländern*, p. 133.

POESCHEL, E., "Frühchristliche und frühmittelalterliche Architektur in Churrätien," in *Frühmittelalterliche Kunst in den Alpenländern*, p. 119.

REINHARDT, H., *Das Münster zu Basel* (Deutsche Bauten), Burg, 1928.

———, *Der St. Galler Klosterplan*, Sankt Gallen, 1952.

REINLE, A., "Neue Gedanken zum St. Galler Klosterplan," *Zeitschrift für Schweizerische Archäologie und Kunstgeschichte*, XXIII, 1963–64, p. 91.

SCHÖNE, W., "Das Verhältnis von Zeichnung und Massangaben im Kirchengrundriss des St. Gallener Klosterplans," *Zeitschrift für Kunstwissenschaft*, XIV, 1960, p. 147.

SENNHAUSER, H. R., *Romainmôtier und Payerne*, Basel, 1970.

SULSER, W., "Die Luziuskirche in Chur," in *Frühmittelalterliche Kunst in den Alpenländern*, p. 151.

WECKWERT, A., "Die frühchristliche Basilika und der St. Galler Klosterplan," *Zeitschrift für Schweizerische Archäologie und Kunstgeschichte*, XXI, 1961, p. 143.

ITALY

Atti del primo congresso internazionale di studi longobardi, Spoleto, 1952.

CREMA, L., "Übersicht über die wichtigsten Grabungen in Italien," *Kunstchronik*, VIII, 1965, p. 126.

DECKER, H., *Romanesque Art in Italy*, New York, 1959.

ENLART, C., *L'Art roman en Italie. L'Architecture et la décoration* [Paris, 1924].

FRACCARO DE LONGHI, L., *L'architettura delle chiese cistercensi italiane*, Milan, 1958.

Guida d'Italia del Touring Club Italiano, 23 vols.

KELLER, H., *Die Kunstlandschaften Italiens*, Munich, 1960.

Reclams Kunstführer: Italien, 5 vols. to date, Stuttgart.

RICCI, C., *Romanesque Architecture in Italy*, New York, 1925.

SALMI, M., "L'architettura in Italia durante il periodo carolingio," *Problemi della civiltà carolingia*, Spoleto, 1954.

THÜMMLER, H., "Die Baukunst des 11. Jahrhunderts in Italien," *Römisches Jahrbuch für Kunstgeschichte*, III, 1939, p. 141.

TOESCA, P., *Storia dell'arte italiana dalle origini alla fine del secolo XIII, Vol. I: Il medioevo*, Turin, 1927.

WAGNER-RIEGER, R., *Die italienische Baukunst zu Beginn der Gothik*, 2 vols., Graz and Cologne, 1956–57.

——— "Italienische Hallenkirchen (Zur Forschungslage)," *Mitteilungen der Gesellschaft für vergleichende Kunstforschung in Wien*, XII, 1960, pp. 127–135.

Periodicals, series:

Palladio, Arte Lombarda.

Studi medioevali (Centro Italiano di Studi sull'alto medioevo, Spoleto), 1954 ff.

NORTHERN ITALY

ARSLAN, E., "L'architettura dal 568 al 1000," in *Storia di Milano*, vol. II, Milan, 1945, p. 499.

———, "L'architettura romanica milanese," in *Storia di Milano*, vol. III, Milan, 1954, p. 395.

———, "Remarques sur l'architecture lombarde du VIIᵉ siècle," *Cahiers archéologiques*, VII, 1954, p. 129.

CECCHELLI, C., *I monumenti del Friuli dal secolo IV all'XI, vol. I: Cividale*, Milan, 1943.

CESCHI, C., *Architettura romanica genovese*, Milan, 1945.

KLUCKHOHN, E., and PAATZ, W., "Die Bedeutung Italiens für die romanische Baukunst und Bauornamentik in Deutschland," *Marburger Jahrbuch*, XXVI, 1955.

KRAUTHEIMER, R., "Lombardische Hallenkirchen," *Jahrbuch für Kunstwissenschaft*, VI, 1928, p. 176.

MAGNI, M., *Architettura romanica comasca*, Milan, 1960.

PORTER, A. K., *Lombard Architecture*, 4 vols., New Haven, 1915–17 (reprinted 1967).

QUINTAVALLE, A. C., *Romanico padano, civiltà d'Occidente*, Florence, 1969.

REGGIORI, F., *Dieci battisteri lombardi minori, dal secolo V al secolo XII*, Rome, 1935.

RIVOIRA, G. T., *Lombard Architecture, Its Origin, Development and Derivatives*, 2 vols., 2nd ed., Oxford, 1933.

Stucchi e mosaici altomedioevali: Atti dell'ottavo congresso di studi sull'arte dell'alto medioevo, Milan, 1962.

VERZONE, P., *L'architettura religiosa dell'alto medioevo nell'Italia settentrionale*, Milan, 1942.

———, *L'architettura romanica del Vercellese*, Vercelli, 1934.

———, *L'arte preromanica in Liguria*, Turin, n.d.

———, "Le chiese deuterobizantine del Ravennate nel quadro dell'architettura carolingia e protoromanica," in *Corso di cultura sull'arte ravennate e bizantina*, VII, 1960, p. 335.

CENTRAL ITALY AND SARDINIA

BRACCO, M., *Architettura e scultura romanica nel Casentino*, Florence, 1971.

DELOGU, R., *L'architettura del Medioevo in Sardegna*, Rome, 1953.

KRÖNIG, W., "Hallenkirchen in Mittelitalien," *Kunstgeschichtliches Jahrbuch der Biblioteca Hertziana*, II, 1938, p. 1.

MARINELLI, M., *L'architettura romanica in Ancona*, Ancona, 1961.

MORACCHINI-MAZEL, G., *Les églises romanes de Corse*, 2 vols., Paris, 1967.

MORETTI, I., and STOPANI, R., *Architettura romanica religiosa a Gubbio e nel territorio della sua antica diocesi*, Florence, 1973.

———, *Architettura romanica religiosa nel contado fiorentino* (in preparation).

———, *Chiese romaniche dell'Isola d'Elba*, Florence, 1972.

———, *Chiese romaniche in Valdelsa*, Florence, 1968.

———, *Chiese romaniche in Val di Cecina*, Florence, 1970.

———, *Chiese romaniche in Val di Pesa e Val di Greve*, Florence, 1972.

———, *Chiese romaniche nel Chianti*, Florence, 1966.

———, *La Pieve di Santa Maria in Chianti*, Florence, 1971.

MORETTI, M., *L'architettura romanica nel Senese*, Parma, 1962.

SALMI, M., *Architettura romanica in Toscana*, Rome and Milan, 1928.

———, *Chiese romaniche della Toscana*, Milan, 1961.

SOUTHERN ITALY AND SICILY

BERTAUX, E., *L'Art dans l'Italie méridionale*, Paris, 1904.

BOTTARI, S., *Monumenti Svevi di Sicilia*, Palermo, 1950.

DI STEFANO, G., *Monumenti della Sicilia normanna*, Palermo, 1955.

SCHWARZ, H. M., "Die Baukunst Kalabriens und Siziliens im Zeitalter der Normannen," *Römisches Jahrbuch für Kunstgeschichte*, VI, 1942–44, p. 1.

———, *Sizilien*, Vienna and Munich, 1961.

WILLEMSEN, C. A., and ODENTHAL, D., *Apulien*, Cologne, 1958.

———, *Kalabrien*, Cologne, 1966.

ITALY: SPECIFIC LOCALITIES

ARSLAN, W., *L'architettura romanica Veronese*, Verona, 1939.

AURINI, G., "Architettura romanica piacentina," *Strenna Piacentina*, 1924.

BAJ, G., *La vetusta basilica di San Vincenzo in Prato*, Milan, 1936.

BARGELLINI, P., MOROZZI, G., and BATINI, G., *Santa Reparata. La Cattedrale risorta*, Florence, 1970.

BELTING, H., "Die Sophienkirche in Benevent," *Dumbarton Oaks Papers*, XVI, 1962, p. 175.

BERETTA, R., *La basilica e il battistero di Agliate*, Carate Brianza, 1929.

BETTINI, S., *L'architettura di San Marco (Venezia)*, Padua, 1946.

BOGNETTI, G. P., CHIERICI, G., and DE CAPITANI D'ARZAGO, A., *Santa Maria in Castelseprio*, Milan, 1948.

CECCHELLI, C., *I monumenti del Friuli dal secolo IV all'XI: Cividale*, Milan, 1943.

DALISCA, A., *La basilica di San Zenone in Verona*, Verona, 1956.

DI STEFANO, G., *Il duomo di Cefalù*, Palermo, 1960.

DYGGVE, E., TORPS, H., L'ORANGE, H. P., "Il Tempietto di Cividale," *Atti del II Congresso internazionale di studi sull'altomedioevo*, Spoleto, 1952–53, p. 75.

HORN, W., "Romanesque Churches in Florence," *Art Bulletin*, XXV, 1943, p. 112.

JACOBS, F., *Die Kathedrale S. Maria Icona Vetere in Foggia*, 2 vols., Hamburg, 1968.

KRÖNIG, W., *The Cathedral of Monreale*, Palermo, 1965.

La Chiesa di San Salvatore in Brescia. Atti dell'ottavo Congresso di studi sull'arte dell'alto medioevo, vol. II, Milan, 1962.

LEHMANN, E., "Zum Typus von Santo Stefano in Verona," *Stucchi e mosaici altomedioevali: Atti dell'ottavo congresso di studi sull'arte dell'alto medioevo*, Milan, 1962, vol. I, p. 287.

PAATZ, W., "Die Hauptströmungen in der florentiner Baukunst des frühen und hohen Mittelalters," *Mitteilungen des Kunsthistorischen Instituts in Florenz*, VI, 1940, p. 45.

———, and E., *Die Kirchen von Florenz, ein kunstgeschichtliches Handbuch*, 6 vols., Frankfurt, 1940–53.

PANAZZA, G., and PERONI, E., "San Salvatore in Brescia," *Stucchi e mosaici . . .*, Milan, 1962, vol. II.

ROMANINI, A. M., "Romanico Piacentino," *Palladio*, I, 1951.

SALMI, M., *La basilica di San Salvatore di Spoleto*, Florence, 1951.

SCHETTINI, F., *La basilica di San Nicola di Bari*, Bari, 1967.

SWOBODA, K. U., *Das florentiner Baptisterium*, Berlin and Vienna, 1918.

TOESCA, P., *Monumenti dell'antica abbazia di San Pietro al Monte di Civate*, Florence, n.d.

SPAIN

DE PALOL, P., and HIRMER, M., *Early Medieval Art in Spain*, New York [1966].

DURLIAT, M., *L'Architecture espagnole*, Toulouse, 1966.

———, and DIEUZAIDE, J., *Hispania Romanica*, Vienna and Munich, 1962.

GÓMEZ MORENO, M., *Arte Califal hispanoárabe, Arte Mozárabe* (Ars Hispaniae, vol. III), Madrid, 1951.

———, *El arte románico español*, Madrid, 1943.

———, *Iglesias Mozárabes*, 2 vols., Madrid, 1919

GUDIOL RICART, J., and GAYA NUÑO, J. A., *Arquitectura y Escultura románicas* (Ars Hispaniae, vol. V), Madrid, 1948.

LAMPEREZ Y ROMEA, V., *Historia de la arquitectura cristiana española en la edad media*, 3 vols., 2nd ed., Madrid, 1930.

PUIG I CADAFALCH, J., *L'Art wisigothique et ses survivances. Recherches sur les origines et le développement de l'art en France et en Espagne du 4e au 12e siècle*, Paris, 1961.

Symposium sobre cultura asturiana de la Alta Edad Media, 1961, Oviedo, 1967.

TORRES BALBÁS, L., *El arte de la alta edad media y del periodo románico en España*, Barcelona, 1934.

WHITEHALL, A. M., *Spanish Romanesque Architecture of the Eleventh Century*, London, 1941.

Inventories, periodicals, series:

Archivo Español de Arte y Arqueología.

Catalogo Monumental de España.

DE AZCÁRATE, J. M., *Monumentos españoles*, 3 vols., 2nd ed., Madrid, 1953–54.

Guías artísticas de España.

Los monumentos cardinales de España.

CATALONIA AND NORTHEASTERN SPAIN

CANELLAS LOPEZ, A., and SAN VINCENTE, A., *Aragon roman* (Zodiaque), La Pierre-qui-Vire, 1971.

Congrès Archéologique, 1954 (Roussillon); 1959 (Catalogne).

DE LOZENDIO, L. U., *Navarre romane* (Zodiaque), La Pierre-qui-Vire, 1967.

DURLIAT, M., *Roussillon roman* (Zodiaque), La Pierre-qui-Vire, 1958.

JUNYENT, E., *Catalogne romane* (Zodiaque), 2 vols., La Pierre-qui-Vire, 1960–61.

PUIG I CADAFALCH, J., *La Géographie et les origines du premier art roman*, Paris, 1935.

———, FALGUERA, A., DE, and GODEY Y CASALS, G., *L'arquitectura romànica a Catalunya*, 3 vols., Barcelona, 1909–18.

SÓTIL BIURRUN, T., *El arte románico en Navarra*, Pamplona, 1936.

CASTILE AND NORTHWESTERN SPAIN

ALCOLEA, S., *La catedral de Santiago de Compostela*, Madrid, 1948.

CONANT, K. J., *The Early Architectural History of the Cathedral of Santiago de Compostela*, Cambridge, Mass., 1926.

GARCIA GUINEA, M. A., *El arte románico en Palencia*, Palencia, 1961.

GAYA NUÑO, J. A., "El románico en la provincia de Logroño," *Boletín de la Sociedad Española de Excursiones*, 1942, p. 81.

———, "El románico en la provincia de Vizcaya," *Archivo español de arte*, 1944, p. 44.

LAYNA SERRANO, F., *La arquitectura románica en la provincia de Guadalajara*, Madrid, 1935.

LOUIS, R., "Les fouilles dans la cathédrale Saint-Jacques de Compostelle," *Bulletin de la Société nationale des antiquaires de France*, 1954/55, p. 152.

PEREZ CARMONA, J., *Arquitectura y escultura románicas en la provincia de Burgos*, Burgos, 1959.

RODRIGUEZ ESCORIAL, J., *El arte románico en Segovia*, Saragossa, 1918.

VÁZQUEZ NUÑEZ, A., *La arquitectura cristiana en la provincia de Orense durante el periodo medieval*, n.p., n.d.

VINAYO GONZALEZ, A., *León roman* (Zodiaque), La Pierre-qui-Vire, 1972.

ASTURIAS

FRISCHAUER, A. S., *Altspanischer Kirchenbau*, Berlin and Leipzig, 1930.

MANZANARES RODRIGUEZ MIR, J., *Arte prerománico asturiano. Síntesis de su arquitectura*, Oviedo, 1957; 2nd ed., 1964.

MENENDEZ PIDAL, L., "Influencia y expansión de la arquitectura prerománica asturiana," *Boletín del Istituto de estudios asturianos*, XV, 1961, p. 417.

SCHLUNK, H., *Arte visigodo, Arte asturiano* (Ars Hispaniae, vol. II), Madrid, 1947.

———, and MANZANARES RODRIGUEZ MIR, J., "La iglesia de San Pedro de Teverga y los comienzos del arte románico en el reino de Asturias y León," *Archivo español de arte*, XXIV, 1915, p. 277.

PORTUGAL

DE LACERDA, A., *Historia de arte em Portugal*, vol. I, Oporto, 1942.

DE VASCONCELLOS, E., and MARQUES DE ABREU, J., *Arte românico em Portugal*, Oporto, 1918.

DOS SANTOS, R., *Architectura em Portugal*, Lisbon, 1929.

———, *Historia del arte Português*, Barcelona and Madrid, 1960.

Inventario artistico de Portugal (Academia nacional de belas artes, Lisbon).

GREAT BRITAIN (ENGLAND, SCOTLAND, WALES)

BILSON, J., "Durham Cathedral and the chronology of its vaults," *Archaeological Journal*, LXXIX, 1929, p. 101.

BOASE, T. S. R., *English Art, 1100–1216*, Oxford, 1953.

BOND, F., *An Introduction to English Church Architecture*, 2 vols., Oxford, 1913.

BONY, J., "Le voûtement de la cathédrale de Durham," *Urbanisme et architecture: Mélanges P. Lavedan*, Paris, 1954, pp. 41–47.

BROWN, G. B., *The Arts in Early England*, vol. II (Anglo-Saxon Architecture), London, 1925.

CLAPHAM, A. W., *English Romanesque Architecture after the Conquest*, Oxford, 1934 (reprinted 1964).

———, *English Romanesque Architecture before the Conquest*, Oxford, 1930 (reprinted 1964).

COOK, G. H., *English Collegiate Churches of the Middle Ages*, London, 1959.

———, *English Monasteries*, London, 1961.

———, *Mediaeval Chantries and Chantry Chapels*, London, 1947.

ESCHER, K., *Englische Kathedralen*, Munich and Berlin, 1929.

FISHER, E. A., *An Introduction to Anglo-Saxon Architecture and Sculpture*, London, 1959.

———, *The Greater Anglo-Saxon Churches*, London, 1962.

FREY, D., *Englisches Wesen in der bildenden Kunst*, Stuttgart and Berlin, 1942.

HARVEY, J., *The English Cathedrals*, London, 1950.

HÜRLIMANN, M., and MEYER, P., *Englische Kathedralen*, Zurich, 1948.

LEHMANN-BROCKHAUS, O., *Lateinische Schriftquellen zur*

Kunst in England, Wales und Schottland vom Jahre 901 bis zum Jahre 1307, 5 vols., Munich, 1955–60.

PETZSCH, H., *Architecture in Scotland*, London, 1971.

PEVSNER, N., *The Englishness of English Art*, London, 1956.

RICE, D. T., *English Art, 871–1100*, Oxford, 1952.

RIEGER, R., "Studien zur mittelalterlichen Architektur Englands: Alte und neue Kunst," *Wiener Kunstwissenschaftliche Blätter*, II, 1953, pp. 15–31.

TAYLOR, H. M., and T., *Anglo-Saxon Architecture*, 2 vols., Cambridge, 1965.

WEBB, G., *Architecture in Britain. The Middle Ages*, Baltimore, 1956.

Inventories, series:

Ancient Monuments and Historic Buildings (numerous brochures, especially on abbeys, priories, and castles), London, Her Majesty's Stationery Office.

Illustrated Guides to Ancient Monuments (England, Wales, Scotland), 6 vols.

PEVSNER, N., *The Buildings of England*, 42 vols. to date, Harmondsworth.

Royal Commission of Ancient and Historical Monuments: County Inventories, 1910 ff.

IRELAND AND ULSTER

Ancient Monuments of Northern Ireland, 2 vols., Belfast, 1962–63.

HENRY, F., *L'Art irlandais* (Zodiaque), 3 vols., La Pierre-qui-Vire, 1963–64.

LEASK, H. G., *Irish Churches and Monastic Buildings*, vol. I, Dundalk, 1955.

SCANDINAVIA

CINTHIO, E., "Der Dom zu Lund in romanischer Zeit," *Arte Lombarda*, VI, 1961, p. 178.

DYGGVE, E., "Tradition und Christentum in der dänischen Kunst zur Zeit der Missionierung," in *Karolingische und Ottonische Kunst*, Wiesbaden, 1957.

FETT, H., *Norger kirker i middelalderen*, Oslo, 1909.

HAHR, A., *Architecture in Sweden*, Stockholm, 1938.

KRINS, H., *Die frühen Steinkirchen Dänemarks*, Hamburg, 1968.

Kyrkliga Byggnader (Nordisk Kultur), ed. V. LORENZEN, Stockholm, Oslo, and Copenhagen, 1933.

LUND, H., and MILLECK, K., *Danmarks Bygningskunst fra oldtid til nutid*, Copenhagen, 1963.

MACKEPRANG, M., and JENSEN, C., *Danish Churches*, Copenhagen, 1940.

Inventories:

Danmarks Kirker, numerous vols., 1933 ff.

Norger Kirker (Norges Minnesmerker), numerous vols., Oslo.

Sveriges Kyrkor, numerous vols., Stockholm.

POLAND

ŠWIECHOWSKI, Z., *Budownictwo romanskie w Polsce*, Wroclaw, Warsaw, and Cracow, 1963.

———, "Les plus anciens monuments de l'architecture religieuse en Pologne d'après les fouilles et les travaux récents," *Cahiers Archéologiques* (Paris), IX, 1957, p. 301.

CZECHOSLOVAKIA

CIBULKA, J., "Grossmährische Kirchenbauten," in *Sancti Cyrillus et Methodius: Leben und Wirken*, Prague, 1963, p. 49.

———, "Zur Frühgeschichte der Architectur in Mähren (800–900)," in *Festschrift Swoboda*, Vienna and Wiesbaden, 1959, p. 55.

Das Grossmährische Reich, Acts of the Congress of the Archaeological Institute of the Czechoslovakian Academy of Sciences (Brno, 1962), Prague, 1966 (includes relevant articles by J. POSMOURNI, p. 107; V. RICHTER, p. 110; and J. POULIK, p. 11).

MENCL, V., "Praha prerománska a románska," in *Praha románska*, Prague, 1948.

———, *Stredoveká architektura na Slovenska*, Prague, 1937.

MERHAUTOVÁ, A., "Les débuts de l'architecture du haut moyen-âge en Bohème," in *Mélanges offerts à René Crozet*, Poitiers, 1966, p. 111.

———, *Raně středoveká architektura v Cechách*, Prague, 1971.

MERHAUTOVÁ-LIVOROVÁ, A., "Rotunda Knizete Vaclava na Prazskem Hrade," *Uméní*, XIII, 1965, p. 88.

Österreichische Kunsttopographie, Vienna, 1907.

HUNGARY

BOGYAY, T. VON, "Der Eintritt des Ungartums in die christlicheuropäische Kulturgeschichte im Lichte der Kunstgeschichte," *Südostforschungen*, XVIII, 1959, p. 6.

———, "Die kunst- und kirchengeschichtliche Bedeutung der Ausgrabungen von Mosapurc-Zalavár," *Neue Beiträge zur Kunstgeschichte des 1. Jahrtausends*, p. 131.

GAL, L., *L'Architecture religieuse en Hongrie du XIe au XIIe siècles*, Paris, 1929.

KAMPIS, A., *Kunst in Ungarn*, Budapest, 1966.

PÁL, V., *Heves Magye Müemlékei*, vol. I (Magyarország Müemléki Topográfiája VII), Budapest, 1959.

Inventories, periodicals:

Magyarország Müemléki Topográfiája, Budapest.

Acta Academiae Hungaricae.

YUGOSLAVIA (DALMATIA AND SLOVENIA)

MARASOVIC, T., "Carolingian Influence in the Early Medieval Architecture in Dalmatia," in *Congrès International d'Histoire de l'Art*, Paris, 1958, p. 117.

MONNERET DE VILLARD, V., *L'architettura romanica in Dalmazia*, Milan, 1910.

ZADNIKAR, M., "Die romanische Baukunst in Slovenien und ihre Kunstgeographische Stellung," *Südostforschungen*, XX, 1961, p. 74.

———, "L'architecture romane en Slovénie," *Cahiers de civilisation médiévale*, II, 1959, p. 469.

———, *Romanska Architektura na Slovenskem*, Ljubljana, 1959.

PALESTINE

DESCHAMPS, P., *Terre Sainte romane* (Zodiaque), La Pierre-qui-Vire, 1964.

ENLART, C., *Les Monuments des Croisés dans le royaume de Jérusalem. Architecture religieuse et civile*, 4 vols., Paris, 1925–28.

CIVIL ARCHITECTURE

SIMON, O., "Der mittelalterliche Profanbau Deutschlands und seine Bedeutung für die Geistesgeschichte," *Architecture*, I, 1933, pp. 86–92.

STIEHL, O., *Der Wohnbau des Mittelalters*, Leipzig, 1908.

TOWN AND CITY

ENNEN, E., *Frühgeschichte der europäischen Stadt*, Bonn, 1953.

GANSHOF, F. L., *Étude sur le développement des villes entre Loire et Rhin au moyen-âge*, Paris and Brussels, 1943.

HERZOG, E., *Die ottonische Stadt*, Berlin, 1958.

HUBERT, J., "Évolution de la topographie et de l'aspect des villes de Gaule du Ve au Xe siècle," in *La città del medioevo: Settimane Altomedioevo*, VI, 1958, p. 529.

MRUSEK, H. J., "Bautechnische Einzelheiten in der mittelalterlichen Profanbaukunst," *Wissenschaftliche Zeitschrift der Martin-Luther-Universität, Halle-Wittenberg*, VI, 1956–57, pp. 641–672.

———, "Zur städtebaulichen Entwicklung Magdeburgs im hohen Mittelalter," *Wissenschaftliche Zeitschrift der Martin-Luther-Universität, Halle-Wittenberg*, V, 1955–56, pp. 1219–1314.

THE MONASTERY

ARENS, F., "Das Kloster bei St. Emmeram in Regensburg. Seine Anlage und Baugeschichte im Mittelalter," *Thurn-und-Taxis-Studien*, I, 1961, pp. 186-296.

BRAUNFELS, W., *Abendländische Klosterbaukunst*, Cologne, 1969.

BURG AND CASTLE

ARENS, F., *Die Königspfalz Wimpfen*, Berlin, 1967.

BOASE, T. S. R., *Castles and Churches of the Crusading*

Kingdom, Oxford, 1967.

BROWN, R. A., *English Medieval Castles*, London, 1954.

BRÜHL, C., "Königspfalz und Bischofsstadt in fränkischer Zeit," *Rheinische Vierteljahrsblätter*, XXIII, 1958, p. 161.

DESCHAMPS, P., *Les châteaux des croisés en Terre Sainte. Le crac des chevaliers*, 2 vols., Paris, 1934.

EBHARDT, B., *Der Wehrbau Europas im Mittelalter*, vol. I (Britain, France, Germany), Berlin, 1939; vol. II, pt. 1 (Spain, Portugal, Italy), 1958; vol. II, pt. 2 (North and East), 1958.

———, *Deutsche Burgen*, Berlin, 1899–1907.

———, *Die Burgen Italiens*, 6 vols., 1971–72.

GRIMM, P., *Stand und Aufgaben der archäologischen Pfalzenforschung in den Bezirken Halle und Magdeburg*, Berlin, 1961.

HAHN, H., *Hohenstaufenburgen in Süditalien*, Ingelheim, 1961.

HOELSCHER, U., *Die Kaiserpfalz zu Goslar*, Berlin, 1927.

HOTZ, W., *Burg Wildenberg im Odenwald*, Amorbach, 1963.

Kirche und Burg in der Archäologie des Rheinlandes, Düsseldorf, 1962.

MÜLLER-WIENER, W., *Burgen der Kreuzritter im Heiligen Land, auf Zypern und in der Ägäis*, Munich and Berlin, 1966.

Pfalzenexkursion des Instituts für Vor- und Frühgeschichte der Deutschen Akademie der Wissenschaft zu Berlin, vom 10. bis 14. Oktober 1960, ed. W. UNVERZAGT, Berlin, 1960.

PIPER, O., *Burgenkunde*, Munich, 1912.

RIEDBERG, L., *Deutsche Burgengeographie*, Leipzig, 1939.

SCHUCHHARDT, C., *Die Burg im Wandel der Weltgeschichte*, Wildpark-Potsdam, 1931.

SCHÜRER, O., *Die Kaiserpfalz Eger*, Berlin, 1934

TUULSE, A., *Burgen des Abendlandes*, Vienna and Munich, 1958.

VERBEEK, A., and MERIAN, H., "Das romanische Haus in Münstereifel," *Jahrbuch der rheinischen Denkmalpflege*, XXVI, 1966, p. 108.

Periodicals:

Der Burgwart: Zeitschrift für Wehrbau, Wohnbau und Städtebau, ed. B. EBHARDT, Marksburg, vols. I–XL.

SOURCES AND ICONOLOGY

BANDMANN, G., "Ikonologie der Architektur," *Jahrbuch für Aesthetik und allgemeine Kunstwissenschaft*, 1951, pp. 67–109.

———, *Mittelalterliche Baukunst als Bedeutungsträger*, Berlin, 1951.

———, "Zur Bedeutung der romanischen Apsis," *Wallraf-Richartz-Jahrbuch*, XV, 1963, pp. 28–46.

EVERS, H. G., *Tod, Macht und Raum als Bereiche der Architektur*, Munich, 1939.

KRAUTHEIMER, H., "An Introduction to an Iconography of Medieval Architecture," *Journal of the Warburg and Courtauld Institutes*, 1950, p. 163.

LEHMANN-BROCKHAUS, O., *Lateinische Schriftquellen zur Kunst in England, Wales und Schottland vom Jahre 901 bis zum Jahre 1307*, Munich, 1955–60.

———, *Schriftquellen zur Kunstgeschichte des 11. und 12. Jahrhunderts für Deutschland, Lotharingen und Italien*, 2 vols., Berlin, 1938.

MORTET, V., *Recueil de textes relatifs à l'histoire de l'architecture et à la condition des architectes en France au moyenâge: XIe–XIIe siècles*, Paris, 1911.

PEVSNER, N., "Terms of Architectural Planning in the Middle Ages," *Journal of the Warburg and Courtauld Institutes*, 1952, pp. 232–237.

———, "The term 'Architect' in the Middle Ages," *Speculum*, XVII, 1942, p. 549.

SAUER, J., *Symbolik des Kirchengebäudes und seiner Ausstattung in der Auffassung des Mittelalters*, 2nd ed., Freiburg, 1924.

TECHNICAL PROBLEMS

ABRAHAM, P., *Viollet-le-Duc et le rationalisme médiéval*, Paris, 1934.

AUBERT, M., "Les plus anciennes croisées d'ogives. Leur rôle dans la construction," *Bulletin monumental*, 1934.

FRIEDERICH, K., *Die Steinbearbeitung in ihrer Entwicklung vom 11. bis zum 18. Jahrhundert*, Augsburg, 1932.

HORN, W., "On the Origin of the Medieval Bay System," *Journal of the Society of Architectural Historians*, XVII, 1958, p. 2.

———, and BORN, E., *The Aisled Medieval Timber Hall*, Berkeley, 1966.

RAVE, W., "Über die Statik mittelalterlicher Gewölbe," *Deutsche Kunst und Denkmalpflege*, 1939, pp. 193–198.

SAGE, W., "Frühmittelalterliche Holzbau," in *Karl der Grosse*, vol. III, Düsseldorf, 1965, p. 573.

PLASTER AND PAINT

AUBERT, M., "Les enduits dans les constructions du moyen-âge," *Bulletin monumental*, CXV, 1957, pp. 111–117.

PHLEPS, H., *Die farbige Architektur bei den Römern und im Mittelalter*, Berlin [1930].

SCHÖNE, W., "Über den Beitrag von Licht und Farbe zur Raumgestaltung im Kirchenbau des alten Abendlandes," *Evangelische Kirchenbautagung, Stuttgart 1959*, Berlin [1961], pp. 89–154.

INDEX

Specific buildings are cited under the name of the city or town in which they are located.

The following abbreviations are used:

B (Belgium), DBR (West Germany), DDR (East Germany), E (England), F (France), I (Italy), N (The Netherlands), S (Spain), SW (Switzerland).

LIST OF PHOTOGRAPHIC CREDITS

Photographs by Bruno Balestrini. All those supplied by other sources are gratefully acknowledged below. The numbers listed refer to the plates.